IN THE SHADOW OF AD

In the Shadow of Adam Smith

Founders of Scottish Economics 1700–1900

Donald Rutherford
Director of Studies
University of Edinburgh, School of Economics

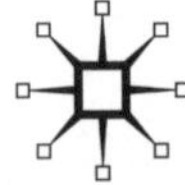

First published 2012 by
PALGRAVE MACMILLAN

Palgrave Macmillan in the UK is an imprint of Macmillan Publishers Limited, registered in England, company number 785998, of Houndmills, Basingstoke, Hampshire RG21 6XS.

Palgrave Macmillan in the US is a division of St Martin's Press LLC, 175 Fifth Avenue, New York, NY 10010.

Palgrave Macmillan is the global academic imprint of the above companies and has companies and representatives throughout the world.

Palgrave® and Macmillan® are registered trademarks in the United States, the United Kingdom, Europe and other countries.

ISBN 978–0–230–25209–7 hardback
ISBN 978–0–230–25210–3 paperback

This book is printed on paper suitable for recycling and made from fully managed and sustained forest sources. Logging, pulping and manufacturing processes are expected to conform to the environmental regulations of the country of origin.

A catalogue record for this book is available from the British Library.

A catalog record for this book is available from the Library of Congress.

10 9 8 7 6 5 4 3 2 1
21 20 19 18 17 16 15 14 13 12

Printed and bound in China

Contents

Preface

This book is the consequence of encounters with a large and rich literature on economics by Scottish writers and an attempt to integrate their principal ideas. One would expect Edinburgh, Scotland's capital, to hold many of the old books of Scottish economists, and its collections are indeed fruitful. Edinburgh University Library, for example, has the large book collections of Dugald Stewart who, as professor of moral philosophy, lectured on political economy in the first decade of the nineteenth century, and of William Ballantyne Hodgson, the first professor of political economy. In addition, the Thomas Chalmers collection in the university's New College includes many rare economics pamphlets – promising material for the historian of economic thought to visit. Obviously, the big figures such as Adam Smith, Francis Hutcheson and David Hume are housed there too, but so are scores of the eighty writers discussed in this book, who were often prolific enough to fill many shelves. It is the aim of this work to combine the theories and views of these writers to show how the more obscure can contribute much to the discussions more often associated with the leading figures. In short, this book is a presentation of two hundred years of Scottish economics in all its breadth.

It is difficult to write a book of this kind without constant encouragement. Fortunately, I have been repeatedly spurred on by Martin Hogg, Gary Koop, Lise Tole, Furuya Yutaka, Graham Richardson, John Gordon, Peter Smaill and Scott McCombe, to name only a few.

Abbreviations used in the text

LJ	Adam Smith, *Lectures on Jurisprudence*
Principles	James Steuart, *Principles of Political Economy*
System	Francis Hutcheson, *A System of Moral Philosophy*
TMS	Adam Smith, *Theory of Moral Sentiments*
WN	Adam Smith, *The Wealth of Nations*

1 Introduction

The contribution of Scottish writers to the development of economics in the eighteenth and nineteenth centuries is outstanding and one of the greatest achievements of the Scottish nation.

The particular stimulus to writing on economics in Scotland was the proposal to create a union of the Scottish and English parliaments. This was not a new idea. In the commercial crises of 1667, 1681 and 1689 there were efforts to create a trade area embracing Scotland and England (Smout 1964), but it was not until 1707 that it came about. There was great scope for change in the whole of the Scottish economy, not only in trade. Carstairs (1955) argues that the Scottish economy in 1707 had changed little since the Middle Ages. It had primitive agriculture, little manufacturing, and primary product exports of raw materials and foodstuffs to European countries. Not until 1718 was a Glasgow ship to venture on a journey to America. But through the union of parliaments in 1707 three economic entities were established: a free trade area, a currency union and a fiscal union.

The two-hundred-year period covered by this book bridges two phases in the development of economic thought: mercantilism, which existed in many European countries from the sixteenth to mid-eighteenth centuries, and classical economics, which succeeded it and waned in the last quarter of the nineteenth century. The mercantilists believed in encouraging states to be powerful through trade and to accumulate gold and silver. The state, like the merchants it promoted through monopoly trading privileges, was concerned with adding value to its investments. Merchants sought profit, nations a surplus of wealth through trade. The length of the mercantilist period, about 1550–1750, was enough for transitions in thought from trade protection to free trade and from crude bullionism to a general balance of payments surplus. In order to strengthen the power of nation-states, mercantilist writers devised a multitude of economic policies for interventionist governments, not only on population, trade and currency, but on employment and welfare. By contrast, the classical economists were more interested in natural processes independent of state action and in the establishment of an exchange economy freely trading with other countries. As with all 'revolutions' in thought, there is no firm date for the beginning or end of the classical school, because new ideas coexist for a long time with the old. But there is little disagreement that the major writers David Hume and Adam Smith were present at the birth of the school in the 1750s. The date it ended could be claimed to be 1870, when Stanley Jevons in Manchester and Carl Menger in Vienna used new methodologies, especially calculus in the case of the former, to produce theories of exchange and value based on subjective utility and so founded neoclassical economics. But today some economists would still be regarded as classical economists. Alfred Marshall (1842–1924), the great early neoclassical economist, had a 'continuity thesis' to explain the smooth transition from classical economics. Neoclassical economics looked different from previous writings on the subject because of its increasing use of mathematical techniques to make the subject more precise.

Classical economics was expounded in a literary way. There was awareness of some functional relationships, especially in their price and value theories, and hints of geometrical representations of concepts such as the demand curve; but it was words and words alone that conveyed their theoretical ideas. As with mercantilist writers, there was diversity of opinion in classical economics, which brings an element of heterogeneity into their version of the subject. There was a also greater unity of purpose in their aims. They wanted economic growth, greater economic welfare, through attending to the underlying mechanisms of a national economy, not through an all-wise government imposing policies in a way the mercantilists would have done. To achieve their ends they had to dig deep into what information there was about economic life and clarify previous attempts at economic theory. These writers had, to varying extents, a classical education, certainly Latin at school and often Greek at university, giving them access to the earliest attempts at economic theory. Plato and Xenophon could make them think hard about the division of labour, and Aristotle about value and money. This ancient stimulus could also give them an interest in property rights, trade, the rate of interest and currencies. Remarkable as many Scottish authors were, there was a limit to home-grown knowledge in so small a country: some ideas had to be imported. Through reading and European travels they received new ideas. James Steuart, David Hume, Adam Smith and James Maitland Lauderdale were not the only Scottish writers on economics who travelled to France and major European countries. Crucial to the classical school was its encounter with the Physiocrats, the French group of economists of the second half of the eighteenth century who introduced the idea of laissez-faire economics, investigated natural processes in the economy, began macroeconomic modelling and tidied up trade and value theories. The English influence was smaller but at times important. John Locke (1632–1704), the English philosopher, was important for the Scots in monetary, value and property theories. Later, in the nineteenth century, the Scots, especially William Smart, used Austrian economics.

It is interesting to ask why people take to writing on economic theory and economic policy. It can be a job requirement, as with the academics discussed below who were expected to continue teaching an established curriculum, for example, Thomas Reid when he succeeded Adam Smith at Glasgow. There is a larger group of people who want to influence public policy. Many of these writers held seats in the Scottish or British parliaments and were expected to contribute to the debates of the day. Other prominent members of society such as clergy or lawyers were expected to provide intellectual leadership. The professional men of letters were alert enough to the issues of the day to include comments on population, currency, trade and other matters of general interest. Richard Fredrick Teichgraeber (1978) argues that Scots took to economics in the Scottish Enlightenment because they identified human personality with labour and that after 1707, deprived of their own parliament, they dropped their interest in politics in favour of economics. Discussion of economics was not confined to within university walls, however. Shinichi Nagao (2007) surveyed the eighteenth-century clubs of Edinburgh, Aberdeen and Glasgow and identified the economic themes of their debates. They discussed luxury, whether happiness of a nation is promoted by trade and manufacture, and the relative contribution of the landed and commercial interests to the tranquillity and stability of the state.

The profession of economist did not exist before the twentieth century, but that did not prevent people in a range of professions writing on matters of economic theory and policy. They built on their education or reflected on their experience in many walks of life to contribute to this emerging subject. It might be surprising to learn that several of these Scottish academic writers wrote on economics as part of their calling, despite the fact that chairs in political economy were not established in Edinburgh until 1870, Glasgow 1892, Aberdeen 1921 and St Andrews 1946. But it was legitimate to teach political economy because the scope of the moral philosophy then professed often included a political economy element which embraced many of the branches of modern economics. Men of education who spent their lives as lawyers, ministers of the Church of Scotland, landowners, men of letters, bankers and industrialists also participated in the economic debates of this long period. What most of them had in common was a Scottish university education.

Whereas earlier economics writers, especially the mercantilists, favoured the pamphlet as a vehicle for expressing their ideas, these writers had enough to say to write books hundreds of pages in length, although the pamphlet form did not disappear. A reason for the longer work was the advent of the comprehensive survey of political economy which, with the exception of Richard Cantillon (1680–1734), had not been attempted before Steuart and Smith. Later, Scottish users of the *principles of political economy* format included Dugald Stewart, Ramsay McCulloch and Shield Nicholson. In addition to the pamphlet and the book, the journal article emerged as a method of presenting the subject. 'Reviews' that discussed an economic issue on the basis of a cluster of related books were established in the early nineteenth century. Scotland was in the lead with the foundation of the *Edinburgh Review* in 1802; *Blackwood's*

Magazine from 1818 also afforded another place for the Scottish publication of economics.

The creation of a trade area, a monetary union and a fiscal union in Scotland in 1707 inspires the first group of themes of this book. Aspects of trade to be discussed include the purpose of trade, the nature of the exchange economy and the determination of the values used in exchange. The second change examines money through considering its function, the nature of paper credit and the problems of banking. The third discusses the functions of government giving rise to public expenditure, taxation and the national debt. Apart from these themes, which are taken from early eighteenth-century economic debates, there are subjects which can loosely be described as the 'condition of the people' – population, property rights, the distribution of income as rent, profits and wages, and poverty – and as the 'condition of the economy' – economic growth and economic development. Dow, Dow and Hutton (2000) observed that the Scottish tradition sees history as important, theory as limited and economic and political issues significant insofar as they inform the policymaker. However, this book on Scottish economic thought presents Scottish contributions to the development of both economic theory and policy. These writers became so dominant in British economics that popular authors such as Thomas Love Peacock, William Cobbett and Thomas Carlyle mocked economics for being Scottish (Grampp 1976: 544). The march of time from the eighteenth to the nineteenth centuries brings an ideological dimension to economics with the clash between varieties of capitalism and socialism.

The major figures in these developments were Hutcheson, Wallace, Hume, Steuart, Ferguson, Smith, Millar, Reid, Anderson, Stewart, Lauderdale, Sinclair, Chalmers, Nicholson and Smart: their short biographies appear in the appendix at the end of the book, while in the text the less significant writers are portrayed where they first appear.[1] The ideas of these many writers, however, are covered as relevant in the thematic chapters that follow.

[1] See 'Appendix: Biographical sketches of the major Scottish writers' on pages 308–11.

Trade

2

International trade

Trade is a good starting point for a discussion of post-1700 Scottish economic thought. The parlous state of Scottish trade both prompted the search for new policies to make the Scottish economy grow and changed the country's constitutional position with England. Discussions then and since have included a review of the good and bad effects of increasing a country's trade. For a small country like Scotland, with an economy open to the constant flows of imports and exports, trade is a necessity without which it would be unlikely to obtain the full range of goods its inhabitants desire and establish industries large enough to become efficient producers. William Playfair (1759–1823), an inventor from East Linton who devised statistical methods of presentation including the bar chart and pie chart, wrote about economics in a work on the rate of interest in 1785, and later published much on the rise and fall of nations. He neatly states: 'The smaller a district, or an island is, the exports and imports will be the greater, when compared with the number of inhabitants. Commerce is necessary because of the diversity of soil and climate, and of taste and manners' (1807: 270 footnote).

There was an awareness of the civilizing effects of trade. Francis Horner (1778–1817), who was educated at Edinburgh High School and at the University under Dugald Stewart, helped to found the *Edinburgh Review*. He was called to the English bar at Lincoln's Inn and entered parliament in 1803; as a Whig (member of a contemporary anti-Tory political party) he supported the liberal causes of the day and was particularly famous for recommending the appointment of a House of Commons Committee to inquire into the high price of bullion in 1810. He went to Pisa to cure his lungs, but died there soon after. In his journal entry for 19 February 1801 (commenting on a paper read at the Speculative Society of Edinburgh on 'the consequence of free commerce and intercourse between China and the rest of the civilised world') he wrote, 'There cannot be a more splendid prospect, than that of this new world being unfolded to the curiosity and the observation of European science . . . The mutual collision of diversified manners, opposing opinions, separate experience, will strike a reciprocal stimulus into each' (Horner 1843 I: 142–3).

To enter trade is to meet new people, encounter new goods and be aware of the possibilities of a different lifestyle. Through trading, new relationships are established between countries, which can either make for peace or raise jealousies leading to war, and the desire to stabilize trading patterns to its own advantage can encourage a country to colonize distant and less developed countries. However, when cheaper substitutes for domestic products become available this has a negative impact on home producers, who then tend to insist on fiscal and other protection for their industries. Increasing the amount of trade within a country is, therefore, potentially disruptive.

For a long time England had been reluctant to allow Scots to enter its trade. England's Navigation Acts of 1660 and 1663 specifically kept Scots out of the trade with the American plantations and the English coastal trade: the legislation ensured Scotland was treated as a foreign country. Scotland had mooted the possibility of a trade agreement with England in the crises of 1667, 1681 and 1689. The Darien venture of the Scotland Company (founded in 1695), which attempted, through voyages in 1698 and 1699, to establish a Scottish company to trade with Panama, collapsed, not least because England thwarted the whole enterprise by withdrawing royal permission. Scotland could not exploit its geographical position to the full due to the Alien Act of 1705 passed by the English parliament, which forbade the import of Scottish goods into England and its colonies, stopping half of Scotland's exports.

According to T. C. Smout (1963), at the union of the English and Scottish Crowns in 1603, King James VI of Scotland and I of England had wanted a customs union between the two countries, but the English had insisted that the commercial barrier remain. Through the union of Scotland and England, Scotland lost control of its foreign policy. It would never have started the three British wars against its best customer, the Dutch, in 1652–54, 1665–67 and 1672–74. As the Unionists had the strong argument that English trade was Scotland's largest trade, there were high Scottish hopes for the Union of 1707 – that the halcyon days which had preceded 1660 would return. After 1707 there would be an English market for Scottish linen and cattle, and Glasgow, free of English restrictions on Scottish trade, could supply Europe with American tobacco.

Discussions of trade abounded after 1700 in Scotland. A major argument for Scotland entering into a union with England had been the improvement of Scottish trade, even the continuance of it given England's proven hostility. Sir John Clerk of Penicuik (1676–1755), who had a university education at Glasgow and Leiden, was a prominent supporter of the proposed union, a large landowner and agricultural improver, an expert on public finance in the Scottish parliament and a member of the new parliament for Great Britain. Writing in 1705, he was sceptical about reviving Scotland's economy through a revaluation or debasement of the coinage, preferring to rely instead on trade policy. Because credit rather than money financed trade he advocated the expansion of bank credit based on land security; he also advocated ending the importation of luxuries, although he doubted if the benefits of this policy would be swift. Clerk, in his *Letter to a friend* (1706), argued that shipping on the Firth of Forth would increase and imports from abroad would fall because English goods would be bought instead of foreign products. Trade with the West Indies would be opened up and exports to England would increase as Scottish black cattle and linen would be admitted and herring exports would soar, supplanting the imports from Sweden, Norway and Denmark. There would be no customs on trade within Great Britain but the application of a common external tariff would mean changes to some tariffs on Scottish imports, although some of these changes would be reductions, for example, on tobacco, sugar and tar.

According to James Hodges, collaboration between Scotland and England would help both countries. Hodges, a Scottish clergyman and pamphleteer based in London and writing at the turn of the seventeenth and eighteenth centuries in 1706, argued that the union would enhance the trade of both Scotland and England. Joint British factories (trading stations) could push the Dutch out of fishing. Prior to the Aliens Act English and Scottish traders had the same access to markets; after the union that policy would be reinstated. Using the analogy of defence, whereby it would be ridiculous if Scotland prohibited England recruiting for the army and the navy north of the border, he argued that it would be absurd for each country to have special privileges in any area of national policy, including trade policies.

David Black, in his *Essay on industry and trade* (1706), put forward many trade proposals. In general he wanted to retain previous agreements, and to promote free trade. Direct trade with Spain was recommended and the scope for more trade with Holland was considerable as Scotland exported improvable, presumably semi-finished, goods. Despite the failure of the Darien scheme he still thought that Scotland could gain more from trade with the West Indies than with India – in his view Scotland had failed in the former only because of the jealousy of the English. Also, after the union, he argued that Scotland should still have its own Council of Trade.

Sir William Seton of Pitmedden (*c*.1673–1744) was a member of the Scottish parliament for Aberdeenshire and a critic of the Union of 1707. In *Scotland's Great Advantages* (1706) he recognized many trade advantages from Scotland's union with England, including access to English ports, a cheaper planting of colonies and participation in trading companies. In *Some thoughts on the ways and means for making this nation a gainer in foreign commerce* (1705) he pointed out that an advantage Scotland would gain from the union would be participation in a trade council that represented the whole of Britain – Scotland's trade had suffered from being subject to the Scots Privy Council, which had a pro-English bias. Instead there should be a nine-person Judicature of Trade elected by parliament. It would fix the duties on malt, flour and meal and use them for promoting Scottish fishing and other export professions. A trade policy would impose some import duties to benefit the national and not the merchants' interests, while export markets would be of Scotland's choosing and embrace Africa, America and all of Europe. He envisaged Scottish exports to be principally fish, wool, flax and corn. Goods for re-export would be free of import duties; imported goods that could not be improved would be heavily taxed. Also, granaries for both Scottish and foreign corn would avoid oscillations in the supply of corn from scarcity to plenty. As a rule he suggested, in standard mercantilist language, 'To sell more to Strangers yearly than we consume of theirs in value' (p. 19).

Thus trade could be improved by Scots having as great an access to markets as the English, and all the benefits of colonies' participation in trading companies. A new trade area made a new trade policy possible. Seton advocated a selective trade policy that argued that no trade with the East Indies was sensible for European countries because goods could be obtained in nearer places; he also maintained that there must be exemptions to free trade to prevent a profusion of inessential imports and the exhaustion of the British stock of money. In *The Interest of Scotland* (1700: 76) Seton elaborated on the various roles for a Council of Trade: encouragement of manufactures and fisheries, termination of wool exports, a lowering of interest rates and a fixing of grain prices, neither too much nor too little. Prior to the establishment of the council the nobility by their frugality and industry would set an example to manufactures and trade. He wanted education to be modernized, and Latin to be replaced with modern languages. According to Seton, agrarian reforms should include the enclosure of land for division into larger farms: this would reduce the problem of a high turnover of tenancies and financial ruin. Seton in his *Some thoughts* (1705) asserted that Scotland would have gained more by trade than by trusting in the security and strength of gold and silver. Using the small country argument, he writes that a society confined within narrow bounds is incapable of producing enough sustenance and is obliged to search for necessaries in neighbouring countries.

A dissenter from these views was William Black, clerk to the regality of Dunfermline. He was sceptical about the benefits of a union of the Scottish and English parliaments in his *Answer to a letter concerning trade* (1706), where he argued that Scots laws should regulate Scottish customs, that the extension of Scottish trade to trading through English companies would cost 5 or 10 per cent in the case of the East India Company, and that Scotland would have an imbalance with England because of the importation of English textiles and the expense of Scots attending court in London. In *Some overtures and cautions* (1707) he argued that after the union Scottish exports should be taxed at no more than the highest rates prior to the union, especially for linen and wool and that, for seven years, imports of silk, woollen and linen goods to Scotland should be banned. He thought a council of trade, which would consist of tradesmen and lawyers chosen by parliament and with powers to settle trade controversies, essential.

The quest for export-led growth was difficult. Rossner (2008) argues that trade did not stimulate economic growth in Scotland because it was evident, given the fact that the ratio of re-exports to total exports exceeded 50 per cent, that the country's overseas trade was an entrepôt one, that is, goods were imported then re-exported without charging import duties. Thus there was scarcely a linkage between trade and the economy as a whole and the national income was stagnant in the 1700–60 period. However, transit trades, especially in tobacco, were encouraged by the implementation in Scotland, after 1707, of the English Restoration Customs System of 1660. Thus the course of Scottish trade might be summarized as the English thwarting the Scots before 1707 and the effects of the union being slow to produce substantial benefits. Scotland had tried a westward trade expansion in the Darien scheme and failed, but by the nineteenth century the westward trade for tobacco was to become a pillar of a successful trading country.

Trade – general advantages

Trade theories try to explain why trade is undertaken: they examine the motives for exporting and importing and the consequences of doing so. Steuart, revelling in an extensive knowledge of foreign countries painfully acquired through fourteen years of exile, regards trade as tending to improve the world in general 'by rendering the inhabitants of one country industrious, in order to supply the wants of another, without any prejudice to themselves' (*Principles* I: 137). 'The object of trade . . . is no more than a new want, which calls for a set of men to supply it; and trade has a powerful effect in promoting industry, by facilitating the consumption of its produce' (I: 191). A reason for foreign trade is to obtain cheaper goods from countries whose established industries are more productive: in a sense this resembles Smith's linking of international trade to more specialization through the division of labour. In trade, Steuart says, what is traded is the surplus of labour, a kind of barter on an international scale. With a hint of what was later called the reciprocal demand theory of trade, Steuart thought that the regulator of trade between particular countries is their wants: trade will cease when the wants can be satisfied elsewhere.

Steuart plays down the importance of natural advantages in determining trade: 'Industry and labour are not properties attached to place, any more than oeconomy and sobriety' (I: 290). He lists the principles to be followed to make a country a powerful trading nation. First, sufficient labour should be applied to natural produce to keep prices of necessities low for those engaged in manufacturing. Second, profits should not be consolidated in higher prices; this presumably could be prevented by the entry of more firms, which would push down profits. Third, the demand, for luxuries must be maintained – if the export demand for them languishes private domestic demand is discouraged; failing that the statesman buys unsold exports or places bounties on exports. Thus what makes trade flourish is a mixture of private and state initiatives. Steuart described a positive trade balance as 'rivers of wealth . . . in brisk circulation . . . returned to this trading nation as blood returns to the heart' (*Principles* I: 226). When there is less exporting, there is more domestic circulation, which encourages the building of palaces and cities, leading to inequality, great private wealth and the need for more public credit. Conversely, with foreign trade, the whole of the industrious society benefits. He writes that trade is 'a scheme invented and set on foot by merchants, from a principle of gain, supported and extended among men, from a principle of general utility to every individual, rich or poor, to every society, great or small' (I: 200). 'Trade allows distant consumers to be supplied and intercourse among nations, bringing both private and public gain. The best trade policy is to encourage frugality and simplicity of manners at home so much can be exported and a taste for luxury abroad to create a demand for our exports' (I: 279).

The great apostle of free trade, David Hume, in his essay *Of Commerce*, laid down the advantages of foreign trade:

> in augmenting the power of the state, as well as the riches and happiness of the subject. It encreases the stock of labour in the nation; and the sovereign may convert what share of it he finds necessary to the service of the public. Foreign trade, by its imports, furnishes materials for new manufactures; and by its exports, it produces labour in particular commodities, which could not be consumed at home. In short, a kingdom, that has a large import and export, must abound more with industry, and that employed upon delicacies and luxuries, than a kingdom which rests contented with its native commodities. It is, therefore, more powerful, as well as richer and happier. The individuals reap the benefit of these commodities, so far as they gratify the senses and appetites. And the public is also a gainer, while a greater stock of labour is, by this means stored up against any public exigency; that is, a greater number of laborious men are maintained, who may be diverted to the public service, without robbing any one of the necessaries, or even the chief conveniences of life.
>
> (1987: 263)

State power, more industry and employment, and widespread public benefit are the consequences of trade. In other words, everyone wins through trade. He even suggests a divine sanction for trade: in his essay *Of the Balance of Trade*, when criticizing protective measures, Hume says 'they deprive neighbouring nations of that free communication and exchange which the Author of the world has intended, by giving them soils, climates, and geniuses, so different from each other' (1987: 325).

The principal immediate benefit of trade is the expansion of markets. Lauderdale in his notes on *WN* wrote 'The advantage of Foreign Trade to any Country certainly consists alone in its opening a more extensive Market and thereby encouraging the increase of Annual reproduction' (1996: 110). And, 'it is evident that the true policy of every nation is to encourage the commerce of its neighbours and to endeavour by opening a new market to their productions to contribute to the increase of their wealth ... attempt to impoverish our neighbours if attended with success must recoil upon ourselves' (p. 125). To the mercantilist, trade and industry are established because of war and ambition – princes hope trade will enrich them – but Lauderdale lacked the narrow view of trade associated with mercantilism: in his *An Inquiry into the Nature and Origin of Public Wealth, and into the Means and Causes of its Increase* (1804a) he writes that commerce, by promoting the interchange of commodities, internationally extends demand as well as 'exciting a quantity of industry that would otherwise have remained dormant' (p. 353). Commerce is 'the great cause of putting the means of increasing wealth into action' (p. 356) and 'cannot exist betwixt any two countries, without equally exciting the industry of both' (p. 359). He firmly asserts that wealth progresses according to the distribution of wealth in the growing countries. Thus, while there was extensive support for international trade, there were also detailed discussions on where and on what terms.

Mercantilism and its critique

Trade was obviously a beneficial activity but there was the ingrained idea that one country could do much better than others if it followed a policy of maximizing its trade surpluses and established trading monopolies at the others' expense. A closer examination, and refutation, of that view was needed in order to establish free trade.

In discussing how a simple trade in necessities can grow to the point that a nation has a trading superiority, Steuart utters sentiments similar to early mercantilists by discussing gaining superiority over neighbouring nations: 'by diminishing, on one hand, the quantity they have of this general equivalent (wealth); and increasing, on the other, the absolute quantity of it at home' (*Principles* I: 318). Further, he gives the statesman of a successful trading country the task of conducting himself 'so as to prevent the exportation of any part of that wealth which the nation may have heaped up within herself' (I: 337). Steuart makes the new point that it was through precious metals entering into foreign trade that, as an universal equivalent, 'they became the measure of power between nations, then the preservation of a proportional quantity of them became the more prudent, an object of the last importance' (I: 344). He claimed that imports have to be checked to see that they are necessary in the sense of leading to re-exports, or being intermediate products or supporting trade with a neighbouring nation; otherwise they must be cut off. Furthermore, he argued that exports of food that lead to population decline are the fault of the statesman.

Between trading countries there is the balance of trade, which can be in surplus, deficit or equal. Steuart says 'The balance of trade is the national profit, or the national loss' (III: 78), suggesting that it can be favourable or unfavourable. He was keen to distinguish a balance of trade from the balance of payments, a rare subtlety for the eighteenth century. Three elements must be added to the balance of trade – expenses of natives in foreign countries, payments of debts to foreigners and lending of money to other nations – to form the general balance of payments. A 'grand balance' is when a 'wrong' trade balance (where imports exceed exports) is added to those three elements.

Steuart both expounded and enhanced mercantilist thought, arguing that the benefit of a favourable balance of trade was not in terms of more specie (coin made of precious metals) but more employment, more subsistence, more shipping, the indebtedness of other countries and the importation of many durable commodities. The amount of specie is a poor indicator of the balance of trade because specie could be invested in foreign trade or hoarded, and paper currency instead of specie could be used domestically. No country, Steuart pointed out, has ever been drained of its specie as it would not spend its last shilling. He was further sceptical about the influence of the balance of trade on prices as 'the true influence which trade ought to have upon prices is never exactly known but to the merchants; who seldom fail to profit of their knowledge instead of communicating it for the benefit of the society' (III: 25). His emphasis is on demand rather than monetary factors: 'what turns the balance of trade in favour of a nation is the demand which foreign markets make for her commodities; now this demand, as it raises the value of her coin above her bullion, so it raises the price of her commodities, by increasing foreign competition to acquire them' (III: 55).

Smith in the *WN* conceded that the receipt of specie, prominent in mercantilist reasoning, is a benefit of trade; nevertheless, his trade theory had a different thrust. He thought trade provides a market for surpluses, giving us in return something we want. By providing a larger market there can be more division of labour and productivity competition to acquire such items.

Trade discussions of the time inevitably mentioned the East India Company, the largest British trading company and a pillar of the mercantile system. Mercantilism was a system for benefiting the trading monopoly – and the Company strove to be this monopoly. Steuart examined the Company's export of bullion to India to finance trade with China, a concern of the mercantilists of the seventeenth century because it violated the basic mercantilist doctrine of aiming to accumulate specie through trade. He argued in the Company's defence that such trade made Britain prosperous and brought in imports of desired consumption goods. In this attack on the Company's critics, Steuart rejected the idea of equating a pile of coin with wealth because

> People commonly estimate the wealth of a nation by the quantity of its coined money. Some go farther, and imagine that the quantity of the coined money is the representation, and even the measure of its wealth. I cannot be of this opinion . . . coin, like every other thing, is made in proportion to the occasions people have for it.
>
> (III: 60)

Steuart noted that the great monopoly trading companies gave merchants greater force by uniting several capitals, and that the elimination of competition increased the profits of the members of each company. But the exclusion of private adventurers raised prices for domestic buyers and gave retailers only the small advantage of being able to buy at the same price. Ever ingenious,

Steuart, mindful of the dubious conduct of companies, suggested a framework of company law for them, consisting of seven principles: (1) the competence of the directors of a new company should be examined, (2) the state should have the right to inspect as it would give public assistance to cover unforeseen losses, (3) creditors should become associates as a way of increasing capital without borrowing, an early recommendation of the securitization of debt, (4) to keep prices down, new members should be admitted to a company, (5) dividends should reflect the value of the fund and the industry of those managing the fund, (6) only merchants should unite into such companies, (7) public assistance should be given to existing, not outside, investors. This was a clever way of trying to make a controversial institution publicly acceptable by constructing a scheme of regulation. It was a scheme far ahead of its time but it was not enough to take pressure off the company.

In *WN* Smith was a critic of the East India Company for oppressing Indians, harming the interests of Britain, who could not benefit from trade competition, distorting the allocation of capital and taking on the role of defending merchants who would have been safer under the protection of the Crown. Smith regarded monopoly companies as a nuisance in every respect.

A stronger way of mounting an attack on mercantilism was to devise the theory of the price-specie flow mechanism. Hume's exposition of the mechanism is famous but he had his precursors in Isaac Gervaise (1680–1720) and Richard Cantillon (1680–1734). This theory linked a balance of trade surplus or deficit with flows of bullion and consequential price changes to demolish the early mercantilist doctrine of trade surplus. In *Of the Balance of Trade* Hume states his celebrated version of the mechanism:

> Suppose four-fifths of all the money in GREAT BRITAIN to be annihilated in one night, and the nation reduced to the same condition, with regard to specie, as in the reigns of the HARRYS and EDWARDS, what would be the consequence? Must not the price of all labour and commodities sink in those ages? What nation could then dispute with us in any foreign market, or pretend to navigate or sell manufactures in the same price, which to us would afford sufficient profit? In how little time, therefore, must this bring back the money which we had lost, and raise us to the level of all the neighbouring nations? Where, after we have arrived, we immediately lose the advantage of the cheapness of labour and commodities; and the farther flowing in of money is topped by our fullness and repletion.
>
> (1987: 311)

He also considers the contrary case when money is increased fivefold. As there is an associated price mechanism in exchange rates that can correct wrong balances of trade: 'When we import more goods than we export, the exchange turns against us, and this becomes a new encouragement to export; as much as the charge of carriage and insurance of the money which becomes due would amount to' (p. 312 footnote).

At the outset of discussing this mechanism it is important to note that it ignores time, incredibly suggesting flexibility and swift adjustment in a slow-moving traditional society. Hume writes that we can understand the balancing of trade throughout the world by looking at the communication between the provinces of a country, which bring money to the same level proportionate to 'the commodities, labour, industry, and skill, which is in the several states... The only circumstance that can obstruct the exactness of these proportions, is the expence of transporting the commodities from one place to another; and this expence is sometimes unequal' (p. 315 footnote). The analogy makes the mechanism seem more reasonable because adjustments within a country are easier than those between nations.

Early commentators on Hume questioned his theory. This dance of the three variables – the price level, the balance of trade and the quantity of money – was criticized in a number of ways. Steuart, in his powerful attack in the *Principles* on the quantity theory of money, expressed doubts about Hume's famous example of the effects of four-fifths of money in Great Britain being annihilated in a night because exportation of bullion would ruin the inhabitants. He argued that an economy could be sealed off from the effects of a balance of trade surplus if the surplus were left stagnant in the hands of money gatherers and not in circulation to raise prices. The effects of price rises would be ephemeral as foreigners would develop substitute goods. This view had the support of Henry Home, Lord Kames (1696–1782), a friend of David Hume and patron of Adam Smith. He acquired his knowledge of law in a private college then was admitted as an advocate in 1723, rising to become a judge in 1751. From 1728 he published collections of legal cases and books on moral philosophy that included his views on economics, farming and literary criticism. He asserted that 'it is not the quantity of gold and silver in a country that raises the price of labour and manufactures, but the quantity in circulation' (1796 I: 115), and that can be regulated by the state.

James Oswald of Dunnikier (1715–69) was at school with Adam Smith and was later MP for Kirkcaldy. In the most severe of contemporary criticisms, Oswald, writing to Hume in 1750, said he did not like the prediction that a fall in the quantity of money by four-fifths would cut the prices of labour and commodities by the same proportion. He thought that Hume misjudged the effects of a change in the quantity of money. An increase in the quantity of money could reduce wages because the price of imported goods had fallen; therefore, there could be an equalization of the prices of transportable goods without a similar stabilization in the amount of money. A drain of people and industry is not related to the quantity of money: a very small increase in the quantity of money would be sufficient to encourage cultivation and the inflow of workers attracted by higher wages. Oswald's survey of Holland, France and Spain indicated that price changes are not related to changes in the amount of money and so he thought that Hume's theory did not hold up with regard to the trade and money flows between a country's capital and its provinces. But Oswald did agree with Hume that trade restrictions raise the prices of labour and commodities.

Was Smith aware of Hume's price-specie flow mechanism? Viner (1927) had argued that the mechanism is mentioned in Smith's *LJ*, a view considered by Robert Eagly in his 1970 article, 'Adam Smith and the Specie-Flow Doctrine'. Smith might have ignored the effects of an influx of specie from abroad but he knew of the relationship between the foreign trade sector and an international specie flow, and analysed international monetary adjustment. Petrella (1968) says that Smith thought the influx would affect the price level but not relative prices, thus having no effect on output and real variables. Smith, as Hill (1997) reminds us, thought it expensive to shift goods internationally – thus there would be trade flows only if there were a big difference in national price levels.

In the modern debate on the price-specie flow mechanism Humphrey (1999) gives the standard praise that Hume showed the impossibility of a permanent trade surplus and that there would never be a scarcity of money because any quantity of money could drive trade, given price adjustments. However, Cesarano (1998), in pointing out that Hume uses the law of one price, states that the international adjustment occurs only if the increase in money is unexpected. Thornton (2007) thought that Cantillon was superior to Hume in his exposition of the mechanism because the latter used a cash balance effect, not a relative price effect. Samuelson (1980) condemned the Humean mechanism as wrong and incomplete for several reasons: the allocation of money ignores the cost of transporting gold and, also, unless there is a change in the terms of trade, the gold drain will stop when people run out of excess money. Further, Hume needed to consider the transfer problem, changes in tastes for goods, a reduction in the supply of an important good and the Marshall–Lerner condition, which insists on imports and exports being responsive to price changes.

Hume did not produce an attack-free theory of trade but he did something more: he showed how one can produce and play with an economic model.

Trade and colonies

In international terms, a country can avoid all trade, trade with a few selected partners or attempt to trade with everyone. The contrast is usually between the first and the third: between protection, or autarky, and free trade. The middle position, selective trading, can be achieved in the relationship between a European country and its colonies, or through trade treaties between pairs of countries.

Mercantilist writers on trade and Scottish pamphleteers examined the role of colonies. Colonial expansion had long been considered by the Scots, and as economics gradually shed its mercantilist clothes the attitude towards these foreign possessions changed. Insh (1932) chronicled early Scottish colonial ventures, beginning with seventeenth-century schemes including the Covenanters' colony in South Carolina in 1684 at Stuart's Town. Memories of Scotland's Darien venture of the 1690s to establish a colony on the Panama isthmus were fresh in 1707.

Early in the eighteenth century the acquisition of colonies was central to Scotland's trade policy. Such territories could provide a source of raw materials and be a market for Scottish manufactures. Patrick Lindsay (1686–1753), son of the rector of St Andrews Academy, who traded in Edinburgh, had colonies in mind when he advocated many legislative changes to boost trade. Plantations, or colonies, in his selfish view existed only for the benefit of Britain. He argued that

> Foreign Colonies are a great Benefit to a Nation, especially in Countries where commodities may be raised as a subject for foreign Commerce that cannot be had at home. But great Care must be taken to encourage them to employ all their own Trade and to prevent their making of any manufactured Goods of their own; for that would be to drain us of our People, and our Wealth, instead of increasing it.
>
> (1736: 129)

In Lindsay's view, colonies could extend the range of goods we consume and expand trade and manufacturing.

The colonies were expected to provide a constant fund of raw materials to keep British manufactures employed. Realizing that demand for exported manufactured goods could be increased only by selling at low prices, or by increasing the wealth of foreign customers, in 1785 James Anderson argued that Britain could only change prices. He dismissed the idea that free trade, which would have increased wealth all round, as a policy of colonization is contrary to the liberty of trade.

Support for colonization continued after 1800. Henry Brougham (1778–1868), educated at Edinburgh University and called to the Scottish and English bars, participated in the founding of the *Edinburgh Review* and wrote controversial political articles for it. In 1810–12 he sat in parliament as a Whig for Camelford, and for Winchelsea from 1815; he was Lord Chancellor from 1830 to 1834. He supported many liberal causes, including education – helping to found Birkbeck College, London – and he was a legal reformer. In a book of 1803, he broadly approved of colonization, regarding its first object as the preservation of the union between parts of an empire. He contrasted agricultural colonies, which expand rapidly, are less liable to invasion and rely less on the receipt of commerce and credit from the metropolis, with the smaller, more valuable colonies peopled by merchants and planters. Brougham opposed the opinion that colonization caused the wars of 1739, 1756 and 1778, and was eager to assert the benefits to a nation of having colonies. One benefit was that the exchequer of Great Britain derived an income from its colonies, including payment of premia for the renewal of Britain's charters. Also, West Indian proprietors brought colonial wealth under government control, supported British industry and contributed to tax revenue by residing in Britain; rich colonies widened the market for British produce; the colonial trade created reciprocal markets, speculations were safer and there was more confidence in debtors. While admitting that there would be slower returns than from the home trade, because new settlements were undercapitalized and distant, he claimed that their establishment gave children more social prospects, enabling 'persons of rank' to be able to afford to marry and the colonies to absorb the excess population of the mother country. In response to Smith's criticism that colonization created monopolies, Brougham replied that Britain was like other European countries in having monopolies: a British monopoly would replace one from Europe. The privileges of these monopolies he thought were exaggerated because their rights were often superfluous, ephemeral and unreciprocated. Free trade was unlikely to produce more flows of goods than a monopoly could.

According to Archibald Alison (1792–1867), who was educated at Edinburgh University, became an advocate and sheriff of Lanarkshire from 1835, and wrote on European history and economic policy, colonies thrived on trading privileges. In his book of 1840, *The Principles of Population and their connection with human happiness*, he argued that there has to be a preferential reciprocal relationship between a parent country and its colonies otherwise the colonies would cease their allegiance. This was the basis of the Navigation Acts, which excluded foreign ships from the trade between Britain and its colonies. Alison noted that trade flourished better under the colonial system, proved by the expanding trade between Britain and Australia, and the East and West Indies.

But there was opposition to colonization. Anderson, in his *The Interest of Great Britain with regard to the American Colonies considered to which is added An Appendix containing the outline of a plan for general pacification* (1782), detailed important objections to such acquisition of overseas territories. Colonies distort the pattern of world production; for example, crops that could have been grown more cheaply in Africa were instead grown in the West Indies, where there were British colonies. Anderson further argued that colonies were difficult to defend, liable to be an issue in wars and had a grave effect on British public finances because they were not a source of tax revenue but the cause of high public expenditure – half of which could have been avoided if there had been no settlement and defence of American colonies. Taxation would have been lower in Britain if it lacked colonies and there would not have been a loss of British capital and labour abroad. What was spent on defending Gibraltar, for example, would be better invested in removing tolls from British canals. Great private fortunes came from the colonies but in the eighteenth century the national debt rose because of wars involving colonies. In Anderson's view, if those who made fortunes out of colonies had been taxed more heavily then colonies would have been more generally acceptable.

Alison, too, could appreciate the disadvantages of colonies. He thought the reciprocity system failed because it attempted to encourage trade between European states with similar jealousies and desires. As it lacked the real reciprocity of lowering duties for all goods entering into trade it prevented each country trading according to its comparative advantage. Ideal reciprocity arrangements, he thought, should be with countries similar to and competitive with Britain, not between old and new countries. The system of reciprocity, however, was broader in concept than the Navigation Acts or the colonial trade in that it was flexible enough to establish a variety of links between countries by treaty.

Smith had strong views on colonies. In the *WN* he contended that there was no necessity for European countries to set up colonies in America and the West Indies, and that, as a result, British trade became roundabout through colonial produce first being exported to the mother country then elsewhere, as with tobacco. He regarded the restriction of particular exports under the colonial system to suit the merchants' interests as a violation of the sacred rights of mankind and could see in the colonial trade what he disliked intensely – the misallocation of capital. According to Smith, capital that could have been used in Britain got tied up in the colonies for several years and the monopoly established by the Navigation Acts drew capital from other trades, with the colonial trade disproportionately benefiting from unnaturally high profits. These profits – in a departure from the natural course of things – caused capital to be diverted from improving land. A trader, Smith argued, naturally wants to employ capital at home, saving the trouble, risk and expense of exportation and enjoying the frequent returns to home, in contrast to colonial investment with its distant and slow rewards. Furthermore, if investment were at home, employment in Britain would rise. Smith also disliked the public financial consequences of a country possessing colonies. The public expense of defending a colony with a peacetime military establishment made colonies undesirable. Smith therefore suggested a major constitutional reform for the colonies: the British parliament should decide what proportion of the colony's revenues raised by the assembly the colony should pay to Britain then the provincial assembly would decide on appropriate taxation and the colonies should send representatives to Westminster. He wanted a gradual relaxation of the laws to move from exclusive trade with the colonies to free trade with foreign competition in order to keep the rate of profit down to the common rate. Smith was unable to persuade the British government to implement his proposals for America but his idea of taxation linked to participation in the British parliament was adopted for Ireland. Smith was right in seeing colonies as a relic of the mercantile system he despised: once the argument for free trade had triumphed there was no justification for exclusive trading relationships with colonies.

Protection and free trade

Put crudely, the contrast between classical economic and mercantilist trade policies is regarded as a battle between free trade and protection. But it is more complicated than that because a disposition towards free trade was evident in late mercantilism, and, in matters of policy, including trade policy, classical economists had exceptions to their general principles. In the period of classical economics the debate between free trade and protection was mainly centred on opposition to and support for the Corn Laws. Adam Smith argued for free trade most of the time but did not invent free trade doctrine in 1776 with his first edition of *Wealth of Nations* – he had his precursors. One of these was William Paterson (1658–1719), who had promoted the Darien scheme to establish a Scottish colony on Panama and had founded the Bank of England, and was, according to Steel (1896), a free trader at the beginning of the eighteenth century with a liberal attitude to other races.

Another such was Francis Hutcheson. In matters of international trade policy, Hutcheson was, for the most part, a free trader, although he admits minor exceptions to achieve other economic ends. He hints that imposing a tariff can be beneficial:

> Goods prepared for export should generally be free from all burdens and taxes, and so should the goods be which are necessarily consumed by the artificers, as much as possible... Where one country alone has certain materials, they may safely impose duties upon them when exported; but such moderate ones as shall not prevent the consumption of them abroad.
>
> (*System* II: 318)

He was willing to contemplate a moderate departure from free trade principles to exploit an advantage in supply. Eighteenth-century writers were aware of what can be called the principal arguments for a tariff – an increase in tax revenue, higher employment, a change in income distribution, improved national security, a change in the balance of trade and the nursing of infant industries. Although Hutcheson hinted at worries about creating a trade deficit, he emphasized the employment effects:

> Foreign materials should be imported and even premiums given, when necessary, that all our own hands may be employed; and that, by exporting them again manufactured, we may obtain from abroad the price of our labours. Foreign manufactures and products ready for consumption, should be made dear to the consumer by high duties, if we cannot altogether prohibit the consumption; that they may never be used by the lower and more numerous orders of the people, whose consumption would be far greater than those of the few who are wealthy.
>
> (p. 319)

After 1707 the Scots had mixed attitudes towards international free trade. Steuart, long labelled a protectionist, had in fact a subtle approach to trade policy. Sen (1957) said Steuart wanted government policy to be adjusted to the type of trade as inland trade requires the encouragement of luxury at home but foreign trade the discouragement of such goods in order to increase exports.

Hume was one of the pioneers of free trade policy at home and abroad, according to Hardin (2007). Like Smith, he wanted large international markets to increase the division of labour and hence prosperity.

Free trade emerged as a policy to get rid of the bad effects of protection. Duncan Forbes of Culloden, in a 1730 pamphlet, *Considerations on the state of the nation, as it is affected by the excessive use of foreign spirits*, was deeply critical of contemporary protectionism, arguing that high import duties caused smuggling, and that manufacturing was not encouraged because bounties (subsidies) were often obtained by fraud so the exports did not materialize. For example, he contended that the smuggling of brandy caused a glut of spirits and that, if the gentry of Scotland switched to the consumption of brandy, this would threaten Scottish agriculture and lower the value of estates because reduced demand for other alcohol – beer, ale and spirits – would lower their prices. According to Forbes, the gentry of Scotland should vow not to purchase or drink brandy. In a further pamphlet of 1744 he argued that after 1707, in order to evade tariffs, smuggling had replaced fair trade in most of Scotland. Another consequence of smuggling was the shrinking of the fishing industry, as men turned from fishing to smuggling. Forbes argued that it was up to landlords to exert pressure on fishermen and tenants by writing to each other about smugglers, encouraging smugglers to take up honest trades such as linen manufacture, thus increasing employment and the money in circulation, and encouraging farmers to stop sheltering smugglers' boats.

Both protectionists and free traders believed trade brings national greatness and benefit. Whereas mercantilists might believe that trade was a zero-sum game with one country gaining only at the expense of another, another view of trade – that it need not be based on rivalry – gradually emerged. Thomas Melvill, a weaver writing in 1734, asserted that 'Trade is the only Thing that can make a Nation truly Great in itself, and amiable in the Eyes of its Neighbours' (p. 39).

Hume used many arguments to advocate free trade. In his attack on protection in *Of the Balance of Trade* he focuses on those wanting to prohibit exports: 'They do not consider, that, in this prohibition, they act directly contrary to their intention; and that the more is exported of any commodity, the more will be raised at home, of which they themselves will always have the first offer' (1987: 308). Hume thought little of the relentless striving for trade surpluses and raises the sophisticated point that statistical deficiencies make the balance of trade unknowable: 'all calculations concerning the balance of trade are founded on very uncertain facts and supposition. The custom-house books are allowed to be an insufficient ground of reasoning; nor is the rate of exchange much better; unless we consider it with all nations, and know also the proportions of the several sums remitted; which one may safely pronounce impossible' (p. 310), referring to the 'numberless bars, obstructions, and imposts' (p. 324). But Hume is aware of the several arguments for a tariff: 'A tax on GERMAN linen encourages home manufactures, and thereby multiplies our people and industry. A tax on brandy encreases the sale of rum, and supports our southern colonies. And as it is necessary that imposts should be levied, for the support of government, it may be thought more convenient to lay them on foreign commodities, which can easily be intercepted at the port, and subjected to the impost' (*Of the Balance of Trade* 1987: 324). This was not strong support for protection but the beginnings of a practical fiscal policy.

Free trade is defended more forcefully in his *Of the Jealousy of Trade*, where he writes that domestic industry cannot be hurt by the greater prosperity of its neighbours: 'where an open communication is preserved among nations, it is impossible but the domestic industry of every one must receive an encrease from the improvements of the others' (p. 328). And, 'If our neighbours have no art or cultivation, they cannot take them [from others]; because they will have nothing to give in exchange... The riches of the several members of a community contribute to encrease my riches, whatever profession I may follow. They consume the produce of my industry, and afford me the produce of theirs in return' (pp. 328–9). Hume says that he is against protecting a staple industry as industry can be diverted from one branch to another: a people is happier if there is a variety of manufactures. Protection produces sloth and ignorance because, where no commodities are exchanged, 'Our domestic commerce itself would languish for want of emulation, example, instruction' (p. 331). Thus Hume sees that individual prosperity and income depend on mutual prosperity. It is a short-term view to try to ruin another country in order to make gains for oneself, since exports can be sold only to countries rich enough to buy them. By this reasoning Hume helped to make markets central to trade theory.

The central theme of Smith's trade theory, underlying arguments for free trade, was the extension of the division of labour principle from a single country to the world in order to produce widespread benefits through specialization. Smith reasons in Book IV of the *WN* that a kingdom, like a household, should be prudent. 'If a foreign country can supply us with a commodity cheaper than we ourselves can make it, better buy it of them with some part of the produce of our own industry, employed in way in which we have some advantage' ([1776] 1976: 457). This is the absolute advantage theory, or explanation, of trade. One country often has great natural advantages over another, so it is absurd to have trade restrictions to encourage, for example, the production of wine in Scotland. But, more so than Hume, Smith recognized exceptions to free trade. In *LJ* Smith wrote, 'A free commerce on a fair consideration must appear to be advantageous on both sides. We see that it must be so betwixt individuals unless one of them be a fool and makes a bargain plainly ruinous; but betwixt prudent men it must always be advantageous. For the very cause of the exchange must be that you need my goods more than I need them, and I need yours more than you do yourself... it must be profitable to both' (p. 390). All that is produced is for the sake of consumption, which makes it useful. What commerce does is to produce the greatest quantity of necessaries for domestic consumption or exchange for something which is wanted more. 'The whole benefit of wealth and industry is that you either employ a greater number or give those already employed a more comfortable subsistence...' (p. 391). Trade can be bilateral or multilateral: 'if you stop the importation of claret, you stop the manufactures which would be sent to Spain no less effectually than by a direct prohibition. These prohibitions hurt ourselves more than they do the French... By our prohibiting French wines we are supplied intirely by the Portuguese at a higher price and in inferior quality than we would be from France' (pp. 391–2).

This multilateral argument is far-sighted and was to lead to the founding of international trade organizations in the twentieth century. However, interestingly, Smith was willing to allow exceptions to completely free trade. In his view, trade restriction is permissible for the defence of the country, as with the Act of Navigation, which expanded the merchant fleet by insisting on British goods being shipped in British boats, and an import tariff is permissible to match a similar tax on home-produced goods; he argues that retaliatory tariffs are used to induce a negotiation for the removal of tariffs between countries. Free importation of goods where British exports had a bounty would not, according to Smith, be a problem as British exports were cheap enough to meet competition.

Smith also used the 'vent for surplus' argument to justify trade:

> When the produce of any particular branch of industry exceeds what the demand of the country requires, the surplus must be sent abroad, and exchanged for something for which there is a demand at home. Without such exportation, a part of the productive labour of the country must cease, and the value of its annual produce diminishes. The land and labour of Great Britain produce generally more... than the demand of the home-market requires. The surplus part of them, therefore, must be sent abroad, and exchanged for something for which there is a demand at home.
>
> (p. 372)

This doctrine reflects the idea that the division of labour makes a great increase in production possible and that the amount of division will depend on the extent of the market. John Stuart Mill thought the doctrine erroneous as it suggests that a country is under some necessity to produce a surplus (*Principles of Political Economy* 1848: Book III, chapter XVII). A more sympathetic view of Smith would be that this describes enterprising producers who will attempt to expand their markets to release their output as producing at a higher volume lowers unit costs and reduces prices to more appealing levels. It is a realistic account of any enterprising growing business that tries to create a large market.

In *WN*, Book IV, chapter II, Smith admits that freedom of trade would cause great disruption in the economy. It is like the ending of the war, he observed, mentioning the 100,000 without work when the Seven Years' War ended in 1763. But the people leaving the army and navy were not entirely deprived of employment and subsistence; ex-servicemen were absorbed into different occupations, and wages did not fall nor did the number of vagrants increase.

This was helped by the fact that ex-soldiers and seamen had the liberty to enter trade, if corporations allowed them to do so. Although Smith admits that completely free trade is as likely as establishing Oceana or Utopia in Great Britain because of all the private interests in favour of protection, he was still an advocate for it. Smith contends that the wealth of a neighbouring country is dangerous in war but in peace it will 'enable them to exchange with us to a greater value, and to afford a better market' (p. 494). He further argues that, even if free trade produces a bilateral trade deficit, Britain can re-export some of the imports.

Smith is famous as an apostle of free trade but was not entirely original in the position he adopted. He was inspired by Hume but did not hold as wholehearted a libertarian policy. Winch (1996) notes that Smith, in his fourth book, *Wealth of Nations*, describes the wider benefits of trade in unifying the world, communication of knowledge and improvement, and creating respect between nations. Sen (1957) finds that Smith used many of Steuart's views on trade. Distinctively, Smith's views had a practical tinge and Teichgraeber (1978) rightly reminds us that Smith was influenced by his observation of the commercial growth of Glasgow where he spent the formative years of life. Consquently, he did not adopt an extreme position on trade but argued for domestic trade as being more secure than foreign trade (Grampp 2000).

After Smith, many Scottish writers were keen free traders but, like Smith, their attitudes could be ambiguous. James Dunbar, for example, who taught moral philosophy at King's College, Aberdeen, and died in 1798, asserted his free trade creed: 'commerce ought to be free, and monopolies of every kind are against the general interest of the commercial world. The late commercial treaty between this country and France seemed to be the result of an enlightened policy' (1789–94: 46).

David Buchanan (1779–1848), a Montrose man who edited the *Caledonian Mercury* and then the *Edinburgh Courant*, wrote on political economy and for *Encyclopaedia Britannica*, and was also a printer. He praised Smith's absolute advantage theory because international specialization means 'the bounties of Providence are distributed in a fair proportion among all nations . . . The only encouragement which trade requires is a free market for its produce, in which the best articles will always command a ready sale . . . Protecting duties, as well as bounties, are imposed for the benefit of the ignorant and incapable . . . Such manufactures as cannot stand their ground without protection should be left to their fate . . .' (1844: 113–15). In other words, protecting some commodities raises the profits of dealers at the expense of others; consequently, prices are raised for the British consumer.

But the Scots increasingly questioned free trade. Chalmers, in his 1808 *An Inquiry into the Ixtent and Stability of National Resources*, seemed to favour protection, dissenting from much of the classical trade position. Writing when Napoleon, through his Continental System, was attempting to exclude Britain from trading with Europe, Chalmers thought it erroneous to regard foreign commerce as essential to national survival. He hoped that this cessation of trade would make Britain aware of the sufficiency of its natural resources and that, in this isolated state, a higher communal ideal would be pursued in a spirit of Spartan self-denial. As his biographer Brown (1982) notes, his vision was rural and static: he was unable to see the dynamic effects of industrialization. Later Chalmers professed himself to be a free trader wanting to abandon all tariffs in favour of an increased land tax. But such trade would entail the industrialization he abhorred. Hilton (1988) contrasts Thomas Robert Malthus (1766–1834) – who was a protectionist most of his life and, through publishing his *An Essay on the Principle of Population* in 1798, inspired a long debate in economics between the relative growth rates of population and subsistence – with Chalmers, who was a fervent free trader from at least 1819, when he joined the cries for the abolition of the Corn Laws.

In an attack on free trade, Alison argued that even the most cautious trader is exposed to great risk because of the periodic contractions of credit, and that it is vain to expect manufactured exports to balance agricultural imports:

> Ages must elapse – generations go to their graves – before the serfs of Poland, or the half-savages on the Mississippi, have either acquired the wealth to purchase, or the habits to desire, the manufactured luxuries of this country. (1847: 78)

In an article entitled 'Free Trade and Protection' for *Blackwood's Magazine* of March 1844 Alison had little praise for free trade. He said that reciprocity occurs under free trade only in retrospect and that commerce and manufacturing are so high in Great Britain there is no point in further expansion. Objection after objection to free trade flowed from his pen. Free trade is fatal to the manufacturing of the younger state and to the agriculture of the older; as in ancient Rome, cheap grain prices will ruin domestic agriculture. He suspected that the motivation of the free traders was a desire for a system of falling grain prices so that wages could be lowered. In his *Blackwood's Magazine* article of July 1848 he praised the wisdom of the Navigation Laws for giving England unparalleled maritime strength and colonial empire: if repealed, income would be transferred from shipbuilders and seafarers to merchants and purchasers. To blast free trade he tried to quantify its effects: he thought it had caused 8,000 to be unemployed in Manchester and over 10,000 in Glasgow, contrary to the free traders' predictions. Asserting that free trade does not encourage industry in both countries, he summons in support Adam Smith, who had argued that home trade is worth all foreign trade put together. Free trade, Alison said, had caused ruinous competition, which affected West Indian sugar and Canadian grain, lost half of the realized wealth of Liverpool, Manchester and Glasgow and created 100,000 paupers. In *Blackwood's Magazine*, December 1849, he blamed free traders for causing a decline in the British population: in the previous three years 250,000 to 300,000 annually had left to seek food abroad. According to Alison, if unchecked the free traders would reduce 'the immense empire of England to two islands, oppressed with taxes, eaten up by paupers, importing a third of their annual subsistence from foreign states, brought in foreign bottoms (ships)' (p. 660).

Overall he had a gloomy insular view. He had tried to measure the impact of liberalizing international trade but he lacked the talents of a successful controversialist: he did not expound his opponents' views with an earnest attempt to understand them before rushing to demolish them.

Trade tariff debates were central to British politics at the end of the nineteenth century following the Colonial Conference of 1887 when the idea of imperial preference was suggested. Joseph Shield Nicholson, professor of political economy at Edinburgh University 1880–1925, using his knowledge of Adam Smith, steered a course between free trade and protection. Nicholson's article, 'Free Trade and Protection. A Reconciliation', of 25 November 1916, reveals Smith's middle position between full trade liberalization and protection, saying that Smith championed 'fair trade' as a combination of both trade policy positions. Nicholson did not revive the old leading arguments, thinking that bounties (subsidies) in practice offered little extra employment and infant industries grew up to be established industries with vested interests. But he did advocate protection for defence industries and wanted free trade within the British Empire, partly to encourage manufacturing industry. He was not a rabid imperialist – his scheme could still work in a smaller empire if commercial treaties with Britain continued. Nicholson, in his *The Tariff Question* (1903), attempts to make mild protection acceptable, despite disliking the term 'protection', which suggests inferior goods produced at home and unable to face international competition. He points out that the foreign exporter often pays the import tariff; if tariffs were reduced, the revenue would have to be found from other sources by the Treasury. Writing later, Nicholson reveals how mixed Smith's views were on free trade:

> the present-day Free Trader will find in his Adam Smith a series of shocks and surprises. Instead of being cosmopolitan, Adam Smith was intensely nationalist, or rather imperialist ... The real strength of Free Trade lies in the stress laid on the character and initiative of the individual. Its great danger is that unlimited competition may destroy the ideas of nationality and national welfare.
>
> (1917: 416–17)

Corn Laws

The specific policy issue that dominated trade discussions until the mid-nineteenth century was the Corn Laws. The policy provided an opportunity for economics writers to raise many of the issues in the eternal debate of free trade versus protection. Article VI of the Act of Union of 1707 granted a bounty of two shillings and sixpence on beer or bigg (barley) and on oatmeal, when the price at the time of its exportation from Scotland was at or under fifteen shillings. The restrictions on the import of grain in various forms and the subsidization of exports had existed for centuries but the debate on whether the corn trade should be free was intense in the eighteenth and early nineteenth centuries in Scotland.

Two teams lined up: the supporters of the Corn Laws, which had the twin objects of boosting exports and curbing imports, and the opponents. The supporters' team had many members.

The Corn Laws were expected to boost corn production. Steuart favoured this form of protection to feed a population that had become larger through an expansion of the manufacturing sector. He argued for cutting off hurtful trade by restrictions, duties and prohibitions to keep wealth higher in Britain than in other countries. Anderson (1785) in a postscript to Letter 13 praised the bounty on corn, *contra* Adam Smith, for encouraging the production of corn, thereby enriching the nation and giving farmers security. He argued against Smith's view that the price of corn is fundamental as manufactures can regulate the price of corn and there is not a correlation between corn prices and wages.

As a leading agricultural reformer Sir John Sinclair could be expected to observe and analyse the Corn Laws in great detail. In a pamphlet of 1791 he extols the importance of agriculture: 'Our acres, when once improved, cannot be run away with; whereas the arts of manufacture and those machines on which their superiority in this country so much depend, may be filched from us by our neighbours... With a productive territory, we may unquestionably consider ourselves as independent of every other power' (pp. 9–10). In another work of 1822 he argues that landowners must unite to preserve the value of their properties in the face of low product prices. There was much he disliked in the Corn Laws, which had not protected agriculture: Britain imported 19.5 million quarters of corn even in the war conditions of 1792 to 1813. Sinclair questioned the warehousing system used to keep foreign grain out of the domestic market until domestic prices rose, because it encourages merchants to speculate, incites smuggling and causes discontent in the populace, as they know that cheap grain is stored. However, he conceded that if Britain gave up its scattered warehouses, the Dutch or others would assume that function. He tackled the familiar criticism of the Corn Laws that they promoted the cultivation of inferior land, thinking it absurd to say that the value of the produce depends on the value of the produce of inferior soils. According to Sinclair, the most fertile crop is harvested first and through its superiority commands a greater price. He believed that, by keeping prices high, the higher return to capital encourages improvement and that Britain was more able to produce grain because of enclosures, better cultivation methods, threshing, and better knowledge of the diseases of wheat. Furthermore, in his view, people consume a broader range of foodstuffs. Thus no foreign grain is required if farmers are treated with confidence and kindness.

Overall, Sinclair was on the side of protection. He concluded that high duties should remain on corn unless there is a dearth. In another work of 1833

Sinclair uses multiplier analysis to trace the effects of the prosperity of one class on others, stating that the abolition of the Corn Laws would be the undoing of the farming and landed interests – and that the manufacturing and commercial classes would be affected if their customers were reduced to poverty and ruin. The inflow of imports after abolition would send unemployed farmers into the town to become cotton spinners and weavers; consequently the textile industry would be hit by a fall in demand and an excessive labour force. Buying imported wheat means that the sales proceeds go into the circulation and wealth of another country. Only rarely do foreigners exporting grain to Scotland buy Scottish manufactures, therefore, 'Our great object . . . ought to be, to discover the best means of increasing the supply at home, by means of *domestic industry*, and not to depend on the winds and the waves, or the good-will of other nations, for the means of our subsistence' (1833: 8).

Protection, Sinclair thought, would not have the bad effect of creating an agricultural monopoly: British agriculture with more than half a million competing farms was hardly in a state of monopoly and imports could still be allowed at times of great scarcity, while warehoused stocks could be used to stabilize prices. Sinclair also argued in the 1830s that a farmer cannot decide how much to cultivate without a firm expectation of the price: farmers would need a level of duties of at least 28 shillings per quarter but the maximum proposed was 12 shillings. Sinclair claimed that duties should be linked to average prices to protect the British farmer from price fluctuations, and he found an indirect supporting argument in Adam Smith (*WN* II), who said that the increase in wealth coming from agricultural improvement is more durable than that from commerce, a cyclical industry. Sinclair appears forceful because he specifically examines agriculture in a period of protection; nevertheless, the theorectical foundation for the free traders' view is left undamaged by his arguments.

As late as 1815, as Paglin (1946) notes, Lauderdale showed his protectionism in his strong support for the Corn Bill of that year. He believed that the Corn Laws protected British agriculture from the effects of foreign surpluses and gave Britain an independent food supply, as well as stimulating employment and demand. He questioned whether free trade could come into being merely by removing the Corn Laws, as other taxes on agriculturalists would remain.

A strong argument used for the Laws was the possibility of great price stability. Through subsidizing corn exports, *The Bee*, 16 February 1791, stated: 'The great objects to be aimed at in a corn law are, to encourage the growth of grain in this country, to keep the average prices of that commodity, as nearly the same as possible, and as low as circumstances can permit' (Anderson 1791–94: pp. 305–6).

The legislature thus should encourage that which leads to wider cultivation and more prosperity. The success of the two sectors, agriculture and manufacturing, march together, *The Bee* argued, and an increased demand for grain increases its price and leads to the cultivation of barren lands. To increase the stabilization impact of the bounty, Anderson wanted it to be variable and based on an average price high enough to stimulate production on less fertile soil, enabling enough food supply in severe years. According to Prendergast (1987) Anderson's predominant motivation in supporting the Corn Laws was a desire to stabilize grain prices and show that Smith was wrong in failing to appreciate that subsidizing exports would increase production.

Price stabilization also concerned George Skene Keith (1752–1823), an Aberdeen graduate and a Church of Scotland minister who wrote on agricultural matters. He produced an analysis of the Corn Laws in 1792, which is full of criticisms and recommendations. Because the bounty on oats was insufficient to pay the canal dues, it impeded the export of corn from the east side of Scotland to Glasgow and to the north-east of England. He suggested that the bounties on exports and taxes on imports should be determined by the average prices of the kingdom, not the prices of each district. With price stabilization as the goal, he suggested that, at a time of good harvests when the price of corn is low, the bounty should only ensure payment for labour and transport; the bounty should be granted gradually and when the domestic price is high, exports should be banned and imports permitted. In general Anderson thought bounties are justified because the supply of corn produced at home is more reliable than foreign corn and bounties are a stimulus to labour. He saw no evidence that Britain would benefit from free trade.

Lauderdale, on the other hand, adheres to the free trade principle in general: 'That perfect freedom of intercourse, unimpaired either directly or indirectly by legislative interference, must ensure a state of the greatest commercial prosperity, is a proposition I wish you to understand me as admitting in its utmost latitude...' (1814: 4), but argues that free trade in corn would injure the corn trade if other trades were still protected. He also reminds us that, in ancient Rome, encouraging imports ruined domestic production, and suggests that granting a bounty on corn can be justified as an exception to the rule that 'the supply of every article suiting itself to the extent of the demand for it' (p. 19), because foresight and industry in cultivation is not enough to cope with the scarcity arising from an unfavourable season. According to him, it was more important to recognize that the Corn Laws had enabled an abundance of subsistence in the face of seasonal variations in corn production than accuse them of distorting the pattern of investment.

Kames (1796) argued that widespread prosperity came from the Corn Laws, because the bounty on corn increased the demand for workers and lowered the domestic price of corn. Alexander Dirom (1725–88), provost of Banff in north-east Scotland, in his posthumous tract (1796) in favour of the Corn Laws, linked protecting the corn trade to maintaining the prosperity of the kingdom. He would tolerate corn imports, a threat to Scottish agriculture, only in times of dire need: in his view, every person in agriculture had to raise enough corn to support himself and four others. The Corn Laws both expanded exports and provided plenty of food at home, enabling population increase. Furthermore, if exports were subsidized both employment and demand for shipping would rise.

The Corn Laws provided a kind of reserve corn supply, as in the bad harvests of 1756 and 1757, when grain was diverted from the export to home market. In the 1750s and 1760s, and in 1772, the ban on exports and the lifting of import duties had destroyed Scottish agriculture. Dirom wanted a bounty on exports when prices indicated a plentiful supply of corn: the bounty would be raised when prices rise and ultimately imports are permitted. According to him, self-sufficiency should be Great Britain's policy. This familiar argument for protection had a particular poignancy when Dirom was writing as the destruction of Poland meant that it could not be Britain's supplier, and seeking corn from America or the Baltic states might be impossible because of the terms which would be exacted, including the abandonment of the Navigation Acts. He went on to challenge the assumptions of Adam Smith. First, he claimed that it was not proven that the money price of corn determines other prices in Great Britain; second, that it was wrong to say that produce rises in proportion to the number employed; third, that the high prices of corn after 1763 were caused not by bad crops but by increased wealth raising the demand for corn through larger cattle herds to satisfy the demand for meat, having more horses, which needed to be fed, and increasing human consumption. Dirom argued that farmers with common sense would reject Smith's view that low prices bring about the increased employment of domestic servants and output, and that in rich and populous countries agriculture needs to be supported as a monopoly more so than manufactures.

The alleged effects of the Corn Laws could, I believe, have been exaggerated. If their effects were small, much of the debate was pointless. Lauderdale, in his notes on *WN*, attempted to weigh the advantages and disadvantages of the Corn Laws. He saw that the bounty on exportation of corn had reduced the money and real prices of grain during the period (1688–1766) in which the laws were in force. After 1766, when bounties were abolished, both the price of grain and volume of imports rose. In his *A Letter on the Corn Laws* (1814), Lauderdale argued that there had been practical freedom in the internal corn trade since the 15th Act of Charles II. The bounty on grain 1688–1757 was efficacious in creating demand and increasing supply. In years of scarcity an ample supply was obtained by stopping exportation. He argued that the Corn Laws, especially those of 1791 and 1804, had failed because the price at which imports on low duties were permitted had failed to keep up with the inflation of the Napoleonic Wars period. In 1844 Buchanan stated that the Corn Laws of 1773–1815 were inoperative as the market price was more than the intervention price. He argued that participants in these Corn Laws debates exaggerated the effect of foreign supply, which had a trifling influence on price. Low prices should have accompanied foreign imports, but the facts show the opposite was true.

With the repeal of the Corn Laws the Corn Laws debate intensified. The protectionist Alison argued that it is doubtful if free trade would lower food prices in the long run as British farmers would have to compete with farmers producing from better soil in a better climate. With prices lowered, he contended,

British farmers would abandon high-cost farming on marginal land, reducing overall supply. The fall in British production would thus raise demand for foreign corn and higher prices for Scottish imports; once foreigners gained a monopoly of supply to Britain they would raise prices further. Alison thought little of the argument that cutting tariffs encourages others to do so: there was no guarantee that the large grain exporters such as Russia and Poland would in turn lower their duties against British manufactures so that Britons could use manufacturing as a substitute industry for agriculture. (When Britain abolished the Navigation Acts in 1849 foreign countries did not reciprocate with a reduction in duties.) He tried to adapt the established arguments for the Corn Laws to his times. Because of its capital and machinery, British manufacturing could stand competition from imports much more easily than agriculture. Using the national security argument for a tariff, he argued that, with Britain living in a perilous world, it was unwise for it to depend on foreign countries for food supplies. He thought it was unwise to endanger British agriculture as at the time it was capable of a yield triple the amount produced, thus making a larger population and an increased domestic market for British manufactures possible. When domestic grain is cheap through increased domestic production, argued Alison, there is not the loss of specie to buy from abroad so trade becomes a matter of nations trading luxury manufactures with each other. Alison concludes that the true policy for both commerce and agriculture is based on three maxims: agricultural protection, encouragement of colonies to expand world trade, and maintaining a powerful navy to protect sea lanes and distant dependencies. With continued doubts about trade liberalization, Alison (1847) argued the case for protection because grain imports to Great Britain and to Ireland were bought with bullion, not manufactured articles. Also, under a free trade regime, less grain was imported, which injured the commercial classes and increased rural unemployment.

With so many possible benefits springing from protection, could it be opposed? Whatever the arguments for free trade its implementation can be gradual. John Craig (1766–1859), a manufacturer near Edinburgh who had been educated at Glasgow University and was the nephew of John Millar the jurist, had mixed views on free trade. He approved, in his 1814 book, of free trade in general and of the corn trade in particular and disliked the idea of one industry being protected at the expense of others. Although supporting free trade he could see the merits of the bounties under the Corn Laws because of their contribution to the stabilization of corn prices. He thought the cost of bounties worthwhile compared with the cost of fluctuating corn prices, for example, in poor relief; furthermore, he saw bounties as encouraging agricultural improvement and healthy rural living.

There were stauncher champions of a free corn trade. Robert Wallace (n.d.), the Church of Scotland minister who anticipated the principal elements of Malthus's population theory, preferred to keep grain cheap at home to help manufacturers, a powerful reason in a country which was industrializing, as he feared that there would be excessive export for storage in foreign granaries under the Corn Laws, causing a dearth and higher prices at home. In general he wanted subsidization for agriculture or manufactures only to assure profitability.

Later, in 1804, Francis Horner approved of a free corn trade. He examined the arguments for a bounty – a reserve from years of plenty for years of bad harvests, adequate profits for the farmer and prices that are lower, uniform and steady – and said they amounted to giving a farmer a real advance on the price of corn. The bounty was wrong, although the Act of 1773 had virtually abolished it. He therefore argued that, although destruction of foreign demand by raising export prices would be a temporary inconvenience, the bounty was wrong. It increased tillage, diverted national capital into a losing trade and constantly diminished real wages. Horner thought that the better alternative to bounties for stimulating agriculture was home demand, which would raise average corn prices to be higher at home than abroad. Smith, he says, made the mistake of thinking that a bounty immediately increased domestic prices, overlooking the interval between the higher money price of corn and changes in the money price of labour and other commodities. According to Horner, both Smith and the pro-bounty lobby, in assuming that the amount of the bounty enlarged the money price even in the home market, ignored the forces of competition and failed to explain how home demand would increase. Perhaps a rising population would boost demand but rising incomes would not be a great help, because as income rises the proportion of it spent on food declines.

In a speech in the House of Commons on 16 May 1814, Horner continued his attack on the Corn Laws, arguing that free trade could be trusted because imports would never be enough to extinguish domestic corn production and imports of a bulky good would have expensive transport costs. In another speech in parliament he explained the crisis in agriculture was temporary, a case of adjusting to the fall of demand after the war. During the war, rents had risen and great outlays had been made on land; protection had not kept out imports even in 1810–12 when Britain was considerably cut off from Continental Europe; therefore, Horner argued, the national security argument was thus irrelevant. He went on to say that, even with protection, the thin soils of Scotland recently devoted to agriculture were depressed through competition from the more fertile lands in England and Ireland. Horner cleverly argued that consumers would be most confident of a steady price if the corn dealers had the impression that too high a price would be pointless as imports would flood in and depress it.

The relative transport costs of different products were also mentioned by Ramsay (1836) as determinants of patterns of trade. Sir George Ramsay (1800–71) was a Perthshire landowner and philosopher who became professor of philosophy at Glasgow University in 1863 and, like Thomas Reid, was a member of the Scottish commonsense school of philosophy. He argued that as the produce of soil is limited by the extent of territory, and there is no boundary to the increase of manufacturing, it is better to import food than force land into production at home. The Corn Laws, he thought, had mixed effects, keeping prices steady but lower than in previous years; if they were abolished Ramsay believed that migration to towns would accelerate.

Another discussant of the Corn Laws, Buchanan, in his 1814 edition of the *WN*, noted that the importation of corn lowered corn prices in 1794–96 in Great Britain, making subsistence cheaper. He raised issues of income distribution, thinking it unjust to have higher prices simply to raise farmers' profits and thus landlords' rents and mentioning that country gentlemen and farmers, in wanting a law in 1813 to ban imports, demonstrated their support for any scheme of monopoly. He feared that encouraging agriculture through the Corn Laws was an invitation for other trades to demand protection.

Foreign trade then was mainly an exchange of manufactures. Smith, too, notes that corn is bulky to trade and even in times of great scarcity little is imported. It is important, I believe, to be reminded that manufacturing dominated international trade, thus making the fuss about the corn trade appear excessive. Further, to have a perpetual law against the importation of corn and cattle is to restrict industry and the population to what the soil can produce. This is all standard free trade talk.

Smith did not write as much on the Corn Laws as many of the other Scottish writers. He did, however, point out the drawbacks of taxes on exports, which, in his view, are only useful if the goods are really going to foreign countries; they are permissible when otherwise the trade could not be carried on. He saw bounties as, in many ways, objectionable as they distorted the pattern of production: in the case of herrings the bounties were too high and discouraged home production to the detriment of the poor. He further argued that corn bounties were expensive and led to two burdens: the tax to finance it and higher prices for consumers. Thus, they either reduce the subsistence of the poor or cause money wage increases. He noted in Book I, chapter XI of the *WN* that the bounty on exports, after its introduction in 1688, had contributed to the scarcity of corn in the home market.

The case for free trade, and against government intervention through the Corn Laws, could be made from experience. Dugald Stewart (1840) thought that 'public magazines', in other words buffer stocks, were no more successful than private speculators in stabilizing prices and had the disadvantage of being expensive. An easier way to have a reserve stock, he contended, would be to stop distilleries' processing of corn in order to make more corn available for human consumption; thus in a sense providing a reserve stock of food.

To sum up what turned out to be one of the lengthiest debates in economics, the supporters of protectionism principally stated that the Corn Laws would increase subsistence, keep corn prices stable at their average level, encourage the cultivation of barren lands, expand exports through the bounty and increase the demand for labour and shipping, recognize that food is so important it cannot be subject to the vagaries of free trade, maintain farm incomes and ultimately those of the manufacturing and commercial classes, and ensure that Britain would not be at the mercy of foreigners who could raise their prices, partly through timing the release of grain from their granaries, if we reduced home production. But the free traders disliked the expensive cultivation of inferior lands encouraged by the Corn Laws, the diversion of capital into agriculture, the continuance of measures that had little effect, the exaggeration of the prospect of swamping the home market when corn was so bulky it would not be imported in great quantities, and the favouring of landlords who enjoyed unjustifiably high profits and rents. The debate seems to be a last stand of the agricultural interest with every conceivable issue raised. It was a discussion largely conducted when Britain was at war and likely to adopt any measures, including protection, on the grounds of national security. However, in the hundred years of peace after 1815 the large volume of manufactured exports made it easy to afford foreign corn and the Corn Laws were gradually repealed from 1846 to 1849.

Evaluation of trade

Trade could stimulate industry, improve society and spread prosperity throughout the world. Anderson (1789) says that trade is only beneficial to a state 'which tends to excite the industry of the people, and promote the manufactures of the country' (p. 60). Although the home market is as important as foreign demand it does not provide employment for the merchant and the custom house. In his lectures on political economy Dugald Stewart (1840) emphasized the fact that there was a limit to a nation's income through trade and that because of the cost of transport it is not worthwhile having distant trade in many goods which are not widely consumed. Thus, I would argue that only a small state could be supported extensively by trade; the large nation needs a large agricultural sector to provide the revenue it requires. Nevertheless, despite Stewart's scepticism about trade he did concede it was important to Scotland.

The great champion of free trade, David Hume, in his essay *Of the Rise of Arts and Sciences*, says that when neighbouring and independent states are connected by commerce and policy there is a rise in politeness and learning: 'The emulation, which naturally arises among those neighbouring states, is an obvious source of improvement' (1987: 119). Similarly, he writes in his *Of National Characters* that where neighbouring nations have close communication by policy, commerce or travelling they acquire similar manners. Hume says in *Of Commerce* that 'Foreign trade, by its imports, furnishes materials for new manufactures; and by its exports, it produces labour in particular commodities, which could not be consumed at home' (1987: 263). Thus, according to him, trade creates employment and happiness, allowing a great amount of labour to be stored up against a public emergency, and arouses men from their indolence.

A big issue was whether trade spread prosperity around the globe to bring about a convergence between the fortunes of previously rich and poor countries. In the urbane discussions of economics of the eighteenth century, Hume linked trade with civilization and the dispersal of economic prosperity throughout the world, to the point of a narrowing in the gap between the incomes of different countries, creating what became known as the 'rich country–poor country' debate. Hume, in his essay *Of Money*, suggested that manufacturing activity would move to cheap labour countries, naturally causing convergence:

> Where one nation has gotten the start of another in trade, it is very difficult for the latter to regain the ground it has lost; because of the superior industry and skill of the former, and the greater stocks, of which its merchants are possessed, and which enable them to trade on so much smaller profits. But these advantages are compensated, in some measure, by the low price of labour in every nation which has not an extensive commerce, and does not much abound in gold and silver. Manufactures there gradually shift their places, leaving those countries and provinces which they have already enriched, and flying to others, whither they are allured by the cheapness of provisions and labour; till they have enriched these also . . .
>
> (1987: 283)

It is hard to tell from this passage how much convergence will occur. Increasing returns in industry seem to favour the unending growth of the large rich country but Hume believed, as shown in his essay *Of the Rise and Progress of the Arts and Sciences* (1987: 135–6), that arts and sciences would grow to a peak then decline; he employed the argument that importing excellent arts from other countries would discourage endeavour at home. Hume's arguments were attacked by Josiah Tucker (1713–99), a Church of England clergyman and Dean of Gloucester, who contended that a poor country such as Scotland would need more than reliance on natural forces. According to Tucker, measures such as low-interest loans and joint partnerships in large firms were required to enhance Scotland's growth rate. Hume, writing to Kames on 4 March 1758, conceded Tucker's points about rich countries, but not his view that limitless expansion was possible. Semmel (1965) stated that Hume would be right if England's prosperity were based on the discovery of rich mines rather than on the state of its industry. Founded on a prosperous home market, a rich country would, in my view, have sufficient capital to lower interest rates and provide longer credit, as well as make experiments regarding intensive division of labour. As with his exposition of the price-specie flow mechanism, Hume needed to spell out many assumptions, for example on the flexibility of resources, to justify his position.

Robert Wallace, in his *Characteristics of the Present Political State of Great Britain* (1758), thought that a rich country could maintain its trade superiority but felt, like Hume, that there was a limit to a country's expansion in the world. James Oswald (1750), more optimistically, believed a rich country could maintain its trade superiority.

The background to the debate is, of course, mercantilism, which thought that the great goal for a nation would be permanent prosperity through a continuous trade surplus. Like the price-specie flow mechanism idea, the rich country–poor country hypothesis discusses how much the fortunes of nations oscillate. Experience shows that rich countries can enjoy their superiority for a long time, and poor countries endure deprivation for years.

Exchange economy

The end of feudalism, and the growth of towns, launched the exchange economy. Instead of central control of the pattern of production and trade to the lowest level of society there could be a free society based on voluntary exchanges. We need to look at what such an economy is, how important self-interest and the invisible hand are to it, whether an equilibrium emerges in markets, and in what ways the exchange economy has been criticized.

The nature of an exchange economy can be understood by its evolution. The most primitive of societies has individuals and small groups living in isolation from each other but when the number of persons involved in exchange increases, a market is created; when those markets are extensive in the allocation of goods and services, a commercial society based on exchange exists. In his account of the aims of political economy, Steuart mentions employing inhabitants 'in such a manner as naturally to create reciprocal relations and dependencies between them, so as to make their several interests lead them to supply one another with their reciprocal wants' (*Principles* I: 21), a succinct description of exchange. When persons became less self-sufficient, the economy becomes more specialized and exchange is necessary if individuals are to acquire a wide range of goods to satisfy their needs and desires. In his examination of the most primitive type of exchange, barter, Kames succinctly described it as 'what is wanted by the one, and what can be spared by the other' (1778: 126). Exchange is thus a swapping of surpluses. In his 1849 book, John Hill Burton (1809–81) explains that exchange has wide benefits. (Burton was an Aberdonian who, failing to make a mark as an advocate, turned to journalism and to writing on history and political economy. He subsequently became a leading figure of the Edinburgh literary scene.) As he saw it, there is a gain in a good passing from someone who does not want it to someone who does 'in making a commodity change its place. It is a fallacy that one person only gains at the expense of another. A person such as an inventor shows that is possible to do good to the community as well as oneself' (p. 51).

All exchange means service for service, whether embodied in material products or not. Buchanan (1814) asserted that mutual profit is the foundation of all exchange. Adam Ferguson, in his *Institutes of Moral Philosophy* (1785), has a dynamic view of exchange: 'Commerce, by accommodating all parties with what they want in exchange for what they can spare, enables and encourages them to increase their produce' (p. 268).

We can explain Ferguson's comment partly by appreciating that exchange creates specialization, which results in productivity gains. A reason for this is that the division of labour leads to a widespread network of exchanges and also a different type of society because the humblest occupation is of significance as part of an interconnected whole. Millar (1787) said it was the separation of trades that caused traffic and exchange. Inspired by Smith, Craig noted that through exchange there can be a division of professions and increase of skill and 'the condition of the poorest member of a civilized state is superior to that of the most powerful chief of a barbarous tribe' (1814 I: 12). Hodgson thought the basis of economic science was the relations between persons unknown to each other, bound merely by justice and voluntary agreements, while Horner reduced the rules of exchange to one: 'the competition of the contracting parties' (Bourne and Taylor 1994: 164).

These writers saw exchange as something natural. David Hume analysed commerce, in other words exchange, in his essay *Of the Rise of Arts and Sciences*, stating that it is easier to account for the rise and progress of commerce than of learning. 'Avarice, or the desire of gain, is an universal passion, which operates at all times, in all places, and upon all persons' (1987: 113). Davie (1994) asserts that Hume understood it is gradually, through experience, that the exchange economy becomes valued. According to Hume, this experience leads to the awareness that the extension of specialization has the unintended consequence of economic benefit in the long run. Furthermore, he contends that equality before the law slowly grows out of the piecemeal accommodation of individuals engaged in exchange, despite the fact they had only the narrow aim of mutual convenience. What Hume was doing, Hardin (2007) thinks, was sowing the seeds of modern game theory. He was considering cooperation in exchange and coordination, with regard to the difference between transactions involving two or a few people and large-scale interaction throughout society.

To Adam Smith, exchange arose from natural propensities to truck and barter, which are human, not animal, traits. In *LJ* Smith argues that exchange is a natural thing: 'it is clearly the naturall inclination every one has to persuade. The offering of a shilling, which to us appears to have so plain and simple a meaning, is in reality offering an argument to persuade one to do so and so as it is for his interest' (p. 352). In *WN* (p. 26) Smith contrasts human beings with the dog who will not engage in exchange.

Was Smith exaggerating natural propensities in explaining exchange? Lauderdale, commenting on *WN*, said 'That disposition to truck barter and exchange as natural to man I suspect to be undoubtedly the effect of a certain degree of civilization and even of political arrangements, independent of the existence of political authority it might be demonstrated that the natural, and most advantageous mode of disposing of any superfluity was to give it to the person who wanted it' (1996: 26). In other words, in his view the beginning of exchange had institutional determinants. In a sense Lauderdale is using the familiar nature-versus-nurture argument to challenge Smith.

According to Kitagawa (1994), Thomas Reid believed people change fundamentally when they engage in the commercial society: in the solitary state man engages in exchange for personal benefit, but in the social state he regards the desires and wants of others. Dugald Stewart (1840) said the exchange economy would be a social union. This point was expanded by William Ballantyne Hodgson (1815–80), the distinguished principal of education institutions and later the first professor of political economy at Edinburgh University, who stated in 1871 that exchange is a phase of human brotherhood both directly helping others and indirectly helping oneself.

Tribe (1999) wrote that Smith was unusual for his times in arguing that in the impersonal process of the market and extension of commerce liberty was advanced, making wealth and virtue compatible. According to Samuels (1977), in Smith's works the market was a regulatory system, part of a wider system of social control through the impact of moral and legal rules, but, nevertheless, a mechanism operating without central direction. Siemens (1997) considered economic exchange to be based on linguistic exchanges, and an important mechanism for human interaction. The stipulation of contracts is particularly important in the transition from linguistic to economic exchange.

Self-interest

The great motive for exchange is self-interest, which is often called self-love and is famously connected with Adam Smith because of his much quoted opinion that by pursuing their self-interest participants in markets promote the public good. However, many precursors relied on the concept. Fleischacker (2004) points out that Locke, Mandeville and Hume assigned it a greater role in human life than Smith, who was not totally reliant on self-interest as the spring of human action: Smith did consider other motives including charity and friendship, which bring about the lending of money, and public zeal, which encourages sacrifices for the state.

In common with Hume and Smith, Steuart founded his economics on a view of human nature and its motivations. Steuart actually says 'self-interest is the ruling principle of my subject' (*Principles* I: 183) because of the universality of human desires: 'Man we find acting uniformly in all ages, in all countries, and in all climates, from the principles of self-interest, expediency, duty, or passion' (p. 24).

In governing a country, the statesman, he says, should always assume that people act from private interest, and in fact he would be bewildered if public spirit motivated them unless a government is so ill-administered that individuals have to be public spirited. Steuart believes self-interest and the public interest are compatible. He asserts that the advancement of the common good is 'a direct object of private interest to every individual' (I: 285) and defines the public good as 'the combination of every private interest...' (p. 184 (also II: 170)). A harmony between the public and the private occurs because being self-interested requires being considerate: 'You must love your country. Why? Because it is yours. But you must not prefer your own interest to that of your country' (I: 184). It is not beneficial, he says, to neglect self-interest, for example, through selling goods without profit to the ruin of trade or selling grain at low prices and discouraging farming. This self-interest can be safely pursued because of the rule of law: he thought that the ruling principle of political economy was that 'the only public spirited sentiment any statesman has a right to exact of his subjects, is their strict obedience to the laws' (II: 170). Law reinforces the link between private and public interests.

Steuart can cope with the difficult issue of self-interest in the sense of the constant pursuit of self-gain. He says that it is 'the allurement of gain', which will determine which industry a worker joins and explains the shift from agriculture to manufacturing, which are uncontroversial activities. He asserts that 'It is the desire of becoming rich, which produces frugality' (II: 30). People engaged in trade reinvest their gains rather than engage in luxury expenditure; without trade the rich turn to luxury consumption. A strand of the self-interest debate discusses the role of luxury. The desire for luxuries, he argues, comes from competition inherent in human nature, which needs to be correctly harnessed: 'emulation is inseparable from the nature of man; and if the citizens cannot be made to vie with one another in the practice of moderation, the wealth they must acquire will soon make them vie with strangers, in luxury and dissipation' (I: 282). He claims that men are induced to labour not through 'want but through the avarice or ambition which makes them want to possess luxuries' (I: 199). Although luxury has bad effects – moral, physical, domestic and political – viewed as a form of consumption luxury can be praised: 'no man can become luxurious ... without giving bread to the industrious, without encouraging emulation, industry, and agriculture; and without producing the circulation of an adequate equivalent for every service ... the agreeable band of union among free societies ...' (I: 326–7). In the end, on balance, Steuart believes that self-interest has economic and social benefits.

That self-interest means helping others appealed to several writers apart from Steuart. Hutcheson in his *System of Moral Philosophy*, as Skinner (1998) reminds us, regarded human life as a mixture of the selfish and the benevolent. German jurist Samuel von Pufendorf, in his *De Officio* (ii: 89), mentioned the great comfort that results from helping one another. On the other hand, Ferguson, according to Hill (1997), argued that private interests lead to the public good instinctively, not through deliberate planning; possibly as a consequence of the contemporary culture in which participants in the economy were expected to be moral. Teichgraebe (1978) was aware that, at the time, Scotland was very religious – the land of the Bible – thus sympathy was an expression of keeping the biblical commandment to love one's neighbour.

As Nakano (2006) notes, Hume, in his *Enquiries Concerning Human Understanding*, seeing the importance of mutual dependence, thinks that actions are performed with reference to others. Davis (2003) perceptively observes that Hume and Smith developed different conceptions of the self. They both agreed on self-interest per se but Smith, in *The Theory of Moral Sentiments*, attributed human motivation to reason and conscience, rejecting Hume's link between motivation and various types of passion. In *TMS* Smith writes, 'How selfish soever man may be supposed, there are evidently some principles in his nature, which interest him in the fortune of others, and render their happiness necessary to him, though he derives nothing from it except the pleasure of seeing it' (p. 9). Later, in *WN* (p. 27), he recognized that the Scots need the help of others and when they ask tradesmen for provisions they do not make the request on the basis of need but by appealing to their self-interest. This is a clear affirmation of the view of the innocuous nature of self-interest. He clearly explains why it is important to follow self-interest:

> Regard to our own private happiness and interest, too, appear upon many occasions very laudable principles of action. The habits of oeconomy, industry, discretion, attention, and application of thought, are generally supposed to be cultivated from self-interested motives, and at the same time are apprehended to be very praise-worthy qualities ... Proper care of his health, his life, or his fortune ... Carelessness and want of oeconomy are universally disapproved of, not, however, as proceeding from a want of benevolence, but from a want of the proper attention to the objects of self-interest.
>
> (p. 304)

Self-interest is being concerned with the self for laudable reasons. We can see that the opposite of self-interest is not unselfishness but self-neglect. The neglectful person disregards health and opportunity and is not maximizing their potential. This insight could not be better expressed than by Smith.

> The care of the health, of the fortune, of the rank and reputation of the individual the objects upon which his comfort and happiness in this life are supposed principally to depend, is considered as the proper business of that virtue which is commonly called Prudence ... Security ... is the first and the principal object of prudence ... The methods of improving our fortune, which it principally recommends to us, are those which expose to no loss or hazard ...
>
> (*TMS*: 213)

This gives a guide as to how a self-interested person behaves, sensibly but not viciously. The self-interested person, by striving for the best, will incidentally make the community as a whole better. Smith was writing with knowledge of life in his small town, Kirkcaldy, where a corrupt use of self-interest would soon be curbed by observant neighbours; but in larger modern societies there is more human behaviour to be monitored.

There is the tired argument, known as the *Das Adam Smith Problem* after Georg Feder and the Germans who devised it, that there is a conflict between *TMS* and *WN because* Smith discards the principle of sympathy for self-interest. Winch (1992) calls it an old fallacy as the prudent man of the *TMS* is the same person as the participant in the commercial society. Macfie (1959) says that Smith always considered society from the individual's standpoint: individuals are bound emotionally in society, loving society and finding it agreeable. Self-love is used more often in the *TMS*, Fitzgibbons (1995) calculates, than in the *WN*, although self-interest is a richer concept than self-love as it includes some virtue.

Why self-interest is so often criticized is because it is equated with selfishness. Smith often used the term self-love but referred to the selfish only three times in *WN*. He calls the man who spends his income on frivolous trinkets and not on hospitality selfish, and criticizes the character of the people, particularly merchants and manufacturers, in nations like Holland, for 'narrowness, meanness and a selfish disposition, averse to all social pleasure and enjoyment' (p. 668) – much like the Calvinists he would know only too well in Scotland. Also he contrasts simple hospitality with selfish pursuits like cockfighting, which can be ruinous. It seems that Smith is applauding conviviality within limits when criticizing selfishness, not commenting in general on self-interest. Self-interest is a complex idea because of the many things of advantage to the individual, including cooperation with other people.

Robert Flint, a fervent opponent of socialism, writes at the end of the nineteenth century that self-love is not selfishness opposed to benevolence, as every class in promoting its own interest does what is best for the community: 'Self-love ... is a rational regard to one's good on the whole. It involves a general notion of happiness or well-being, and not a mere loss of pleasure or aversion to pain' (1894: 364). Flint's justification for self-love or self-interest is derived from his three-dimensional view of man as a rational and responsible agent obliged to perfect himself, a social being with social duties, and a creature of God with religious duties.

Other comments on self-interest include Stabile's (1997), that self-interest in itself is not enough for markets to function: there has to be trustworthiness and the market has to act as an impartial spectator. What self-interest does, as Thomson (1965) suggests, is impart 'the motion to society ... considered as a powerful human sentiment ... an instrument of economic progress ... in refinement and in creative activity' (p. 227).

The invisible hand

A much discussed aspect of the exchange economy is its coordinating mechanism in the form of the 'invisible hand'. An increasing amount of ink is spilt on the analysis of this concept, which was first mentioned in an offhand way by Smith in his essay 'History of Astronomy', where he writes: 'Fire burns, and water refreshes; heavy bodies descend, and lighter substances fly upwards, by the necessity of their own nature; nor was the invisible hand of Jupiter ever apprehended to be employed in those matters' (*Essays* 1980: 49). This fails to state the function of the invisible hand. What could that hand have done? Presumably effect a miracle, a departure from the usual course of nature. Macfie (1971) suggests that Jupiter represents the pre-Enlightenment view of the ignorant savage who is unaware of the divine and social order.

The expression 'invisible hand' is an example, he says, of Smith's love of pithy forceful phrases.

Next, in the *TMS*, Smith writes:

> The rich . . . are led by an invisible hand to make nearly the same distribution of the necessaries of life, which would have been made, had the earth been divided into equal portions among all its inhabitants, and thus without intending it, without knowing it, advance the interest of the society, and afford means to the multiplication of the species.
>
> (Section IV I: 185)

This suggests that the hand operates independent of will and intentions: what it does is to act as an equalizing force, providing sufficient subsistence to enable population growth.

In the *WN* Smith writes:

> By preferring the support of domestick to that of foreign industry, he intends only his own security; and by directing that industry in such a manner as its produce may be of the greatest value, he intends only his own gain, and he is in this, as in many other cases, led by an invisible hand to promote an end which was no part of his intention. Nor is it always the worse for the society that it was no part of it. By pursuing his own interest he frequently promotes that of the society more effectually than when he really intends to promote it. I have never known much good done by those who affected to trade for the public good.
>
> (p. 456)

Again unintended actions are mentioned; maximizing behaviour is founded on self-interest. The power of the invisible hand is not restricted to the direction of investment: there are the 'many other cases'. Smith wanted the invisible hand to have a wider application in economic matters.

A starting point for considering the invisible hand is the use of the word 'invisible', which does suggest something divine, or spiritual and not material, or part of an unseen world. The opposite, the visible hand, is presumably the exercise of power by the state. The invisible hand seems to mean some inherent underlying mechanism of a society or a gentle movement in a state bringing about improvement. Smith based whatever happened in a free economy on human nature: that is the clue to his idea of the invisible hand.

Many critics of the invisible-hand concept seek to diminish its significance. Kennedy (2009) lists seventeen versions of the invisible hand stretching back to Homer's *Iliad* and dismisses it as a meaningless metaphor. Rothschild, another surveyor of the concept, in *Economic Sentiments* (2002) regards it as a hope, or a hint. Stimson (2004) argues 'The invisible hand is what men *would* recur to in order to explain such events *if* they did not understand the character of those chains which bind hidden events.' Lindgren (1969) thinks the invisible hand was a rhetorical device to communicate with men who were uninterested in the interests and motives of members of society.

According to Grampp (2000), however, the invisible hand is more interesting than important. He summarizes the leading interpretations of the role of the invisible hand – conducting economic affairs in a market to produce a mutually beneficial society, the price mechanism, the unintended consequence of individual human actions, competition, mutual advantage in exchange, a joke, an evolutionary process acquiring knowledge, skills and habits to inform buying and selling, providence, the prime mover of economic and other behaviour, and a contribution to national security by reducing capital exports.

The idea of the invisible hand was not exclusively an economic idea: the concept helps us to understand social change. Andriopoulos finds a process of that nature described in the *WN* passage:

> But what all the violence of the feudal institutions could never have effected, *the silent and insensible operation of foreign commerce and manufactures* gradually brought about. These gradually furnished the great proprietors with something for which they could exchange the whole surplus produce of their lands, and which they consume themselves without sharing it either with tenants or retainers. (Andriopoulos's italics)
>
> (1999: 746, quoting *WN* 418)

He argues that the language of the supernatural pervades both gothic novels and Smith's economics. Succinctly he writes, 'Smith implicitly postulates by this figure a hidden or imperceptible *supernatural* intervention that is already at work within the economic sphere, thus rendering external interventions by the state unnecessary' (p. 747). This opinion neatly links together the idea of the spiritual with the idea of negative liberty. Inevitably, this concept has to be considered again in a later chapter of *In the Shadow*. Winch (1996) thinks Smith in his *TMS* is using the idea to describe the secret concatenation, or link, between the rich and the poor.

Equilibrium in exchange

A modern reader, especially when fed on neoclassical economics, will search in Scottish economics writings for the notion of the exchange economy as the theatre in which market forces produce equilibrium states. When there is an equilibrium state, a market has settled down, with demand and supply matching each other and a price agreed. This can happen in countries with little change in population and technology, with a strong belief in following custom, or where there is some mechanism to match demand and supply. Otherwise various disequilibria can exist and shortages of demand or of supply can persist for years. There can be so many prices for the same thing that prices are not set by a market but by negotiation.

Keynes in his *General Theory* (1936) says that Hume stressed the importance of the equilibrium position, not the changing transition to it. But Vickers (1957) sees Hume's essay *Of Money* contrasting a general equilibrium position with the transition to it: time lags are introduced to examine the impact of an increase in the supply of money. Smith, it is true, in *WN*, uses the word 'equilibrium' only once but he does speak of movements towards equality. He analyses, as Recktenwald (1978) instructs us, the forces moving to and from one equilibrium for an individual and one for society. Furthermore, Joseph Schumpeter (1954), not a leading cheerleader for Adam Smith, as Watson (2005) reminds us, does concede that Smith was presenting a rudimentary equilibrium theory in showing that market prices gravitate to natural prices, which will be discussed in the chapter on value of *In the Shadow*.

To Steuart, the 'balance' of an economy may, or may not, be in an equilibrium state. He writes 'when we say that the balance between work and demand is to be sustained in *equilibrio*, as far as possible, we mean that quantity supplied should be in proportion to the quantity demanded, that is wanted' (*Principles* I: 235). That is, an increase or diminution of either work or demand will overturn the balance. The picture he presents is not of natural but governmental forces achieving an equilibrium. He recommends that when there is excess demand, the statesman increase supply to make 'the balance come even of itself, without any shock, and that as soon as possible…' (p. 240). In his view, without state intervention the demand will be cut by a price increase or foreign supply, which will 'leave the balance in an equilibrium, disadvantageous to trade and industry' (p. 240): this is a clear idea of a lower level equilibrium. In the short run, when imports cope with excess demand, he argues that 'the balance would still be found in a kind of equilibrium at home' (p. 251). When discussing the balance of wealth, Steuart states how the balance reaches equilibrium:

> …the industrious classes who furnish consumable commodities for the price of their overplus, must constantly have the balance of wealth turning in their favour; and when once they arrive at a certain degree of ease, proportional to their ambition, then they give over working, and become incorporated into the class of those who have enriched them… Thus matters go on a perpetual cycle. The industrious become easy, and the public lays the consumer under a perpetual contribution in proportion to their expence.
>
> (IV: 141)

In this example an undirected labour force oscillates between one equilibrium and another, without any prodding by government. Steuart is constantly concerned about achieving full employment and seems to restrict government intervention to such matters. He is optimistic about the time it takes to adjust to equilibrium. In an examination of the effects of opening up foreign trade on wages and prices in agriculture and industry, he writes 'in a short time accounts will be balanced on all hands' (*Principles* I: 228).

In his work on taxation and exchangeable value David Buchanan (1844) clarified the idea of an equilibrium price, when the price is at rest with demand and supply exactly equal: 'The demand and supply are like equal weights in opposite scales, which are never at rest until they come to an even balance' (p. 322). This equilibrium price is the natural price, 'the point to which the price continually tends amid all its variations' (p. 322).

Reid, who was the successor to Adam Smith as professor of moral philosophy at Glasgow University, gave a detailed account of the movement towards equilibrium:

> Every one is divided betwixt the desire of a high price & the fear of having his Commodity ly on his hands while others rend theirs at a lower price. The Buyer is agitated by like hopes and fears as the Seller however bargains will be Strict. Some at a higher price some at a lower till at last after vibrating for a while the price will settle nearly at a Medium betwixt the highest and the lowest.
>
> (Kitagawa 1994: 339)

Equal value of commodities, Reid says, lets labourers purchase the conveniences and accommodations of life at the prices the custom and opinion of the country believe they deserve. He suggests that an equilibrium is a settled state of affairs. Therefore, to regard equilibrium as the goal of exchange activity suggests a static view of commercial society and a fear of embarking on a new economic path. Reid's observations are not used as the basis for an economic theory, as in neoclassical economics, but they did show an appreciation of the existence of equilibria and their creation.

Evaluation of the exchange economy

These Scottish writers were interested in evaluating the commercial system and society that had emerged from primitive times. To this day there is a suspicion of commerce and markets: murmurs about 'market forces' still express the deep concern that the consequences of letting demand and supply operate unchecked will be unpleasant. Commerce is disliked and even seen as a new form of slavery, replacing the more leisurely pace of work in cottage industries and in agriculture with the discipline of life in shops, offices and factories. Also there is an entry condition for entering the exchange economy: you have to possess things to exchange or have access to money. If you are poor you are excluded; to succeed you have to be competitive, making some gainers and some losers. There is no sympathy for the weak, society is divided between achievers and non-achievers, and lives can be destroyed. Thomas Carlyle is more strident than many a modern writer in attacking the exchange economy. He is very different from the leaders of the Scottish Enlightenment who lauded commerce and the liberation it brought. Cohen (1989) used three criteria for assessing commercial society – citizenship, polite conversation and taste, and natural law. All these are present in Smith's principal works. Smith did not think that the development of commerce is a smooth process: he saw that many obstacles existed – the despising of merchants despite their useful function, imperfections in the law of contract, the difficulties of conveying goods in lawless countries, laws that confined commerce to particular fairs and markets, staple towns with exclusive privileges, taxes on importation and exportation, and monopolies and exclusive privileges of corporations.

Exchange was central to Smith's thinking. In *LJ* (1762) he praises the outcomes of an exchange economy, saying that under commerce and manufacturing the poor get higher wages and the rich have an opportunity to spend more money as they have fewer servants. However, it is fair to say that 'For Smith the market economy has no essential features of its own. It is merely an aggregation of the social relationships of which it is constituted' (Watson 2005: 148). Market exchange was discussed in *TMS* and Young (1985) thinks that Smith thought market exchange is a social process based on social consensus; that an interdependence of utility functions comes about because we want the approval of others – in other words, that psychology is more important than sociology. Several writers, according to Lamb (1974), try to reconcile the different themes of the *TMS* and the *WN* on the basis of market psychology. However, moral questions lurk beneath Smith's treatment of exchange, including that of moral propriety so important to his argument in *TMS*. This is especially so in Smith's famous statement that 'It is not from the benevolence of the butcher, the brewer, or the baker, that we expect our dinner, but from their regard to their own interest' (*WN*: 26–7). Viner, in his 1927 article, wanted this to be about exchange and not about the moral issue of benevolence, but Smith included both.

In a detailed attempt to explain why Smith morally approved of the commercial society, Fleischacker (2004: 55) provides a fourfold reply. Through commerce there is a broadening of markets, which provides cheaper food, and through international trade there is international peace. Unlike living under feudalism individuals are not servilely dependent on superiors and instead conform to the rule of law. In the *Wealth of Nations* Smith wants economic transactions to be constrained by justice so that participation in markets leads to self-reliance and self-government. We could argue that 'Smith saw no need for defining in great detail the idealized operation of a market system and for evaluating this system in terms of strict efficiency criteria' (Buchanan 1976: 4). However, despite his general affirmation of the system, Smith could descend to specifics. Cropsey (1957) notes that Smith contrasts liberal capitalism with the medieval social order, where commerce was not a 'normal or completely legitimate activity' (p. 40). He had a varying regard for the different participants of the commercial society: Cole (1958) notes that he was critical of merchants and manufacturers but liked bankers and farmers.

However, the exchange economy had its critics, including Ferguson who, Hill (2007) reminds us, was an early critic of commercialization and its attendant alienation. He preferred to think of human beings as naturally cooperative, uniting for a common purpose in a way different from the impersonal association of the exchange economy. Like Smith, Ferguson believed in a spontaneous order: in his *Essay in the History of Civil Society* he says that in many societies, including ancient Rome, commerce was despised and the warrior admired more than the merchant. He argued that in the commercial state 'man is sometimes found to be a detached and solitary being; he has found an object which sets him in competition with his fellow-creatures, and he deals with them as he does with his cattle and his soil, for the profits they bring. The mighty engine which we suppose to have formed society, only tends to set its members at variance, or to continue their intercourse after the bands of affection are broken' (1767: 24) but admits that it raises the level of the human condition throughout society and creates new pursuits.

The exchange economy needs intermediaries who have often been regarded as parasites, not producing anything themselves and not promoting the public good. Merchants following the principle of self-interest sometimes gave exchange a bad name. However, Hume, in *Of Interest*, describes merchants as 'one of the most useful races of men, who serve as agents between those parts of the state, that are wholly unacquainted, and are ignorant of each other's necessities' (1987: 300). Communication becomes more difficult when there is an increase in numbers and industry so it is 'reasonable, that a considerable part of the commodities and labour should belong to the merchant, to whom, in a great measure, they are owing' (p. 300). Experience of commercial life forces us to agree with him.

The Scot who was the most strident critic of the exchange economy was Thomas Carlyle (1795–1881), an essayist and historian who, after an education at Edinburgh University, failed to become a Presbyterian minister but spent much of his life in a pulpit of his own preaching about the woes of society. Carlyle's objections to the modern exchange economy were the strongest denunciations he made of economic life. In *Chartism* he mourns the change to the modern exchange society. In his view, the whole nature of society was being perversely changed.

> *Cash Payment* had not then grown to be the universal sole nexus of man to man: it was something other than money that the high then expected from the low, and could not live without getting from the low. Not as buyer and seller alone, of land or what else it might be, but in many senses still as soldier and captain, as clansman and head, as loyal subject and guiding king, was the low related to the high. With the supreme triumph of cash, a changed time has entered…
>
> (1840: 58)

He is lamenting the switching from traditional to modern social relationships. In such an economy and society all that counts is having cash, but that is not in itself able to satisfy all human needs:

> there are so many things which cash will not pay! Cash is a great miracle; yet it has not all power in Heaven, nor even on Earth. 'Supply and demand' we will honour also; and yet how many 'demands' are there, entirely indispensable, which have to go elsewhere than to the shops, and produce quite other than cash, before they can get their supply!
>
> (1840: 66)

In 'The New Downing Street' (1850) Carlyle asks: 'Is there no value, then, in human things but what can write itself down in the cash-ledger? . . . there are invaluable values which cannot be sold for money at all' (p. 150). Ultimately, he is suggesting that the cash economy is dehumanizing. In *Past and Present* he laments that 'Cash payment never was, or could except for a few years be, the union-bond of man to man. Cash never yet paid one man fully his deserts to another' (1843: 188). But once people have cash they have immense power. In *Sartor Resartus*, Carlyle argued 'whoso has sixpence is sovereign (to the length of sixpence) over all men; commands cooks to feed him, philosophers to teach him, kings to mount guard over him, – to the length of sixpence' (1831: 31). Meanwhile, in 'Signs of the Times' Carlyle seems to be hinting at the economics of a later economist, Marshall, who in his *Principles of Economics* argued that in the first stage of examining an economic problem a mechanical, not biological, approach should be used. Carlyle writes:

> this age of ours . . . (is) . . . the Mechanical Age.
>
> (1829: 60)
>
> Men are grown mechanical in head and in heart, as well as in hand. They have lost faith in individual endeavour, and in natural force, of any kind.
>
> (p. 63)
>
> . . . There is a science of *Dynamics* in man's fortunes and nature, as well as of *Mechanics*. There is a science which treats of, and practically addresses, the primary, unmodified forces and energies of man, the mysterious springs of Love, and Fear, and Wonder, of Enthusiasm, Poetry, Religion, all of which have a truly vital and *infinite* character . . .
>
> (p. 68)
>
> . . . the wise men, who now appear as Political Philosophers, deal exclusively with the Mechanical province; and occupying themselves in counting-up and estimating men's motives strive by curious checking and balancing, and other adjustments of Profit and Loss, to guide them to their true advantage: while, unfortunately, those same 'motives' are so innumerable, and so variable in every individual, that no really useful conclusion can ever be drawn from their enumeration.
>
> (p. 69)

> Fantastic tricks enough man has played in his time ... but to fancy himself a dead Iron-Balance for weighing Pains and Pleasures on, was reserved for this his latter era. There stands he, his Universe one huge Manger, filled with hay and thistles to be weighed against each other ... In Earth and in Heaven he can see nothing but Mechanism; has fear for nothing else, hope in nothing else: the world indeed would grind him to pieces; but cannot fathom the Doctrine of Motives ... and mechanise them to grind the other way?
>
> (p. 176)

Too much of the mechanical destroys the moral force. Carlyle is striking at the very heart of the exchange economy as many economists see it. He sees an economy as a broader entity, not based on self-interest and the mean-minded calculation. What upsets him is the contrasting of pain and pleasure, profit and loss, at the heart of utility-based economics.

In the modern exchange economy he says the quality of production declines. He denounces, in 'Shooting Niagara', the doctrine of 'cheap and nasty' in the new religion of free trade. London bricks crumble in sixty years but Etruscan pottery is still fresh after three thousand years:

> no good man did, or ever should, encourage 'cheapness' at the ruinous expense of *unfitness*, which is always infidelity, and is dishonourable to a man ... if the price is too high for me, I will go without it ...
>
> (1867: 32)

> Build it once *rightly*, the expense will be, say fifty per cent more ... Every seventy years we shall save the expense of building all England over again! ... The money-saving would ... pay your National Debt for you ... – and all this I reckon as mere zero in comparison with the accompanying improvement to your poor souls ...
>
> (p. 34)

Carlyle is worthy of extensive quotation. His powerful denunciations could still be employed by many a critic of the modern economy. A commentary provided by Welch explains that Carlyle believed that people are bound together by a 'mystic miraculous unfathomable union' (2006: 386), which is neither pecuniary nor based on self-interest. Carlyle admitted that people were better fed, clothed and lodged in his age than in previous ages but incapable of doing the noble thing.

We can see desperation in Carlyle's violent criticism, and echoes of contemporary socialism. He appears to be objecting to the modern monetized society without appreciating the functions of money. There is also a great deal of romanticism, which was to occur later in the Arts and Crafts Movement's promotion of craftsmanship. Perhaps Carlyle had not studied the literature that extolled the many benefits of the commercial age.

Consistent with their belief in economic development reaching its peak in the age of commerce, the Scots were quick to praise the exchange economy, which brought greater economic freedom. It provided a form of allocation devoid of the controls that rationing brings and it had emerged through the natural instinct of self-interest, and was based on common sense with a built-in incentive mechanism. That some succeed and others fail was not seen as a criticism but a fact of life. It had its own ways of reaching equilibrium and, although based on self-interest, was not widely regarded as immoral until critics of the calibre of Carlyle exposed its darker side for excluding the poor and debasing production.

Value

Value theory is not as prominent today as it used to be in economics, as it appears to have been overtaken by price theory; but there is a case for revisiting the long debates on value to see if there is a basis for prices and whether they are fair. This quest to understand value is very old in economics, going back at least as far as Aristotle's *Nicomachean Ethics*, Book V. So much of microeconomics is concerned with the mechanics of price theory that the justification for market valuations can be forgotten, but any accusation of unfairness in a market does require a return to an examination of the basis for pricing. The discussion of prices is unavoidable because in an exchange economy we need prices to effect the transactions that constitute its life. This examination of value begins with the objective approach of considering value in use: that is, utility and intrinsic value. This leads to the contrast between natural prices and market prices, the labour theory of value, the hunt for a standard of value, the role of demand and supply, and the link between the theories of aesthetics and of subjective utility as a foundation for value. In the Scottish discussion of value, battle lines were drawn between prices based on the cost of production and those related to utility.

Utility and intrinsic value

We can begin examining the connection between prices and utility in Hutcheson's writings. His contribution to value theory attempts to base value on what is intrinsic in a good. He considers utility, in the sense of usefulness, and the cost of production as alternative foundations for value theory, mentioning goods that 'yield a great and lasting use in life, and have cost a long course of labour to acquire and cultivate'(*System* II: 53). This anticipates Smith's labour disutility theory, which links the value of a good to the toil and trouble of producing it. Then Hutcheson moves to the Aristotelian distinction between value in use and value in exchange:

> The natural ground of all value or price is some sort of use which goods afford in life; this is prerequisite to all estimation. But the prices or values in commerce do not follow the real use or importance of goods for the support, or natural pleasure of life.
>
> (p. 53)

In this curious sentence he contemplates prices departing from their natural basis. He is hinting at the distinction between objective utility, which perhaps can be measured by natural sciences such as physiology or chemistry, and subjective utility, which can be based on something as unpredictable as a whim and anticipates Smith's distinction between natural and market prices. Necessaries as well as luxuries feature in his value theory. Pesciarelli (1999) is rightly cautious about identifying Hutcheson's value theory entirely with utility, although he appears to measure value by the quantity of goods required to produce subsistence. For Hutcheson, utility is the prerequisite not the standard of value.

The next major Scottish writer on value, Steuart, is rarely presented as a founder of price theory, which is a serious oversight as he theorized a great deal about prices and their application. He takes up the issue of intrinsic value, the basis for usefulness, early in his *Principles*, regarding it as 'the simple substance, or the production of nature' (I: 41), echoing the view of the medieval scholastics that the intrinsic substance was a substratum. The intrinsic price is the real value, the minimum price, which takes into account what the workman must receive for subsistence and the materials used. If a switch in production from agriculture raises food prices the intrinsic value will increase. Although changes in demand will generate price fluctuations 'the intrinsic value of the commodity stands immoveable; nothing is ever sold below the real value; nothing is ever bought for more than it may probably bring. I mean in general' (p. 222). However, prices for foreign markets are not based on real value but on the 'eagerness of acquiring, or the capacity of paying... The spirit, not the real wants of the people' (p. 205).

Later, in the nineteenth century, utility was regarded as the subjective experience of the consumer, not as a basic intrinsic value. But the objective and subjective views of utility can coincide when the consumer receives satisfaction from the usefulness of the thing. It is indisputable that consumer opinion will have a powerful and immediate effect on value and prices but as time goes on there emerges an irreducible value related to the minimum reward to factors of production. This view is expressed in the idea of natural prices.

Natural prices

The natural price is central to Smith's discussion of value. The concept both enables us to see his equilibrium thinking and raises issues of fair prices and the construction of prices through adding up different elements of cost.

Smith asserts that every society or community has ordinary or average or natural rates of wages, profits and rent. These will be determined by local circumstances, whether there is economic growth or not, and the nature of each employment of labour and capital. The natural price of a good is determined by the factors of production being paid their natural rates, that is, what it really costs to bring the good to market. The profit provides subsistence to the provider of capital and wages subsistence for the worker. Contrasted with the natural price is the market price: this is created by the quantity of goods brought to the market and the 'effectual demand' (the demand of those willing to pay the natural price). If there is a shortage of the quantity supplied, the price will rise, and the opposite when there is a shortfall in demand. Market price will equal natural price when 'the quantity brought to market is just sufficient to supply the effectual demand' (*WN*: 74). 'The natural price, therefore, is, as it were, the central price, to which the prices of all commodities are continually gravitating' (p. 75). This is Smith's notion of an equilibrium that is more long term than short. He suggests that the aim of a market is to establish such an equilibrium: 'The whole quantity of industry annually employed... naturally aims at bringing always that precise quantity thither which may be sufficient to supply, and no more than supply, that demand' (p. 75).

However, variations in output make actual produce different from the average produce that constitutes effectual demand. Great fluctuations in market prices affect rent less than wages and profits because rent is certain in money terms or steady in yearly terms if paid in produce. When the market price is less than the natural price, Smith says that factors of production are under perfect liberty to withdraw, pushing up the market price towards the natural price, and vice versa. In other words, he argues that competition can provide all the regulation needed, but that this mechanism cannot operate if there is regulation of the prices of provisions and other goods or price-fixing by exclusive corporations.

Smith's analysis was shared by other Scots. Ferguson hints at natural prices: 'Commodities that are the work of labour, time, and skill cannot continue to be sold for less than will maintain the workman, and pay the whole of his advance' (1785: 266).

Samuel Read (1779–1835), son of a Linlithgow linen bleacher and a partner in a bleach field business at Roslin near Edinburgh, equates value with price and regards value as the same as the vendible power of commodities. Looking in detail at prices, he thought the cost of production to be 'the indispensable condition or cause of their existence' (1829: 10), and that, ultimately, supply and demand depend on the cost of production, which brings value into contact with human conduct. According to him, although prices are determined through exchange they are ultimately regulated by the cost of production.

A natural price thus came to be a cost of production-based price. This is consistent with Smith's suggestion that it is something of more permanence than the market prices fluctuating around it. Young (1985) looks at the natural price in the context of the earlier medieval debate about value: 'The natural price has normative significance as both a sort of just price and as an economically efficient price in directing society's allocation of resources' (1997: 77). He thinks Smith distances himself from his alleged precursors in that Smith was concerned to present humanistic policy proposals and not moral objectives like the medieval writers. The all-pervasive word 'natural' in Smith's writings does make attempts to link his economics to his philosophical background inevitable, but in value theory it is quite an extension of Smith's modest statement that the natural price is the central price, a kind of trend price which could represent a long-run equilibrium price, to including a normative element in his theory. There is some support for the normative view of the natural price in Watson, 'For Smith, the gap between market and natural prices has its origins in the moral basis of society . . . a failure to socialise all individuals into the just principles that create a society devoid of harm' (2005: 147). But there needs to be a systematic accumulation of evidence from Smith's books to support this opinion.

The contrast between value based on costs and value based on market prices recurs in these theoretical writings. It is illuminating to compare factor prices (another term for costs) and product prices. If product prices are regarded as based on costs then we have to contrast their determination with the forces creating underlying factor prices: this entails comparing the processes of price formation in factor and product markets. These two types of price could move at the same rate, for example, when an increase in a cost is passed on proportionately in the product price, but the conditions of the product market might be such as to permit no price increases because of declining demand. The strength of demand and the flow of supply in each type of market, product or factor need to be looked at together. Sometimes demand for a factor of production is derived from a demand for its product; sometimes not.

Labour theory of value

The most famous cost of production theory is the labour theory of value. Relating the value of a good to the amount of labour needed to produce it did not originate with Smith. It was clearly explained by Sir William Petty in his *A Treatise of Taxes and Contributions* (1667) that the silver price of corn is related to the quantity of labour needed to produce both silver and corn. An early Scottish example of a labour approach to value is Patrick Murray's. Murray, fifth Lord Elibank (1703–78), was an advocate and an army officer, and later a leading member of Edinburgh literary circles and close friend of Lord Kames and David Hume. He believed that the value of manufactured goods which will 'arise from the labour of Men, is determinable by the time employed in working them. If a certain piece of work shall employ a Man two days, it must bear some proportion to the quantity of provisions required to maintain a Man for that time . . . When the practice of an art is confined to a few hands, it depends on them to put what price they please in their skill; and then, as happens in all monopolies, the Purchaser being at the mercy of the Seller' (1758: 3). Hume, in his *The Stoic*, also suggests a kind of labour theory: 'Every thing is sold to skill and labour; and where nature furnishes the materials, they are still rude and unfinished, till industry, ever active and intelligent, refines them . . .' (1987: 147).

Smith, at the outset of his presentation of value theory, having distinguished value in use and value in exchange, argues that because of the division of labour most of what we consume is produced by the labour of others. In Book I, chapter V of the *WN* he sets out his three labour theories of value – the labour command theory, the labour disutility theory and the labour quantity theory. The first of these says value is 'the quantity of labour which it enables him to purchase or command' (p. 47). Second, the real price is 'the toil and trouble which it can save to himself, and which it can impose upon other people' (p. 47). He argues that labour will measure values at different times; that is, that labour is the real price of all commodities but not how goods are commonly valued. The 'higgling and bargaining of the market' (p. 49) is needed to allow for labour of different qualities. The third theory claims that value is 'the value of a certain quantity of labour' (p. 49). But Smith restricts the quantity version of labour theories to simple societies. In his example of the 'rudest', that is, primitive, society, the relative values of beavers and deer are proportionate to the days or hours of labour of each hunter. He admits that labour quantities have to be qualified by the amount of hardship and training of the labour, although the latter is itself the product of labour. What Smith has to say about labour in relationship to value is diffuse. It would have been simpler if he had opted for a quantity theory but he is reluctant to apply that version of labour theories of value to more advanced societies because of his awareness that, in these, labour has to share the fruits of production with other factors of production.

After Smith, criticisms of his labour – especially labour quantity – theory soon accumulated. Kames criticizes Smith's attempt to account for 'the comparative value of commodities, by reducing them all to the labour employ'd in raising food' (1778: 132) because not all the raw materials worked upon by labour are of equal value. Another of his concerns is the supposition that every sort of labour is of equal value, ignoring skill (which in fact Smith had considered). Like many other critics Kames does not appreciate how cautious Smith was in his labour theories.

Francis Horner, in his review of *Canard's Principles* in the January 1803 issue of the *Edinburgh Review*, vehemently opposed the linkage between exchangeable value and stored-up labour. He too wants raw materials to enter into value because labour and raw materials are exchanged. 'The value of raw materials, like that of manufactured articles and of labour itself, varies with the proportion of supply and demand. The ratio of labour to raw material inputs varies from good to good' (1803: 56). In Horner's view, labour does not measure exchangeable value, which is a varying proportion of the amount of labour employed. What he appreciates is that there is not a stark choice between determination of value by cost of production or by supply and demand: costs are themselves determined by supply and demand – market determination all round. Horner wrote, 'it is improbable that quantities of labour accurately equal are ever exchanged for each other . . . there is no strict proportion between the quantity of labour exchanged in any one bargain, and those exchanged in any other' (Bourne and Taylor 1994: 160). Similarly, Craig also opposed the labour theory of value because the cost of labour is no judge of exchangeable value.

The great error of Smith's system, according to Lauderdale in his notes on *WN*, is to say that a commodity's value is based on the cost of labour and not what necessaries can be procured for it. Continuing with his attack Lauderdale says it is impossible to say that real price equals toil and trouble, as in the labour disutility theory, because price would then vary according to the skill and dexterity of the person wanting it. To the seller, real value is based on the costs of raw material and sustenance of workers; labour is not the real measure of value and comparative values are not based on labour alone. Lauderdale tries to devise a new way of attacking the labour quantity theory by reminding us that the quality of each commodity must be considered, a point of Smith's that is often ignored, and applies his reasoning to the most primitive rude society where quality is a determinant of value not reducible to a quantity. He denies that value can be intrinsic because comparative value depends on the proportions between the quantity of each commodity and the extent of the demand for it or, what is the same, the proportion between buyers and sellers. Value depends on the proportions between quantity and the extent of demand as 'constituted by Opinion' (1996: 22), as is shown by the variation in value with circumstances: a siege can make water or gunpowder more valuable than silver.

> labour must procure subsistence and subsistence in a civilized society as [it] involves a habitation and utensils makes it necessary that the price of labour itself should be composed of rent and something to keep up stock as well as the mean food and clouths [*sic*] of the animal. The component parts of the necessary price of that sea fish were then 1st a share for rent of a house – 2dly – to keep up furniture stock 3dly what in an uncivilized state would be the only component part of the price food in a warm climate...
>
> (p. 30)

However, whilst reducing the importance of labour in value theory, Lauderdale fails to pay enough attention to the natural and market price distinction.

Samuel Read thought it an error to regard labour as the sole cause of value with the consequence that all reward should go to labour, because both labour and capital deserve their shares. In other words, he criticized the view that there is a production function linking only one input (labour) to output. Pashkoff (1993) thinks that Read was following Smith's adding-up approach to value, most visible in his idea of the natural price, in stating that labour is not the sole determinant of exchange value as wages are only part of price.

Labour was bound to be thought of as the major foundation of value in the eighteenth century given the primitive technology then determining production. When the machinery age swept in, labour became less and less important. Smith's shrewd comment that labour quantity mattered most in primitive societies was in a sense a forecast forgotten by his critics: he could have been anticipating post-labour theories. Perhaps the remaining attraction of a labour theory is that in pursuit of fairness we want the prices of products to reflect the worth of the people who produce them.

The measure and standard of value

In times of inflation there is a call for a method of measuring price changes. Early attempts, for example that of William Fleetwood, Bishop of Ely, in 1707, at constructing a price index were crude because there was not then a method of judging the relative importance of each of the many thousand price changes that can occur in an economy; this is done now by weighting the price change of each good according to its relative importance in consumer expenditure. A different, and earlier, way of ascertaining the extent of inflation or deflation was to take a commodity with a stable value and use it as a standard to judge price changes.

Hutcheson deals with the issue of the measure of value in a practical way, by considering what can serve as an acceptable measure and whether money is suitable. He thought that in everyday life major currencies are stable enough to be trusted to measure value. The important qualities of money he lists are general desirability, portability, divisibility, durability and rarity. Precious metals such as bullion or coinage meet these criteria. Despite the usefulness of precious metals in exchange, he was aware of their fluctuating values and the importance of considering other options:

> the value of labour, grain, and cattle, are always pretty much the same, as they afford the same uses in life, where no new inventions of tillage, or pasturage, cause a greater quantity in proportion to the demand. 'Tis the metal chiefly that has undergone the great change of value, since these metals have been in greater plenty, the value of the coin is altered tho' it keeps the old names.
>
> (*System* II: 58)

As the practical use of an inflation indicator is to keep real incomes at least constant, Hutcheson suggests, consistently with the above, that:

> The most invariable salary would be so many days labour of men, or a fixed quantity of goods produced by the plain labours, such goods as answer the ordinary purposes of life. Quantities of grain come nearest to such a standard.
>
> (*System* II: 62)

The idea of an invariant standard of value did not appeal to Steuart: 'the unit in money can have no invariable determinate proportion to any part of value ... it cannot be fixed to perpetuity to any particular quantity of gold, silver, or any other commodity whatsoever' (*Principles* II: 214), which seems to warn other writers to stop the quest for an invariant standard.

In *WN* Smith was to conclude that 'Labour ... is the only universal, as well as the only accurate measure of value, or the only standard by which we can compare the values of different commodities at all times and all places' (p. 54). Dugald Stewart, Smith's first biographer, and one of his first critics, argued that as precious metals are divisible and fusible they are admirable for forming a scale of value but that relative value is much more precise. He contended that Smith was seeking a universal standard, not measure, of value, and chose labour as he wanted a unit fixed in 'the unalterable principles of human nature' (I: 352). However, the real price, that is, toil and trouble, is only true of a primitive society. He thought Smith would find it hard to hold both ideas: that there is a labour quantity theory of value and that there is intrinsic value based on labour and two other components. Stewart regarded value as being value in exchange, in usual parlance, and not intrinsic value, and he questioned labour as being the basis of the standard of value when labour is only one class in society. All commodities, not just labour, have real and nominal prices. He laments Smith's failure to provide a rule to calculate comparative prices at different times and places, and suggests wages as a measure of value because they are related to the necessaries of life.

In his annotation of *WN* Lauderdale states that a real measure of exchangeable value can never exist: 'there is no such thing as a Standard of real value and that the idea of price or value always arises from the comparison of two different things, the price of all Commodities will be found to depend on the relative state of the proportions with regard to plenty and demand that subsists betwixt any two Commodities compared with a view to exchange' (1996: 31). Lauderdale also firmly asserts that 'nothing can be a real measure of the value of other commodities, which is constantly varying in its own value' (p. 27).

From another angle, Playfair attacked the idea of absolute value, writing that 'The real essence of all wealth, and that which determines its value, is the necessity under which the consumer lies to purchase it' (1809: xxxv). He points out that the consumption of agricultural and manufactured goods is interdependent and, as such, the joint products cannot be separated. In his view, this is a natural standard based on human need, not human labour.

To talk about labour as the standard of value is easy; to implement such a proposal is tougher. Robert Owen (1771–1858), the pioneer of cooperative communities, made an attempt in his *Report to the County of Lanark* (1820). He was born in Wales but is chiefly famous for the model factory, New Lanark mills, twenty-three miles from Glasgow, which he ran from 1800. Many Owenite cooperatives and socialist communities copied his ideas, despite the fact that his later attempts at idealistic communities in Indiana and Hampshire failed. Writing at the time when Britain was about to return to the gold standard ('resume cash payments') he assumes that 'the natural standard of value is, in principle, human labour, or the combined manual and mental powers of men called into action... the average physical power of men as well as of horses (equally varied in individuals), has been calculated for scientific purposes...' ([1820] 1970: 207). To make labour the practical standard of value it is necessary to calculate how much there is of it in articles to be bought and sold: 'the prime cost... or the net value of the whole labour contained in any article of value' (p. 222), then count how many units of labour 'the exact value of the unit or day's labour which society ought now to fix as a standard of value ... [This] need not represent a less value than the wealth contained in the necessaries and comforts of life which may now be purchased with five shillings' (pp. 223–4). Of course this scheme did not gain general acceptance. There was no reason to expect that labour would retain its value and be a guide to the value of goods. Given the many types of labour needed to produce a complex good and the existence of subcontracting the calculations to implement Owen's proposal would be impossibly difficult.

Samuel Read argued that a better measure of value is necessary to regulate contracts. Writing on the subject in 1821, he recommended a statement of the value in standard money of the pound sterling for the period of the Bank Restriction from 1797 as part of a plan for reforming the currency. In a table he compared the value of sterling to the price of gold. He suggested that there should be legislation enabling all persons liable to pay money under contracts created during the Restriction to leave those obligations and pay the amount in gold or standard money, thus reducing the amount in sterling that the contracting party had to pay. The standard money was proposed because 'the derangement of contracts and debts is so various and complicated' (p. 298). Throughout the debate concerning the effect of paper money on inflation, the lack of a price index complicated discussion but at least Read attempted an approximation to it. Later, in 1829, he came closer to Owen's view: 'The natural wages of common labour, or determinate quantities of corn, are the only defined or definable articles which could then be appealed to with certainty to perform the office of correctors, or to determine the value of previous contracts' (p. 217). Given the high proportion of workers' wages then being spent on corn there is some plausibility in Read's proposal.

Demand and supply

In all these discussions of value the lengthy debates seem to skirt round the simple and obvious truth that value is merely a price determined by demand and supply. This idea has a long ancestry. Gershom Carmichael, according to Taylor (1955), provides a crucial link between Aristotle, Grotius, Pufendorf and Hutcheson. Carmichael (1672–1729), a graduate of Edinburgh and Glasgow universities and a prominent natural rights philosopher, was regent at St Andrews in 1693 and at Glasgow in 1694 then the first professor of moral philosophy (1727–29) at Glasgow; he was succeeded by Hutcheson. Carmichael said that 'In general we may say that the value of goods depends on these two elements, their scarcity and the difficulty of acquiring them ... Furthermore, scarcity is to be regarded as combining two elements, the number of those demanding the good and the usefulness thought to inhere in the good or service and which can add to the utility or pleasure of human life' (Taylor 1955: 254). Later Carmichael places more emphasis on the subjective element, saying that usefulness can be real or imagined. Hutcheson, according to Taylor (1965), followed Carmichael's notes on Pufendorf.

John Law (1671–1729) was a writer on trade also interested in land banks. He was born and schooled in Edinburgh, where his father was a merchant, and fled to France after being sentenced for murder in 1694; he then made a career by inventing paper money in order to reform the catastrophic public finances of France, after creating a bank in 1716 and becoming Controller General of Finances for France in 1720. The collapse of his scheme caused one of the largest share price bubbles of all time and made later writers cautious about paper money. In Thweatt's (1983) view, Law was the first writer to use *demand* in conjunction with *quantity* to state that prices are in proportion to demand not quantity. Thweatt goes as far as to suggest that Steuart and Smith invented the actual expression 'demand and supply'. Steuart takes up the examination of quantity and demand and by the time he wrote *Considerations of the interest of the County of Lanark* (1769) was speaking of demand and supply. Steuart was aware that prices were not a feature of primitive societies like the Scottish Highlands of the early eighteenth century but of later more industrial societies. His argument was that 'Sale alone can determine prices, and frequent sale only can fix a standard' (II: 74). In later society money would be more equally distributed, boosting the prices of necessaries purchased by the workers and reducing the prices of luxuries consumed by the rich. The determinants of value were listed by Steuart as 'First, The abundance of things to be valued. Secondly. The demand which mankind make for them. Thirdly. The Competition between the demanders and Fourthly. The extent of the faculties of the demanders' (*Principles* II: 215). In other words value is determined by how much is supplied, demand, competition and ability to pay. Prices will be within the limits of the cost to the seller of bringing it to market and the resale price, which for subsistence goods will be determined by the number who must buy it. Steuart asserted that value in exchange depends on the proportion between demand and supply. The proportionality theory of price, a legacy of Aristotle, had been widely used previously, especially by John Locke. For there to be demand there had to be real or apprehended intrinsic value, which could be beauty, fashion or curiosity. A combination of scarcity and demand are essential to value in exchange: any conceivable price can emerge.

Hutcheson firmly explains price determination by a demand and supply mechanism:

> prices of goods depend on these two jointly, the *demand* on account of some use or other which many desire, and the *difficulty* of acquiring or cultivating for human use. By the use causing a demand, we mean not only a natural subserviency to our support, or to some natural pleasure, but any tendency to give any satisfaction, by prevailing custom or fancy, as a matter of ornament or distinction in the more eminent stations; for this will cause a demand as well as natural use. In like manner by difficulty of acquiring, we do not only mean great labour or toil, but all other circumstances which prevent a great plenty of the goods or performances demanded. Thus

> the price is increased by the rarity or scarcity of the materials in nature, or ... accidents ...
>
> (*System* II: 54)

What is particularly interesting is he tries to explain the determinants of demand and supply by going beyond using 'demand and supply' as a slogan. He considers both actual demand and potential demand as arising from natural tendencies; supply is more than the consequence of labour. Prices will thus be determined by current demand and supply and expectations arising from underlying determinants.

According to Kames 'it is the demand chiefly which fixes the value of every commodity'. Value 'rises in proportion to the excess of the demand above the quantity'; value is not intrinsic. Prices will be brought down to 'the lowest value that can afford any profit' (1796: 101). This is not to say that the proportion fixes the price for that would make equilibrium prices, where demand equals supply, always with the value of one. (But the movement of prices will be determined by the proportionality, with excess demand pushing up prices and excess supply reducing them.) Kames asserted it is 'a general rule, that the value of goods in commerce depends on a demand beyond what their quantity can satisfy; and rises in proportion to the excess of the demand above the quantity' (p. 136). He reminds us that a commodity is more valuable the greater the excess of demand over quantity. Hence water is valuable in arid regions. If utility or the intrinsic nature of a good, and not demand and supply, determined value, a pound of iron would be worth ten pounds of gold.

In his *Institutes* Ferguson claimed: 'The price of commodities in trade is as their scarcity combined with their demand ... Articles, in the production of which, labour, time, and skill are required, continue to multiply, while the price is sufficient to maintain the labourer during the time he is employed to reimburse his apprenticeship and other expenses and to furnish an adequate reward' (1785: 37). Manufacture would stop if the price were less. It is not clear if these are natural or market prices: market prices are determined by demand and supply but natural prices are long-run equilibrium prices based on the costs of maintaining humans. Also, Ferguson writes, 'The price of commodities fluctuates and keeps pace with the quantity of money in circulation with the scarcity of the commodity, with the demand, and with the riches of those who consume it' (p. 266). This view considers both the general ability to pay because of the amount of money in circulation and the individual consumer's ability to pay determined by his personal income.

A strange discussion of market prices occurs in the work of Thomas De Quincey (1785–1859). He was notorious as the most famous drug addict of the nineteenth century, through publishing *Confessions of an English Opium-Eater* (1821). He moved to the Edinburgh area in 1830, where he spent the rest of his life as a journalist, and he published an extended version of his *Blackwood's Magazine* articles as *The Logic of Political Economy* (1897: 118–294). Most of this appallingly prolix book, which could be set as a punishment for errant students of the history of economic thought, is devoted to his value theory: 'The question of value is that into which every problem finally resolves itself' (1897: 148). In the *Logic* he uses his sharp analytical mind to dissect familiar classical concepts of value, correct Smith and give depth to his own price model. He asserts that exchange value or price consists of intrinsic utility and the difficulty of attainment, and that these elements create a motive for purchasing, with utility as the latent force and difficulty ruling the price. 'It is the *power*, the affirmative worth, which creates a fund for any price at all; but it is the *resistance*, the negative worth or what we call the cost, which determines how much shall be taken from that potential fund' (p. 166). Unusually, he explains 'value in use' as being teleological, for it is 'value derived from the purpose which the article contemplates' (p. 190). He argued, in a sense explaining Smith's idea of market price, that market values are disequilibrium values not equal to the cost price. Because supply cannot be abruptly adjusted to demand there is an 'oscillating market price' (p. 205) around 'the steady central price, or natural price'. He writes that it is 'technical market value (that is, not value in a market, but value in a market whose equilibrium has been disturbed) ... [that] must be *Binomial*' (p. 207). That is, both cost and the relation of supply to demand determine price. De Quincey, in his value theory, thus considers value in use as it relates to a host of possible effects and is one of the earliest writers to acknowledge the disequilibrium nature of many prices.

In a marketplace it is easy to see prices being determined by demand and supply with repeated price adjustments during the day as traders and customers come and go, but most prices are in fact calculated by a formula in advance of goods being taken to market. Hutcheson carefully explains the formation of prices in commerce, using a cost-plus approach with a profit margin for the person organizing production determined by custom:

> to fix the price we should not only compute the first cost, freights, duties, and all expences made, along with the interest of money employed in trade, but the labours too, the care, attention, accounts, and correspondence about them; and some cases take in also the condition of the person so employed, according to the custom of our country.
>
> (*System* II: 63)

This seems to be a departure from the idea that the free forces of demand and supply determine prices but the cost components can reflect market conditions and anticipate future changes.

Steuart, too, moves towards pricing on a cost-plus principle, taking into account the cost of 'employing the workman, the value of materials and profit upon alienation' (*Principles* II: 173), but his greater contribution to price theory was to indicate how competition fixes prices. He saw demand both under barter and in a monetized economy as a reciprocal relationship between two parties. If there is one interest there will be simple demand but, if several interests, compound demand. He is fond of the idea of 'double competition', the competition both among the buyers and among the sellers. The sellers through their mutual competition depress prices; buyers in competition with each other will raise prices to the point of exhausting their means of payment or hitting a price ceiling imposed by magistrates. 'All that can be said with certainty, is, that competition on the part of consumers will make them rise, and that competition of the part of furnishers will make them fall' (III: 30). Perhaps this is his greatest contribution to price theory, that perfect competition has a large number of buyers in competition with each other, and that a large number of sellers will also compete among themselves. The extreme opposite of this is bilateral monopoly, when there is only one buyer and one seller. Steuart, through using the idea of double competition, which can vary in degree, can classify all the different types of market structure whether competitive, oligopolistic or monopolistic.

Hodgson claimed that the assertion that prices are fixed by supply and demand means they are fixed by competition. 'Competition', he reminds us, is derived from a Latin word meaning aiming or seeking together. In a competitive system individual interests seek their respective objects without any outward restraint. Competition is not a principle but 'the free play of as many self-interests' (1870: 5) and is only excessive if dishonest; otherwise it has the merit of removing undue power. At every stage of production competition keeps prices near actual costs, or natural prices. An increase in price has a double effect, reducing demand when poorer consumers are excluded and increasing production when profit margins rise. (Thomas Chalmers (1832 II: 40) had pointed out that the immediate determinant of the price of food is not the quantity produced but the quantity brought to market. But even a small shortcoming of a crop stimulates more production.) The opposite of competition, monopoly, the parent of scarcity, dearness and badness, removes the incentives to honest effort, and encourages fraud as well as indolence. Hodgson (1877), noting that demand is desire and the ability to give something in exchange for what is desired, argued that man desires less at a higher price, a suggestion that the demand curve is downward sloping.

Often these Scottish writers tried to explain the reasons for price changes in terms of forces within a particular market or in the economy as a whole. In his discussion of value Murray looks at both types of force: 'the prices of things can never increase, unless when the demand exceeds the quantity to supply it... plenty of money may make some delicacies and superfluities dearer, because as it enables more individuals to aspire to them, it may increase the demand for them', but only when production 'cannot be increased by art' (1758: 22–3).

An increase in demand stimulates greater supply. Whereas plenty of money from the West Indies, he observes, caused higher prices for scarce commodities, in other cases a high price leads to more employment and prices coming down.

While Murray hinted at a changing relationship between demand and supply, Lauderdale, in his *Inquiry*, looks in more detail at the dynamic relationship between demand and supply, which shows the movements between the demand and supply curves until an equilibrium is reached, or not:

> when the quantity of any commodity is diminished, demand operates in restoring the usual supply, not only from the encouragement it gives to those who are concerned in producing that article, by the great rise in its value; but with augmented energy, from the circumstance, that the necessary fall in the price of other commodities calls off a portion of industry from the formation of them, whilst it points it to the production of the article whose quantity is reduced.
>
> (p. 3)

Steuart, however, wanted price flexibility in an economy:

> The whole delicacy of the intricate combinations of commerce, depends upon a just and equable vibration of prices, according as circumstances demand it. When principles are not understood, prices cannot gently fall, they must be pulled down; and merchants dare not suffer them to rise, for fear of abuse, even although the perfection of an infant manufacture should require it.
>
> (*Principles* II: 313–14)

The weaver will push the price as high as the profits of the merchant and competition dictate; some merchants will fix prices according to demand and not the real value of their goods. Also price flexibility can be the inevitable result of the type of economy. Murray noted that a more agricultural economy will have more price fluctuations because of variations in weather, unlike an industrial country.

Because of the prominence of labour theories of value in *WN*, Smith's earlier reliance on a market view of value can easily be ignored. In *LJ* he has a clear demand and supply analysis, making use of the idea of abundance. He writes that plenty and cheapness are inseparable: 'we see that water, which is absolutely necessary for the support of mankind, by its abundance costs nothing but the uptaking, whereas diamonds and other jewels, of which one can hardly say what they serve for, give an immense price' (p. 333). He goes on to write, 'When goods are brought to the market we seldom enquire what profits the person will have if he get such or such a price' (p. 357), for what counts is the demand or need, abundance proportionate to demand and the wealth of the demanders. According to Smith's argument, if market price is higher than the natural price many will crowd into the trade, the number employed will increase, there will be greater output, poorer people will be able to afford it and the price will fall to the natural price. Impressed by the force of demand, Smith stresses its importance in examining the movement away from the natural price: 'Those things which are scarcest bear the highest price, as they become the purchase of the richest persons who can afford to bid highest. They alone purchase diamonds' (p. 361).

Smith, through using the idea of market price, transformed value theory into demand and supply analysis. According to Taylor (1956), Smith in his *LJ* used market price to link together utility, scarcity and demand. But how far did he progress in his analysis? Laidler (1981) complained that Smith lacked a market demand function, preferring to regard demand as a force and market prices as responding to variations in the ratio of demand to supply.

In Smith's *WN* there is a movement from the demand and supply analysis of the *LJ* to attempt to produce a satisfactory labour theory of value. This is a reverse movement in economics: from 1870 the labour theory of value was largely abandoned when neoclassical economics started. However, Horner used demand and supply analysis to kill off the labour theory of value much earlier: 'The reciprocal value of any two commodities . . . is determined in every instance of exchange by the competition; or by the proportion between the supply and demand of each of two commodities . . . in the actual exchange of any one commodity for any other, no regard is paid to the quantity of labour employed in producing either; the quantities reciprocally exchanged are proportioned by the competition between the supply and demand for both' (Bourne and Taylor 1994: 160–2). It could be Jevons speaking in 1871.

With the tools of demand and supply it was possible to dethrone cost of production theories. Ramsay's 1836 work firmly stated that value is immediately determined by the proportion between demand and supply. Certainly it is not labour alone that is the dominant cost, because the use of fixed capital is important. Ramsay, according to Prybyla, regarded the cost of production as only a remote regulator or cause of value: 'his discussion of how cost of production fits in with supply and demand, reveals a groping towards the concept of supply and demand schedules, shifts in demand and supply, and the notion of elasticity' (1963: 312–13).

Demand and supply analysis became more precise with the employment of the idea of elasticity, the responsiveness of one variable to another such as the response of changes in demand to changes in price. Lauderdale saw that there is an inelastic demand for necessaries and that the elasticity of a particular demand curve is determined by consumer preferences and the nature of a commodity. The use of elasticity analysis caught on. De Quincey (1897) was aware of three classes of elasticity when a market contracts or expands through a price change, and traces the different effects of price changes of various magnitudes. Patrick James Stirling (1809–91), famous for his translation of the extreme, laissez-faire economist Frederic Bastiat, played with the idea of different supply elasticities, stating that changes in supply would not cause proportionate changes in price: 'The proportional differences will depend upon whether the article is a luxury or a necessary, of a durable or perishable nature, portable or bulky, of partial or general use' (1846: 25).

Another tool emerging from discussions of demand and supply is the demand curve. Steuart has some notion of the inverse relationship between price and quantity demanded, which underlies the idea of a downward-sloping demand curve. There can be price discrimination, he writes, on the part of a merchant who wants to increase profits and sales and who will 'make a kind of auction, by first bringing down the prices to the level of the highest bidders, and so descend by degrees, in proportion as demand sinks . . . The traders will profit as much as possible, and sell off as much of their goods as profits will permit' (*Principles* I: 213). Also he hints at an inelastic (unresponsive to price) demand curve in a particular case, 'Things of absolute necessity must be procured, let the price be ever so great . . .' (I: 214). Sen (1957) argues that Steuart develops price theory further through his awareness of demand and supply elasticities, and that he regarded demand as more important than supply.

These writers were anticipating the modern ideas of market analysis, with curves expressing functional relationships and elasticities employed to show the power of demand and supply. The most outstanding contribution to demand and supply theory in Scotland in the nineteenth century came from (Henry Charles) Fleeming Jenkin (1833–85), who was a pioneer of telegraph cable engineering and was appointed professor of civil engineering at University College, London, in 1866 and then at Edinburgh University in 1868, where he held the chair until his death. His sudden demise was regarded as a tragedy. His five essays on political economy are notable for a graphical application of demand and supply analysis to the determination of prices, wages and tax incidence. His demand and supply diagrams appeared first in a footnote to his article on trade unions, which he sent to Jevons, who was inspired by it when writing his *Theory of Political Economy*. Jenkin's 1870 article, 'The Graphic Representation of the Laws of Supply and Demand, and their application to labour', especially, shows him to be crucial in the development of microeconomics. What John Stuart Mill could sketch in words about the nature of the demand curve Jenkin illustrated in a way that helped Alfred Marshall in 1890 to provide a demand and supply apparatus fundamental to economics textbooks ever after. Jenkin sought to show specifically what determined the price of a commodity at a given time in a given market, with demand and supply relating to particular prices. He plots demand curves against a vertical axis, showing quantities demanded and supplied, and a horizontal axis, to indicate different prices. He then goes on to devise three laws of supply and demand. First, 'In a given market, at a given time, the market prices of the commodity will be that at which the supply and demand curves cut.' Second, 'If the whole supply be increased, it will most frequently, but not always, happen that the supply at a price will, throughout the whole scale, be increased; prices will then fall . . . If the purchase fund be increased it will often happen that the demand at a price will rise throughout the whole scale; prices will then rise . . .' Third, 'In the long run, the price of the manufactured article is chiefly determined by the cost of its production, and the quantity manufactured is chiefly determined by the demand at that price' (Colvin and Ewing 1887: 78). He admits that his first and second laws are applicable only in the short run. There is a realism in his account of how prices are determined in markets – he admits that the actual price at which there is a sale is only an approximation to the theoretical price. Thus the 'laws' are only a matter of probability. Also he applies his analysis to English auctions, in which bids ascend from the lowest, and Dutch auctions, where the opposite occurs. Nevertheless, by considering wages as a price, Jenkin could apply his supply and demand analysis to the labour market.

In Scottish economics Fleeming Jenkin might be considered the patron saint of demand and supply analysis. Jenkin got about as far as Marshall in constructing demand and supply curves but Perlman (1995) writes that Jenkin did not change classical price theory, relying instead on the theory in J. S. Mill's *Principles of Political Economy*. Jenkin's critics, Brownlie and Lloyd Prichard (1963), quote Joseph Schumpeter's opinion that he was not rigorous in his examination of demand and supply functions, thinking they were subjective and only existed in the mind. But this is a view not far removed from Marshall's idea that most of the demand curve is conjectural ([1890] 1959: 110) as we know only the immediate vicinity of a point on the demand curve. Jenkin was probably the first in Britain to discuss demand functions and able to use the idea of consumers' rent in analysing taxation and showing the influence of trade unions on wage rates.

Aesthetics and subjective value

The eighteenth-century debate about value coincided with the discussion of the basis for aesthetic judgements. There is a connection between value in economics and value in art because both disciplines seek to determine what something is worth. The task of valuing a good is acutely difficult when that good is a 'work of art' or of exceptional beauty. As Michael says, there is a link between aesthetic theory and value theory: 'aesthetic pleasure serves as a mark of the value of the exciting object. Objects are of value either as instrument, i.e., as means to an end, or in themselves' (1984: 251). Writing about aesthetics, Santayana, in 1904, observed that 'aesthetics' is a loose term with various meanings as it can be concerned with a sense of beauty or works of art. When speaking of the phenomena of art and taste aesthetics is *factual* but it is *ideal* in cases such as the intent of poetry or the interpretation of music. He thought that aesthetics does not provide a separable value because what entertains the imagination depends on the exercise of the senses.

Francis Hutcheson made an early and distinctive contribution to the theory of aesthetics through introducing the notion of a human sense capable of appreciating what is beautiful. In his *An Inquiry into the Original of our Ideas of Beauty and Virtue* (1738) he writes 'the Word *Beauty* is taken for the *idea rais'd in us*, and a Sense of Beauty is for *our Power of receiving this idea*' (p. 7). 'But what we call Beautiful in Objects, to speak in the Mathematical Style, seems to be a compound *Ratio* of *Uniformity* and *Variety*: so that where the Uniformity of Bodys is equal, the Beauty is as the *Variety*; and where the Variety is equal, the Beauty is as the *Uniformity*' (p. 17). If Hutcheson thinks there are conditions in the object to make us call it beautiful he is either returning to an intrinsic view of value or describing the determinants, not the nature, of taste.

A much respected writer on aesthetics at that time, Alexander Gerard (1728–95), first professor of moral philosophy at Marischal College, Aberdeen, included some economics in his lectures and sought to establish the basis for aesthetic assessments in his *An Essay on Taste* (1759). He clearly asserted that the natural powers of the mind, helped by proper culture, produce a fine taste, but qualified this by stating that tastes differ from person to person and that the quality of one's internal sense is variable. He argues that some people will admit they are incapable of making a judgement through prejudice or personal imperfections and need to follow a standard of taste that cannot reconcile all tastes but determine which are best. In this view, a taste that is common to all mankind is generally approved in all places and in all ages but 'The sentiments of those only are to be taken into the account, who have a good natural taste, who have not allowed it to be vitiated, who have improved it by study or conversation, and by such extensive acquaintance with works of imagination, as enable them to compare one with others, and to judge of its relative as well as of its intrinsic merit' (p. 227). According to Gerard, few people are the discerning leaders in aesthetic matters. His view is like the study of consumers: a few prominent people, like leading critics, with their preferences widely advertised, can have a powerful effect on the nature of demand.

In references to taste in his essay *Of the Standard of Taste* Hume too has a mental approach: 'Beauty is no quality in things themselves: It exists merely in the mind which contemplates them and each mind perceives a different beauty' (1987: 230), which reminds one of the long search for a standard of value and the rejection of the notion of intrinsic value. But 'there are certain general principles of approbation or blame, whose influence a careful eye may trace in all operations of the mind. Some particular forms or qualities, from the original structure of the internal fabric, are calculated to please, and others to displease' (p. 233). This sounds like a return to the intrinsic value and has echoes of Hutcheson: he admits that 'Though it be certain, that beauty and deformity, more than sweet and bitter, are not qualities in objects, but belong entirely to the sentiment, internal or external; it must be allowed, that there are certain qualities in objects, which are fitted by nature to produce those particular feelings' (p. 235). However, he believes that these intrinsic qualities are too minute to have much effect. Later he states that experience makes a feeling more exact and nice when we judge objects for their beauty and that men of delicate taste are rare but are usually distinguished by the soundness of their understanding and the superiority of their faculties to the rest of mankind. This is a mixed approach to the appreciation of beauty dependent on both subjective feelings and, to a small extent, the qualities in objects that produce feelings.

Jones (1976) pointed out that Hume discusses aesthetics within the context of man as a social being and summarizes Hume's position: it is by comparison, not intrinsic worth, that we judge beauty. Utility can, Jones argues, make us call something, for example a fertile field, beautiful and what is beauty can vary from culture to culture. In his view the rules of art are founded on experience and observing general points of view, perhaps like the medieval idea of the just price depending on the common estimation. Furthermore, what is beautiful is derived from a uniformity of sentiment; it cannot be too eccentric as private states are expressed in a public language governed by public criteria: language as a social institution makes communication intelligible and objective. Hume's criteria for assessing beauty are 'exactness of perception, freedom from prejudice, and what he calls "good" sense' (p. 58). Hume, who was, according to Halberstadt (1971), influenced by Hutcheson's internal sense view, thought utility and esteem are the bases of beauty and that visible beauty gives a uniform pleasure.

Adam Smith's philosophical interests were wide enough to include aesthetics, allowing us to consider the links, if any, between aesthetic and market judgements of value. Smith writes about aesthetics in his essay *Of the Imitative Arts*, suggesting that the exact resemblance of component parts of an object constitutes beauty. In *TMS* he repeats the popular view that utility is a principal source of beauty, for example, the convenience of a house gives pleasure. However, Smith had a sociological view of ethics: 'to live in society . . . we constantly pay more regard to the sentiments of the spectator, than to those of the person principally concerned' (p. 182). According to Macfie (1959), Smith equates propriety and beauty. Further, in *TMS*, in a commentary on the relationship between beauty and the average, he writes:

> in each species of creatures, what is most beautiful bears the strongest characters of the general fabric of the species, and has the strongest resemblance to the greater part of the individuals with which it is classed . . . the beauty of each species, though in one sense the rarest of all things, because few individuals hit this middle form exactly, yet in another, is the most common, because all the deviations from it resemble it more than they resemble one another.
>
> (pp. 198–9)

But Smith rejects the view that one's idea of external beauty depends entirely on custom, although grudgingly admitting that nothing which is called beautiful would be contrary to custom. Thomson (1965) thinks that a striking feature of Smith's system is that he regards his own standard of judgement as aesthetic rather than rational. Smith, according to Jones in Mizuta and Sugiyama (1993), said that utility is one of the principal sources of beauty: property owners value the fitness of their possessions for purpose.

Thomas Reid, in the view of Robbins (1942), follows Joseph Addison (1672–1719), the English essayist who used the aesthetic categories of the new, the grand or sublime, and the beautiful. All aesthetic values were, according to Reid, derived from the qualities of the mind. In his *Essays on the Intellectual Powers of Man*, Reid distinguished what immediately strikes one without any reflection as beautiful from that which, based on the rational judgement, possesses a specified agreeable quality. Reid's analysis could be applied to the distinction between impulse-buying and the careful purchases that absorb a large proportion of a consumer's income. Dugald Stewart, according to Hipple (1955), seems to think that beauty refers chiefly to objects of sight, especially colours. This would correspond to the idea of valuing goods when they are displayed in a market. He thought that the most common form of a species is the most beautiful, which seems to refute the idea that the scarcest is the most valuable.

Hugh Blair (1718–1800), a prominent Church of Scotland minister in Edinburgh and the first professor of rhetoric and belles-lettres at Edinburgh University, a noted literary critic and friend of the leaders of the Scottish Enlightenment including Hume and Kames, said in his lectures 'Taste may be defined, "The power of receiving pleasure from the beauties of nature and of art"' (1825: 10). He goes on to explain in detail the mental approach of Hutcheson and others.

> Taste ... is a faculty common in some degree to all men. Nothing that belongs to human nature is more general than the relish of beauty of one kind or other; of what is orderly, proportioned, grand, harmonious, new or sprightly. In children, the rudiments of Taste discover themselves very early in a thousand instances; on their fondness for regular bodies, their admiration of pictures and statues and imitations of all kind; and their strong attachment to whatever is new or marvellous ... We must, therefore, conclude the principles of Taste to be deeply founded in the human mind. It is no less essential to man to have some discernment of beauty than it is to possess the attributes of reason and of speech ... Taste ... is ultimately founded on an internal sense of beauty, which is natural to man, and which, in its application to particular objects, is capable of being guided and enlightened by reason ... [But a consensus emerges] ... the common feelings of men carry the same authority, and have a title to regulate the Taste of every individual. (p. 19)

According to this idea, sense and perception count more than reason. When the Blair view is applied to value theory in economics we see that subjective valuations are not perverse and eccentric but fundamental to human nature. The consequence of this is that there is something predictable about the behaviour of consumers in markets because few tastes are eccentric: herd-like behaviour rules.

Later Patrick Geddes (1854–1932), the city planner who tried to relate the natural to the social sciences, contributed to the aesthetics and value debate. In his attempt to link economics to the physical sciences he classifies ultimate products as necessaries or super-necessaries. Whereas necessaries replace structures and maintain energies, super-necessaries stimulate the sense organs. 'In any at all civilised community, in short, every ultimate product has visibly superadded its *aesthetic sub function* of visual stimulus...' (1885: 35). This does not state that value is an aesthetic judgement alone but that appearance does count, as Dugald Stewart said.

Subjective utility

Without going to the lengths of devising a theory of aesthetics many of these writers on value saw that utility was a subjective entity.

Lindsay had observed that 'Glass Beads and Diamonds may be in themselves equally useless and unnecessary; but their real Values are severally settled by the Opinions of Mankind' (1736: 61–2). Hume, on the other hand, is inclined to a subjective theory of value. In *The Sceptic* he writes 'But though the value of every object can be determined only by the sentiment or passion of every individual, we may observe, that the passion, in pronouncing its verdict, considers not the object simply, as it is in itself, but surveys it with all the circumstances, which attend it' (1987: 172); citing the case of the joy which possession of a diamond gives, chiefly because of its rarity. When pronouncing blame or approbation, he writes that 'those qualities are not really in the objects, but belong entirely to the sentiment of that mind which blames or praises' (p. 163). More strongly he contends, 'no objects are, in themselves, desirable or odious, valuable or despicable; but that objects acquire these qualities from the particular character and constitution of the mind, which surveys them' (p. 171) and that 'Objects have absolutely no worth or value in themselves. They derive their worth merely from the passions' (p. 166).

As ever, Steuart had a distinctive approach, which is relevant to the subjectivity of value: he saw that export and domestic prices are differently determined. Vanity and caprice move domestic prices but export prices will depend on merchants demanding goods from domestic producers in order to obtain a desired level of profits (*Principles* III: 31). This is an interesting contrast between the subjective valuations of the ultimate consumers and of their merchant intermediaries, but it does not challenge the view that value is ultimately subjective, because the merchants engaged in international trade will have to anticipate, or even research, the nature of demand abroad.

Things have value, according to Lauderdale, because 'the commodity, as being useful or delightful to man, should be an object of his desire' (1804: 12); 'exchangeable value...is...merely the practical means of expressing the degree of desire for any particular article of wealth...' (p. 107).

In further support for the subjective approach, Seligman (1903a) claims that Craig regarded subjective utility as the basis of all value because price is related to the estimation of the purchasers. Bruce even suggested that Craig's analysis of utility almost reached the notion of marginal utility. 'He (Craig) sees that with every decrease in value or price there is a new group of purchasers whose lower estimate of utility is now available for consuming the increased supply. This new group . . . is the marginal group as we know it in the modern doctrine of value' (1938: 699).

In Kauder's (1953) view, Smith undid the thinking of two thousand years by stating that water has a great utility and small value in *WN*. Thus the year 1870, the start of what is sometimes called the 'Marginal Revolution', which distinguished total from marginal utility to explain the relative values of water and diamonds, was a more important year than 1776 when *WN* was first published. It is a pity Smith abandoned his swift dismissal of the so-called water and diamonds paradox in *LJ* because he would have avoided Kauder's severe judgement. In support of Smith, Skinner quotes *WN*, Book I, chapter XI, c.31, 'The merit of an object which is any degree either useful or beautiful, is greatly enhanced by its scarcity' (1995: 165–82).

The change in value theory occurring in European economics after 1870 in the often called 'Marginalist Revolution' was led by Stanley Jevons in Manchester, Carl Menger in Vienna and Leon Walras, founder of the Lausanne school of economics, in Switzerland. Hodgson, first professor of political economy at Edinburgh University, recognized a movement away from previous theories by his assertion that it is not scarcity that raises prices but the 'mental conviction or apprehension' (1870c: 8).

The eighth Duke of Argyll, George Douglas Campbell (1823–1900), was one of the largest landowners in Scotland with 175,000 acres, a promoter of mass emigration to the USA and a Liberal politician who rose to be Secretary of State for India (1868–74), then abandoned politics through opposition to Liberal land reform proposals. A devout Christian, his interest in science took him into evolution debates in an attempt to put economics on a scientific basis. On the issue of value he shared John Stuart Mill's view that there is a mental element in all kinds of value: 'the mental adaptation of all work and of all effort to the corresponding needs and desires of the society in which we live' (Argyle 1893: 348). Later he writes that value depends on the great categories of the desires of humanity, and the conceptions and inventiveness of men.

Towards 1900 the subjective utility approach moved more to the centre of Scottish value theory when William Smart attempted to make Glasgow the Vienna of the North by putting the early Austrian school firmly on the university curriculum. This occurred, according to Davie (1991), because Edward Caird at Glasgow wanted libertarian Austrian economics to counter the Marxism of Smart's colleague William Wallace. Smart, in *An introduction to the theory of value* (1910), rebuked his colleagues for playing down the economics descended from Jevons, the English writer closest to the early Austrians. With much truth Smart notes 'the history of economic science is strewn with the wrecks of theories of value' (p. 1); he then proceeds to repeat the central views of the Austrians: that value is a relation and not an inherent property of things and that subjective value is what is 'valuable to me when I consider that my wellbeing is associated with or dependent on the possession of it' (p. 5), whereas objective value is a power or capacity, 'power of exchange', or 'purchasing power', a price in a market. He argues that value refers to human life, to the satisfaction of a want, and has an element of scarcity in most cases. Obviously influenced by Carl Menger, the founder of the Austrian School, Smart classifies goods into necessaries, comforts and luxuries (Scottish writers such as Chalmers had also used that taxonomy) arguing that the classification is based on 'the consequences which will ensue to our lives if these wants go unsatisfied' (p. 21). Without food we die but without tobacco we merely have discomfort. Smart, concerned to show a break from the classical view of value, accused Adam Smith of confusing utility and value in his value-in-use concept. There was a transition in the idea of utility, he observes, from the consideration of physical life to the spiritual life as value depends on a 'felt want' (p. 25). Following in the footsteps of Jevons and Friedrich von Wieser (1851–1926), who succeeded Menger as professor in 1903, Smart relates value to marginal utility. Like Jevons in his famous attack on the labour theory of value, Smart rejects the cost of production as the basis of value: 'value comes, not from the past of goods but from their future' (p. 68). He claims that value is not a conscious process as a businessman naturally uses ideas of marginal value and price (pp. 63–4).

This tour of value theorizing in Scotland shows the variety of Scottish approaches and emphasizes the fact that these writers were pioneers of methods that are still prominent in microeconomics today. The cost of production approach, particularly in the form of the labour theory of value, had died out and the subjective utility strand, long in the background and linked to aesthetic theory, triumphed.

Value is both a practical and a moral issue. We need prices for allocation within a market and we want the 'right' prices. Were the Scots trying to tidy up the three philosophical issues bequeathed by the Ancient Greeks – the creation of just prices, which would now be called fair prices; the distinction between substance and accidents expressed in the difference between natural and market prices; and the question of aesthetics, which searches for the reason for our judgement that something is valuable? They perhaps scored worst on establishing just prices, as many of these writers had a matter-of-fact acceptance that prices come from the working of markets. In looking for the substance beneath fluctuating prices, however, they stumbled on something more convincing than intrinsic value – some kind of long-run equilibrium price. And yet it was aesthetics that proved the more promising philosophical approach in the journey towards modern theories of price – perhaps because this was the area on which, of these three philosophical issues, the Scots worked hardest.

Money

3

Functions of money

In 1707 Scotland lost its own currency, the Scots pound, and entered into a monetary union with England. To have one's own currency is a great mark of independence because a currency sets the prices at which the country trades with the rest of the world. In such currency mergers, there is always the problem of the weaker country having an inappropriate exchange rate, as well as less influence on its monetary affairs. However, the creation of a free trade zone gave Scotland a chance of improving its trading performance so that it could cope with a British currency. Important issues, of perpetual interest to the student of monetary economics, were discussed repeatedly by the Scots: the nature of money, whether it is neutral with respect to the real economy, the validity of the quantity theory of money, the use of a standard for the value of money, the price for using money (the rate of interest) and whether usury laws should regulate interest rates.

The nature of money

In the increased activity of the exchange economy, barter was soon found to be too clumsy a method for conducting transactions. There was the problem of the 'double coincidence of wants', that is, the problem that the surplus output one party had needed would be wanted by another party, who had a surplus of what the first party wanted. It was better to choose something regarded as valuable for use as an intermediary. Thus money emerged as an institution noted for its efficiency. Aristotle had suggested that money has the function of being a medium of exchange, as well as a unit of account and store of value, setting the agenda for much of monetary economics.

In Book I, chapter IV of the *WN* Smith explains the inconvenience of using barter as an exchange mechanism without first having established a universally acceptable medium of exchange. He noted that, in order to barter, either there has to be a coincidence of wants or each party has to maintain stocks of many goods. Also money is divisible, unlike in barter, when, for example, a large beast, which is more than potential buyers want, is offered by one party.

In *LJ* Smith writes that money has two purposes – a measure of value and a medium of exchange – and many advantages. He argues that when commerce becomes complicated through the exchange of numerous things it is difficult for people to remember relative values: they need money as a common measure. Also, it is easier to carry a small amount of silver than the equivalent in linen. Money has a dynamic effect 'as an instrument of commerce. It by that means promotes the exchange of commodities; this exchange again promotes the industry of the people and facilitates and encourages the division of labour' (p. 374). He writes that we can estimate the money needed to carry on its circulation by the amount of rent of land estates: the landowners in turn pay all the other classes. There are hints here of François Quesnay's – (1694–1774), court physician and leading Physiocrat – *tableau économique*, which shows the circulation of rents.

Smith distances himself from mercantilists and their obsession with accumulating specie with the dismissive assertion, 'There can be no fear of want of money, for if their [*sic*] be too little it will soon be supplied by the exportation of goods, and if too great it will be sent abroad for goods either in specie or melted down' (*LJ*: 386).

He thinks that specie is not necessary for the financing of wars because refined manufactures can be used in payment – there is rarely excess subsistence, thus agricultural produce would not be used as a way of paying. Despite his aversion to mercantilism, he admits (*WN*: 438) that money is part of the national capital, albeit a small part.

In *Of Money* Hume has a basic view of money. It is 'only the instrument which men have agreed upon to facilitate the exchange of one commodity for another. It is none of the wheels of trade but the oil which renders the motion of the wheels more smooth and easy' (1987: 281). Kames shares this view: 'Money may be justly conceived to be the oil that lubricates all the springs and wheels of a great machine, and preserves it in motion' (1778: 145). Having argued that barter became deficient when wants multiplied and that a generally accepted commodity was needed in exchange, he explains that money is needed to pay wages so that people can go to market. If there is a shortage of money then industry and manufactures must decay: if we fail to confine our expenses, the balance of trade moves against us, causing a drain of gold.

Considering what kind of thing is usable as money leads to the debate about intrinsically valuable money versus fiat money (valuable because of the prestige of the issuing authority). Sir James Steuart wrote extensively about money, distinguishing different types of money: 'Money, which I call of account, is no more than an arbitrary scale of equal parts invented for measuring the respective value of things vendible', but real money is 'coin, or a modification of the precious metals, which by general agreement among men, and under the authority of a state, carries along with it its own intrinsic value' (*Principles* II: 44). He was a supporter of the idea of fiat money: 'money is any commodity, which purely in itself is of no material use to man' (I: 51), although he did apparently hanker after specie as money.

Dugald Stewart argued that it was an accidental circumstance that precious metals' intrinsic value makes them money. For artistic purposes, intrinsic properties add to value but this is a minor use of gold and silver: it is the adaptation of gold and silver to being media of exchange that gives them utility. He appreciated that the characteristic of money, as is seen in English and Scottish paper money, is 'general consent' (1840 I: 336–8).

Neutrality of money

David Hume initially appears to think that money has little impact on economic activity. In his essay *Of Money* he says, as we have seen, that money is merely an instrument and of no consequence: 'If we consider any one kingdom by itself, it is evident, that the greater or less plenty of money is of no consequence; since the prices of commodities are always proportioned to the plenty of money…' (1987: 281). Also, he asserts that 'money is nothing but the representation of labour and commodities, and serves only as a method of rating or estimating them' (p. 285). But Hume does concede in that essay the mercantilist view that the public gains in having plenty of money at time of war because it is cheaper to buy the services of mercenary troops than use one's own inhabitants to fight; at other times it is more important to have a great industrious people than a great amount of money.

He does argue, though, that any power money has is quite short term. Admitting that an increase of gold and silver will ultimately raise prices, Hume says,

> it is only in this interval or intermediate situation, between the acquisition of money and rise of prices, that the increasing quantity of gold and silver is favourable to industry. When any quantity of money is imported into a nation, it is not at first dispersed into many hands; but is confined to the coffers of a few persons, who immediately seek to employ it to advantage…They are thereby enabled to employ more workmen than formerly, who never dream of demanding higher wages, but are glad of employment from such good paymasters…the money must first quicken the diligence of every individual, before it encrease the price of labour.
>
> (pp. 286–7)

Conversely, in the short term a fall in the quantity of money can be pernicious to industry with less employment and cause difficulties for farmers trying to sell corn and cattle. In case the reader gets the idea that money is more important than Hume thinks it is, he firmly states: 'the want of money can never injure any state within itself: For men and commodities are the real strength of any community' (p. 293). In *Of Money* there seems to be a contradiction between his view that money has a real effect only in the short term and the opinion that 'The good policy of the magistrate consists only in keeping it [money], if possible, still encreasing; because, by that means, he keeps alive a spirit of industry in the nation, and encreases the stock of labour, in which consists all real power and riches' (p. 288). He seems to be worried about the deflationary effects of a falling money supply; perhaps he was not worried about *some* inflation if that kept industry lively.

Hume, in raising the issue of the neutrality of money, that is, that changes in the supply of money do not affect real incomes, consumption, production and employment, provoked a major monetary discussion. Vickers (1957) is firm in his conviction that Hume in his *Essays* was keen to say that the money supply does not affect the price level, economic activity or the rate of interest. Paganelli (2009) asserted that at least in the long run Hume regarded money as neutral and claimed that money was merely an instrument to facilitate exchange; like Montesquieu, Hume considered money as a sign of all commodities. Money is therefore regarded by him as the consequence, not cause, of trade dutifully matching the amount of money to the demand of commerce.

Smith, too, according to Laidler (1981), viewed money as an endogenous variable responsive to prices, not their cause. Simmel bluntly asserts 'Adam Smith's theory [is] that gold and silver are merely tools no different from kitchen utensils and that their import increases the wealth of a country just as little as the multiplication of kitchen utensils provides more food' (2004: 173). In *WN* Smith regards money as having a passive role, increasing as a consequence of the rise in the value of annual produce. But part of the increase in output has to go to buying gold and silver to provide the circulating medium.

Regarding this subject, we look at a final word from Kames, who saw in his *Sketche* the stimulating effects of an increased amount of money: 'Plenty of money elevates our spirits, and inspires an appetite for pleasure' (1778: 146), leading to exertion in building, husbandry and manufactures. In his *Sketches* he argues that before money was introduced, under barter there was a demand only for necessaries: 'Money prompts men to be industrious; and the beautiful productions of industry and art, rousing the imagination, excite a violent desire for grand houses, fine gardens, and for everything gay and plentiful . . . money is a species of property, of such extensive use as greatly to inflame the appetite (1796: 91).

Much of this debate can be resolved only by statistical analysis, especially in order to determine how lasting the effects of changes in the quantity of money are. What is most useful in Hume's analysis is his emphasis on the importance of time, which the economic model builder had to address when introducing time lags to indicate the speed of response to changes in economic variables.

Quantity theory of money

Linked to the debate about the neutrality of money is the more famous theory, the quantity theory of money. All these writers were aware of countries, such as their own, with a shortage of money and others, such as Spain, famous for an excess. The simplest quantity theory of money linked the amount of money in an economy to the price level in order to explain inflation.

Hume has a crude quantity theory of money in *Of Money*:

> It seems a maxim almost self-evident, that the prices of every thing depend on the proportion between commodities and money, and that any considerable alteration on either has the same effect, either of heightening or lowering the price…It is the proportion between the circulating money, and the commodities in the market, which determines the prices.
>
> (1987: 290–1)

This was an elementary theory because it did not mention the velocity of circulation, that is, the number of times a stock of money turns over in a given time period. Hicks (1967) stated that Hume regarded the quantity theory of money as merely an equilibrium condition.

Hume opposed repeated debasements and the inflationist projects of the mercantilists and John Law. Low (1952) asserts that Hume always thought in terms of an instantaneous quantity theory of money while Vickers (1957) said that Hume described the nature and structure of the empirical monetary system, explaining the modes of causation.

Steuart was more subtle. He avoided the simple assertion that more money soon meant higher prices because the state of demand and competition are crucial in explaining price increases. Taking issue with Hume and Montesquieu over the quantity theory of money, Steuart opposed the simple notion that prices are proportionate to the quantity of money, insisting that 'it is the complicated operations of demand and competition, which determine the standard price of every thing. If there be many labourers, and little demand, work will be cheap' (*Principles* II: 78). In the short run, he argued, foreign trade will increase prices as it encourages industry and transfers labourers from farming to manufacturing, bringing about increases in wages and higher product prices through the expansion of cities and increased competition between purchasers for a supply of commodities. Other reasons for price increases, according to Steuart, are the amount of credit, especially through more paper currency, and the ability of bankers and merchants to economize on the amount of money they need for their transactions. Money, he writes, has the passive role of entering into circulation only if there is an increase in demand, otherwise extra coin will be hoarded or melted down into plate and paper money will return to the issuer under what was later to be called 'the law of reflux': 'it will return upon the debtor in it, and become realized; because of the little use found for it in carrying on circulation…it is the desire of spending it (money) alone, which will raise prices' (p. 79). He also argues that a country can only absorb a determinate quantity of money: 'the less use they make of coin, the more use they will make of paper, and vice versa' (III: 191), so if trade diminishes the solid property melted down will be consolidated again. Consistent with his general view, he says grain prices are not raised by an increase in money because 'the proportion of wealth found in the hands of the lowest class of the people' determines such prices (II: 80). But with luxuries, he contended that more money could raise their prices. Where Steuart can agree with Hume is that 'the price of every commodity is in proportion to the sum of money circulating in the market for that commodity' (p. 83) because money is merely the measure of demand. Demand would cease, he argues, if prices were raised by sellers as high as the quantity of money justified; price increases are in proportion to the urgency of demand. Also, in his view, if prices are raised too high then the rich will buy the goods they want from abroad. However, in a closed economy Steuart saw that there are many ways of selling produce without using specie, such as by exchanging goods for other goods or services; consequently, prices would not be proportionate to the amount of money. Because of frictions and political resistances, he believed that the changes in the prices of precious metals would not cause a proportionate change in other prices. What Steuart is doing is steering us away from a crude notion that more money means higher prices, through emphasizing the fact that prices are the consequence of the working of markets where the force of demand is very important.

Dugald Stewart, in his *Lectures* (1840), realized that there was no simple proportionality between money and price increases, arguing that the distribution of money was as important as its amount. In support of his opinion he cited Smith, who had noted occasions of both increased and decreased prices of provisions following an increase in the amount of paper money, because the state of the harvest was more important than the money supply. Later, in Stewart's discussion of the Bullion Report – the report of the House of Commons Select Committee on the implications of Britain being off the gold standard – he questioned the idea that more money meant higher prices, citing the authority of Steuart, Hume and Smith.

Discussion of the price-specie flow mechanism (examined at length in Chapter 2) includes the real effects of changing the money supply. Wennerlind (2005) says that Hume, in the *Political Discourses*, wanted to promote employment at a time of surplus labour, believing that an inflow of money and more employment would result from a trade surplus rather than from a domestically generated increase in the money supply. Mayer (1980) said that Hume's quantity theory of money applied to the whole world, not a single country, because of the price-specie flow mechanism, while Lucas (1996) regarded Hume's parable of the annihilation of money in one night as a statement of the quantity theory of money and deduced the theory from people acting rationally.

There was the suspicion that the Bank of England, without a curb on issuing paper money, would generate inflation after the 'suspension of cash payments' in 1797, when the Bank of England and the Scottish banks went off the gold standard, dropping the requirement that banknotes could be exchanged at banks for specie (coin minted from precious metals). Monetary specialists and general economists reacted to the Bullion Report of 1810. Stewart had many quibbles with the Bullion Committee's views. He wondered how the superabundance of money, as described by the Committee, could bring about increases in prices and why some commodities were affected more than others. Aware of a more sophisticated way of expressing the quantity theory, to take into account the velocity of circulation, he noted that the amount of money failed to keep up with the rise in prices and doubted if the cause of the greater velocity of circulation was the high state of confidence; he believed it was due to money passing between more persons. Also, he argued, it has to be recognized that much of the increased circulation arose from small notes being circulated.

Bimetallism

Several writers played with bimetallism – the use of both silver and gold as a standard of value. Smith was a bimetallist favouring a currency based on both silver and gold (see especially in *WN*, Book I, chapter V) but Steuart was sceptical: it is 'impossible for any law to keep the standard attached both to the gold and the silver coin at once, without preserving constantly the market proportion of the metals at par, with the numerary value of the coins' (*Principles* II: 300). However, he concluded that as an invariable measure there could be a pound of national credit specified in troy grains of fine silver and fine gold bullion: 'the sums shall be borrowed or acquitted, according to the market price of one half in gold and one half in silver, at the respective requisitions of the creditors or of the state, when borrowing' (p. 311). In other words, he thought the best way to change the standard would be for the government to come to an agreement with public creditors.

Another opponent of bimetallism was Joseph Hume (1777–1855) of Montrose. He had studied medicine at Aberdeen and Edinburgh universities then made a fortune in Bengal as a paymaster after being a ship's surgeon for the East India Company. As MP for Weymouth from 1812, and for Aberdeen burghs from 1818, he was a leading Radical politician, espousing causes such as parliamentary reform, Catholic emancipation and economy in government expenditure. In an 1816 pamphlet he argued against two metals being used for legal tender as the cheaper metal would always be used. He doubted if one needs to know the intrinsic par value of sterling as the commercial par is determined by demand and supply: a gold monometallism is superior. Because of its stable price, he said, gold is agreed to be the general physical standard or measure of value. It is more convenient for making payments because silver, if used, would have be transported in cartloads to make larger payments. The coins cannot be worth more than the bullion they represent and in fact are less valuable as they cannot be exported or melted down.

Conversely, Nicholson was attracted to bimetallism (see 1895: 246–75). Friedman called Nicholson one of the ablest of British economists in favour of bimetallism (1990: 96). In his *A Treatise on Money* (1895) Nicholson favoured a ratio of 15:5 between gold and silver, supported by an international agreement. The American economist Irving Fisher (1894) explains bimetallism in terms of two reservoirs of liquid gold and liquid silver flowing into a single reservoir to obtain a static equilibrium between the two precious metals. If the two metals are coined at a fixed ratio the debtor, unless contractually prohibited, can use either metal; if the appropriate ratio is chosen, bimetallism can be successful for generations. A wrong ratio would represent a depreciation of gold. He argued that demonetization of silver had caused a serious appreciation of gold and with both silver and gold in use the price level would be steady at its previous level. To bring bimetallism into effect he suggested that there needs to be an international agreement that on a certain day parties to the agreement will coin the silver and gold brought to them at a fixed rate, probably 15½:1 gold to silver. Germany happily used that ratio for seventy years until legislation ended it. But in his *Principles* (1893–1901), volume II, chapter XVIII, Nicholson admits that the case for bimetallism has been weakened though not overthrown by the great increase in gold supplies and countries' increasing use of a gold standard.

Rate of interest

The reward for using someone else's money was originally called 'the use', or 'usury', but later the 'rate of interest'. From ancient times the rate of interest has been a major matter of contention in economics: one can question its justification, determination and appropriate level. In the eighteenth century the Scots considered, in particular, the role of the market in determining interest rates and whether it was sensible to have the legal fixing of maximum interest rates through the usury laws, which were in force from 1660 to their repeal in 1854.

To justify the payment of interest, Hutcheson uses the ideas of the productiveness of capital and opportunity cost:

> If in any way of trade men can make far greater gains by help of a large stock of money, than they could have made without it, 'tis but just that he who supplies them with the money, the necessary means of this gain, should have for the use of it some share of the profit, equal at least to the profit he could have made by purchasing things naturally fruitful or yielding a rent. This shews the just foundation of interest upon money lent…
>
> (*System* II: 71)

> They should be satisfied if it surpasses the annual profits of purchases, as much as compensates the greater troubles or hazards attending the loans…
>
> (p. 73)

Thus, because borrowers benefit from the financial help a loan affords them, they should pay. He also raises the deeper issues of finance being productive and the idea of opportunity cost – comparing the employment of money in different ways – and highlights the fact that interest is related to the amount of risk. In Hutcheson's view, both the rate of profit and the supply of loanable funds are crucial to the determination of interest rates. Thus, in a newly settled country where small amounts of capital have a great return and land rents are high, lenders demand high interest; when trade has expanded, there is more money and more land is being purchased, lenders are content with less interest.

Steuart justified the payment of interest because credit is necessary: 'Without good faith there can be no credit; without credit there can be no borrowing of money, no trade, no industry, no circulation, no bread for the lower classes, no luxury, not even the conveniences of life, for the rich. Under these circumstances, there can be no rule for the rate of interest; because borrowing cannot be frequent and familiar' (*Principles* III: 133). He had an acute awareness of money as finance and offered this unusual reason for freely determined interest rates – that they do not matter much because borrowing is an unusual event.

Many writers wanted a market analysis of interest rates. Murray, one of the first Scottish writers to discuss the determination of the rate of interest on money, argued, 'The price of money is the interest it bears ... [which] ought to rise and fall in proportion to the demand and plenty' (1758: 25). Kames regarded interest as the 'price or premium given for the loan of money' (1778: 137) and regulated by demand. Ferguson, in his *Institutes*, thought that the rate of interest in wartime is more than in peacetime, thus interest can become independent of gross profits (1785: 201).

Steuart analysed the loans market and was concerned that the demand for loans by spendthrifts would push interest rates too high, to the detriment of merchants. Although he argued that the statesman should hurt the credit of the extravagant he was aware that excessive suppression of prodigality and dissipation could hurt the workers who supply luxuries. The statesman himself can help to lower the demand for loans:

> He should abstain from borrowing himself, and even from creating new outlets for money, except from the most cogent motives. By this he will, in a short time, gently reduce the rate of interest. Then he may by statute ... bring it down a little ...
>
> (*Principles* III: 141)

However, he notes that much of manufacturing and trading does not rely on borrowed money (returning to his previous argument that borrowing is not a continuous activity) so the level of the rate of interest is not always crucial (although purchases of raw materials and machinery are financed through borrowing). He suggests the demand in money markets for loans by the landed classes could be reduced if a land bank could lend, with payments paid through land being let by the acre: this would take such transactions out of the money market, an early example of the idea of 'the own rate of interest' where the principal and return in interest are measured by the same commodity.

The actual rate of interest emerges as a compromise between borrowers' desire for interest to be as low as possible and lenders' wish for it to be high as all parties act from self-interest. Double competition occurs. (Smith has a parallel account in his bargaining theory of wages.) But Steuart provides the argument that the rate of interest, or price of money, is more stable and uniform than other prices, as units of money, unlike commodities, are, or ought to be, the same. This is strange as commodities can be as homogeneous or heterogeneous as money. Steuart realistically concludes that in modern commerce the important determinants of the rate of interest are demand and competition.

Steuart, in his *Principles* III, according to Low, saw the actual market rate of interest fixed by the demands of those borrowers 'as having most pressing occasion for money (and who) will offer the highest interest and by the offers of those lenders with . . . the most pressing occasion to draw interest for their money (and who) will offer it at the lowest interest' (1954: 119), making it an early example of marginal analysis. Steuart did not think of the rate of interest in non-monetary terms. To him it was not 'the reward for abstention from consumption . . . [but] one way of converting a sterile asset (cash)' (p. 129). The most striking aspect of Steuart's analysis was 'his decision to view the rate of interest mainly as a phenomenon of the market for paper claims rather than a result of the flows of real savings and real investment' (p. 133).

Although Hume did not cover the whole of economics in his writings, he chose the rate of interest as an important topic, analysing the forces determining an interest rate at length. In *Of Interest* he dispels a mercantilist fallacy:

> Prices have risen near four times since the discovery of the INDIES; and it is probable gold and silver have multiplied much more: But interest has not fallen much above half. The rate of interest, therefore, is not derived from the quantity of the precious metals.
>
> (1987: 296)

Instead:

> The encrease of lenders above the borrowers sinks the interest; and so much the faster, if those, who have acquired those large sums, find no industry or commerce in the state, and no method of employing their money but by lending it at interest.
>
> (p. 305)

He explains why interest is high or low:

> A great demand for borrowing; little riches to supply that demand; and great profits arising from commerce: And these circumstances are a clear proof of the small advance of commerce and industry, not of the scarcity of gold and silver.
>
> (p. 297)

He also argues that where there is only landed interest in a state there will be little frugality, borrowers will be many and the rate of interest higher. This is again a firm endorsement of the idea that there is market determination of the rate of interest.

Commentators on Hume praise his analysis of interest. Checkland (1956) believed that Hume's theory of interest moved from the mercantilist emphasis on the supply of money to a consideration of real saving. Vickers (1957) supports Checkland because, throughout his *Essays*, Hume says that the supply of money alone does not affect the interest rate: interdependent forces in the monetary system, including industry, determine it. His theory is a real theory, which looks at supply and demand for capital resources and also includes a class analysis: he argued that demand comes from the prodigal landlord and savings from the merchant and trading classes. Consequently, Berry (2006) asserts that Hume, in explaining changes in the rate of interest, distinguished commercial and non-commercial ways of thinking.

To Smith in *WN* interest is the compensation for letting someone else employ one's capital. Unlike Hutcheson, Smith does not regard money on loan as useful finance to make a profit because, he noted, in fact money is lent mainly as loans to country gentlemen on mortgages to pay off tradesmen's bills. According to Smith, the borrower runs the risk but the lender is paid for giving the borrower the opportunity. He observes that the legal rate of interest is the same throughout Great Britain but the market rate is higher in Scotland than in England, and argues that it will be high, in general, where the law does not enforce contracts, because everyone is like a lender to a bankrupt, with little certainty of payment.

According to Low (1954), Smith did not synthesize two theories of the rate of interest – a theory of real resources and a theory of the prices of securities connected to market expectations (which appears in his discussion of the national debt). In his view, monetary changes are surface phenomena; frugality and the technical advantages of investment are more important. Hutcheson and Hume provided Adam Smith with a theory of long-term trends in interest rates.

As both Hume and Smith believed, Dugald Stewart said the rate of interest was not the consequence of the quantity of precious metals but of demand for borrowed money because of patterns of consumption. The extent of a country's riches and poverty is not the sole cause of interest rates – it is rather the poor enforcement of contracts as, for example, persons of bad reputation will be charged high interest. In his discussion of the Bullion Report, Stewart bluntly stated that 'The natural and equitable rate of interest will be determined by the demand there is for borrowing, and the plenty there is to supply that demand... The *primary* cause of the depreciation is the artificial cheapness of the rate at which, in consequence of the laws of usury, the use of money may be obtained, combined with the security the Bank enjoys, in yielding to the public demand, in consequence of the stoppage of cash payments' (1840 I: 447).

Overall, these Scots largely recognized that the rate of interest is a price, varying, as all prices do, when market conditions change. There are some hints at an analysis of the borrowers and lenders but not enough, perhaps because financial institutions had not sufficiently developed.

Usury laws

The nature of banking was affected by the centuries-old debate about usury and the payment of interest. This was an example of price regulation that was more common in corn markets. In practical terms, usury laws, which fixed the maximum rate of interest, directly affected only a small portion of the population because few people had access to finance; however, in the long term, the statutory fixing of interest rates could retard the development of finance and banking.

Steuart, a strong opponent of these laws, interestingly observes that before the expansion of trade and industry money was often lent without interest because it was regarded as barren stock. He asserted that regular payment of interest became essential to the obtaining of credit. Forbidding lending on interest, he said, would be like locking up money rather than supplying the wants of society. He thought the case for usury laws is not to protect the person wanting a loan for productive purposes, as he will not pay an excessive rate of interest, but to keep borrowers who want money for dissipation from the grasp of usurers. Thus, sensibly, Steuart thinks the task of the statesman is to keep credit from extravagant people to maintain the rate of interest at reasonable levels; no state ever suffered by interest rates being too low. He traces the chain of consequences forged by spendthrifts who borrow – the rate of interest will rise to the injury of merchants, extinguishing trade and hurting the spendthrifts themselves because the higher interest rates depreciate property: this occurs in countries that have put their land into circulation through land banks. If interest is too low then potential lenders will invest elsewhere. Steuart believed that the usury laws were unenforceable because idle people who want to borrow can always evade a legal maximum interest rate by devices such as discounting and making gifts.

As for Smith, in *WN* (Book II, chapter IV) he opposes the complete prohibition of the charging of interest because the debtor would have to borrow at higher rates to compensate for the penalties that could be imposed on the creditor. He could see some merit in interest rates: keeping them down means that sober people, not projectors and prodigals, borrow, and the capital of the country is much safer (another example of security justifying departures from laissez-faire). He thought that a legal rate of interest should be a maximum rate fixed above the market rate, not a minimum, because it is impossible to reduce interest below the lowest ordinary market rate. Thus capital would not be wasted but be put to the best use, always one of his primary concerns.

In his *General Theory* Keynes stated: 'Even Adam Smith was extremely moderate in his attitude to the usury laws. For he was well aware that individual savings may be absorbed either by investment or by debt. Furthermore, he favoured a low rate of interest as increasing the chance of savings finding their outlet in new investment rather than in debts. Bentham's criticisms were mainly on the ground that Adam Smith's Scotch caution was too severe on "projectors" and that a maximum rate of interest would leave too little margin for the reward of legitimate and socially advisable risks' (1936: 353). Winch (1997) also reminds us that Smith wanted a maximum rate of interest to encourage capital accumulation and drive out projectors who would want higher returns for their investments.

Dugald Stewart (1840), on the other hand, greatly objected to legislative interference in the setting of interest rates, as he believed the interest rate should be proportionate to the loss: it is the lender, not the legislator, who has the knowledge to set the appropriate rate. He cited authorities in favour of usury as diverse as ancient Romans and Calvin. Rather than have a maximum interest rate, what he saw as being needed was a rate that represented what was convenient and agreed between lender and borrower as, in principle, there is no difference between the gain from selling a house and the return from lending money. He also lists the practical difficulties of fixing an enforceable interest rate. Stewart thought that a decrease in the rate of interest is the only stimulus a statesman can give industry because it affects all industries and does not interfere with the actual employment of capital. Because of usury laws, he noted, agricultural improvement was financed through annuities at very high interest rates. According to Milgate and Stimson (1996), Lauderdale followed Stewart's argument that anti-usury laws, which kept down interest rates, produced a crisis of over-investment in fictitious capital without a reduction in consumption.

A historical context for the usury laws is provided by a Scottish advocate, James Grahame (1790–1842). He recognizes that the term usury once meant any rate of interest but now refers to excessive interest. In primitive societies, he argues, spare money was used only to give temporary aid to those in distress but later the rich insisted on remuneration for the risk they took if they assisted the poor. However, he says that the poor could not borrow at affordable rates. The code of Justinian, he says, is instructive in that a structure of interest rates is laid down: 4 per cent for persons of illustrious rank; 6 per cent as the ordinary, legal rate; 8 per cent for the convenience of manufactures and merchants and 12 per cent for nautical insurance. Grahame noted that Steuart had asserted that a proper legal rate of interest could not be set until borrowing was more frequent, suggesting that interest rates were not truly market rates in the past. In a wide-ranging discussion of the usury laws he notes that they enabled government to contract huge debts, allowed private financing of property purchases at low interest rates, and that landowners were preferred to merchants as their security was better. But the laws prevented useful loans to the poor and to ingenious speculators. Of course, abolition of the laws could lead to harassment of debtors, who would be asked for higher interest rather than immediate repayment; something which was later to be the common practice of the loan shark. However, in his view, the weak could be protected from the strong by following the example of the Dutch and instituting a Tribunal of Conciliation.

Grahame observed that opponents of usury laws have discovered that usurers 'trade, like other merchants, in buying and selling . . . the worst they can do is to buy as cheap as they can find men willing to sell, and to sell as dear as they can find men willing to buy' (1817: 9). This view takes some of the mystique out of interest rates: they are merely prices for lending money and those who work to provide the service of lending should have remuneration.

When an economy becomes monetized it changes. That was very much the case for Scotland as it made the shift from agriculture to industry. Money eases the running of a modern exchange economy, but it can also take on a life of its own, expressing its own innate power and creating changes in the real economy that are not always intended. There was reluctance, certainly on the part of Smith, to allow free money markets because they could send a national economy in the wrong direction if the markets provided finance for those who would diminish rather than increase national capital. But if, I would argue, the reason for interfering in money markets through setting maximum interest rates was to improve the quality of lending, then instead of usury laws there could have been other controls such as banning lending for some undesirable purposes or excluding certain types of borrower.

Paper credit

In the centuries before banknotes and other paper money were used there was often a shortage of money because the supply of precious metals was insufficient to meet the demand for coin. Providing money in paper form seemed a major advance in economic institutions, but inevitably the amount, value and quality of the new instruments would be questioned. Those who believed that money must have an intrinsic value were suspicious of paper money and quick to point out its defects, but there were optimists eager to extol the change from coin to notes. Smith, especially in his doctrines of real bills and reflux, believing that the amount of paper money would not be in excess of the gold and silver it replaced, seemed to be on the side of the modernizers. The debate within Scotland on the merits of paper money moved to a larger arena when the Bank of England went off the gold standard – 'suspended cash payments' – in 1797.

Early in the eighteenth century Scottish writers proposed new ways of increasing the money supply in Scotland. Usually they contrasted increasing the amount of paper money with other options. An anonymous writer of 1705 suggested calling in half of Scotland's plate, then mixing it with copper to make an alloy and prevent it from being melted down or exported. But something more was needed too, the writer thought: a new bank, approved by the Committee of Trade, which would issue bills guaranteed by a half of the new coinage. Providing there was good credit, money would be lent at 3 per cent.

Clerk, also writing in 1705, lamented the shortage of money and saw difficulties in using changes in the coinage to solve the problem. A debasement of the coinage would be followed by foreigners doing the same; conversely, a higher value of Scottish coinage would have an immediate benefit in inducing money out of hoards into circulation but the disadvantage of that would be foreign money flowing into Scotland, raising prices to the ruin of trade and making life difficult for debtors. Clerk thought a good alternative to changing the value of the coinage would be using paper credit. He argued that credit on good security is worth as much as gold and silver and that the Bank of Scotland could issue £200,000 or £300,000 sterling on the security of land.

Seton, in *Some thoughts* (1705), mentioned the need for money in Scotland to undertake new projects, cope with bad seasons and deal with the consequences of unregulated trade. He reminded his readers that an independent government can let anything serve as money: only custom made gold and silver money. Rather than have debasement of the currency, he wanted the government to increase the money supply by issuing bills or 'talleys' on the security of money or land. He also suggested a 10 per cent appreciation of large denomination gold and silver coins.

In his proposals to reduce the scarcity of money, Hodges, once employed in the Darien expedition, asserted 'Credit is undoubtedly one of the best and readiest ways of supplying the want of *Money*' (1705: 1), recommending that the Treasury issue bills to create an Exchequer credit to pay its debts. In this way, ordinary taxes, customs and excise would increase by 10 per cent but there would be a discount of the same percentage if payments, when due, were made in such bills. He also wanted the African Company to issue bills, with government backing, of up to £100,000 or £120,000 to finance fishing and manufacturing industries. Thus the security for this paper credit would be two funds, of the national revenue and of the African Company, which he saw as better than using land as a security.

To understand the attractions of paper money it is essential to understand the nature of credit and paper money as a type of it. Steuart took a broad view of money, seeing it as comprehending banknotes, bank credit, bills, bonds and merchants' books (i.e. balances). He appreciated that credit, a temporary advance of money, could make up for a shortage of coin and, indeed, was a fundamental aspect of society: 'Credit is the basis of all contracts between men: few contracts can operate so instantaneously as not to leave some performance, or prestation [paying money that is due] . . . at least for a short time, in suspence' (*Principles* II: 212). Steuart's examination of credit is shrewd and illuminating. He distinguishes three types of credit – private, mercantile and public – and shows that whereas mercantile and public credit are usually based on confidence, personal credit requires a security as its basis. He also notes that public credit is a late invention and differs from the other two in that it can be easily transferred, because one unit of it is as good as another.

Interestingly, Steuart, like Plato, was aware of the idea of parallel currencies, that is, having one currency for domestic purposes and another for international transactions: 'Coin we have called the money of the world, as notes may be called the money of the society' (III: 181). This view reflected the practice of the time of using bullion to settle balances with foreigners. Steuart thus thinks that paper money is principally of use domestically, ignoring bills of exchange, which are a major form of paper money in international trade.

In *The principles of money applied to the present state of the coin of Bengal* (1772), which was composed for the use of the East India Company, Steuart observed that the paper of the Bank of England is secured 'upon a value in *money* belonging to the trade of England lodged in the Bank' (p. 75 footnote), but the Scottish issues are secured '*upon land and personal estates* in the possession of individuals, not lodged in the banks, but mortgaged to the banks' (italics in original). Both types of note issue are, Steuart argued, secure and not money: English bank paper represents money; Scottish paper represents land and personal estates, not money. Thus, he believed that most English notes have to return in less than sixty days because they are issued on the discount of bills; by contrast Scottish notes are issued on permanent obligations and may not return for years. The Scottish banks, to satisfy the public, must have 'a certain fixed and perpetual fund of annual income' (p. 76 footnote), which the tolls on bridges and highways provide. What Steuart is doing is to show that there can be extensive creation of paper credit with a variety of bases – specie, land and pledged tax revenues.

Taking a slightly different viewpoint, Murray used the nature of money to argue for the justification for paper credit:

> As Money, it has no intrinsic value in itself; the value is in the things purchaseable by it; and it is only a general letter of credit, payable to the bearer for goods to a certain amount, or an universal ticket that gives the owner an option to possess whatever he chuses to a certain extent. In this sense, it is no more than the figure or character that represents the things it can procure...
>
> (1758: 8)

According to his argument, bills of exchange make money go further and are popular in international transactions because of the difficulty of transporting money between countries, and a settlement of a debt in specie is needed only in the case of a trade deficit. Within a country 'A certain quantity of ready money is necessary to carry on circulation; more than that, it is of little use' (p. 19).

Like Steuart and Smith, Wallace, acutely aware of the great advances in contemporary Scottish banking, was an enthusiastic advocate of paper money as a creator of employment. He had no fear of overissue even if there were no convertibility into gold or silver, providing borrowers gave good security, which he (appearing to be hinting at the real bills doctrine) lists carefully as corn, bullion, lands, goods and good debts. Contrary to Hume, he saw the transmission mechanism for an increase in bank credit as a way to increase economic activity through a rise in prices, which would stimulate industry and consumption.

Although several writers favoured more use of paper money, their analysis of it was slight. David Hume and Adam Smith, however, set out the basic advantages of a paper currency. Hume, in *Of the Balance of Trade* (1987), could find many reasons for it. Paper money banishes specie and bullion, he writes, and it is advantageous for merchants to discount his bills upon occasion: facilitating the circulation of money favours the general commerce of a state. He explains that private bankers can give credit on the basis of money deposited in their shops and that bank credits based on the surety of assets are in a sense the coining of houses, ships at sea and the rest. Paper, with the banknote as the best-known type of paper money, Smith explains in the *WN*, is a less costly and sometimes as convenient form of money as gold and silver. He reports that the trade of Scotland quadrupled after the foundation of the Bank of Scotland in 1695; it doubled in fifteen years after banks were established in Glasgow for merchants to trade with greater facility. The Scottish merchant keeps no money unemployed, he says, and has the flexibility of repaying or using the line of credit. Smith's defence of paper currency is based simply on the relationship between the increased paper money supply and the expansion of commerce.

Sir John Sinclair, a strong supporter of paper currency, in a pamphlet (1810a) went as far as to assert that the country could not carry on its business if paper currency were annihilated. In his scheme, notes would be issued only on undoubted security; paper currency in circulation would be enough to meet the demands of increasing wealth, population and the revenue of the country, and both small and large notes would be issued. Writing to the Bullion Committee he expressed the opinion that Britain had the pecuniary resources to carry on the war against Napoleon for twenty more years if paper currency were on a proper footing: because of the circulation of paper money within a country in times of war, coin/bullion can be exported to prosecute the war without causing monetary crisis at home where there would be prosperity and employment. In another pamphlet of that year (1810b), Sinclair admits that precious metals are part of wealth and have the important uses of enabling individuals to obtain the value of their labour, transferring property in goods, and enabling the government to obtain revenue and defray the public expenses, but argues that it is only in the early states of society that precious metals are needed as currency. Civilized societies will manage on a well-regulated paper currency and a small proportion of metals in coins. To control the amount of paper money, he writes, the circulating medium should be proportionate to the quantity of labour to be paid, the quantity of goods and property transferred, and the total amount of demands and expenses of the Exchequer. Thus, in his view, it was wrong that the Bank of England restricted credit before the suspension of cash payments.

In a speech in the House of Commons on the Bullion Report in 1811 Sinclair divided currencies into the intrinsic and the ideal. He says that a large currency can function without circulating precious metals, using the example of China whose currency was called 'cash' and consisted of coins six parts copper and four parts lead with a hole to allow them to be strung together. In Britain the advantages of paper currency included the low cost of producing it, the ease of increasing it if the nation required it, the greater ability to export it, the addition to the revenue and an independence from other countries, which is important in time of war. He said that paper money, even at the time of an expensive war, allows industry to abound and the rate of interest to be low. He was impressed by the quality of British paper money compared with the paper currency of America and the assignats of France because British currency was issued by a responsible corporate body under the control of parliament against deposited securities, and, as it was based on temporary securities founded on real transactions, it was not issued excessively. Sinclair, writing later in 1819, summed up his thinking: inconvertible paper is better than gold for internal circulation providing it is limited in its amount and founded on solid property, making it as valuable as coin. Furthermore, the worth of a currency depends on common consent, which means it is better to have private rather than public issuers of money, as ministers of the Crown could abuse their power.

Real bills doctrine

A way of answering critics of paper money afraid of its overissue was the real bills doctrine, which virtually said that such a state of affairs is impossible because of the correspondence between monetary and real transactions.

Both Steuart and Hume hinted at Smith's real bills doctrine. In *Of Money*, Hume warned against overissue and comments that it can 'never be the interest of any trading nation; but must lay them under disadvantages, by encreasing money beyond its natural proportion to labour and commodities, and thereby heightening their price to the merchant and manufacturer' (1987: 284). Whether there was an automatic adherence to the natural proportion was, he said, yet to be considered.

Boldly, Smith writes in the *WN* that an excess issue of notes, more than what the circulation would have been in gold and silver, would return to the banks to be exchanged for gold and silver because it could not be sent abroad and a bank gains no interest through an excessive issue. Gradually Smith moves to his exposition of the real bills doctrine, the central feature of his discussion of paper credit:

> When a bank discounts to a merchant a real bill of exchange drawn by a real creditor upon a real debtor, and which, as soon as it becomes due, is really paid by that debtor, it only advances to him a part of the value which he would otherwise be obliged to keep by him unemployed and in ready money for answering occasional demands. The payment of the bill, when it becomes due, replaces to the bank the value of what it advances, together with the interest. The coffers of the bank, so far as its dealings are confined to such customers, resemble a water pond, from which, though a stream is continually running out, yet another is continually running in, fully equal to that which runs out; so that, without any further care or attention, the pond keeps always equally, or very near equally full. Little or no expense can ever be necessary for replenishing the coffers of such a bank.
>
> (p. 304)

With this repetition of the word 'real' Smith emphasizes that money in the form of a bill is not in danger of inflating the money supply. To reinforce the idea that the note issue is safe he mentions that the Scottish banks are careful to monitor their customers and ask for frequent and regular repayments, which was possible because it is used to finance circulating capital – bank lending for fixed capital was financed by mortgages or bonds as the loans would be for several years. Thus the doctrine appears to work because paper money is concerned with short-term finance. This optimistic picture of aiming to rid anyone of the fears of overissue can be true only if it is based on a correct description of banking and if in practice banks never fail through overissue, which was certainly not the case.

A prominent critic of the real bills doctrine was Henry Thornton (1760–1815), author of *Paper Credit* (1802). Murphy (2003) mentions that Thornton accused Smith, along with Hume, Steuart, Locke and Montesquieu, of ignorance of the actual mechanisms of the monetary economy. Smith had a unidimensional view of the money supply, he says, and did not appreciate the importance of the velocity of circulation. It was wrong to say that the whole supply of paper money could never exceed the equivalent amount of gold and silver because there was a wide range of different paper media of exchange with differing velocities of circulation. After Thornton's criticisms, Laidler (1981) summarized the problems with the real bills doctrine: any number of real bills could be created on the basis of the same alleged security (which depended on how many transactions between merchants occurred when bringing goods to market), and nothing is said about the determinants of the value of goods used as collateral for the bills. Francis Horner states that 'Smith seems to have nowhere explained the principles and history of that private commercial credit which is the foundation of paper money which would subsist though there were no paper, but which that kind of money contributes both to facilitate and to enlarge' (Bourne and Taylor 1994: 248).

Control of the note issue

Whatever the perceived benefits of paper money there was the fear that it was potentially dangerous and needed to be supervised by imposing rules on banks for its issue. Anderson's *The Bee*, 2 October 1793, observed that nations, like individuals, can overtrade, partly because British trade is conducted through the use of artificial stock in the form of paper currency. Merchants were discounting trade credits at 7.5 per cent, higher than the 5 per cent legal maximum for the rate of interest. He proposed the setting up in every town of a charter bank with a capital of £100,000 to provide the trading part of the nation with real stock. Before issuing any notes these banks would lodge four-fifths of their capital with the government at 3 per cent as a security for the note issue; the remaining fifth would be kept in the bank to purchase bullion or bills of exchange. By following this idea, only the Bank of England, not a single person or a trading house, could hold more than £5,000 of the bank issue of a particular bank.

Smith was prepared to depart from his central doctrine of natural liberty by linking the issue of banknotes to national security. In *WN* he distinguishes circulation of notes between dealers and between dealers and customers. In London when notes have a minimum value of £10 most of the circulation is between dealers, a kind of wholesale money market. He suggested a £5 minimum for banknotes everywhere to keep paper money circulation between dealers. This would also have the advantage of reducing the reserves a bank needs.

What made the question of controlling the note issue urgent was the suspension of cash payments in 1797. During the period that followed, a profusion of pamphlets and articles, many by Scots, spewed from the presses. A Scot, Francis Horner MP, proposed the setting up of a House of Commons Bullion Committee to investigate the effects of this suspension. In a letter to John A. Murray on 26 June 1810 he wrote dismissively of the Bullion Committee's report, 'stating nothing but very old doctrines on the subject it treats of, and stating them in a more imperfect form than they have frequently appeared in before' (Horner 1843 II: 47). In another letter to Murray on 29 November 1810, he wrote, 'I suspect ... that convertibility alone of all paper into specie, without an actual interchange of a certain portion of specie circulating along with the paper, is not sufficient to secure the permanent value of the paper' (I: 63). When the Committee reported, Horner, in the House of Commons on 6 May 1811, pointed out that in monetary debates there are the two extremes of wanting paper currency to be based on confidence alone and not precious metals, and the ancient system of coinage using precious metals. He wanted a well-regulated paper currency instead of the Bank lending according to demand. In his view it had been wrong to restrict cash payments even in war because of stagnant internal credit. In articles for the *Edinburgh Review* he used his detailed knowledge of the monetary system and, considering the banking system and paper credit in the light of Henry Thornton's critique of Adam Smith, he agreed with Thornton that an excessive issue of paper would raise the market price of gold above its mint price, the equivalent of the debasement of the currency. Horner said that London banks encouraged country banks – a kind of subdivision of labour – but that an excessive local issue by country banks pushed up local prices, leading the population of country areas to request specie or notes of the Bank of England: the Bank would ruin credit if it did not expand its note issue. In 1793, when the Bank had not increased its paper, the direct loan of Exchequer bills to mercantile firms with proper security had relieved a commercial crisis. But the usury laws limited the Bank's ability to restrict the amount of its loans by putting a ceiling on interest rates. Noting that there had been an increase in the note issue after 1797, Horner was cautious in connecting price increases to the state of the paper currency because, as he said, Scots have to investigate the 'first appearances of this recent increase of prices, and to trace its progressive diffusion over all the relations of internal exchange... To specify in what proportion this rise is locally confined to our own island, or common to us with the Continent of Europe; and to distinguish in what proportion that local rise consists of a real increase in the bullion price, and of a nominal increase only in the currency price' (1802c: 201). Horner was not rushing to condemn the Bank of England, more to explain life under a paper currency.

Later, reviewing Lord King's pamphlet on the Bank Restrictions in the *Edinburgh Review* of July 1803, Horner stated that an enlargement of the paper currency beyond the demands of trade has the same effect on prices as an increase in precious metals, one with a local effect and the other affecting the whole commercial world. Without convertibility into specie, he says, there is no limit to the excess of paper currency, which retains the confidence of the public. The benefit of paper currency is not essentially because it is a substitute but 'in saving a certain portion of so costly an article, and, what is of far greater consequence, in facilitating exchanges between places remote from each other, and economizing the time and the labour of large payments' (1802c: 201). He recognized that specie, because of its intrinsic value, is the ultimate element of a currency and, as measures of depreciation, the market price of specie and adverse exchanges might just be temporary. We have to see, he wrote, if the excess of the market price over the mint price is steady and the depression in the course of exchange great. Thus Horner expresses little confidence in the real bills, as in his view overissue is clearly possible.

The Earl of Lauderdale, keen to enter the monetary debate, warned that paper money can be dangerous. In a pamphlet (1805b), he uses the analogy of Ireland and argued that the increase in the Bank of Ireland's paper issue was the sole cause of Ireland's currency depreciation. Because, he says, the Bank of Ireland was legally compelled to discount at 1 per cent below the legal rate of interest within Ireland, the cessation of cash payments in Ireland, together with this practice of discounting, meant there was no check on overissue. He goes on to generalize, saying that the constant and invariable symptoms of an unfavourable exchange produced by an excess of paper are an accompanying proportional rise in the value of bullion, banishment of gold coin from circulation and debasement of small money, and an unfavourable exchange caused by overissue, which is different from one caused by a balance of debt. To correct overissue credits to customers and to agents of country banks, he suggested that credits should be cut off and bank capital increased. It was important to stop discounting below the legal rate of interest.

In a further pamphlet of 1812 Lauderdale wrote that 'a Bank of England Note possesses, and can possess no value, differing from, or independent of, the coin it engages to pay' (p. 7). He says that a test of depreciation is that the exchange rate falls so low that it is profitable to export gold without loss. Sarcastically he added

> It was, however, reserved for the ingenuity of the present times to discover, contrary to all authority and experience, that paper not payable in coin on

> demand, was capable of conducting the circulation of a country, with an uniformity of value which could not belong to it, if tied down to a metallic currency as the standard.
>
> (p. 69)

In 1819 Lauderdale argued that the current plan for the resumption of cash payments was based on the false view that there had been an overissue of Bank paper. He was confident that at any time cash payments could be resumed if the mint proportions between gold and silver adjusted to their market proportions, and if silver coined at the old mint price was made the sole legal tender and gold allowed to circulate with an agio (charge for its circulation).

The alternative to relying on the real bills doctrine was adherence to the gold standard, but this could be an unnecessary and dangerous policy. Sinclair, in his letters to the Bank of England in 1797, argues that if more gold coins had been produced in the previous three years the demand for specie would have been met and there would have been no need then to leave the gold standard. But off the gold standard the capital of the Bank of England should be increased through a proportion of Exchequer bills being subscribed into bank stock and two pound and three pound notes issued. He thought that his proposal was not inflationary, as the tax on coining could be as low as 5 per cent.

Sinclair (1819) noted that returning so quickly to the old gold standard was responsible for distress and unemployment and might never have occurred if the two parliamentary committees had not overlooked the provision of a statement of the relative merits of metallic and paper currencies. A way of conducting this comparison was to count, from the Reformation of the sixteenth century, the cost of the coinage with compound interest, the profit to the revenue of stamps on paper currency, the variations in the value of gold and silver to see if they are fit to be a permanent standard of value, funded and unfunded debt incurred since 1797, the amount of money borrowed by the public and paid in banknotes, and the size of the Bank's circulation if cash payments resumed. Given his support for paper money he outlined a plan to issue £40 million in inconvertible notes by the Bank and private bankers, with a stamp to make them secure and limited, to create a general national tontine (a joint annuity with the survivor gaining all the shares), with contributions according to income from all to add £14 million annually to the public revenue, to increase money in circulation by following the Scottish practice of *cash accounts* (borrowing on the basis of a deposited bond and two sureties), and to pass legislation to limit paper circulation to the real wants of the country. Sinclair's untidy scheme was a response to a temporary downturn in the economy rather than necessarily a permanent way to manage the currency.

Samuel Read was another writer concerned with the quality of the paper currency and how to issue it in such a way that it would maintain its worth. In 1818 he observed that the Bank of England had offered a plan to the government, based on a measured price for each unit of a paper currency to avoid overissue. He proposed that the government set up a commission, which would independently manufacture and issue paper currency for delivery to the public in return for the stock that constitutes the national debt. Rather than Bank of England notes, he proposed that this paper money, with a minimum note worth £25, would be legal tender, with a seignorage on gold coins of 7 or 8 per cent to prevent melting down. Furthermore, the interest rate on this new money would be slightly cheaper than for specie. Read addresses here an important issue – that there was so much distrust of the Bank of England – and thus suggests that it should pass its note-issuing powers to an independent body. Like Smith, he was, however, cautious about the issue of notes of small denomination.

After the Bullion Report debate and the return of the British banking system to a pyramid of credit based on gold the question of how strict a system of paper credit should be occurred in the debates leading to the Bank Charter Act 1844, and its Scottish equivalent in 1845. Alison (1847) pointed out that paper credit was the answer to banking crises. The 1844 Act had made money even tighter, creating a money famine; nevertheless, as he pointed out, there was no shortage of credit as the government was able to issue bonds at par. All previous crises, including that of 1793, were alleviated by an increase in paper. In Alison's view, instead of a gold currency Britain needed 'a safe and regulated paper currency . . . any half dozen practical men in London will in half an hour be able to devise a system' (p. 72). He argued that bank notes are needed to represent gold and silver coin when coinage is insufficient for the necessities of commerce.

Concluding remarks

The existence of paper credit was always questioned. At the beginning of the eighteenth century Paterson, according to Steel (1896), was a persistent critic of inconvertible paper currency despite being a contemporary of John Law, a major founder of paper credit. Hollander (1911) points out that David Hume and Joseph Harris (1702–64) denounced paper money, obviously affected by the reckless contemporary extension of banknote issues and circulating credit. Hume, Paganelli (2009) reminds us, called paper money 'counterfeit money' and condemned money-jobbers who conducted open market operations. Aware of the abuse of bank credit, Hume almost recommended a public bank with a 100 per cent reserve requirement to support its note issue. Thomas Reid's view on paper credit was similar to Hume's: his message appeared to be that market prices fluctuate because of their inherently unstable nature.

Smith, writing under the shadow of John Law and *after* the Ayr Bank collapse, suggested Law's scheme would lead to excess banking, but Law himself, in *Money and Trade* (1705), did consider safety, to the extent of suggesting a restriction on the note issue and the exclusion of some landowners from his scheme. Law was reacting to the chronic shortage of money, not helped by the Darien scheme, of his times. It could be said, according to Humphrey (1999), that Law's idea of a bank-issued paper to replace a deficient metallic one was an attempt to address the problems of the depressed Scottish economy.

In the end, the critics of paper money seemed to have won the day, largely through tightening the rules for banking. But there was a kind of inevitability that the new money would survive. Once there is an awareness of the merits of fiat money, its cheapness to issue and its growing acceptance there is no turning back to a world of coin. Paper money is most under scrutiny, as happened after 1797, when the rules for issuing it change and bring about a larger note issue. The pamphleteers debated with fury the departure from a currency convertible into precious metals, but paper money passed its greatest test when it became acceptable to the general public.

Banking

Scotland made a notable and unique contribution to the development of banking. The Scots proposed numerous types of bank: land, joint stock, branch and savings banks. By 1810 Scotland, a small country, had thirty-seven banking institutions, only eight of which had failed since 1772 (Checkland 1956). This was the period of free banking – banking without central bank direction – which was in tune with the libertarian mood of the times. The Scottish writers noted the expanding view of the role of banks and the fact that they were vital partners in economic and commercial activity.

For Smith, the great merit of banking is to make what would otherwise be dead capital active, by substituting paper money for gold and silver. He was keen to outline the many innovations that made Scotland a leader in banking, and to encourage the expansion of banking. The increase in the number of banking companies throughout Great Britain, he thought, increases the security of the public because such banks are more careful in keeping the correct proportion of cash, have a smaller effect if they fail as they are smaller banks, and have to be more liberal with their customers to be competitive.

A supporter of Scottish banking, Hume, in *Of the Balance of Trade*, praises the bank credit or overdraft, a Scottish invention:

> This money, or any part of it, he has the liberty of drawing out whenever he pleases, and he pays only the ordinary interest for it, while it is in his hands. As a man may find surety nearly to the amount of his substance, and his bank-credit is equivalent to ready money, a merchant does hereby in a manner coin his houses, his household furniture, the goods in his warehouse, the foreign debts due to him, his ships at sea; and can, upon occasion, employ them in all payments, as if they were the current money of the country.
>
> (1987: 319)

This far-sighted comment shows that Hume understood the changed concept of money: that making bank deposits is very important in the money supply.

Despite his long foreign exile Steuart was interested in Scottish banking. In Scotland, he noted in his *Principles*, the Scottish banks were founded on private credit with notes issued on land and other securities and were 'banks of circulation upon mortgage' unsuitable for England where mercantile credit was the basis of confidence. He outlined the practical principles of banking: that experience teaches the banker the proportion between coin in their reserves and paper in circulation and that the banker's profit will be the excess of interest on money advanced over loss of interest through retaining coin, management expenses and the cost of providing funds abroad to pay balances. He advocated transparency in a bank's operations as ignorance of the state of banks saps confidence and causes bank runs. But all was not well in Scottish banking. Commenting on the controversial 'option clause' in Scottish banking, which meant that banks could avoid paying on demand by using the option of delaying payment for months, Steuart wrote sternly that the practice 'stops trade, ruins manufactures, raises the interest of money and renders the operation of melting down property quite ineffectual' (III: 219). But, on balance, he thought it best to retain option clauses because the coin needed to honour banknotes could be obtained from abroad, increasing the grand balance against the nation.

Kames praised the existence of banks, using the old argument of scarcity of money to urge their establishment. Banks stimulate industry by increasing the quantity of money. Using Smith's real bills doctrine to separate the good from the bad banks he tells us 'the only bank that will not injure foreign commerce, is what is erected for supplying the merchant with ready money by discounting bills ... bills really granted in the course of commerce'. In the case of a bank 'erected for lending money there is great danger of extending credit too far' (1778: 159–60), because it will damage the nation and cause the prices of labour and manufactures to rise.

Land bank

Any system of credit needs a solid base to ensure the soundness of the money created. Precious metals have long been regarded as a sure foundation but countries wanting to expand credit and short of gold and silver have to resort to another basis. Hence the attraction of land, which is universally acknowledged under a system of private property to be valuable and is owned by the members of society most likely to want to found banks because of their repeated need of credit.

John Law proposed a land bank, boldly asserting that 'a LAND MONEY may be established upon a voluntary acceptance so as to serve the uses of money better than silver money and to us to have a currency preferable to it' (1705: 55). He realized that land is more uncertain in quality but of a more certain value than silver; however, such quality differences were less than the changes in value due to supply and demand. He maintained that 'nothing can supply the uses of land and unless the consumption of the product of the earth diminish the demand for land and will not be less, so land cannot be less valuable [than silver]' (p. 66). His idea was that the scheme, run by a land mint set up as a company by an act of parliament, would run the land bank issue. He argued that land notes are more easily delivered than silver money. In his Piedmont proposals, Law, according to Wasserman and Beach (1934), wanted a government-controlled national bank but later abandoned the idea of land as security for paper money in favour of basing credit on confidence.

In a similar way, Hugh Chamberlen (1705) proposed that a sum of £300,000 should be circulated in talleys (pieces of wood representing the amount of the debt) or notes of different denominations. They would be lent for twenty-five years at 5 per cent on the security of land; at the end of twenty-five years the land would be free of the charge. The heritors borrowing the money would repay it in equal annual sums so that the talleys could be progressively destroyed; one percentage point of the interest rate would be used to defray the costs of the issuing office. Rubini (1970) explains that only Chamberlen wanted a pure land bank; other proposers suggested some specie to redeem note issues. The scheme was doomed because ministers disliked land banks, which would compete with the Bank of England: without ministerial support, a land bank was bound to fail.

The attraction of creating new banks is to increase competition in the financial sector, ensuring fairer access to finance. Playfair remarked that 'A rival bank is certainly the best remedy for the inconveniences arising from monopoly and uncontrolled power…' (1797: ix). Noting that a new bank gains support if magnificent to behold and profitable to individuals, he suggested that a new bank could be a land bank with a solid foundation; nevertheless, he recognizes the shortcomings of land banks. They are supported by men of landed property who want money to repay debts or to squander their resources, not by men in trade who sustain trade and manufactures, and they violate the principle that every bank should grant only temporary loans. He cites the case of the Bank of Ayr, a land bank that lent for land improvement until it was ruined when the borrowers were unable to pay. Instead, he thought a bank could remedy the shortage of gold if its notes represent goods and services because goods are constantly being changed into money. Under prudent management only one tenth of securities need to be converted into cash and there is a low probability of default if there are three solvent names on each note. The notes the bank issues would be used by commercial men for the purposes of trade.

Land banks were not a vague suggestion but a carefully constructed proposal. Playfair's criticism, born of the Ayr Bank collapse, is not a reason for abandoning such banking. These banks do have a solid security and could lend for long periods as building societies (savings and loans associations) have successfully done for many years. Of course land, the collateral for the loan, can vary in value but so can precious metals, which no one thought unsuitable as reserve assets. Strict rules for withdrawing deposits would prevent sudden liquidity crises and there would be a solid security for the note issue and little chance of a bank run if bank lending were confined to large transactions.

Savings banks

Another Scottish innovation in banking institutions was the establishment of the parish, or savings, bank. Henry Duncan (1774–1846), the founder of Scottish savings banks, describes the institution he created in his pamphlet (1816) on parish banks. In his early life he had experience of banking in Liverpool before following his grandfather and father into the Church of Scotland's ministry. In 1810, as a parish minister, he founded a bank in Ruthwell, south-west Scotland; others were soon set up in Edinburgh, Dumfries, Hawick and Kelso. Building on the idea of a friendly society he wanted flexibility in the size of deposits and, to encourage saving, cash prizes for regular savers. Deposits in the parish bank, made by employers deducting a portion of employees' wages, would attract 5 per cent compound interest and could be withdrawn without restriction, and an annual publication of statements of accounts would give depositors a sense of security. In addition to the deposits an auxiliary fund, built up from surplus interest, unappropriated money from other sources, and charitable contributions for distribution to the poor, would finance better management than the friendly societies'. It was not Duncan's intention to supplant the friendly society, a mutual fund that provided insurance for sickness and old age, when implementing his changes. Although the parish bank idea spawned a large savings movement throughout Scotland it was less successful as a solution to the problem of poverty: better-off workers could afford to save, not those likely to be destitute.

Central banking

In the early eighteenth-century beginnings of modern banking, when the state had a minor role in economic life, it was unusual to think of central banking, but Steuart did. He saw a broad role for the Bank of England beyond what was permitted in its charter – issuing notes for discounting bills of exchange, trading in gold and silver and advancing money to the government on the security of tax revenues. He suggested that bank paper be made legal tender to reduce the role of coin in settling indebtedness to other nations. Another recommendation was that the Bank should have offices in cities, in order to make subordinate banks redundant, and have funds in Holland, Antwerp, Hamburg and perhaps Cadiz and Lisbon, to borrow money abroad without having to export English coin. As for monetary and banking policy, he argued that if there were little money then the statesman should increase the velocity of circulation (the number of times a stock of money turns over) to provide food for all.

Steuart thought that the best methods of borrowing would be either paper money or a fund of credit from annual taxes. He recommended repayment of domestically raised loans short term to keep up the circulation, and punctual payment of only the interest, in the case of foreign loans, to pay foreign expenses. Such an active monetary policy would, he thought, enable the statesman at any time to curb prodigality and hurtful luxury as well as extend industry and domestic consumption. He attempted to justify the statesman's intervention in banking: 'Upon the right establishment of banks, depends the prosperity of trade, and the equable course of circulation' (*Principles* III: 168). The government would facilitate the use of bills 'by declaring the security upon which they desire the loan to be good, and by becoming answerable to the public for the solidity of it' (II: 232). In a sense, this is a description of the lender of a last-resort function in a banking system. Steuart was also aware of the need for a cheap money policy when government borrowing was necessary:

> As the object of the borrower is to have interest low, the statesman who intends to borrow, must use all possible means to increase the quantity of money in circulation.
>
> (IV: 119)

In 1798, Lauderdale saw the perils of not coordinating monetary and fiscal polices. He argued that it was a 'ruinous and inconsistent policy of coupling a loan from the Bank with a project of taxing income, as means of raising the supplied. Raising a loan increases the amount of money in circulation but increased taxation lowers it' (p. 18).

Free banking

Free banking is commercial banking with the absence of restrictions imposed by a government or a central bank. In regarding freedom in a negative way – as the absence of constraints – Briones and Rockoff (2005) identify types of freedom that could be curtailed: freedom to lend, freedom to issue banknotes, freedom to set up a bank, and freedom from the regulation and help of a central bank. The peculiar feature of Scottish banking was that it allowed innovations absent from other banking systems.

Smith wanted to apply free trade to banking. As Arnon puts it, Smith thought that 'under competition bankers should be allowed to behave freely according to their own best interests...' (1987: 270), albeit not entirely freely, as Smith wanted regulations for the issue of small notes. Smith praised the halcyon early days of Scottish banking but was aware of the failure of the Ayr Bank: Dwyer (1998) mentions that many of Smith's friends, including the Duke of Buccleuch, lost investments in it. Nevertheless, Smith did not use his personal experience as a reason for banking regulation: instead he explained that the Ayr Bank had foundered through excessive lending and ruinous replacement of its cash in the London money market. Sargent and Wallace (1982) argued that Smith could have made a case for unregulated banks because the interest they charged on loans would have been lower and their gold reserves smaller than under an integrated British banking system. There were other reasons for free banking. According to Rothbard (1988), Sir John Sinclair supported free banking in the 1820s and 1830s as the alternative to a return to the gold standard.

Whether there was free banking in Scotland is a matter for debate. The period of 'freedom' is usually dated from 1716 or 1727 and ends with the Peel Act of 1845. Because the Scottish banks held their own specie reserves it was alleged they could evade outside control and have unrestricted competitive issue of notes. However, there was some regulation of the Scottish banks, especially with the Usury Law 1714 setting a legal maximum of 5 per cent to the interest rate. Also the Bank Notes (Scotland) Act 1765 abolished the peculiar Scottish banking practice of the 'option clause', which gave banks six months to redeem notes if they wished. Further, the coinage used daily for transactions in Scotland was controlled by the Bank of England and the Royal Mint. It could be said that there was a pyramid of credit as the London money market, including the Bank of England, was the principal source of liquidity for the Scottish banks.

Any attempt to curb the note-issuing powers of Scottish banks was a sensitive matter for Scots. The first great Scottish novelist, Sir Walter Scott (1771–1832), wrote three letters to the *Edinburgh Weekly Journal* under the pseudonym of Malachi Malagrowther, which were later published as *Thoughts on the Proposed Change of Currency* (1826). Scott, who had personally gone bankrupt through investment in his publishing house, criticized the banking legislation of 1826, which, in a response to the 1825 banking crisis, proposed to abolish notes of less than £5 in value. His plea for the retention of these small notes was made within the context of a laudatory description of Scottish banking, which he said had helped the industrious and enterprising convert Scotland from poverty to prosperity. According to Scott, the circulation of Scottish banknotes was free and unlimited so that want of specie did not inconvenience Scotland; the system was based on banking companies with many persons, including men of landed property, supplying a considerable fund of credit. Issuing small denomination banknotes, he believed, apparently prevented runs on Scottish banks, produced profits, permitted liberal advances to individuals, and made the transport of cash more secure, for example, cattle drovers could safely carry a banker's receipt. Furthermore, he argued that as bank branches could exist without specie drawn from London they could exist in remote areas, and that small note issues were also cheap, as the £1,500,000 cost of purchasing and maintaining gold for small coinage was avoided. The Scottish banking system was well ordered, Scott said, with inter-bank indebtedness settled in notes or in specie, and a reporting twice a week to a tribunal in Edinburgh of the note circulation. Scott won his point, small notes were kept, and he was given the accolade of having his portrait on the notes of the Bank of Scotland.

The matter of the issue of small notes was raised again within twenty years. In 1844 Hugh Miller (1802–56), a geologist, a bank agent for five years and a Free Church leader alongside Chalmers, published, like Scott, a plea for the retention of small notes. He noted that 60 per cent of Scotland's note issue consisted of £1 notes and that Sir Robert Peel proposed to substitute gold coins for them. Miller's opposition was based on several arguments: that the banks would lose the benefit of issuing their own paper, that bank lending would fall if banks could not give interest, that cash credits would cease, and that trade and commerce would go into convulsions. He forecast that joint stock companies, encouraging speculators, would spring up.

Despite the moving pleas of Scott and Miller Scottish banking largely went the way of English banking over the next hundred years. But banks in Scotland did retain their small notes, although after 1846 their quantity would be controlled by the Bank of England. Banking, like any economic institution, can have a varying amount of freedom from the state, hence the abiding interest in 'free banking'.

Standing back to survey Scotland's banking institutions we can see their imaginative diversity. Because individuals in society have different financial needs they make different demands upon banks. Entrepreneurs of the financial sector recognize this and create different types of bank. The poor want to save what they can for a rainy day and have no need of a whole range of financial services: savings banks will suffice. A landed aristocracy suffers from having a large capital tied up in land and unavailable for the immediate discharge of debt, hence the appeal of a land bank, which uses their greatest asset as the foundation of credit. Commerce constantly under the pressure of irregular cash flows requires short-term financial accommodation, which commercial banks are ideally suited to provide. In a country like Scotland, with regional economic imbalances between Highland and Lowland, city and countryside, a mechanism for linking the cash-rich to the cash-poor areas was essential. Thus, we see the appeal of a national bank with branches throughout the country to even out regional differences in liquidity.

Public Finance

4

Functions of government

In practice, governments had few roles until late in the nineteenth century. But this did not prevent a widespread debate to establish whether governments should confine their activities to the most basic roles, mainly defence and law and order, or, on the other hand, whether they should extend their remit to include roads, education and welfare.

These Scots wrote in the age of a minimal state, a state which itself spent little and restricted its activities. A minimal state has many attractions, including an absence of interference in the economic activities of firms and households, and low taxation because it has few activities of its own to finance. The size of a government can be estimated by measuring the ratio of its spending to national income; what it is doing is evident in the distribution of that spending over different functions. It is possible to have governments that prescribe economic conduct without engaging directly in the country's activities; for example, a government may achieve its objectives by tightly regulating an industry instead of taking it into public ownership. In earlier times central governments had varying degrees of control over their populations. If there were powerful local barons then the centre would impose little and have less justification for spending.

It was difficult for a Scottish view of the economic functions of government to be exercised in this period through purely Scottish institutions. The abolition of the Scottish Privy Council in 1708 meant there was no Scottish administration until the Scottish Office was established in 1885. Nor was there much support for an expansion of government activity. Campbell quotes a writer in the *Caledonian Mercury*, 21 April 1783: 'it is to *trade, industry and improvement of the soil*, that poor Scotland must look for salvation and not to the nonsense, and distraction, and the turmoil of politics' (1964: 468).

This is a simple agenda, with nothing for the government to do. Any advice from these writers would have to be aimed at the British government in London.

Francis Hutcheson, tutor and mentor to Adam Smith, considered the possibilities for government action: 'The law of nature requires the doing whatever most tends to the good of mankind, as far as human prudence can discern: and no doubt obliges too to constitute the best sorts of polity' (*System* II: 285).

This prompts the questions: who should promote what is good? A government or individuals, and in what ways? Hutcheson thought civil rights prevent further injury and keep individuals subservient to the general interest. To explain his position he uses the example of the inventor: any reluctant or shy inventors should be compelled, if the invention is for the preservation of life or advancement of general happiness, to publish their breakthrough but be given compensation according to the labour incurred, the profit expected or the good to society.

Hutcheson concedes strong powers to the state – to compel each person to work so that they are not a burden on the industrious, and to compel parents to educate their children to make them self-sufficient in due course. Austerely, Hutcheson exempts no one from the duty 'to follow some profession or business subservient to some common good' (p. 113), otherwise he sees them as corrupt and useless. Concerned that great inequalities of wealth grant disproportionate power to individuals and threaten the state as a whole, Hutcheson proposes a remedial policy:

> there should be such Agrarian laws as will prevent any immoderate increase of wealth in the hands of a few, which could support a force superior to the whole body. 'Tis vain to talk of invading the liberty of the rich, or the injury of stopping their progress in just acquisition. No publick interest hinders their acquiring as much as is requisite for any innocent enjoyments and pleasures of life. And yet if it did, the liberty and safety of thousands or millions is never to put in the ballance with even the innocent pleasures of a few families; much less with their vain ambition, or their unjust pleasures, from their usurped powers or external pomp and grandeur.
>
> (p. 248)

For his time, this attitude is radical. It follows the modern view that the state should devise policies to correct inequalities. To contrast political liberty and economic liberty and consider wealth redistribution between social classes was an agenda too far for his Scottish successors, while his emphasis on the common good has a medieval ring to it. Interestingly, his proposals did not require the state to do anything but compel others, with the consequence that the state achieved extensive goals without incurring large public expenditure. This is consistent with the view of Taylor (1956), who argued that laissez-faire principles were embedded in Hutcheson but seemingly absent from Hume.

The minimal state

With little reference to the French Physiocrats, who had invented the notion of laissez-faire, Scottish writers independently set out the case for small government and little interference in the running of economic affairs. Hume, in his essay *Of the Original Contract* (1987), claimed that no individual in government was entitled to make violent innovations, in other words, interfere with ordinary activities. Hume, Wolin (1954) explains, was a conservative who disliked reform. In his view, government merely protected society and executed its purposes; rules of society were mere contrivances to meet human needs.

Adam Ferguson, without debating the role of government to the extent of, say, Steuart, proposes in his *Institutes* (1785) that the government should bestow plenty and security through defence and commerce, not through some elaborate matrix of policies. As befits a retired army chaplain he was a fervent supporter of defence expenditure, arguing that 'states must be prepared to incur indefinite expence', and 'safety is to be preferred to profit' (*Principles* 1792 II: 430). In his *An Essay on the History of Civil Society* of 1767 he explains the justification for defence:

> The law of Nature, with respect to nations, is the same that it is with respect to individuals: it gives to the collective body a right to preserve themselves; to employ, undisturbed, the means of life; to retain the fruits of labour; to demand the observance of stipulations and contracts.
>
> (p. 192)

Most of these rights gave rise to no government expenditure except in the case of self-preservation, which requires spending on defence.

Kames was not an advocate of big government, certainly not of governments with grandiose plans and expenditure to match. In an example of minimal government he reports (1778) that the public revenue can be greater than the expense of government and the surplus used to purchase land as in the Canton of Bern in Switzerland; its policy of locking up money in its Treasury allows immense wealth to coexist with frugality and cheap labour. Lehmann (1971) believes that Kames's interest in public economy sprang from his experience as a member of the Board of Trustees and of the Board of Commissioners, which made him aware of bad policy on the Poor Laws and discriminatory regulations on commerce and tax.

In the *WN* Smith begins his discussion of the role of the state by listing the four basic state expenses – defence, justice, public works and maintaining the dignity of the sovereign. Smith devoted 125 pages of that book to discussing public expenditure, compared with ninety-three to taxes and forty-one to debt.

He begins with defence. According to him, alternative methods for conducting defence are either all citizens being engaged in military training ready to serve or professional armed forces. He opts for the latter and says it contributes to regular government and control of the provinces but is expensive. He recognizes that in a society that has switched from agriculture to manufacturing it is less realistic to have the population as a reserve army because sedentary manufacturing work is not as good a physical preparation for fighting as the outdoor life of farming. Smith was controversial in that there was opposition to the creation of a standing army. Andrew Fletcher of Saltoun (1653–1716) was called 'the Patriot' for his fierce defence of Scotland's independence in the debates in the Scottish parliament prior to the Act of Union of 1707. After an education at St Andrews University, he strongly supported William of Orange and the Protestant succession that succeeded the Stuart monarchy and vehemently opposed, as a member of the old Scottish parliament, an incorporating union of the Scottish and English parliaments that would destroy the independence of the Scottish. A learned man, he assembled the largest Scottish private library of his times, of 6,000 books. In his *A Discourse of Government with Relation to Militias* of 1698 (1979: chapter 1) he clearly opposed a defence policy that opted for a standing army rather than a militia. He feared a professional army gives a king increased power to destroy ancient liberties and felt that Britain had never been secure under a mercenary army. Instead he had the idea of national service for all men aged twenty-two years; they would spend two years in a camp at their own expense, if they could afford to do so, or one year at public expense, where they would subsist on bread and occasionally beef, and on water sometimes flavoured with brandy or vinegar. No women would be allowed in the camp; soldiers found engaging in self-abuse would be liable to capital punishment. In plain coarse clothes they would march a great deal and spend their leisure hours reading military histories. In the summer thousands from the same locality would be assembled for exercises and every man of high enough estate would keep a horse suitable for war duties. Perhaps unsurprisingly, this tough policy was never adopted.

The breadth of Smith's notion of the defence function is clarified by Buchanan. Buchanan reminds us that in the *WN* Smith had argued that, on defence grounds, there could be a bounty on sailcloth and gunpowder made in Britain despite the small chance of their production failing. The means of defence, for Smith, was more than the establishment of a professional army; in the case of the navy, the Navigation Acts would boost the amount of merchant shipping, which when necessary could be converted into a navy. But Buchanan in his *Inquiry* (1844) was not willing to follow Smith's concession to the Navigation Acts, because this intervention in the shipping industry cut profit through interfering with the assortment of cargo that could be carried and, by diverting trade and navigation from their natural course, the Acts violated Smith's basic libertarian principle. He also noted that the powers of the Navigation Act were being eroded by commercial treaties from 1811, which conceded navigation rights to other countries.

The second basic role of a minimal state is law and order. In *TMS* Smith wrote bluntly 'society cannot subsist unless the laws of justice are tolerably observed...' (p. 87). In *WN* Smith writes that for commerce and manufacturing to continue to flourish there has to be a regular administration of justice, security of property and legal support for contracts. Smith explains why expenditure on law and order is necessary: great inequality of property requires a system of justice to protect it but law and order cannot be entirely self-financing. In the past the administration of justice used to be a source of profit to the sovereign but that led to corruption: reform meant that justice had to be financed by the state. Ever keen to keep public expenditure to the minimum Smith suggests ways of minimizing the cost of justice; for example, the fees a court charges could meet their expenses. Alternatively, he suggested that there could be fixed salaries for judges paid from the rent of landed estates. Cohen's (1989) reading of Smith leads him to state that to ensure justice, in Smith's view, government and law have to follow the principles of the spectator, policing threats to the functioning of competitive markets through monopoly and privileges and supplementing the market through public works. According to Macleod (2007), in a free market society Smith saw the minimum institutions needed to secure the public interest as property law, the law of contract and a criminal law to forbid force, fraud and theft.

The most controversial form of expenditure on Smith's list, the third, is for erecting and maintaining public works that have great benefit to a society by facilitating commerce and providing instruction for the people, but cannot reasonably be paid for by one or several individuals. However, as I would argue, most of the infrastructure including roads, the coinage and the post office generates revenue, which meets their expense; even poor parents would pay some fees for the schooling of their children. But it could be argued that creating an infrastructure was part of the more basic functions of defence and justice and not a separate function. After 1715, the year of a Jacobite rising, military roads built in Scotland to prevent further insurrections had a beneficial effect on commerce through making inland trade easier. In turn, a flourishing commerce permits the financing of better harbours and other improved transport facilities. This is a neat way of combining the thinking of *TMS* and *WN* on law and order, that is, that there were spillover benefits from the barest of government roles. Bowles (1986) notes that manufacturing was encouraged in the cities because they had law and order while Ferguson wisely comments 'The success of commercial arts, divided into parts, requires a certain order to be preserved by those who practise them, and implies a certain security of the person and property, to which we give the name of civilisation . . .' (*Principles* 1792 I: 252).

The reduced role for the state might explain why Smith was not a favourite source of quotations in parliamentary debate during the period 1783–1800: Henry Thomas Buckle (1821–62), historian, could find only thirty-seven occasions when Smith was mentioned (Milgate and Stimson 1996).

A fourth Smithian reason for public expenditure was that there should be expenditure on the sovereign, to maintain his/her dignity as head of state; this was a time when certain orders of society were expected to have more splendid furniture, dress and so on than others. To some extent Smith seemed to be trying to justify the Civil List, which in Great Britain from 1760 granted the sovereign an allowance in return for his/her ceasing to pay for government ministers and the judiciary and surrendering the revenue from the Crown estates.

We can ask with Winch (1996) whether Smith thought the legislator is one who contemplates the natural order or moulds events. Smith had, according to Samuels and Medema (2005), three models of social control – moral rules, law and the market – thus making his ideas difficult to interpret. 'The point of the *Wealth of Nations* is not that government is bad, but that government was doing bad things in promulgating mercantilist policy' (p. 225). Winch (1992) says that both economic individualism and natural liberty are present in Smith's role of the state: Smith was not very keen on redistribution of income or wealth.

How consistent was Smith on the role of government? Many writers list areas of policy where Smith was interventionist. Harlen (1999) takes agriculture as an example: in Smith's view protection was permissible to avoid a famine, retaliatory tariffs were approved as steps towards free trade, and temporary monopolies were permitted to encourage a risky new trade. Viner (1927) says that Smith was concerned to separate natural government activity promoting general welfare from what was injurious, but his suspicion of government did not give him a faith in voluntary organizations: apart from the Church of Scotland, he was not keen on religious organizations and despised corporate guilds. Nevertheless, Viner finds many roles set for government in the *WN*: the Navigation Acts; sterling marks and quality stamps for woollen and linen cloth; enforcement of contracts; banking regulations; hindering farmers from sending goods to market; public works to facilitate commerce, including government running of canals; temporary monopolies to establish a new trade with a remote nation; public hygiene measures to prevent the spread of disease; compulsory registration of mortgages; colonial laws that prevented the engrossing of land against agricultural progress; a maximum rate of interest; some export restrictions for revenue reasons and to help domestic manufacturers; a heavier taxation of rents in kind than that for money rents; some taxation to effect reforms, as with tax on the retail sale of liquor to stop the proliferation of small alehouses; higher taxes on luxury carriages; taxes on ground rents. Quite a long list!

These exceptions to laissez-faire need classification. Grampp (2000) collects thirty-five or forty measures of government intervention in *LJ* and *WN*, dividing them into five kinds – helping buyers, sellers and people in need; increasing efficiency by regulating or replacing certain markets; taxing to redistribute income, as with house rents, or redirect use of resources, as with land rents; restricting foreign trade, especially that contributing to defence; and regulating the issue of currency and other financial transactions.

As for the many alleged departures Smith made from the idea of a minimal state one has to ask how many of them can be reduced to the basic roles of defence and law and order. Even banking regulation has an impact on a nation's defence. Many of the exceptions to state non-intervention were to provide a framework for free economic activity.

In Scottish economic thought what was the outcome of this debate? Did the minimalists triumph, or was there a movement towards the more modern interfering state?

Thomas Reid, Smith's successor at Glasgow as professor of moral philosophy, seemed to have expansive views about the role of government: 'The duty of a State to promote Industry Agriculture Arts and Science. To provide for the Necessities of the Poor, to Punish idleness Riot and Dissipation. To manage the Public Revenue to provide Ships & harbours and all the Implements of foreign Trade to drain marshes make highways bridges Canals Fortresses...' (1990: 75). But he was cautious about the state's direct involvement: 'it is not...the business of politics to show how men ought to act, that belongs to Morals, but to show how they will act when placed in such circumstances and under such government' (Kitagawa 1994: 167). To promote is not the same as to organize, thus there is no commitment to state expenditure on different industries in Reid, but when he speaks of providing and managing there has to be deeper involvement by the state, making Reid far from an out and out minimalist.

Scottish writers in the nineteenth century had in their ranks supporters of both state action and laissez-faire. Playfair, in his 1807 survey of the decline of nations, comments on Smith's views on government functions and thought there are certain things individuals cannot provide individually but if done collectively are done badly. Individuals need, for example, to combine to provide a postal service, although joint service need not be in the public sector. He points out difficulties in the provision of education. England, he thought, was the country with the worst neglect, by the lower classes, of their children, and although admitting that not many parents could afford tutors for children, he did not recommend employment of publicly financed teachers. However, he wanted the government to ensure that teachers are properly qualified and children are examined, because parents are no judge of schoolmasters and the proficiency of the child; examinations would permit parents to estimate the merit of a school. Despite these modest tasks for government, Playfair hoped there would be specialist schools for each occupation, which would create good members of society, and female education, as women could thus have a good effect on the conduct of their husbands and children. As a general principle, he argued that 'The interference of the law between a man and the use of his property ought to be seldom as possible' (p. 148). Later, in his 1809 edition of *WN*, Playfair takes a more minimalist position, contending that the government should 'direct all its attention to the enlargement of the market, by forming safe and convenient roads, by the circulation of sterling coin, and by securing the faithful fulfilment of contracts' (p. xlv) – these were seen by him as indispensable measures, yet only provided a framework, in order to permit free economic activity. He thinks the government should guard natural liberty and the private interest instead of directing industry. Occasionally Playfair could be more pro-intervention. Unlike Smith, he approved of apprenticeships in a pamphlet of 1814, arguing that the present system had brought good results and that the government's responsibility for education included encouraging apprenticeships to prevent youths from becoming vagabonds and blackguards, to produce good workmen and to advance morality and industry.

Other writers of the early nineteenth century believed in a minimal state more firmly than Playfair. Dugald Stewart said 'the perfection of political wisdom consists not in incumbering the machine of government with new contrivances to obviate every partial inconvenience, but in removing, gradually and imperceptibly, the obstacles which disturb the order of nature' (1854–60 II: 238). This stripping of government down to size would leave it with few functions to exercise.

It was possible at that time to be a political reformer and a follower of laissez-faire principles for the economy. Joseph Hume, a Radical MP, constantly criticized government activity, especially if it entailed more public expenditure and more taxation. He disliked micro-interference by government:

> almost all the acts that have been passed for the regulation of particular trades, appeared to me to be objectionable, and when joined the effect of exclusive privileges in different classes of workmen, to have been productive of the very consequences which the legislature intended to prevent.
>
> (1812: v)

He regarded any interference with a master or with a buyer or a seller – for example, statutes of apprenticeship, privileges of corporations, exclusive charters – as injurious to the progress of art and industry. Custom and practice, he thought, already provided procedures for settling disputes, avoiding the need for legislation. Thus as it is rare to pay wages in goods or truck, legislation to cover this is unnecessary. Where specific acts of parliament had been passed in relation to, for example, tailors and leather workers, he pointed out that disputes between men and masters were frequent. He also provided the example of the knitting industry, a stationary trade after the 1664 Royal Charter created a monopoly for framework knitters and limited types of production. Consequently, he stated:

> Let it [the industry] be protected, and leave the rest to be managed by ourselves . . . every one in general being the best judge of his own abilities how to employ his stock in trade.
>
> (p. 26)

In his view, every master and every artisan should have full discretion in trade to employ capital and labour; the fixing of wages with penalties prevents paying the industrious and ingenious more. If landlords and tenants are free to increase rents, he says, there can be an improvement in agriculture. In other words, freedom and competition in trade and manufactures lead to an increase in profits. To sum up, Joseph Hume could see substantial benefits in most economic activities being conducted without government activity.

Education was always to be a battlefield between supporters and opponents of active government. Craig (1814) determined as far as possible to keep education out of the hands of the state, wanting a private approach because differences in occupations, wealth and talents, in his view, ruled out a general and permanent educational plan. He suggested that parental affection would produce more constant and efficient education, and that the father should be compelled to educate his children and threatened with disgrace if he neglects them. He believed private education is affordable because in most places the inhabitants can support a schoolmaster whose wages need be no more than a mechanic's; low wages would make the teacher teach better through relying on scholars' fees. Under state education, he argued, the young acquire useless attainments, retarding national improvement, and scientific progress is impeded if the law prescribes the conduct of science. Only basic education should be given to the whole nation: strangely he believed that if the 'lower orders' can read they are unlikely to promote political revolution, despite socialism flourishing in trade unions where members were better educated. Public examinations and public reward would lead to general emulation. A way of encouraging education would be to exclude the illiterate from employment in a manufactory under the age of twelve unless an orphan: a simple scheme of compulsion costing nothing to the government. For universities Craig had a private competitive approach, advocating low salaries to stop the neglect of teaching in favour of research. In Scotland, he observed, where professors are idle private lecturers appear. He also argued that universities do not have a monopoly of knowledge because they do not teach everything.

In the prosperous, industrialized nineteenth century there were strong supporters of laissez-faire. Stirling, in his *The Philosophy of Trade*, approved of a minimal state that does not interfere with markets. The state should

> afford protection to industry and security to property, preserving strictly the standard of money once established, enforcing covenants, and thereby maintaining credit, but leaving demand and supply to perform their appropriate functions, without restraint or encouragement.
>
> (1846: vi)

Robust in his opinions, Patrick Edward Dove (1815–73), an Edinburgh-based writer, argued that 'The genuine essence of all liberty is *non-interference*' (1850: 33). A government can create crimes, he wrote, but 'No action can be *less* criminal than the purchase of the productions of one country, and the transport of those productions to another country, for the legitimate profit of the trader and the convenience of the inhabitants' (pp. 37–8). A possible implication of this view is that smuggling is a legitimate activity giving profit and employment to all involved, or that it is merely a call for free trade. Dove went on to argue that little revenue is actually required by the state: it is because of legislation that more revenue is needed. He saw the source of evil as the doctrine '*that rulers are competent to legislate for every thing and for any thing*' (p. 52; italics in original) and contended that 'When a community begins to emerge from barbarism, and legislation assumes a defined form, *every thing* is legislated for. Food, thought, speech, action, property . . . are all made subjects of enactment; and men thus endeavour to improve the world that God made, by passing laws to amend the order of nature' (p. 57). He also argued, more strongly, that 'Man, in making laws, must have the most clear and perfectly justifying *reason* for so doing; or otherwise he is attempting to controvert the arrangements of the Almighty ...' (p. 245). And that 'It is not man's office to originate laws. God has made the laws, and given man an intellect to *discover* and *apply* them. As well may man make laws in the physical sciences ...' (p. 247). Dove is fairly unusual for employing a theological argument in favour of his minimalist views; it would have been too strong a justification for Enlightenment thinkers to make.

Despite the fervour of these arguments for a minimal state, contrary attitudes were present in this body of Scottish writing. Interventionism had its supporters.

The interventionist state

Smith's views on the functions of the state are so widely known and discussed that it is easy to forget another sturdy strand in Scottish economics which is supremely represented by Sir James Steuart, a great apostle of state action centred on the 'statesman', who gives leadership to a nation and powerfully directs it. That is,

> a statesman at the head of government, systematically conducting every part of it, so as to prevent the vicissitudes of manners, and innovations, by their natural and immediate effects or consequences, from hurting within the commonwealth'.
>
> (*Principles* I: 140)

> I suppose him to be constantly awake, attentive to his employment, able and uncorrupted, tender in his love for the society he governs, impartially, just in his indulgence for every class of inhabitants, and disregardful of the interest of individuals, when that regard is inconsistent with the general welfare.
>
> (p. 168)

> The more he [the statesman] has their [people's] actions under his influence, the easier it is for him to make them concur in advancing the general good.
>
> (p. 339)

Steuart is quite clear that the government has the task of countering the ill effects of human nature that potentially affect general welfare. The statesman is a kind, impartial figure sensitively guiding the governed on the right path by exercising authority according to the 'spirit, manners, habits, and customs of the people' (p. 21). Subject to the rule of law he cannot be a dictator, nor act haphazardly, because his actions are based on data collection to discern where action is needed. Policies spring from his basic economic principles to keep agricultural workers employed in creating a surplus, 'the main spring of all alienation and industry' (II: 144), to conduct industry for the relief of want and subsistence of the needy, and to circulate money. Steuart wavers between a short and long list of tasks for the state. In minimal mode he says:

> A people who depend upon nothing but their own industry for their subsistence, ought to be under no further subordination than what is necessary for their protection.
>
> (I: 259)

In this mode he wanted the statesman to provide a framework for commerce: 'The duty of the statesman is, to support the double competition', that is, between sellers and between buyers, 'every where' (p. 247) and to promote 'a gentle increase of food, inhabitants, work and demand' (p. 248).

In interventionist mode he required the state to prevent the exportation of accumulated wealth, maintain full employment, ensure an equable circulation of domestic wealth, with the rich paying the industrious poor properly for their services, impose taxation that extracts an equitable proportion of annual incomes subject to ensuring an income which meets physical needs, use public funds to keep all industries vigorous, promote foreign trade and defend society at the public expense. Interestingly, much of this list is implemented by modern democratic states. According to Steuart, higher agricultural output would increase the population and tariff protection would expand industries. This expensive programme appears to move towards egalitarian socialism albeit as a mild form of equality of opportunity: 'by being equably distributed, I do not mean, that every individual comes to have an equal share, but an equal chance' (II: 130–31).

Steuart was never short of proposals for government action. He wants colonization, a standing army to avoid expensive mercenaries and the use of men enfeebled by sedentary manufacturing tasks, schemes to take the population out of unemployment by public works at home and by promoting the sale of luxuries abroad through studying foreign tastes, a ban on specie exports to reduce imports and restore a trade balance, price controls to promote agriculture, and the relocation of industry to the provinces in order to cut workers' living costs. Hoping to reduce cyclical fluctuations in the economy he wanted to promote price stability through a fiscal policy of taxes and subsidies in order to keep prices at a uniform standard, or within a narrow range. As he saw it, price stability would promote stable behaviour among manufacturers, who would stop swinging between being 'idle and extravagant' and 'diligent and sober' (IV: 164).

In a commentary on Steuart, Sen (1957) says that Sir James regarded a watchful statesman as necessary to a free society. He had, as levers for controlling the economy, sumptuary legislation (regulation of personal expenditure especially on clothes), money, taxation and public expenditure. Tortajada (1999) thought that the aim of Steuart's economic writings was to propose policy measures, especially on population and its full employment, while Tribe

(1978) believes that Steuart, to some extent, regards the state as being the royal household rather than the national economy, suggesting that his policy proposals were modest.

Later writers could appear to favour the minimal state but in practice give the state a considerable role. For example, Craig could argue that the most just governments 'diffuse the greatest portion of security and happiness, call forth the highest exertions of intellect, and, at the same time, encroach the least on individual liberty' (1814 I: 143), which was hardly the agenda for big government; however, elsewhere he edged towards the modern state's wide view of its functions. Given that the purposes of political society are, as he writes, 'to protect the citizens from injury, to increase by combination the effects of individual exertions, and to improve the moral and intellectual faculties of man' (p. 271), there are three types of duty of government: administering the criminal law to protect from injury, the civil law and national defence. Nevertheless he was willing to countenance directing wealth and industry to their best employments, a proposal which demolished a pillar of Smith's system. Craig elaborated on Smith's third reason for public expense, that is, that some investments unprofitable to individuals can be undertaken by the state, for example, good roads. If the profits are too distant and precarious, the government, in Craig's view, is justified in levying a general tax. He also thought that the government should run the post office because it provides regular communication and enables the conveying of information and, as the population of Scotland is small, it would be too expensive for the public to run. Finally, he wanted a redistribution of wealth to help the poor, and more education to promote religion.

Thomas Carlyle, in his 'The Present Time' pamphlet of 1850, mockingly described the non-interventionist government as following a policy of 'Leave-alone' or 'Anarchy, Anarchy; and only the street-constable' (p. 37). More elaborately, he writes, in 'Signs of the times', of government that 'it is emphatically a machine: to the discontented, a "taxing-machine"; to the contented, a "machine for securing property." Its duties and its faults are not those of a father, but of an active parish-constable' (1829: 67).

In *Past and Present* Carlyle wants a role for government which would overcome the problems of the market economy: 'are not Sanitary Regulations possible for a legislature? The old Romans had their Aediles [magistrates in charge of public works]...in direct contravention to supply-and-demand...' (1843: 264).

To cope with the pollution of urban areas he suggested that

> The Legislature, even as it now is, could order all dingy Manufacturing Towns to cease from their soot and darkness...Baths, free air, a wholesome temperature, ceilings twenty feet high, might be ordained by Act of parliament, in all establishments licensed as Mills.
>
> (pp. 264–5)

We get an idea of his wide range of roles for government by examining the new ministries he recommended:

> I do consider that there must be some Education Secretary, Captain-General of Teachers, who will actually contrive to get us *taught*... again, why should there not be an 'Emigration Service', and Secretary, with adjuncts, with funds, forces, idle navy-ships, and ever-increasing apparatus;... Every willing Worker that proved superfluous, finding a bridge [presumably to America] ready for him.
>
> (pp. 266–7)

He wanted employers to provide entertainment for their workers and not merely grant market minimum wages, provoking strikes. Carlyle's vision was an attack on the industrialization and capitalism of his day. He had anticipated the attitude of some modern governments, who examine every conceivable problem of society and rush to provide a state solution without considering the cost of running such a state and the effects of creating a massive public sector.

The more cautious interventionist John Hill Burton had mixed views on the role of the state, as seen in his *Political and Social Economy* (1849). He too wanted sanitary laws and a government-run post office, as well as better salaries for public servants to prevent theft and laziness. However, he saw a limit to public policymaking: joint stock companies rather than local authorities could provide housing cheaply and custom and usage could take care of agriculture.

As democracy gradually emerged over the two hundred years studied in this book, most of the adult population could express through the ballot box their priorities for government. Instead of welfare expenditure being the exercise of paternalism it could be a government provision demanded by the masses. Anything could be debated – how much to spend on the most basic roles of defence and law and order; whether to develop poor relief and indulge in the modern demands for free education and health care. But more democracy would not automatically mean the launch of expensive new roles for government because the increase in taxation to finance them could deter voters from supporting high expenditure and promote a return to a minimalist view of the state.

The arguments for a minimal state seemed to have more coherence than the appeals for government intervention because of reliance on the simple idea of economic liberty. Arguments for more government action were not based on an explicit economic or political philosophy: they could best be described as ad hoc responses to the problems arising from increased urbanization and industrialization. By 1900 government was still quite a modest affair: UK public expenditure was a mere 14 per cent of the gross domestic product (GDP). That ratio reached peaks of 57 per cent in 1918 and 70 per cent in 1945 at the end of two world wars. Even in the twenty years after 1965, and after 2008, over 40 per cent of GDP was spent by government.

Taxation

After a government has decided what its activities should be it has to choose a method of financing them. It can rely on the income from its assets (many monarchs previously supported themselves mainly from their estates), on charges for services rendered, on raising taxation or, in the short term, on borrowing. In modern times taxation is the most important means of financing a government. In the *WN* Smith chiefly considers taxation and borrowing and, alert to taxation being only one way to finance a government, considers raising revenue from mercantile projects including a post office (although he thinks it is demeaning for a sovereign to be in trade), interest from investments, rents, and the sale of Crown lands, which in many countries could pay off public debt – a sovereign should have lands only for pleasure and magnificence and taxes.

John Millar (1787) reminds us of the late emergence of taxation as the principal way of financing the state. He mentions that taxes were virtually unknown in Saxon England. The public revenues came from the income of the king's demesne and from fines and forfeitures. However, King John of England, like Henry III, raised much Crown revenue from indirect taxes in the form of aids and scutages (under feudalism, money paid to avoid personal service); King John gave parliament exclusive power to impose them. For example, tradesmen needed protection for the transport, sale and store of their goods, therefore the king could demand a portion of goods or other payment. Because such duties were established by long usage they were called customs.

Sinclair, in his *History of the Public Revenue of the British Empire* (1790), notes that 'The power of a State must greatly depend on the income it possesses' (p. 3), and reports that permanent taxes began about 1710; previously taxes lasted only as long as necessary to pay off the money borrowed on the credit of the tax. Particular taxes could have particular purposes. Originally, import duties and customs were paid for guarding the coasts from pirates and by foreign merchants for the liberty of trading in a sovereign's dominions.

Sir James Steuart had a simple notion of a tax: 'a certain contribution of fruits, service, or money, imposed upon the individuals of a state by the act or consent of the legislature, in order to defray the expences of government' (*Principles* IV: 145). He classifies taxes according to what is taxed and how they are levied. For example, he divided taxes into *proportional*, such as customs and excises, *cumulative*, which affect possessions, income and profits such as tithes, land tax, window tax and poor rates, and *personal*, in the form of service; he saw the latter as being a feudal practice replaced by monetary taxes. In his discourse on taxation, Andrew Hamilton, deputy comptroller of excise for Scotland, uses a different taxonomy and claims that there are three types of tax. There is the *political tax* to restrain the use of a commodity, which is rarely effective, as the gin tax shows; the *commercial tax* to prefer one commodity to another, for example, Portuguese to French wines; and a *revenue tax* to produce revenue for the state, the reason for most taxation. From reviewing the types of tax Hamilton examines their justification. In a commercial society Hamilton argues that the state gives the service of security and protection, enabling the merchant to transport goods and customers to consume them:

> No person can reside in a country, without receiving all that security and comfort, which its laws and government afford. There is a claim of justice, therefore, on every individual, to pay his proportional expence for the blessings of his situation.
>
> (1793: 110)

Echoing the sentiments of Hobbes in chapter 30 of his *Leviathan* (1650), Thomas Reid insisted that the state has the duty to lay on taxes equally and manage them rightly:

> There does not appear to me a Shaddow of Reason why the Consent of a Subject should be necessary to his bearing an equal Share of the public burthen which the service of the State demands . . . The burthen of taxes (is compensated) by the advantage of defence by the laws and arms of the State.
>
> (Kitagawa 1994: 197)

Smart similarly regarded taxation as based on an implicit contract, saying, 'the government renders us certain services which we pay for with part of our income' (1900: 5) and 'The government servants buy their bread and butter from us, and we buy justice, defence, education, etc, from them' (p. 7). However, he claimed that we ourselves determine the amount we pay.

Having recognized that taxation is the principal means of financing a government, and having looked at broad classifications of it, we need now to examine in detail major issues in the study of taxation: the tax burden, the canons of taxation, the incidence of taxation, the land tax, profits tax, indirect taxation, income tax and tax reform.

Tax burden

The correct level of taxation avoids destroying a national economy and improves it: 'Sometimes a slight additional burden may prove to be an incentive to labour, and a spur to greater diligence and activity' (Sinclair 1790: 3), but I would argue that if too great a burden the population and wealth decrease. A burden can be regarded in a macroeconomic way as the proportion of national income taxed, or microeconomically as the weight on individuals. As Smart (1900) points out, there is no accurate measure of 'sacrifice' and hence a tax burden is not a justification for refusing to pay taxes. Poverty is not an excuse for avoiding taxation or for refusing to pay for bread, unless one is a pauper.

Having a low tax burden is an attractive attribute of a state. Smith, at the beginning of his career, had advocated 'easy taxes':

> Little else is requisite to carry a state to the highest degree of opulence from the lowest barbarism, but peace, easy taxes, and a tolerable administration of justice: all the rest being brought about by the natural course of things.
> (Lecture in 1755, quoted in Stewart (1858), section IV: 68)

Peace and good administration matter but so does taxation. David Hume and Samuel Read, according to Seligman (1903b), also thought that taxation should be moderate and levied gradually.

Turning to Scotland, we see that after 1707 the Scots, no longer with a separate tax system, had reasons to be suspicious of their tax burden. Although it was a novelty for Scotland to have its taxation fixed south of the border, not much of that Scottish revenue ended up in English hands. Whatley (1989) notes that in the fifty years following the Act of Union only 15 to 20 per cent of tax revenues raised in Scotland went south. The true fiscal impact of the union was the curing of Scotland's finances by introducing the more efficient English revenue system. Whatley admits, 'The days when Olympian pronouncements about the place and impact of the Treaty of 1707 in Scottish economic history could be passed are over, at least for the meantime' (1989: 181). The new tax on linen exports in 1711, Campbell (1964) says, made it difficult for Scotland to compete with Austrian and German cloth re-exported through London, although this problem was less important in 1742 when bounties were paid on British linen exports. The malt tax raised little revenue and was negative by 1724–25. Until 1760, 15 to 20 per cent of Scotland's tax revenue was from land and malt taxes. Nevertheless, Scottish expenditure grew, especially on the law courts.

The new tax regime created by the union had its critics, especially because of the alleged burden of particular taxes. William Black, in his *Answer to a letter concerning trade* (1706a), had argued that the salt duty was too high, twice the English rate, making it almost impossible for Scots to afford to use foreign salt for curing fish. In his *Remarks upon a Pamphlet* (1706) he forecast that numerous taxes would be imposed on Scots as a result of a union, for example a four shillings in the pound (20 per cent) tax on lawyers' receipts. In his *A Short View* (1706) he pointed out that Scots already complained of their taxation being too heavy and feared that union with England would overburden them with heavy taxes on trade in order to service the national debt. In return for much taxation, Scotland only received the empty promise of free trade. In *Some overtures and cautions* (1707) Black said the effects of taxation were heavy because it was not proportionate to what the population could pay; consequently, tenants would lose their possessions, servants when taxed would require higher wages, landlords might have to repossess their land or lower their rents leading to a lower standard of living, and merchants would have less trade.

Hodges (1706) was also concerned about the tax burden. He questioned the uniformity of taxes throughout the newly created Great Britain, given that there were differences in the administration of justice and separate responsibility for national debts. Excises of beer and ale, like the prices of those commodities, could, he argued, be different in England and Scotland and the amount of tax raised in each country should be proportional to the possession of land and capital. Although there should be equality of customs dues, his view was that the excess could be applied to paying off Scotland's public debt.

A method of judging the tax burden is to debate the relative merits of high and low taxation. Steuart, in arguing for high taxes because they would be useful to finance particular policies – for example, to subsidize exports and to give adequate pay to public sector workers – cared little for tax being a burden. In his opinion, full employment is such a worthwhile goal that 'The number of people *well-employed* makes the prosperity of a state; and the profits of the opulent classes, by the augmentation of industry, more than compensates all the burden of their taxes' (*Principles* IV: 206). This, according to him, is the consequence of the public gaining more than the taxpayer loses:

> If the money raised be more beneficially employed by the state, than it would have been by those who have contributed it, then I say the public has gained, in consequence of the burden laid upon individuals; consequently, the statesman has done his duty, both in imposing the taxes, and in rightly expending them.
>
> (p. 178)

It needs courage to believe that the state can spend more wisely than an individual. Steuart set out his reasons for thinking so. He believed that the state is superior to the private sector in entrepreneurship and in supporting every kind of industry because merchants and potential manufacturers are more concerned with their own wants. In a more grandiloquent passage he argues that taxation, when rightly imposed, is capable of 'providing an outlet for many young people, who in time become ornaments to their country, and instruments of her defence; of supporting foreign trade by bounties on exportation; of promoting the improvement of lands, the establishment of colonies, the extension of fisheries, and every other scheme for augmenting the production of subsistence and manufactures' (p. 208).

In *Of Taxes* (1987) Hume argued that taxes are not a burden as they are merely transfers within a country. Taxes, he said, can temporarily excite industry because new taxes encourage work to help us maintain our station in life and position in society: further taxation leads to an inferior condition. Other writers were not as sanguine.

Steuart, although seeing the usefulness of increased tax revenues, admitted that there was a limit to taxation because of the difficulty of obtaining more tax revenue through higher tax rates. Taking the case of France he informs us that when taxes rose consumption fell and reduced tax revenues: high tax rates could make the poor starve and the rich stop buying taxed goods. He thought a clever way to cope with taxpayers' objection to a tax burden is to vary tax rates. Steuart thought that the strategy for proportional taxes should be to impose them gently, gradually raise them until they begin to interrupt consumption, then lower them until consumption resumes its level.

In the examination of the tax burden the effect of taxation on the poor, especially the disproportionate impact of the largely indirect taxes on lower income groups, is repeatedly mentioned by the Scots. John Dalrymple (1720–89), fifth Earl of Stair, advocate, captain and author of political pamphlets, was well aware of this possibility:

> by the lower and lowest Orders of the People, the great Weight and Proportion of the taxes are paid. From their well being, full Employment, and comfortable Situation, even to a little Superfluity, the Riches of a Nation, and, consequently, its Revenues arise . . .
>
> (1782: 21)

> The poorest parts of the Community ought to be the primary objects of the care of every just and humane legislature.
>
> (1784: 25)

His argument was that the type of taxes imposed then were regressive (disproportionately falling on lower income groups). That helping the poor is both humane and of general benefit to a nation is hard to contradict yet, given that indirect taxation continued to be a major contributor to the coffers of the Treasury, this problem did not go away. Socialist writers always regarded the poor as their special remit and repeatedly mentioned this aspect of the tax burden. Campbell (1831: 2) argued that contemporary taxation had widespread bad effects: it lessens consumption, which in turn causes unemployment and reduces wages. Burdensome taxation can continue for a long time because, as Dove pointed out, workers, when taxed by indirect taxes, have little perception of its oppression, which means that taxation of that type 'prevents the community from dwelling on the *cause* of their suffering and thereby retards a revolution against the privileged classes' (1850: 51). (Steuart, too, knew that tax perception could be low, especially when proportional taxes were part of prices.) Although Dove saw little prospect of an abolition of customs and excise, major indirect taxes then, he nevertheless argued that abolition was essential for a country to be free.

Another aspect of the tax burden, compliance costs, concerned Playfair (1807), who observed that total tax revenue is not offset against the loss of time, trouble and inconvenience of the taxpayer. To reduce the tax burden, he said that it was necessary to economize in public spending through cutting war expenditure, reducing interest payments and making the tax system fair, equal and not troublesome. Far-sighted as Playfair was in raising the issue of these costs he did not see that a reduced tax burden could still leave compliance costs high because the continued existence of particular taxes troublesome to the individual taxpayer could continue.

All these critics of tax thought that a burden might be avoided if the tax system were based on sound principles. The Scots worked hard to set them out.

Canons of taxation

The canons, or principles, of taxation advanced by Smith are famous but he was not alone in laying down the fiscal rules a state should follow. Hutcheson was an early deviser of appropriate rules for a tax system:

> these (taxes) are most convenient which are laid on matters of luxury and splendour, rather than the necessaries of life; on foreign products and manufactures, rather than domestick; and such as can be easily raised without many expensive offices for collecting them. But above all, a just proportion to the wealth of people should be observed in whatever is raised from them, otherways than by duties upon foreign products and manufactures, for such duties are often necessary to encourage industry at home, tho' there were no publick expences.
>
> (*System* II: 341)

He proposes what was to be a recurrent recommendation, basing taxation on the ability to pay, but was also keen to consider which goods were to be taxed as, at the time, taxation was mainly on commodities.

Steuart, too, laid down principles of taxation subject to the general principles:

> according to equity and justice, all impositions whatsoever ought to fall equally and proportionally on every one according to his superfluity . . .
>
> (*Principles* IV: 231)

> they will be laid on more equally, and less arbitrarily; providing the theory of them in general be well understood. Here every man must know *what* he is to pay, and *when*; and the amount of the tax must bear a proportion, on one hand, to the exigencies of the state; and on the other, to the quantity of circulation which takes place upon the payment of it: that is, a man must not be made to pay all the state can demand of him for a year, upon his making a trifling, though most essential, acquisition of a necessary article of subsistence.
>
> (II: 32–3)

He raises the issues of equality of imposition, and the importance of the tax system being comprehensible and transparent and relating properly to the circulation of money. More formally he set out his canons for taxation, being aware of their relationship to the tax burden:

> First, That the more such taxes are proportional to the subject taxed, Secondly, the more evident this proportion appears; and thirdly, the more frequently and regularly such taxes are levied; the more they will resemble proportional taxes; and the less burden will be found in paying them
> (IV: 150–51)

Noting that proportional taxes are imposed at the point of sale on idle consumers, he was quick to detail the difficulties arising from such taxation – its effects on wages, foreign trade and consumption, and the expense of collection. So concerned was he with collection costs that he put together practical proposals such as collecting taxes at the gates of towns and villages, prohibiting delivery of goods until the excise on them was paid and confining the manufacture of taxable goods to sea ports; when there are more public officials to collect taxes the rest of population has to increase its industry or suffer privation.

Ferguson in his *Institutes* (1785) explains the reasons for taxes in the different forms of capitation, assessment on property, customs and excise, elaborating on them in his *Principles* (1792), where he sets out his tax maxims (II: 434–7):

1 Real emergencies are to be provided for at any hazard or expense to the subject: 'every one who partakes in the benefit of a public establishment should bear a part in the expence it incurs' (p. 434). Both the state and the people have the same interest in protection.
2 Private estates are not to be unnecessarily taxed, taking from the industrious what can be squandered by the prodigal.
3 Taxes should be fixed subject to the limit that they do not affect the private ability to protect their own property and are not arbitrary.
4 No tax should drain its source, disabling a labourer in labouring, or robbing a trader of his stock or dispossessing a landowner.
5 Avoid every grievance in the imposition of taxes: 'nothing should take place in the exactions of revenue or of public service which has a tendency to alienate the minds of the people' (p. 437).

The fourth canon is new to the Scottish discussion and long-sighted, unlike many of the other canons of taxation, which could apply only to the short term. Taxation, a leading economic policy, does something to an economy in both the current year and the future. Throughout his list of tax principles there is the underlying assumption that taxation is potentially injurious so should be imposed with great care.

Kames, in *Sketches of the history of Man* (1774 I: 474ff), succinctly stated rules for taxation: (1) 'That wherever there is an opportunity of smuggling, taxes ought to be moderate.' (2) 'That taxes expensive in the levying ought to be avoided.' (3) 'To avoid arbitrary taxes.' (4) 'To remedy the inequality of riches as much as possible, by relieving the poor and burdening the rich.'

(5) 'That every tax which tends to impoverish the nation ought to be rejected with indignation.' (6) 'To avoid taxes that require oath of party.' The fourth rule boldly argued for income redistribution; the sixth that the tax system should be apolitical. Overall these canons are more like reasons for reducing taxation than for imposing it correctly.

An advance on previous canons for taxation was the inclusion of a moral criterion. James Anderson discusses the ideal tax: 'No tax is good, nor perhaps will ever be permanently so productive as it might be, if it does not at the same time operate as a regulation of police, that tends to preserve, if not to purify, the morals of the people, and to augment the general prosperity of individuals not the prosperity of a particular class only' (1799: 65). Subsequently, in the spirit of Anderson, taxes on alcohol and tobacco have been called sin taxes. Anderson remarks that when the resources of a wealthy court decline taxes are increased, manufacturing languishes and population declines, as in Spain.

Hutcheson, Steuart, Ferguson and Kames all enunciated a theory for the basis of the tax system, but Smith's is better known. All tax revenue, Smith says, comes ultimately from rent, profits and wages and should be taxed following four maxims of taxation – in accordance with the ability to pay, set at certain not arbitrary levels, levied at the time convenient for the taxpayer, and cheap to administer. This is a neat summary, in a sense, of other writers' lists. Nevertheless, Smith's version of the maxims was challenged. Dugald Stewart was critical of them, saying that the first was too vague as 'equality' might mean 'equitable' and the notion of ability to pay is disputable. He thought, like Ferguson, a fifth canon was necessary: 'No tax should be imposed in such a manner as to drain the source from which it is derived' (1840 II: 224), ensuring that taxation is not on the fund but its fruits, on factor incomes, not capital. Craig, too, in his 1814 work wanted to add to Smith's maxims on taxation: that taxes should not be paid out of capital but out of what could have been spent. He reasoned that taxes on capital are more oppressive than taxes on expenditure as they lead to the loss of future profits and income.

The canons suggested are clear and straightforward to implement. All of them seem to be inspired by sympathy for the taxpayer; even the efficiency criteria, through cutting the cost of collection, could reduce tax rates. But there is something idealistic about these principles: there are many examples, in country after country, of their still continuing to be violated.

Incidence of taxation

Providing an accurate measure of the incidence of any tax is difficult. As O'Brien explains, the incidence of tax is indeterminate except 'under rather strict and empirically unusable assumptions about the price elasticities of demand and supply for commodities and services singled out for taxation' (1988: 16). Nevertheless the specific impact of taxation continued to be debated.

Hutcheson and Steuart looked at the transfer of the burden of taxation from the person who first paid it to another. Hutcheson in his *System* writes about this phenomenon in a variety of circumstances.

> In land-taxes, gentlemen in debt are immoderately oppressed, beyond those of clear estates; and moneyed men contribute nothing. Duties and excises, however the merchant or other wealthy trader first advances them, yet are at last paid by the consumer. The hospitable generous men, or such as have numerous families supported genteely, bear the chief burden here, and the solitary sordid miser bears little or no share of it.
>
> (II: 341–2)

This is a modern discussion of a tax system that has a regard for the incidence of each type of tax and an awareness of the relative burden of tax on different classes of society. Steuart, too, knew that tax could be shifted, for example,

> as the farmer is supposed to have paid the tax upon what he has borrowed and consumed, he must draw it back from those who, in their turn, are to consume his crop and if he draws it back, he cannot be said to pay it, although the state profits of it as much as if he did.
>
> (*Principles* IV: 143)

But the proprietor could not pass on land tax for then he would make his produce more expensive and be undercut by the farmer.

Hume, in *Of Taxes*, appreciates the effects of taxation by raising the fascinating issue of taxes having the power to create disincentive and incentive effects, either discouraging or encouraging effort.

> When a tax is laid upon commodities, which are consumed by the common people, the necessary consequence may seem to be, either that the poor must retrench something from their way of living, or raise their wages, so as to make the burden of the tax fall entirely upon the rich. But there is a third consequence, which often follows upon taxes, namely, that the poor encrease their industry, perform more work, and live as well as before, without demanding more for their labour. Where taxes are moderate, are laid on gradually, and affect not the necessaries of life, this consequence naturally follows; and it is certain, that such difficulties often serve to excite the industry of a people, and render them more opulent and laborious, than others, who enjoy the greatest advantages.
>
> (1987: 343)

Thus he champions the subtle approach of making taxes encourage effort by introducing them stealthily. But that did not make him an advocate of high taxes. In the 1752 edition of his *Political Discourses* Hume qualified this by saying: 'Exorbitant taxes, like extreme necessity, destroy industry, by producing despair; and even before they reach this pitch, they raise the wages of the labourer and manufacturer, and heighten the price of all commodities' (1987: 635). He thinks that an attentive legislature will be aware of the point where benefit ceases but ''tis to be feared that taxes, all over EUROPE, are multiplying to such a degree, as will intirely crush all art and industry...' (p. 235).

Tax by tax Hume considers incidence. In *Of Taxes* he writes that 'The best taxes are such as are levied upon consumptions, especially those of luxury; because such taxes are least felt by the people' (1987: 345) because they are to some extent voluntary, paid gradually and insensibly, and produce sobriety and frugality. The most pernicious taxes, he thinks, are arbitrary taxes, punishing industry and causing inequality. Poll taxes are condemned, because the sovereign can increase them to the point of oppression. If a tax is levied on something an artisan consumes then he can entrench on consumption or increase labour: these effects are more likely than raising wages at the expense of rent. Hume objected to the popular view that taxation ultimately fell on land: 'why the landed gentleman should be the victim of the whole (burden of the tax), and should not be able to defend himself, as well as others are, I cannot readily imagine' (p. 347). In his view, the tradesmen should share the burden with the landlord; it would have to be a very heavy tax which the artisan could not pay without raising the price of his labour. Hume thus traces the possible effects of taxes in terms of industry, equality, oppression and consumption.

Sinclair, on the other hand, held a contrary and controversial view by contrasting what is the best and what is the most productive tax. He thought moderate excises the best but that taxes on the necessaries of life would raise the price of labour, enabling the industrious to pass the tax on but not the idle. He seems to be concerned both with the idle poor and the idle rich. Anderson (1785) recommends measuring the incidence of tax as the per capita tax burden of people in different districts.

Horner made an attempt in his January 1803 *Edinburgh Review* assessment of Canard to discuss incidence as a whole. He wrote:

> the equable diffusion, or exclusive incidence of taxes, cannot be ascertained by any direct induction of particular facts; but must be obtained synthetically, after a just analysis, both of price and of the order according to which the annual produce is distributed among the people.
>
> (1803b: 432)

Conversely, Canard tries to show that 'taxes diffuse themselves equally over all the different branches of revenue, on whatever branch they may nominally be imposed; and whether they are levied at the source of revenue or upon consumption' (p. 63).

He produces as an example a tax upon rent, which claimed to be equally shared between landlord and tenant. Although taxes ultimately come from neat produce they can come circuitously. Taxes on wages or on profits are 'finally paid, either by the consumers in an increase of price, or by the landlord in a diminution of rent' (p. 67).

In his study of the incidence of several specific taxes, Lauderdale, according to Thomson (1970), prefers capital to income taxes. A tax on capital is less inequitable than one on income, promotes more efficient state management and prevents excessive capital accumulation. He thought a tax on income violated natural law and a tax on succession was based on expediency. It seems, according to his 1798 pamphlet, that he thought only indirect taxes were suitable.

In his *Enquiry* of 1808 Chalmers, according to Roberts (1945), believed that taxes were ultimately paid by the landowner: labourers would not lose their comforts through any tax. Furthermore, as Brown notes (1982), Chalmers was in favour of increased taxation on the rich through a 20 per cent tax of landed income for those with more than £50 annually.

Incidence could also be related to the economy as a whole. Lauderdale, according to Paglin (1961), looked more broadly at the macroeconomic relationships between the taxing, spending and debt management of government relative to private saving and spending. There was much wisdom in all these suggestions but a lack of methodology for establishing whether their hunches would turn out to be correct. Without a national income accounting framework these impacts of taxation could not be accurately assessed.

Land and wealth taxation

The taxation of land has an obvious attraction to a revenue authority because many of the richest in society are landowners, apparently with considerable ability to pay and only challenged in the incomes league by the moneyed class. Also, if rent is regarded as a surplus, a less essential income, then the taxation of land is appealing. A land tax could take various forms, including a general wealth tax or a levy on increments in land values.

William Ogilvie (1736–1819), a classicist who was professor of humanity at King's College, Aberdeen (1765–1817) – and also a landowner – surprisingly recommended drastic land reform. He argued that because the original soil was jointly owned by the community, the most equitable tax would be a land tax used to support the expenses of the state.

According to Bruce (1938), Craig was an early exponent of the capitalization theory of taxation, which explains that a land tax causes a fall in the value of the land equal to the capitalized value of the tax. He says the cheapest land tax to collect is based on land areas, as the same survey can be used for a long time. It would be fixed and precise because it was based on the amount, and not quality, of a land area. If the land tax were based on land values that were falsely understated the tax would be recouped later when the land was sold. Although frequent changes in tax revenue would occur as land prices fluctuate, these changes, seldom perceived, would not be a solid objection to the tax. However, Craig preferred to relate tax to the average price of corn, to keep the tax the same proportion of the net rent, as, with a general register of leases, this was the easiest way to ascertain rents. Craig (1821) opposed a tax on gross produce because it would prevent expensive cultivation except on very fertile ground. He thought that land was special in that it is gradually improved, unlike machinery, which depreciates, but doubted the fairness of land taxes because they taxed one class, the landowners, more than others.

Taxation based on the value of land is a type of wealth taxation. Craig, in his 1814 book *Elements of Political Science*, saw insuperable difficulties in having any type of wealth as a basis of taxation because all private transactions would have to be scrutinized. If declarations of wealth were sworn on oath the amount of tax contributed would be in proportion to regard for truth, not wealth. It is very expensive to have government officials inspect accounts and, while the successful could be penalized, the failing merchants might pay too much to disguise the decline in their fortunes.

Stewart considers the 'territorial tax' on net produce of agriculture recommended by the Physiocrats and notes their claim that a tax of that kind would have the three merits of equality, certainty and economy in collection. The tax is proposed because taxation can be placed only on what is productive.

Whatever these writers argued, some taxation of land is inevitable because it appears to be fair to tax landowners, who are often among the richest people of society. The tax base is visible and immobile but, like all wealth taxes, it causes problems of valuation. It is easier to tax rents as part of income taxation.

A form of land taxation is the tithe, the portion of agricultural produce or labour levied by the church. Anderson argued that tithes and rent are alike: 'they are both calculated to draw from the soil the means of subsistence for a body of men who bear no share in the trouble or expence of cultivating that soil' (1799: 408). The tithe eliminates some of the farmer's profits as the farmer can only afford to produce if the price of grain rises. According to Anderson, 'Thus does tythe in every case tend at the same time to enhance the price of grain, and diminish the produce of the country' (p. 410). Although a tithe is supposed to be only a tenth of the free produce of the ground, because it is levied on gross produce, in practice it can be a quarter of the net produce after wages and seed corn costs are deducted from the value of the produce. Anderson noted the bad effects of the tithe on farming practice: farmers had less chance to save and carry out improvements because the tithe prevented them recouping their capital costs from the first harvest, and it becomes worthwhile for them to change from cornfields to grasslands.

Dugald Stewart followed William Paley (1743–1815), archdeacon of Carlisle and influential moral philosopher, in regarding tithes as a tax on industry, causing farmers to reduce their production and hence the amount of food. Craig, observing that church tithes do not discriminate between high and low yield land, said they would discourage the raising of expensive crops as net profit would be destroyed. In their view, tithes could cause a stationary agriculture and prevent the landlord and the tenant from investing enough to create a more ample income in the future.

Another approach to taxing land is a tax on ground rents. In 1814 Craig mentioned Smith's approval of this tax because wealth in land needs no care or attention and the tax burden cannot be passed on in higher prices. However, Craig regarded it as an unjust tax because the value of the land is determined locally but central government reaps the tax revenue; taxes on house rents, he thought, should be considered relative to tenants' incomes.

Smart, in 1900, admitted that it is easy to tax increments in land value. He was opposed to the American Henry George's single tax proposal (a tax on the unimproved value of land) as it violates the principle that taxes are paid by those who benefit. George's proposal amounted to confiscation as it abolished private property in land and seized the revenues of a class without compensation. Smart, however, noted that land taxation would improve profits, with one set of capitalists gaining at the expense of another.

In general, Niall Ferguson (2001) says a land tax has disadvantages because it discriminates against landowners relative to other asset holders, and it is difficult to conduct an accurate land survey as the basis of assessment.

Profits tax

Profits are inevitably considered a suitable basis for taxation because the existence of profits is often questioned and profit is often regarded as a less essential factor payment than wages. But profits taxes are criticized for their effects on investment and the difficulty of their collection.

A taxation authority has to consider the possibility of competition from tax regimes who offer lower tax rates to attract investment. Profits could yield little revenue because of the mobility of capital. Even the hint of such taxes could make capital flee abroad: Dugald Stewart wrote of this capital flight and higher interest rates at home through a shortage of capital. Playfair (1807) also had similar sentiments: 'All taxes then, when they pass a certain point, have a tendency to send away persons, and property, and trade, from a country, which if they do, its decline is inevitable' (p. 105). It is true that rent and taxes can stimulate industry, he says, but if carried too far 'the people become degraded, disheartened, their independent spirit is lost and broken, and industry flies away' (p. 108). Taxation prolongs the operation of necessity. Human exertion, he argues, contrary to Hume and Smith, is like a spring pressed upon; beyond a certain point it gives way: 'it ought to be a general rule to lay on as few taxes as possible; and the giving as little trouble and derangement to the contributor as may be...' (p. 115). Thus, in Playfair's opinion, profits tax is a clear case of a potentially burdensome tax.

With profits taxes, and indeed any tax, it is crucial to select an appropriate rate and levy high rates very carefully and gradually. Andrew Hamilton (1793) raised the issue of the relationship between profit rates and tax avoidance. If profit rates were 40 or 50 per cent, he says, there would be more temptation to avoid a duty than if it were 10 or 15 per cent. He also argues that it is easier to collect tax when there are fewer firms: a trader with a large capital can evade the profits tax through lowering his profits.

Indirect taxation

Much of what the Scots wrote about taxation concerned indirect taxation. In general, Smith, painstakingly examining many different types of tax, thinks that most types have bad effects on factor incomes, achieve little and can be collected with varying difficulty. He does not like variable land taxes, which are not based on fixed values, as they would discourage land improvement, nor taxes on agricultural produce, which ultimately fall on the landlord as the farmer will reduce his rent to pay them. But it is easier to tax land than interest because it cannot be concealed or moved elsewhere. He also criticizes window taxes for tending to promote lower rents, and sees taxes on necessaries, including under the Corn Laws, as like a tax on wages. Taxes on luxuries, he argues, only raise the prices of such goods while high tariffs often raise little revenue because of smuggling. He was aware of the wider and not always expected effects of taxation. In *LJ* Smith writes, 'It is said indeed that taxes on those liquors prevent drunkeness, but the conterary is probably the case. By raising their price they make them an object of their desire, and such as good-fellowship requires them to press on their guests. We see accordingly that in Spain and France, where all liquors are very cheap, there is less drunkeness than in this country' (p. 363).

In *LJ* Smith says that taxes are either on possessions or consumption, and he goes on to repeat common concerns. Possessions, he wrote, can be land, stock or money. In his view it is easy to tax land as it is evident what quantity everyone possesses (a curious view as there are many disputes over ownership), but to tax stock or money means looking at a tradesman's books, an infringement of liberty which could ruin his credit. 'When taxes are laid upon commodities, their prices must rise, the concurrence of tradesmen must be prevented, an artificial dearth occasioned, less industry excited, and a smaller quantity of goods produced' (p. 531). Also, 'The taxes on consumptions are not so much murmured against, because they are laid upon the merchant, who lays them on the price of goods, and thus they are insensibly paid by the people' (p. 533). He argues that people are not ruined as much by taxes on consumptions as on possessions as it is always possible to reduce consumptions. Smith points out that the English are the best financiers in Europe through not using tax farmers: it costs £300,000 in England to raise £7 million but in France, of 24 millions raised, half goes to the costs of levying and the profits of the farmer.

Craig (1814) said taxes on sales are direct if they fall on the seller, indirect if they ultimately fall on the consumer. He had a myriad of objections to indirect taxes. In his opinion, sales tax on trade with a slow turnover, for example, trade to the East Indies or South America, has a trifling effect, but a small retailer could be turning over circulating capital once a month and paying a great deal of tax. A tax on the sales of houses is repugnant, he writes, and adds to the misfortune of the poor as it is usually they who have to sell houses and lands. Furthermore, the window tax, which does not reflect the size or value of a house, is unfair because an additional window makes a greater difference on a small house than on an elegant mansion: this is an application of a diminishing utility argument. A similar tax, the hearth tax, is, he says, unjust as the size of rooms is not taken into account; however, this was abandoned as it required internal inspection of houses. According to Craig, articles such as jewels and paintings denoting affluence and splendour should be taxed but valuation problems make it difficult to do so. Taxation on litigation, he thought, would further diminish national wealth because the costs of going to law are paid out of capital. He argued that it is unfortunate that only taxes on necessaries can raise much tax revenue as there is so much competition to produce necessaries that a moderate tax could ruin manufacturers. Furthermore, a tax on necessaries does not increase the wages fund or reduce labour supply: it will make workmen more frugal. Overall, Craig wanted to tax the luxuries exclusively used by the rich. A tax on brewing, as he argued, does not affect the rich who brew their own.

A problem with indirect taxation was the possibility of tax evasion. Anderson's *The Bee*, 16 February 1791, discusses smuggling, which is a double tax on the public: new taxes are needed to meet the revenue *and* to pay for extra revenue officers. Craig had a different attitude from his contemporaries on smuggling, which he thought does little harm to anyone and offends against positive rather than natural law. According to him, customs officers could be given the incentive of receiving a portion of contraband goods but the cost of repressing smugglers should not take too high a proportion of the tax yield. Competition from illicit trade in smuggled goods, in his opinion, leads to the gradual corruption of the fair trader. He thus suggested that smuggling could be ended by reducing duties, as then the risk would be greater than the profits from smuggling.

In a summary of the many ills arising from indirect taxation, Buchanan (1844) includes its excessive costs: expensive establishments for collection, the employment of more revenue officers to catch smugglers and vexatious interference with most important branches of industry. Also, the property tax, collected once a year, fell heavily on small traders. Detailed taxes on manufacturing, he wrote, interfere to the extent of stopping invention and new modes of working; therefore, although taxation can create revenue, it is also an instrument of monopoly through protective duties and tariffs.

The malt tax was a controversial indirect tax and the cause of social unrest when it was reinstated in Scotland in 1714. Hume wrote in *Of Public Credit*: 'In GREAT BRITAIN, the excises upon malt and beer afford a large revenue; because the operations of malting and brewing are tedious, and are impossible to be concealed; and at the same time, these commodities are not so absolutely necessary to life, as that the raising of their price would very much affect the poorer sort' (1987: 356). He used the practical argument that the tax base could not be concealed and the moral argument that it was better to tax inessentials.

Smith, in *WN*, suggested the lowering of the malt tax and the increasing of the tax on brewing. Sinclair (1834), writing about the need to repeal the malt tax, states that it is laid on the land and labour producing it, on the malt and hops, on the maltster and on the publican who has a licence. Of the final price of malt liquor, he writes, three quarters was taxed. It thus burdens land, reduces the annual consumption of malt, and encourages home production of spirits and the resulting committing of crimes. He thought that, instead of the malt tax in the eighteenth century, there could have been borrowing to reduce taxation and a reduced tax, say on sugar, to increase consumption and maintain total tax revenue. But taxing alcohol was an attractive proposition because it is not taxation of a necessity yet is sure to produce a steady stream of revenue. In some form or other it is unlikely ever to be abolished.

Income tax

A fiscal innovation of the eighteenth century, the income tax, was introduced by William Pitt the Younger in 1799 as a graduated tax starting at two old pennies per pound (1/120th) for incomes over £60 and rising to two shillings in the pound (a tenth) on incomes over £200. It was temporarily removed in 1802, revived in 1803, abolished in 1816 then permanently reintroduced in 1842. Originally the term 'income tax' was avoided in favour of the vaguer description in the statute of 'a contribution of the profits arising from property. This new tax fell on professions, trades and offices', but Peel in 1842 robustly used the words 'income tax' in his legislation.

Many supported income taxes because an income tax was easy to design and had a progressive element. In *Letters of Sidney*, Millar laid down the principle that the British system of taxation is unjust 'unless the proportion which taxes bear to the property of each contributor increases progressively according to the amount of his property' (1796: 73). In a description of the tax system he writes

> The taxes which each inhabitant pays to the state consist of the quantity of enjoyment of which [he] deprives himself for the good of the community. The exertions of government secure to him all his enjoyments and enable him to follow out in quiet such measures as he thinks may increase his comforts... Society may be viewed as a great commercial concern in which the input stock ought to be proportioned to the share of profits to be afterwards drawn by each individual.
>
> (p. 74)

He uses the sacrifice principle: income taxes have an imperceptible effect on people with higher incomes and are just because 'the advantages he derives from government are always increasing and the price he pays for these is always diminishing' (p. 78).

Millar, aware that the purpose of much taxation then was to execute the basic functions of the state, in support of the principle of progression, thought it reasonable for those in the middling ranks of society to pay for general protection but not for them to meet the expenses caused by the immense wealth of others. Progressive taxes should be on income, he believed, because it is more difficult to have graduated taxes on consumables than on assessed incomes. If there were taxes on commodities then he thought it best to have them on luxuries and superfluities but not set too high to prevent consumption or encourage smuggling. Millar fails to see that there could be different tax rates for different price ranges of a good and that taxing luxuries consumed by the rich, and not necessaries bought by the poor, is following the progressive principle.

Was the income tax related to ability to pay? Anderson (1799), writing about the income tax, says that the backbone of the countryside consists of gentlemen with £200 to £500 per annum who reside on their estates and would find a tax of 10 per cent on their income intolerable, leading them to have to sell out to merchants, who in turn would create large estates and leave villages deserted through their neglect of agriculture. His reasoning is an argument about particular tax rates not the tax itself.

In a more detailed analysis of the taxation of incomes Sinclair (1799) argued in favour of a 0.5 per cent tax on capital and a greater, 5 per cent, tax on income. As it is difficult to estimate income and the value of capital, a blended tax system is, he claimed, needed. But he did realize that the better-off could have problems paying such a tax as a landowner already has burdens such as the legal expenses of preserving his property, expenditure on improving his estates and working unpaid as a Justice of the Peace or in another capacity. He also recognized that professional persons can be affected by sickness and public calamity and therefore their income tax of 10 per cent will be paid out of savings, reduced expenditures, reduced capital or borrowings and could lead to emigration, which would reduce the opulence of Britain, diminish the revenue from existing indirect taxes and raise the price of necessaries. He thought it unjust to tax people with property abroad in places such as Ireland and the West Indies as these countries have their own legislatures and, in his view, it was better to lose some tax revenue than have strict regulations that drive men to perjury. Instead of an income tax, which would give a minister power over all the property of the country and would be difficult to get rid of if it were imposed, he put forward the idea that some expenditure economies were possible, as in the navy.

Another critic of the income tax, Lauderdale, argues that an income tax of 10 per cent would decrease national expenditure and affect tax revenue in the coming year:

> Every man of any experience must acknowledge, that the increased price of commodities and the habits of the wealthy in this country, lead them to

> live pretty generally up to their income. In the present state of the monied market, it is perfectly impossible they should borrow; the sum, then, they are assessed, must of necessity be raised by a saving of income. This reduction of annual expenditure must proportionately diminish the receipts of the lower classes, not only for the time; but as habits of economy, when adopted, from whatever cause, are seldom relinquished . . . most probably for ever.
>
> (1798: 35–6)

Furthermore, 'the habit of abstinence which this projected reduction of income for two years and a quarter will generate, may not be easily conquered' (1798: 23). That taxing the rich is bad for the poor who do not benefit from their expenditure is a familiar argument of Lauderdale the macroeconomist but he fails to see that tax revenues can be spent by governments and stimulate a national economy.

Craig added to the mound of opinions of the income tax. Ensuring progression in the tax system was Craig's position in his 1814 book; he wrote that tax burdens on individuals should increase in quick progression according to wealth. The basis of his argument is that all enjoyments can be classified as necessaries, gratifications or superfluities. Taxes on necessaries cause distress and cramp the powers and energies of man; gratifications give pleasure to the senses and delight to the mind so deprivation of them is an evil affecting happiness; superfluities are valued solely as a proof of wealth, a preservation of rank that can be lost without privation.

Taking a broader view of direct taxation, Alison (1850) argued in *Blackwood's Magazine*, February 1847 (p. 625), that a more just system of direct taxation would (1) equalize succession tax on land and personal estate and lower it to half and (2) equalize all direct taxes levied on landed and personal estates. Alison noted that taxes fall with 'peculiar force' upon the growth of capital because they tax the excess of income over necessary expenditure of the middling ranks to 'dry up those little streams whose accumulated flow form the great reservoir of national opulence' (1840 I: 165). Taxation can become so oppressive that the population rebels and the state collapses, as happened in Athens and Rome.

Joseph Hume, the Radical MP, argued, according to Chancellor (1986), for a move from indirect to direct taxation but disliked a graduated income tax, favouring an abolition of assessed taxes on property and the reduction of import duties, permitting the excise to disappear. His proposals reflect the view that indirect taxes are necessarily regressive, which we have seen fails to consider the possibility of multilayered taxes discriminating in favour of the poor, for example, through exempting articles of mass consumption from taxation. Hume might have been hinting at this: in general he wanted lower taxation through lower government expenditure as the route to cutting taxes on candles, soap, paper, windows and trade.

One problem with an income tax is that it cannot produce much tax revenue unless it is levied widely: there are not enough high incomes to avoid taxing people who are not very well off. Realistically, Craig (1814) appreciated this, arguing that progressive taxes on property fall more heavily on the middle ranks of society; a tax as a fixed proportion of income hurts low income groups more than high income groups.

Tax reform

Most writers on taxation were keen to alter the existing tax system. These Scots, many of them engaged in public life, were not short of fundamental proposals for reform, whether to restructure the tax system according to basic principles or to tinker with the taxes in force. With regard to tax theory Steuart, for example, as Sen (1957) mentions, had a benefit theory linked to taxable capacity but opposed the idea of reducing the tax system to a single tax whether on land or trade. Craig wanted an equality of sacrifice with gradation and differentiation through progressive taxes, and saw tinkering with the tax system as the principal way to reform, whether by changing the range of taxation or tax rates to make them more acceptable.

Which goods to tax is a recurrent theme of the reformers. Sinclair thought it wrong to say there should be taxes on the necessaries of life, an uncontroversial idea for few people would dare to recommend taxes that caused starvation. But there is a stimulus from high taxes:

> if manufacturers, from the cheapness of living, could maintain themselves and their families by the labour of only three days in the week, few could resist the temptation, though in consequence of being idle for the other four they would become less expert in their profession.
>
> (1790: 127)

He noted that in manufacturing towns commerce flourishes best and workmen are most assiduous when the price of provisions is high.

A tax reformer usually has a list of taxes to scrap and new taxes to replace them. Sinclair suggested that the existing revenue could be improved by regulating smuggling, consolidating custom house dues, consolidating malt, beer and ale taxes into a malt tax, revaluing houses, using fines and forfeitures not to benefit individuals but to improve North Britain (Scotland) or help the general purpose of the empire, replace coal and salt taxes and revive the hearth tax, and remove tax on drugs and extend the tax on medicines in order to shift the tax burden to the wealthy.

Inventively he proposes new taxes – an income tax in the form of a stamp duty on all receipts of income, an excise on dress (possibly only on male workers as it could fall too heavily on females), an additional tax on sugar, an additional excise on ale, revival of tax on cider and perry, a poll tax in times of public misfortune, a professional tax starting at a moderate rate at the beginning of a career, a licence and profits tax of 25 per cent on stockbrokers, a tax on bachelors, a tax on absentees living abroad, a tax on parliamentary representation of 10 shillings per annum per voter and £100 per district with an MP, a tax on corporations of 25 per cent, taxes on the church, including on a plurality of livings and non-resident clergy, a tax on public amusements in the form of a stamp duty on all admission tickets, a dog tax of 5 shillings per dog, a hide tax but not on pigs so the poor could get cheap meat, tax on half the income of the dead, and miscellaneous taxes on many items, including carpets, lodgings and wearing watches. This amount of detail makes these proposals resemble a modern budget. They have the advantage that they impact on small groups who would not protest as much as the population at large if a general tax were imposed.

Changing tax rates can increase tax yields and, because they are more reasonable, encourage compliance. The most extreme cases of high rate taxes crying out for reform were the customs duties on spirits and tea. Because the duties encouraged extensive smuggling these high rates of tax were widely criticized. The policy response from William Pitt the Younger was the Commutation Act 1784 to reduce custom and excise duties on tea from 119 per cent to 12.5 per cent to destroy tea smuggling and to create for the East India Company a complete monopoly of tea imports. It was estimated that a tax shortfall of £600,000 to £900,000 had to be replaced by a window tax to restore tax revenues. This reform reflected Andrew Hamilton's warning against what he called the 'over-tax system' (1793: 5), which levied taxes so highly that it was impossible to collect them and caused an encouragement of smuggling. Beer tax was an example he cited. He noted that in the 1790s there were seven duties on ale, six on malt, nine on foreign spirits and nine on distilling. With hints of what later was to be called the Laffer curve, a diagram which shows that tax revenues rise with increased tax rates until a rate is reached at which tax revenues have reached a maximum so further tax rises are pointless, he pointed out a 'decrease of quantities on the Revenue books... when the high duties began to operate' (p. 16). Reduced rates of tax can increase revenue, as happened in 1745 when the inland duty on tea fell from four shillings (20p) in the pound to one shilling (5p) and 25 per cent on the price, causing the revenue to almost double. The blessings of prosperity are diffused when the real price of articles falls. Also, when there is over-taxation the cost of tax collection can be as much as twentyfold higher. One could argue that Hume, too, in his *Of the Balance of Trade* (1987), suggests the Laffer curve by saying that a lowering of the duty on wine increased tax revenue.

These reformers recognized the futility of levying taxes with a predictable low yield: the cost of collection in extreme cases could be higher than the tax revenue. A drastic solution was to abolish the taxes that yielded little revenue. Sinclair, for example, discusses a proposal to exempt a district from all existing taxes in return for it paying into the Exchequer the net amount it now gives, thus saving the cost of collection. But this would be difficult for people to pay – paying in a lump sum would make the amount look enormous compared with a gradual levying of taxes, and would still cost something to collect.

Anderson (1785) thought the tax system in Scotland oppressive and unproductive. On 26 December 1792 in *The Bee* it was noted that article XIV of the Treaty of Union required the parliament of Great Britain to have regard to the circumstances and abilities of every part of the united kingdoms – an invitation to consider the position in Scotland. In the Scottish Highlands it then cost £10,000 just to collect customs dues; in nine northern Scottish counties it cost more to collect customs than the revenue raised. It was more difficult to collect taxes in Scotland than in England because the population was dispersed and poor in many parts of Scotland, especially the northern and western coasts of Scotland. In Scotland two-thirds of persons did not pay tax; the whole of tax revenue came from the area between the Clyde and the Forth. A solution could be to charge 800,000 people in Scotland £3 annually in order to raise £2.4 million, but ultimately the way to increase tax revenue would be to have a prosperous people with a growing population.

Anderson wanted recognition of the peculiar circumstances of Scotland in the tax system, and cited the case of the coal tax to make his point. Before 1707 there was a duty on the coal carried coastwise to wealthy London, which raised much tax revenue for Scotland: the union had put an end to that. Poor northern Scotland could not escape the British tax, lacking the major rivers of England and thus being dependent on sea transport. He argued that Scotland would be better off if taxed like the Irish at about a fifth of the usual coal duty, a move which helped the Irish rock salt industry.

A writer, probably Anderson, in *The Bee*, 19 January 1791, recognizing that 'Taxes may injure the *health*, the *population*, the *industry*, the *knowledge* or the *morals* of mankind' suggested that 'The *number* of taxes should be as small as possible, in order to diminish the number of the *tax gatherers*: For they are a class of men of no *direct* use in a state' (p. 86).

Believing that moderate taxes can stimulate greater exertions, the writer wanted governments to use the tax system to discourage unemployment and idleness. He thought every tax is oppressive to certain persons and wanted to reconcile general taxation with justice through taxpayers being able to apply to a 'board of exemption'. Grounds for exemption from tax would include having a large number of children or being engaged in scholarly activity. He realized that in a prosperous nation additional taxes mean increased production by the industrious class.

Excise duties on manufactures, according to Craig, are easy to administer as officers are all over the country and the goods can be traced from manufacture to the delivery to the consumer. However, excises are regarded as a repugnant attack on liberty as inspectors come to business premises, and retail prices are simply increased to pay a sales tax. The poor, he argued, pay more tax as goods pass through more hands – retailers and intermediate dealers – but imported luxuries for the rich are sold only once in Britain. To avoid the costs of an inspectorate he suggested that there could be a general assessment based on dealers giving an annual account of their sales. New taxes on trade can be (1) a tax on each clerk employed in business, which would be paid by the master,

(2) a tax on the number and size of utensils employed by the manufacturer, and (3) a duty proportionate to the rent of the retailer.

> the chief and permanent effect of an increase of taxes is not to diminish wealth, but to deprive the citizens of part of those luxuries or comforts ... they might formerly have enjoyed.
>
> (1814: 359)

Another supporter of low taxes was Benjamin Bell (1749–1806), a surgeon and farmer from Dumfries who, apart from writing books on ulcers and gonorrhoea, interested himself in taxation. He looks at the effect of indirect and direct taxes on the rich and the poor. In his work of 1797 he protested against a proposed tax on road tolls, which he thought would be ruinous to manufacturing, obstruct land development, prevent the formation of new roads, affect the poor who would have to pay more for fuel, and especially hit Glasgow and Paisley who would pay nine tolls on the meal brought from east Scotland. Even tolls on carriages for pleasure, as approved by Adam Smith, were criticized by Bell for not being fair and direct. He wanted public burdens to fall entirely on the opulent and saw that indirect taxation could be progressive. He listed items suitable for taxation: superfluities of the table, dealing in luxuries, public amusements, china, watches, silk stockings, deer parks and hothouses. A tax on watches, owned by a quarter of the population, would, by itself, produce a large tax revenue. Later, in his three essays of 1799, he thought taxation on consumption had gone too far and should be replaced by income taxation, which is more reliable and less expensive than other taxes to collect. He wanted a mild modification of the existing tax: a multi-band tax at 8.5 per cent for incomes of £60–£100, gradually rising to 10 per cent for incomes over £200. An income tax should not, he argued, discriminate between different types of income and should make possible the annihilation of land tax. Having commissioners at the parish level would, he suggested, ensure all incomes were detected.

In his *An Enquiry into the Extent and Stability of National Resources* (1808) Chalmers, according to Roberts (1945), virtually recommended reducing taxable income as a way of diminishing the tax burden, arguing that incomes should be taxed net of expenditure on necessaries and a personal tax-free allowance, and that such taxes should be used to finance judicious state expenditure. This anticipates the modern way of taxing personal incomes.

Tax reform was related to tax incidence. In Hamilton's opinion the landlord would pay less tax and the Exchequer receive more revenue if the tax were imposed on the landlord and not indirectly on the necessary goods consumed by a labourer. Generally he believed that taxes on merchandise are passed on in higher prices with no effect on profits, but he did contemplate cases of merchants unable to pass higher taxes on in higher prices, causing them to cut supply with the result of a later rise in prices and increased competition.

Overall, he thought that improvements and economic growth would enable us to bear higher taxes.

Changing tax rates, abolishing some existing taxes and introducing new ones was certainly reform but not drastic enough for some critics of the tax system. Sinclair, whilst admitting there were objections to particular taxes, wanted to adopt the fundamental reform of reducing the need for much taxation by obtaining revenue from other sources. He wanted the government to embark on lucrative projects such as voluntary contributions to pay off the national debt, employment of the poor, a charge for manufacturing coins, a state-only note issue with notes issued for a year with 5 per cent interest, the sale of guinea lottery tickets to richer households, the granting of life annuities, converting temporary annuities into permanent stock, the sale of minor offices, the sale of Crown lands, the takeover of undemanded stocks, and a 50 per cent profits tax on the Bank. He also suggested that the public should take over the possessions and debts of the East India Company. These were interesting proposals but he did not prove whether they were as reliable as major taxes with a steady flow of revenue.

The tax system could also be fundamentally reformed by concentrating on a single tax and abolishing the rest. Would land taxation alone be sufficient in this role? Dalrymple (1784), aware of contemporary proposals for tax reform, had dismissed the idea of meeting the demands of government through a land tax of two shillings and sixpence in the pound, fearing that the tax rate would soon rise to four shillings. A particular criticism he had of the tax was its burdensome nature because present leases had been granted in time of peace and circumstances had changed: agricultural produce had fallen, foreign necessaries were dear, and payments uncertain and the expense of improvements deducted from them. On the contrary Samuel Read wanted a drastic simplification of the tax system through the imposition of a land tax at 12 per cent to finance all of government, excepting in time of an emergency. A tax of an eighth of the rack rent would provide a surplus for making roads, canals and creating a war chest. In the case of the foundation of new states and colonies this tax would be imposed; in existing states it could replace existing taxation. The poor rate could be replaced by a tax on all property and incomes so it would not fall only on land. Also, he raised an often neglected point: the democratic approval of taxation. Read writes 'in the imposition of *taxes*, as well as in other affairs of government in general, the sense and suffrage of the people ought to be taken as widely and extensively as circumstances will permit, that they may be sanctioned by voluntary consent, or appointment of the *greater number* at least, without which they cannot be altogether just or unexceptionable' (1829: 90). (He cites Hume's essay *On the Perfect Commonwealth* for stating that the extension of the suffrage to parish meetings would not result in mob rule.)

These writers were imaginative in their proposals but many ideas were too extreme to be implemented. The more moderate course of reasoning about taxation often amounted to no more than a plea for a movement from indirect to direct taxation in order to achieve a system based principally on an ability to pay. Implementing a change from indirect to direct taxation could represent a great movement to post-tax equality but this takes the simplistic view that indirect taxation is inherently regressive, that is, it falls proportionately more on those with lower incomes. There is scope for graduated indirect taxes and for exemption of basic goods, such as food, used by the poor. Many of these suggested tax reforms are still to occur but, as Ferguson (2001) points out, after 1815 the British financial system had settled down and had four defining characteristics. There was a professional tax-collecting bureaucracy, parliamentary and public scrutiny of budgets, a funded national debt guaranteed by parliament, and a central bank with a partial monopoly over the note issue.

The Scots set the agenda for tax debates that continue to this day. They were aware that tax is only one of the possible sources of revenue for a government and would become crucial to public revenues when the state expanded its activities and thus its expenditure. Raising more taxation can be done through increasing the types of tax or increasing tax rates. There are dangers in doing both of these as the more complex the tax structure, the greater the effects on the firms and people who pay them. Conscientiously, these writers looked at tax after tax individually. Taxes could discourage effort on the part of taxpayers or might serve as an incentive to reach a desired level of income. Overall the burden of tax could be oppressive for a society as a whole or for particular groups, especially the poor. There was awareness of what was later to be called the Laffer curve, which warns that if tax rates rise to a high level total tax revenue will fall, and that, in extreme cases, capital and labour would leave a country – the ultimate way to avoid a tax.

The study of taxation involves the examination of a mass of details; however, public finance as a subject has coherence if one considers the 'canons' of taxation, ably set out for all time by Steuart, Smith and Ferguson. These writers repeatedly discussed the perpetual issues of taxation: their collection, their type – especially whether direct or indirect – their incidence on one group rather than another and on the population at large, and the complexity of their range.

National debt

The debt accumulated by successive governments in the eighteenth and early nineteenth centuries concerned both governments and contemporary economic commentators. In Scotland at the time of the Union of Parliaments in 1707 there were fears that Scotland would be dragged down by participation in England's debts, hence the special provision through the Equivalent for them in the Act of Union.

In this period war was the cause of much accumulation of national debt, unlike in previous centuries when it was a means of acquiring wealth through seizing slaves, treasure, prisoners and land. The wealth gained through colonial acquisitions was not enough to prevent the increase in the national debt and to cut the net costs of government.

During the reign of Queen Anne (1702–14), the national debt rose by £23 million, and further grew to £52 million in 1727, £132 million in 1763 after the Seven Years' War and £245 million at the conclusion of the American War in 1783. It slightly reduced to £239 million at the start of the French War but increased by £592 million during the war. John Ramsay McCulloch (1789–64), one of the most prolific writers on economics in the nineteenth century, completes this account of Britain's journey into debt (1863) by recording that it was £800,770,238 in 1862. After an education at Edinburgh University McCulloch was editor of *The Scotsman* (1871–21), an early contributor to the *Edinburgh Review* and *Encyclopaedia Britannica*, professor of political economy at University College, London (1828–37), and then comptroller of the Stationery Office from 1837. Elizabeth Schumpeter (1938), considering the split in government finance between taxation and net borrowing, noted that in the early eighteenth century the latter hardly occurred but that in the 1756 to 1800 period it was over 40 per cent of government income; during 1803–15 it came down to 21.6 per cent. The worst year was 1797 when 65.3 per cent was obtained through loans. Another student of debt, Fetter (1945), provides a survey of debt accumulation over the period 1688–1802. During this time, he notes that there were six sub-periods of war, covering sixty-three years when public debt increased at an accelerating rate. In the financial accounts of Great Britain, Stettner (1945) notes that the national debt grew from £16.4 million in the year 1701 to £78.3 million in 1748, to £252.5 million in 1793. Interest payments assumed a higher proportion of government expenditure: even in the peacetime period of 1784–92 it amounted to 56 per cent of government expenditure (O'Brien 1988).

The rising volume of national debt had its critics. In his essay *Of Civil Liberty* Hume regards free governments as degenerate when they indulge in 'the practice of contracting debt, and mortgaging the public revenues, by which taxes may, in time, become altogether intolerable, and all the property of the state be brought into the hands of the public' (1987: 95). Smith adds to the attack on the accumulation of debt in *WN*:

> Great nations are never impoverished by private, though they sometimes are by publick prodigality and misconduct. The whole, or almost the whole publick revenue, is in most countries employed in maintaining unproductive hands.
>
> (p. 342)

He identifies the church and the armed forces as less productive uses of government expenditure and reminds us that governmental prolificacy impacts upon ordinary people.

The argument against the national debt

In his essay *Of Public Credit* (1987) Hume's list of the disadvantages of a national debt is long, and he identifies the narrowly economic and wider social implications of the national debt. First, he argues, national debts cause a migration of people and riches from the provinces, where the interest is paid, to the capital city, where there is disproportionate benefit from interest payments. Second, public stocks, being paper credit, have a host of disadvantages. Third, the taxes to pay the interest on the debt either raise the price of labour or oppress the poor. Fourth, as foreigners hold much of Scottish national debt the British people becomes subordinate to them, and this occasionally causes the migration of British people and riches. Fifth, as most of the public funds are held by idle people they encourage a useless and inactive life. Winch (1978) thinks *Of Public Credit* alarmist and lacking the balance and philosophic stance of Hume's other essays, and, interestingly, Hume did modify his remarks later. Hume writes that as far as national debt is concerned, 'our modern expedient, which has become very general, is to mortgage the public revenues, and to trust that posterity will pay off the incumbrances contracted by their ancestors' (1987: 350), but goes on to admit that in modern times debt has been confined within reasonable bounds of 'frugality, in time of peace, as to discharge the debts incurred by an expensive war' and that 'war is attended with every destructive circumstance; loss of men, encrease of taxes, decay of commerce, dissipation of money, devastation by sea and land' (p. 351).

Other specific arguments against the national debt abounded. An early critic of debt accumulation, Murray, argued in his analysis of the pattern of bond holding that an increase in public debt threatens a domestic currency: 'The Dividends drawn by Foreigners diminish the quantity of *Specie*... A diminution of the funds engaged for the payment of the interest of these debts, would occasion Runs on Banks, and hurt their Credit' (1758: 33), while non-payment of dividends would lead to a 'universal stoppage of payment'. This view put the difficulties posed by a national debt in a broader context.

A national debt could cause the spiralling of taxation. Anderson (1785), giving Spain as an example, warned that a large government debt comes from unwise conduct and necessitates taxes on raw materials and even on manufactures. Consequently, the tax revenue declines and smuggling rises, which encourages the industry of a foreign state, not Britain's own. In 1789 he warned that as the national debt rises there is further oppression of industry through this higher taxation to service the national debt: the price of manufactures rises affecting Britain's position in markets. *The Bee*, 19 January 1791, argued that the public debt diminishes a present evil to transfer it to future generations. 'Every age ought to pay for its own wars, and then statesmen will be careful on what grounds they involve a people in war...' (p. 86).

Lauderdale also complained that the raising of large sums by funding kept taxes low in the short run but that the annual charges for servicing debt were more than the tax revenue collected, requiring further taxes.

Increasing the national debt could distort public finance, avoiding a purge of unnecessary public expenditure. In his pamphlet (1783c) Dalrymple, worried about the national debt, noted that there was a falling off of revenue because the East India Company was not paying its dues, once £1.2 million annually.

He saw little scope for economies in public expenditure apart from in sinecures and payments to office-holders but recognized that long-established commitments made retrenchment difficult. The real economy, he asserted, is to avoid war: a point he had made in his *Facts and their consequences* (1782). The abolition of corruption would also help. Another solution in his 1784 pamphlet was to get rid of foreign possessions, especially Canada and Gibraltar, to save £3.9 million annually, and to help American Loyalists through money not through more colonization. Overall the policy should, he argued, be one of achieving a collective balance between peacetime incomes and the expenditure of the nation. Dalrymple thus had a practical plan for reducing the national debt and a long-term policy to avoid war.

Writing in 1814, Robert Hamilton (1743–1829), a partner in the family paper mill business before becoming rector of Perth Academy in 1769, wanted a strategy to eliminate the need for a state to go into debt. There should, he contended, be surplus revenue in peacetime to pay off war debts or to finance future wars; taxes should be higher in wartime because it is best to tax rather than to borrow to finance the extra expenditure. But he recognized that there are limits to taxation as income is still needed to supply the necessaries of life; he thus argued that some creation of debt should be permitted.

National debt, by causing a financial revolution, changed society and created a new moneyed class. Adam Ferguson, like David Hume, was aware of the change in the structure of the national economy caused by the building up the national debt. In his *Principles*, 1792, he argued that it is nations with ample credit which accumulate debt and that a new trade arises – trade in the public debt, which adds nothing to the national wealth. Sinclair thought that public debts corrupt manners, encourage idleness and immoderate expenses, and cause the population to decline; a selfish moneyed interest of gambling stock jobbers is created, officers have to be appointed to manage the national debt, and foreign stockholding makes us a tributary of another state. He realized that is difficult to get rid of the debt without a public bankruptcy, and that large public debts weaken a nation. Similarly, Playfair wrote that the national debt is 'the great disease of our constitution' (1787: 3). A large portion of industry supports 'a new order of men, who have an ideal property in the funds' (p. 8). Britain was the first country to have accumulated so much debt, he writes, dividing the nation into the industrious and the idle, and every increase in the national debt increases those who are idle and lays burdens on the industrious, crushing industry and trade.

The financial implications of the national debt did not escape these writers. Horner reported that 'during the war we had borrowed money, which was then of small value; and we were now obliged to pay it at a high value. This was the most formidable evil which threatened our finances' (1843 I: 535). He was appalled by the cost of servicing the debt relative to tax revenue collected.

In his 1814 book Craig thought the national debt had a serious impact on capital through converting private capital into immediate government expenditure. The ordinary peace establishment financed out of annual taxes does not diminish national capital but, as Craig realized, current taxes have to be supplemented by borrowing to finance wars. In his view, if war could be financed by current taxation, private parsimony would compensate for public profusion and restore capital. However, during a war, he argued, the reduction in trade allows surplus mercantile capital to be lent to the government and thus, because speculative capital is used productive capital is not diminished. Craig also raised the problems of the bond markets, recognizing that the price of newly issued government stock must fall to sell them, but that if the interest rate is legally fixed then there is little scope for making the bonds attractive. However, he argued, as the price of public stock usually rises when peace returns there is little risk to a banker who subscribes. Consequently, with more borrowing and servicing of the debt and more taxation, the exertions of people will be dampened and the point will come when no more public credit is forthcoming.

In a work of 1821 Samuel Read blames the expenditure of capital in loans during the Napoleonic Wars on higher interest rates, estimating that in 1816 interest rates could have been as low as 2 or 2.5 per cent, and in a later work in 1829 he argued that the liquidation of the national debt would benefit the labouring and other classes.

The benefits of debt

In his *Characteristics* of 1758 Wallace argued against the popular mercantilist idea that a state should hoard up reserves to deal with emergencies. If there is an emergency, he wrote, there is not time to tax, thus making it permissible for a government to borrow. He argues that Great Britain was justified in its wars after 1688 and that increasing the national debt was right. Borrowing, he thought, is acceptable not only to protect the country's trade or liberty when faced by an enemy but to pursue a useful scheme such as draining marshes. Borrowing to execute a popular scheme would be financed by a moderate tax on the proceeds of the investment, which would pay the interest and gradually repay the principal. Optimistically, he states that the limit to a country's borrowing is larger than imagined.

Hume, despite his criticisms of debt, could see its advantages: public securities have become a kind of money and traders can hold their cash reserves in them, enabling them to trade with less profit, which 'renders the commodity cheaper, causes a greater consumption, quickens the labour of the common people, and helps to spread arts and industry throughout the whole society' (1987: 353). It is therefore more convenient, in his view, to invest in government bonds (usually called then 'the funds') than in land.

Another supporter of debt, Steuart, used Hume's argument to assert that people are never exhausted by paying a state's creditors, unless the creditors are foreigners, for the payments pass between one private person and another. He argued for high public expenditure, recognizing that people do not generally spend for the benefit of the public as a whole, thus the statesman is required to tax them in order to 'diminish the fund of their prodigality' (*Principles* II: 142): this, in effect, turns meat and drink into harbours, high roads, canals and public buildings. Borrowing in Britain was easy, he wrote, because the more democratic a state the greater its public credit; in France under an absolutist monarchy where there was tampering with the rights of creditors, interest rates were higher to reflect the risk of that interference.

Interestingly, Steuart sets out the principles a statesman should follow in contracting public debt: the population should understand that debt leads to a reduction in some individuals' incomes; it should be made clear that borrowing is for the benefit of the population and lenders should be assured that promises made to them will be honoured. In a sense Steuart is advocating a publicity campaign to make the national debt palatable to the population.

Steuart's general position on the national debt is described by Sen (1957). Steuart was optimistic about the effects of the debt on the national economy, compared with Hume and Smith who failed to see the growth of income and wealth by the end of their century. Although Steuart knew that a rising debt could lead to state bankruptcy he could see the advantages of debt. To keep interest rates low, he wanted funding, not repayment, of the debt. As Stettner said, 'Only Sir James Steuart saw the social and economic implications of the growing public debt. Smith and Hume could not see its essential and positive role' (1945: 452). Steuart indicated his positive attitude by referring to public *credit* rather than public *debt*. Credit, he wrote, is an asset to the community as both taxes and public credit can stimulate trade, industry and employment, and credit can permanently boost the national income and the trade balance. This was in sharp contrast to the general criticism of the classical economists that public debts and taxes oppress an economy. Nevertheless, he did argue for public credit only when circulation was stagnating or as part of war finance. Hume, on the other hand, thought public debt disrupted the existing social structure and created a class of lazy stockholders. But Stettner (1945) notes that Hume did recognize that merchants could benefit by investing part of their funds in government issues, enabling them to trade on a lower profit, to sell at a lower price and boost consumption. With high praise for Steuart, Stettner writes:

> The classical economists failed to see that the needs of a new and growing industrial and commercial middle class required a sound public credit... They were unable to grasp what Steuart saw so clearly – that the steady development of democratic forms was giving the people a stake and voice in the Government which in itself constituted the primary guarantee of responsible and non-arbitrary public debt management, and provided strong safeguards against the debt abuses of an earlier period.
>
> (p. 474)

However, it is rather early to speak about democracy. Would anyone think of an aristocrat like Steuart, a close ally of the autocratic Stuart dynasty, as a democrat?

Interestingly, Smith tried to be balanced in his treatment of the national debt. He was willing to concede that under certain circumstances public debt was sensible. In the *WN*, after noting that in the past sovereigns would maintain a treasure trove as a contingency reserve, he writes 'The want of parsimony in time of peace, imposes the necessity of contracting debt in time of war' (p. 909) because provision has only been made for a peacetime establishment. Practically, he noted that even if extra taxes are imposed at the onset of the war it will be a while before there is revenue from them, making it necessary to borrow to equip armies and fleets. In such a situation the public is glad to lend. If the state is already overburdened with taxes, he writes, it takes something as serious as a war to make a new tax acceptable. Government borrowing, he thought, would be easy because in a commercial society merchants and manufacturers have spare funds to lend. Initially, he suggested bills can be used to finance the debt, later a fund can be assigned for a short period or perpetuity to finance a loan; the Bank of England lends money to the government in anticipation of the inflow of tax revenues.

Although Smith could see cases when borrowing was necessary and easy he does not like the argument in Melon's *Essai* of 1734 (1761) that increasing the national debt is the route to extending trading, multiplying manufactures and cultivating where there is an insufficiency of capital. Smith says Melon ignores the fact that borrowing turns capital into revenue, and that productive labourers have to maintain unproductive labour. The lender, he argues, has his capital replaced with a government security but the country does not have its productive capital replaced.

According to Roberts (1945) Chalmers was concerned about the effect of the national debt, attacking Smith's view that the national debt reduced a nation's capital. Assuming that demand would remain the same, he said in his *The Christian and Civic Economy of Large Towns*, that lost capital would be recouped by lowering wages or reducing consumption. As servicing the national debt would be costly, higher taxes would result, the money supply would increase and prices would rise. Roberts observes 'the element of truth in Chalmers' theory that public expenditure inflates the national liquid money-capital and thus, to some extent, provides the wherewithal for its own finance' (p. 114). But Chalmers ignored the impact of higher government spending on employment and wealth.

The effects of increasing the national debt were a mixture of good and bad. For Sinclair (1790) the largeness of the British public debt, requiring some of it to be raised abroad, had the unfortunate consequence that the interest was distributed to stockholders and did not circulate in the economy; however, he realized that the foreign holding of British debt left more of its capital for domestic purposes and gave foreigners an interest in British happiness and prosperity to ensure they receive an income from Britain.

Financing and redeeming the national debt

A fund for the gradual extinction of the national debt in Great Britain, first introduced by Sir Robert Walpole's government in 1716, suffered from poor management, causing William Pitt, in 1786, to propose a better system. He proposed that there be higher taxes to maintain the fund and restrictions on its use, which were followed until war broke out in 1793. Soon the very existence of the fund was questioned.

Steuart, in his discussion of public credit and public debt (*Principles* Book IV), is, from the outset, concerned with the method of financing the debt, noting that if an annuity (an investment producing equal annual incomes) is set for a fixed number of years it will be self-extinguishing, but if it is a perpetual annuity the servicing of the annuities will gradually absorb the whole income of the state. Previously, as taxes were approved for short periods, loans had to be of short duration too but loans had become long term. Steuart recognized that government securities provided an investment opportunity for stockholders who cannot find a better way of placing their money, but that they also required the raising of taxes to finance the servicing of a debt. Steuart spelt out the severe implications of a large national debt. It has a limit, he contends, when all income from a country's economic activities is given to public creditors. National bankruptcy is not an attractive alternative to servicing the national debt: everyone, not just creditors, would suffer.

In *Of Public Credit* Hume says that, of relying on an increase in debt to finance the government, 'It would scarcely be more imprudent to give a prodigal son a credit in every banker's shop in London, than to impower a statesman to draw bills, in this manner, upon posterity' (1987: 352). Further, in that essay he discusses a work of Archibald Hutcheson (1660–1740), an Irishman who, in *A Collection of Treatises relating to the National Debts and Funds* (1721), proposed the discharge of the national debt by a levy on the public. Hume sought to demolish that idea: he argued that most of the levy would fall on houses and lands because the poor could not contribute and that much wealth is hidden, therefore, if this scheme were implemented it would damage frail public credit.

With that proposal dismissed, Hume considers the effects of a national bankruptcy, the extreme way to finance the national debt. He argues that an absolute prince can declare a bankruptcy when he pleases but that this is more difficult under a free government. People might prefer to lend after the debts had been cleared. The only check the public has is 'the interest of preserving credit; an interest, which may easily be overbalanced by a great debt, and by a difficult and extraordinary emergence, even supposing that credit irrecoverable' (p. 364). In a footnote (p. 364) Hume quotes an estimate that there are, in total, 17,000 native and foreign stockholders who would become the most wretched of people after a bankruptcy, but claims that the landed gentry have better financial roots. Reviewing foreign expedients for cutting the burden of the national debt Hume mentions increasing the money supply, cutting the interest rate and taxing the debt itself but says no one is deceived by such stratagems.

Sinclair, reminding us that twice in the reign of Henry VIII parliament abolished the king's debts, said this was a bad precedent for bankruptcy destroys the bonds of society and property ceases. Advocating that a state go bankrupt to eliminate the national debt also met with Hamilton's disapproval:

> The interest of the public debt is, for the greater part, drawn from the profits of the industrious part of society, and paid to the idle and luxurious. It is drawn from the merchant, the manufacturer, the farmer, and paid to the stockholder. The amount so drawn may be augmented till it occasion the ruin of those who pay it, and involve the whole community in distress and confusion.
>
> (1814: 33)

He saw the dire consequences of bankruptcy, arguing that it is wrong to be in favour of using public bankruptcy to eliminate the national debt as it would cause great distress, leading to internal insurrections and invasions by foreigners who would take advantage of the turmoil. If the national debt were held by foreigners, then bankruptcy, in Hamilton's view, could lead to invasion.

Steuart debates the ways of repaying redeemable debt. He warns that repayment of debt all at once would lead to serious price effects, for example, if much land had to be sold to repay it. Britain had instead used the method of reducing interest upon capital as a way of dealing with the effects of the national debt without decreasing the principal. The golden time to repay debt is, in Steuart's view, at the end of a war when there is much money in circulation and taxes can be raised. Using a lottery to pay off capital should, he argued, occur only when an increase in the money supply reduces interest rates.

Ogilvie (1781) argued that landed property is ultimately responsible for all debts and thus for redeeming it. He suggested there could be a repayment of the national debt at fixed periods by landlords and that, if land holdings were equalized, everyone would be equally responsible for the national debt.

Setting up a fund to pay off the national debt was the principal scheme offered to cope with the national debt but it needed associated measures. Sinclair (1790) sets out the principles of a beneficial funding system: the public pays only the original principal and should be allowed to pay off the debt over five to seven years if money could be borrowed at a lower interest rate; and wars should be financed by perpetual annuities because moneylenders could charge more for an uncertain contingency such as life. He wanted an unalienable sinking fund financed by taxing every propertied person in England at death half his clear income; the management of this sinking fund was to be by a special committee, individuals without relatives would be encouraged to leave fortune and property to the public, and careful checks would be taken to avoid wasting the money borrowed. He sees the disadvantages of the funding system – a nation is encouraged to be reckless, even going to war, and is at the mercy of the moneylenders; additional taxes are needed to finance even state borrowing for investment in successful enterprises. Sinclair's proposals for the repayment of the public debts included the conversion of the land tax into a rent charge, the issue of annuities for life, a 10 per cent tax on the net personal estate of all inhabitants and an excise duty of apparel until all the national debt was paid off. His analysis of debt redemption usefully contrasted funding with other options.

The sinking fund plan established in 1786 was, Playfair (1807) thought, the most likely way to relieve Britain's financial distress. In future, debts should be raised through annuities, which would be shorter at the beginning than at the end of a war, as people find it easier to pay at the beginning of the war. While interest on annuities is, he argued, much higher than on perpetual loans, over time it is cheaper to have annuities.

A wide-ranging attack on funding came from Lauderdale. What is remarkable is his ability to see the debt in a macroeconomic framework and not just as a problem of public finance. In a pamphlet (1798) he showed his scepticism about funding and other contemporary proposals for coping with the national debt. He thought that the funding system had some merit in defraying costs of modern warfare but that it would push up interest rates, making it impossible to be a borrower. Most of the associated tax proposals were, he believed, dubious: the property income tax was based on imperfect knowledge; a tax on income would reduce consumption and profits; and a tax on profits would fail to distinguish between the rentier and the industrious capitalist. Taxing the rich more would, he wrote, affect the poor when the rich reduced their expenditure. Instead of more taxation, he believed that a way of coping with debt would be to reduce expenditure through abandoning those colonies too difficult to defend.

In his *Inquiry* of 1804 Lauderdale was concerned that contributions to the sinking fund made to reduce the national debt could affect the national economy. He was critical of Pitt's scheme of 1786 to contribute 4 million pounds annually to the sinking fund because, in his view, the management of the national debt had moved the distribution of property away from what was natural and most advantageous:

> the funding System therefore Seems to operate as a means of conveying a large and important portion of the National Property from that State in which a total absence of regulation and restraint secures its natural activity, and of course ensures the exertion of its productive qualities.
>
> (1804a: 164)

Again the macroeconomic consequences concerned Lauderdale. Unlike government expenditure on warfare, which generates demand for commodities, raising money from the public to reduce the national debt will, he argued, have a depressing effect on national demand, with nothing to compensate for this increased saving while Britain's foreign enemies who hold government stock will be furnished with capital. The lessons Lauderdale drew were that there has to be caution in repaying too much debt and that accumulation of capital must have its bounds.

Furthermore, Lauderdale, in his third letter to the Duke of Wellington of 1829, argued that instead of worrying about accumulated public debt and the crumbling of public credit and the setting up of a sinking fund, it should be understood that a large public expenditure increases public wealth.

Lauderdale, Fetter (1945) asserts, wants to discredit the sinking fund policy in the context of his argument about the general and evil effects of saving. Paglin (1946) believes, on the other hand, that Lauderdale's motive in attacking the idea of a sinking fund was because of his fears that the prices of bonds would rise and lower their rate of interest, and that debt reduction would lead to a continuance of heavy taxes. In speeches in the House of Lords, according to Paglin (1961), Lauderdale always linked the sinking fund to taxation; after 1815 he warned that unrestricted peacetime borrowing would be ruinous.

Playfair (1807) supported a sinking fund although its first effect is to turn revenue into capital. He had a different scheme of debt management. Everyone should be compelled, in proportion to their capital, to subscribe to a 2.5 per cent loan, sacrificing 2 per cent of interest to redeem present national debt. At the end of ten years the cost of servicing national debt would be reduced by a half. In 1813 he argued that to preserve national tranquillity there should be economy in public expenditure, perseverance in Pitt's plan to pay off the national debt and abandonment of the plan for the pricing of provisions; furthermore, the wealthy should assist in reducing the debt and all theoretical reforms should be resisted. In his view it is better to pay for the war out of current taxation and find a way of reducing interest.

Craig (1814) was another supporter, with reservations, of the sinking fund, although he believed it was too slow to be fully effective. The positives that he recognized were that a sinking fund prevents a permanent fall in national wealth, stabilizes stock prices and raise their prices, allowing a government to borrow on more favourable terms, and that it also avoids a sudden call on inhabitants and makes resources ready for national service.

Hamilton considered other ways of handling the national debt: his idea was that in abstract a small sum lent on compound interest for a long time will grow immensely; however, such a scheme is limited. Attractive as it first appears, such a scheme would founder through lack of demand for the government securities and the shortage of investment opportunities to invest the vast fund productively; it would be unlikely that the trustees would stick by the scheme for generations. Richard Price's scheme to borrow money at simple interest then to reinvest it at compound interest is delusive. Tontines were tried but were not a great success. Lotteries were used in the 1756–84 period to finance the Seven Years' and American Wars: the profit the government obtained from the lottery being a kind of 'tax on the spirit of gaming'. Hamilton thought the accumulation of debt could be restrained only by taxing more than is needed to pay interest on the debt, leaving some revenue to reduce the debt itself. Also, he argued that the national debt could be reduced by refunding the old debt with a new debt at lower interest rate.

According to Smith, a sinking fund provides a reserve for extraordinary expenses:

> A sinking fund, though instituted for the payment of old, facilitates very much the contracting of new debts. It is a subsidiary fund always at hand to be mortgaged in aid of any other doubtful fund.
>
> (*WN*: 916)

But Smith wanted more than a scheme with the attribute of convenience because funding brings about extra taxation and reduces the private ability to accumulate: more heavily taxed landowners will, for example, be less able to carry out improvements. He thought the funding system pernicious and disliked the idea that the public debt had no effects on an economy because it is merely the right hand paying the left; this ignores the possibility of foreign creditors. A depreciation of the currency could be attempted to reduce the burden of debt but creditors on a large scale would suffer. Instead Smith had remedies for restoring the public finances, including more equal taxes on land and on the rent of houses, and changes to customs and excise so that extra tax revenue could repay the debt. He also recommended extending British taxation throughout the empire – land tax, stamp duty, customs and excise – as, given the cost of maintaining establishments in Ireland and America, he argued it is right to get them to contribute to Britain. If extra revenue cannot be raised then expenditure should be reduced by freeing us of the American colonies. Smith's proposals for imperial taxation had logic but could provoke a political crisis leading to the separation of America from Great Britain. Buchanan, in his 1814 commentary on *WN*, firmly said public bankruptcy is to be avoided not because it weakens the state but because of gross oppression and cruelty to individuals.

A good summary of the debate on the national debt among the Scottish writers can be found in McCulloch (1863); he compared the advantages and disadvantages of public debt. The debt can, he wrote, be easily transferred between individuals; it can be a repository of savings of any size and make possible the running of banks and insurance companies. Debt also avoids the shock to a national economy of paying for all public expenditure within a year; in a national emergency there must be borrowing if that is the only mode of financing the extra public expenditure. Furthermore, not making the public pay immediately for public expenditure leaves money in private hands, where it can be used as capital to increase wealth, and the extra tax to pay the interest can be a spur to industry. But the disadvantages, in McCulloch's view, are greater: the taxes to pay the interest can cause a country severe difficulties and can encourage the migration of capital and manufactures to less taxed countries because the rate of profit is reduced and the public is enervated. The funding system is, according to him, delusive if it does not make clear that increased war expenditure does diminish private fortunes and subsistence. Furthermore, less of a stimulus can be given to industry if war expenditure is presented as less than it is. Also, under a funding system public debt can be accumulated in a reckless way, as in America: it is wrong to assume that a surplus in revenue will always be applied to the sinking fund – temporary demands for extra expenditure will take precedence over the sinking fund. He thought it a delusion to say that the debt would be paid off at the rate of compound interest and it is foolish to imagine that the debt can be eliminated by using borrowed money, as this would increase the total debt still further. Like Hume, McCulloch opposed Archibald Hutcheson's proposal of 1721 to use a 10 per cent wealth tax to pay off the national debt: it was impracticable as it is difficult to get the rich to pay even moderate income taxes; a government following Hutcheson's advice would be overthrown. McCulloch prefers the prudent long-term policy of having surpluses in the public finances in peacetime to meet the demands of war.

Debt can be an element in the financing of a household, firm or government. For all three, borrowing and debt accumulation can be essential as a matter of survival or as part of a strategy to spend more than current income to achieve future improvements. In the case of a national government building up national debt to defend the nation, debt is regarded as essential and uncontroversial. More contentious is debt accumulated to fulfil a grand ambition, because government projects often fail to achieve what is hoped of them. These writers were also interested in the social effects of creating a new moneyed class to hold bonds rather than banks and other firms. The substantial increase in debt in the eighteenth century demanded an urgent examination of its financing, including its abandonment in bankruptcy.

Condition of the People

5

Population

From ancient times, 'population' has been an economic issue. Broadly speaking there are two population problems: a population can be too small, hindering economic development through labour shortages, or it can be too large, pressing on resources and thereby reducing economic welfare. Both these opposing positions recur in the works of the Scottish writers featured in this book. Many remedies were proposed for alleged population problems, including restraining population growth within Scotland and encouraging the emigration of a surplus population.

Much of the opinion on population in the eighteenth century was ill-informed, despite contemporary ambitious attempts to count the population. Alexander Webster (1707–84), a Church of Scotland minister who led a famous revival at Cambuslang, near Glasgow, devised a population census to put demography on an empirical footing. In his *Account of the Number of People in Scotland in the Year 1755* he calculated the population of 892 parishes. (Youngson [1961] tells us that Webster was a friend of Robert Wallace, the great precursor of Malthus.) Webster's estimate for Scottish population in about 1750 was 1.265 million. An official census taken for 1801 gave the figure as 1.6 million; the population rose to 2.8 million in 1851 and 4.5 million in 1901.

In a summary of changes in the Scottish population, Flynn and his co-writers (1977) note that an increase in the population of 28 per cent in the period 1755–1801 was concentrated in the mid-1760s to the late 1790s sub-period. Had it not been for emigration, however, the population would have been larger. Emigration in 1851–60 cut decadal population growth from 11.6 to 6.0 per cent. Another check to population growth was the outbreak of cholera in unhealthy urban settlements: the disease killed 10,000 in 1831–32 and contributed to urban mortality in further outbreaks in 1848–49, 1853–54 and 1866–67. The greatest feature of demographic change in the nineteenth century was the growth of the Western Lowlands, where growth was faster than in the other regions and where interregional migration of males balanced the numbers of males and females.

Underpopulation

Hodges, writing in 1703, mourned the depopulation of Scotland, noting that 'Scotland, tho one of the most fruitful People on Earth, is more lyable to, than any other Nation whatever, great Numbers of People after the Expense bestowed on their Education, being yearly forced out from amongst them, and scattered abroad through the Earth for want of Encouragement and profitable Business at Home' (p. 5).

This lament has been repeated in the modern literature on the 'brain drain', the emigration of the most talented of a nation. Ambitiously, Hodges wanted the present Scottish population to remain within the country, to bring home Scots who had emigrated and to attract immigrants from other countries.

In pursuit of his goal of promoting population expansion, Hutcheson takes up the old mercantilist recommendation of taxing the unmarried and also links population growth to promoting industrial productivity:

> If a people have not acquired an habit of industry, the cheapness of all the necessaries of life rather encourages sloth. The best remedy is to raise the demand for all necessaries; not merely by premiums upon exporting them, which is often useful too; but by increasing the number of people who consume them and when they are dear, more labour and application will be requisite in all trades and arts to procure them.
>
> (*System* II: 319)

It seems, then, that Hutcheson wants a world of sober, industrious, fertile married couples. The pattern of consumption initially makes large families possible; the rise in basic prices is an incentive to work harder and to obtain higher incomes to keep population growth on its upward course.

In his *Essay*, Ferguson, concerned with underpopulation, cautiously asserts that increasing the numbers of mankind can be a worthy object but not if achieved by conquering other countries. He believed that 'The strength of nations consists in the wealth, the numbers, and the character, of their people' (1767: 232). Also in the *Essay* he both justifies population growth as the means of increasing the labour force and suggests a policy to encourage it:

> The value of every person, in short, should be computed from his labour; and that of labour itself, from its tendency to procure and amass the means of subsistence. The arts employed on mere superfluities should be prohibited, except when their produce could be exchanged with foreign nations, for commodities that might be employed to maintain useful men for the public.
>
> (pp. 236–7)

In his *Institutes* (1785) Ferguson writes that man can subsist in any climate, accommodating himself to inconveniences or surmounting them. Population growth depends on physical laws of propagation, the security and means of subsistence: 'Men in every secure situation people up to their resources' (I: 26).

Kames, on the other hand, was concerned by depopulation although, writing in Scotland, he observes that cold countries, presumably including Scotland, have higher population growth. Nevertheless, depopulation in Scotland was still a concern and inequality, in his view, was one of the causes. The prosperous and opulent are 'sunk into voluptuousness... Cookery depopulates like a pestilence' (1778: 112). France, he says, illustrates this: food is wasted on special dishes whereby one person is fed where previously ten were. He notes that luxury intercepts food from the industrious – a view echoing Ferguson's – and weakens the power of procreation. Also, despotism is a greater enemy than luxury as it reduces men and women to slavery and destroys industry, while 'An overflowing quantity of money in circulation' (p. 115) causes depopulation for the price of labour, then the prices of manufactures, will rise, preventing their sale in foreign markets. The remedy, he suggests, is for impoverished manufacturing workers to move into agriculture where cultivation is more efficient and deeper by the spade than the plough.

In the spirit of mercantilism, Anderson states:

> It is universally admitted that the real strength of a kingdom consists in the *number* of its inhabitants, and that its riches will be in proportion to the industry of its people.
>
> (1782: 24)

A decline in population, in Anderson's view, makes taxes more oppressive, causing the population to want to emigrate. But, as he notes, the restless lacked the means to travel abroad: Britain had to subsidize its people to emigrate to a distant place such as America. Anderson (1789) also noted that the population declines where there is slavery because slaves have to be constantly replenished. The population decline, in his opinion, indicates unhappiness. In a reprinted pamphlet he writes, 'To the philosophical statesman, the number of active citizens which can be supported by the state, affords the truest criterion of its power' (1799: 131).

These attitudes towards population growth lingered on throughout the eighteenth century. Dunbar, for example, stated:

> In every country where men are well supplied with the necessaries of life, and happy in their political establishment, population is likely to flourish. Government therefore ought to beware of obstructing population by improper laws. But under a well constituted government it seems unnecessary to encourage it by remuneratory laws. Populousness in most states may be considered as a pretty sure criterion of public prosperity.
>
> (1789–94: 45)

What is especially interesting about this opinion is that he considers both subsistence and political arrangements as causes of population growth.

Overpopulation

What became the central issue in population theory – the race between human population and subsistence growth – concerned the major Scottish writers, who in turn provided inspiration for Malthus's celebrated theory. Lindsay asserted of the poor 'these will multiply and increase, where-ever comfortable Bread is to be earned for labour' (1736: 5)' and Murray that 'money enables a greater number of people to employ labourers, it increases the demand for labour; and if we take it in that light, it must increase the number of People, for Men will always multiply up to the means of supporting them. – another proof that plenty of money does not necessarily increase the price of labour...' (1758: 30–1). Hutcheson, in his *System*, observed that when the population was rising at a faster rate than food supplies, humans have a stronger claim than other animals in a competition for food.

Robert Wallace (1697–1771), minister of New Greyfriars, Edinburgh, is principally known for his contribution to demography. He both challenged David Hume's view of the size of population in ancient times and anticipated crucial aspects of the population doctrine in Thomas Robert Malthus's (1766–1834) *Essay on Population* (1798). David Hume, in his dispute with Wallace, gathered what evidence was available of the customs and population size of ancient Greece and ancient Rome from classical literature for his essay *Of the Populousness of Ancient Nations*. His general theory is that

> Almost every man who thinks he can maintain a family will have one; and the human species, at this rate of propagation, would more than double every generation. How fast do mankind multiply in every colony or new settlement; where it is an easy matter to provide for a family.
>
> (1987: 381)

Hume assembles many arguments for ancient populations being smaller than modern. In those times there were diseases unknown to us; there was slavery, which was not conducive to population growth as many slaves were ill-treated and starved, as they had not being bought for their breeding potential; many were under monastic vows of celibacy; and children were exposed to severe weather. Furthermore, as he argued, ancient republics were often engaged in foreign and civil wars, leading to many being killed.

Wallace's *A Dissertation on the Numbers of Mankind in Ancient and Modern Times*, first published in 1753, was founded on a paper delivered to the Philosophical Society at Edinburgh and issued with an Appendix replying to Hume's speculation about the size of ancient populations. It both sets out a priori reasoning about the determinants of population and checks that theory against the classical literature of ancient Rome and ancient Greece. In the treatise it is immediately obvious that the author is well versed in biblical accounts of ancient history. He assumes the existence of Adam and Eve as the first humans, that there was a great flood at the time of Noah and that the Old Testament establishes a chronology for earliest history. Given these assumptions Wallace indulges in the kind of genealogical thinking present in both the Old and New Testaments of the Bible.

His model attempts to show that there must be special reasons for the population of countries in the eighteenth century being so small. He assumes that the human race begins with a single breeding human pair who, in 33½ years from their first procreative act, produce six children, of whom two die, leaving two males and two females. Subsequent generations follow the same pattern of procreation. In 600 years the total population surviving would be 786,432, after 1200 years, 206,158,430,208. But why is the population actually so much smaller than these projections? Wallace sets out his reasons:

> The causes of this paucity of inhabitants, and of this irregularity of increase, are manifold. Some of them may be called physical, as they depend entirely on the course of nature, and are independent of mankind. Others are moral, and depend on the affections, the passions, and the institutions of men. Among the physical causes, some are more constant: such as the temperature of the air; the extreme heat or cold of some climates; the barrenness of some regions of the earth; and the unfavourableness of the climate or natural product of some soils to generation. Other causes of this kind are more variable: such as, the inclemency of particular seasons; plagues; famines; earthquakes; and inundations of the sea; which sweep off great numbers of men, as well as of other animals, and prevent the quicker replenishing of the earth.
>
> (1753: 12)

These checks amount, he maintains, to the constitution of the earth and natural disasters. But, he writes, curbs to population growth are chiefly moral:

> wars which men have waged against one another; great poverty; corrupt institutions either of a civil or of a religious kind; intemperance; debauchery; irregular amours; idleness; luxury; and whatever either prevents marriage, or weakens the generating faculties of men, or renders them either negligent or incapable of educating their children, and of cultivating the earth to advantage.
>
> (p. 13)

Human beings, not God, in other words, diminish the effects of human generative faculties. Wallace admits that data is lacking to enable an accurate statement of the rate of population growth and of the strength of checks to be set out. All he can do is to enunciate the five basic principles:

1 Populations are greater in agrarian than primitive societies as there will be more food to encourage people to marry.
2 Elimate and soil are important determinants.
3 Land equally divided will support a large population because flourishing industry and commerce pays for food.
4 Where there are many marriages rather than debauchery, the population, *ceteris paribus* (other things being equal), will be greatest. 'Wherever living is cheapest, and a family can be most easily supported, there will be more frequent marriages, and greater numbers of people. Where scarce any thing is needed but simple food, a simple garment, and a little plain furniture, living will be cheapest' (p. 23).
5 Populations are greater when more persons are employed throughout the world in agriculture and fishing. As manufactures increase, simplicity of taste declines, as does the population; manufacturing is not a spur to agricultural productivity, as Hume had argued.

Wallace dismisses as specious the argument that flourishing arts and manufactures are as necessary as agriculture.

After outlining his a priori principles, Wallace turns to histories of ancient times to demonstrate that countries were more populous then than in his own day. In his sources he finds references to sumptuous cities and to fertile agriculture. Using accounts of the size of armies and ratios supplied by the mathematician and astronomer Edmund Halley, he calculates the size of entire populations. Other ways of measuring populations he uses are to multiply land areas by population density or number of houses by average household size. To explain population decline he examines records of smallpox and greatpox outbreaks to establish them as significant causes of increased mortality. But disease is not sufficient, he says, to explain the great decline in population. Again he attributes population decline largely to changes in morality:

1 Religious institutions contributed to population decline in Islamic societies through polygamy and the existence of eunuchs, and in Christian nations through preventing the divorce of childless ill-matched couples and allowing celibacy.
2 Ill-treated servants were often too impoverished to start families and beggars relied on the support of others.
3 Rules of succession to property, especially primogeniture, discouraged matrimony through creating estates of unequal size.
4 The ending of incentives for married couples, as in ancient Rome and Greece, discouraged modern marriages.
5 Large standing armies in Europe caused many young men to be unmarried and debauched women, who became prone to venereal disease.

6 Trade to increasingly distant places through long voyages and exposure to bad climate brought about increased mortality.
7 Decline in the appreciation of agriculture and simple pastoral life cut the produce of subsistence needed for an expanding population.
8 Large, modern states, in contrast to ancient, small states, were noted for their populousness.
9 The Roman Empire caused the ruin of ancient states, devastation of their cities and slaughter of their inhabitants.
10 Luxury replaced simple living from the times of Alexander the Great and his successors; the neglect of land increased the price of food and the change from marriage to debauchery reduced the birth rate: 'it is not the prevalency of luxury, but of simplicity of taste among private citizens, which makes the public flourish...' (p. 162).

Wallace then argues that Scotland is underpopulated because much of its land was uncultivated, despite contemporary improvement schemes, and despite the fact its agricultural exports were considerable. He also argued that population fell through the youth leaving the country in search of greater prosperity; those remaining were discouraged from marriage because they wanted to save bequests for their families. This close summary of the *Dissertation* reveals Wallace's central views on population: that there is a powerful force for reproduction within human beings which could have produced billions of people by the eighteenth century had there not been many checks that diverted people from a simple moral life on small landholdings. Wallace's model of population growth is probably the first attempt to show a geometric progression of population by tracing a population of different age cohorts growing exponentially. It is clear that Wallace had mathematical abilities: in 1720 he was assistant to James Gregory, professor of mathematics at Edinburgh University.

In Wallace's *Characteristics of the Present Political State of Great Britain* (1758) his discussion of population repeats his praise of the simplicity of a largely agricultural country, which increases the size of its population, making it more healthy and virtuous. Luxury, through its power to hinder marriage, is again attacked by him as causing population decline. Wallace anonymously published *Various Prospects of Mankind, Nature and Providence* (1761), another important contribution to the theory of population but one that lacked a mathematical model. Again he argues that more land could be cultivated to increase the population; he also goes further to consider the utopian conditions for maximizing population growth:

> As the complete culture of the earth requires vigorous endeavours, idleness must be banished, universal industry must be introduced and preserved. Labour must be properly and equitably distributed; every one must be obliged to do his part and the earth must be cultivated by the united

> labours of all its inhabitants acting in concert, and carrying on a joint design.
>
> (1761: 26–7)

Once he states these conditions he reveals that it would take many years for the world to emerge from begin underpopulated.

Hume's essay *Of the Populousness of Ancient Nations* contradicted Wallace's central theme that population had fallen since ancient times. There was a superficial agreement of some assumptions between the men – population growth being related to small governments, equality of fortune, importance of agriculture and the universal practice of marriage (Wallace 1753: 169) but there were huge differences between them:

1 Hume alleged that slavery discouraged propagation; Wallace quoted examples from classical literature of the good treatment of slaves, including encouraging to them to have their own families, unlike the severe contemporary slavery practised in Turkey, which was detrimental to population growth.
2 Wars, according to Hume, would have decimated ancient populations if the numbers of those killed were correct or exaggerated but a population usually recovers its size after a conflict; also modern civil and religious wars were more destructive than their ancient parallels.
3 Hume asserted that agriculture was very primitive and the climate extreme in ancient times; Wallace finds modern parallels of equally cold weather and ancient authorities for the wealth of agricultural produce available in the ancient world, again emphasizing that in the Roman Empire extensive subdivision of land, careful laws of succession to property and simple living contributed to population growth.
4 Ancient history suggests that numbers were greater than Hume infers from stated size of armies and slave populations. Also Wallace says that population decline *after* the fall of the Roman Empire has not been disputed.

The English essayist William Hazlitt, in *A Reply to the Essay on Population by the Rev. T. R. Malthus* (1807), identified Wallace as the chief source for Malthusian population theory and anti-utopianism, citing at length *Various Prospects* rather than the *Dissertation on the Numbers of Mankind* (Howe 1930 vol. I: 189). The population theory in *Various Prospects*, although lacking the mathematical section of the *Dissertation* had, according to Hazlitt, the underlying notion of Malthus's version of the principle:

> It seems to me sufficient for Wallace to have said that let the one ratio increase as fast as it would, the other would increase much faster, as this is all that is practically meant by a geometrical and arithmetical series.
>
> (Howe 1930 vol. I: 195)

Despite the earnestness of Wallace's prose and his deep dredging of classical authors to oppose Hume, Hazlitt believed that the population theory was not seriously held. In *The Spirit of the Age: Or, Contemporary Portraits* (1825) Hazlitt surmises that the population discussion in *Various Prospects*

> was probably written to amuse an idle hour, or read as a paper to exercise the wits of some literary society in the Northern capital, and no farther responsibility of importance annexed to it. Mr Malthus, by adopting and setting his name to it, has given it sufficient currency and effect.
>
> (Howe 1930 vol. II: 107)

It was reasonable for Hazlitt to stress Malthus's debt to Wallace heavily but silly to suggest that the theory was not firmly believed by its authors. Hazlitt, if he had studied the *Dissertation* closely, would have also appreciated the parallelism between the account of checks to population growth in both of these population theorists. Also, both of them stressed the influence of morality, but then they did have in common a ministerial role in their respective established churches.

The Wallace–Hume debate, according to Luehrs (1987), is usually seen in the context of the Battle of the Books dispute between ancient and modern authors. Hume thought population growth could be promoted by a government that made the condition of subjects easy and secure. Luehrs goes on to say that Hume's greatest challenge to Wallace's view that the ancient city-state had virtuous stability was that they were not Stoic paradises. However, Wallace conceded Hume's point that ancient simplicity was not barbarism. Both focused much more on moral rather than physical causes of population growth.

Malthus, in the preface to the second edition (1803) of his *Essay on Population*, admitted that he had deduced his population principle solely from the writings of Hume, Smith and Wallace. He agreed with Wallace that the population of ancient Italy was very large but thought that both Hume and Wallace failed to appreciate that 'the more productive and populous a country is, in its actual state, the less probably will be its power of obtaining a further increase of produce, and consequently the more checks must necessarily be called into action to keep the population down to the level of this stationary or slowly-increasing produce' (Malthus 1989 I: 145). He praises Wallace's table of population growth from a single couple, using it as the basis of his calculations of the fruitfulness of marriage in the 1806 edition of his *Essay*.

As an eighteenth-century economics writer, it was not surprising that Steuart also paid so much attention to population matters. From the beginning of his discussion in *Principles of Political Economy* he makes the popular linkage between population and subsistence: 'it is not for want of marrying that a people does not increase, but from the want of subsistence…' (I: 89). 'Every individual is naturally [2nd edition; 'equally' in the 1st edition] inspired with a desire to propagate' (*Principles* I: 174).

What is sophisticated in Steuart's theory of population is that he develops the overplayed subsistence idea, translating it into the concept of agricultural production. In his view, if the population grows in accordance with food supplies, then one needs to go back to investigate the determinants of agricultural output by examining the fertility of the soil and ease of arable work as well as the amount of fish and wild birds. Multiplication, he argues, arises from the statesman inspiring an interest in agriculture, which then provides the food that makes population growth possible. Although the state of agriculture was important to population growth, he noted the perverse case of the Scottish Highlands, where the poor climate and soil required a large population to obtain any produce; the usual relationship between food and subsistence is when industry creates employment and an increased demand then stimulates food production.

Steuart views population growth as a function of the nature of agriculture but refrains from attacking luxury for diverting resources from producing basic foodstuffs. He considers whether luxury production should be discouraged: by reducing the food supply it raises food prices and encourages more agricultural production but it also corrupts the manners of a people. Luxury production is morally neutral, he believes, if its object is the consumption of labour and the ingenuity of man: Steuart opposes the moral reformer who wants a rich man to forgo luxury as it will cut the income of the husbandman.

He argues that the wealthier members of society have a crucial role in population growth: 'It is the demand of the rich, who, coeteris paribus, multiply as much as they choose, which encourages agriculture even in foreign nations…' (p. 177). This is a use of the macroeconomic theme of expenditure encouraging demand for labour and increasing the number of children. Steuart rejects the old mercantilist prejudice in favour of marriage because a bachelor, through his expenditure, provides food for others' children whereas those who get married often reduce the number of their servants. He looks at the argument that slavery is necessary to make men labour beyond their wants to produce a food surplus, stimulating population growth. Admitting that, in the ancient world, slavery was the engine of population growth, he sees, in the modern world, trade and industry as the driving forces. 'Wants promote industry, industry gives food, food increases numbers…' (p. 12). In a society's infancy, spontaneous fruits are, he believes, the efficient cause of multiplication. When agriculture is established 'multiplication is the efficient cause of agriculture' (I: 133): the population through its demand for food stimulates farmers to produce it. If there is insufficient food at home, then food will be imported temporarily until domestic producers improve their lands to eliminate foreign competition. Steuart recognizes that if several nations decide to specialize in manufacturing they will have to import food from further away and the domestic population will decline because food will become more expensive.

Although Steuart praised hospitals for foundlings (abandoned children) and the use of colonies to absorb excess population, he rejected the idea that Europe's population needed a boost, possibly because he thought it was pointless to increase the population if people's standard of living were only at a low subsistence level. He considered the issue of the effect of charity on population but did not regard it as dangerous – as many writers on the Poor Law did – because of a self-correcting mechanism: 'charity cannot extend beyond superfluity, and this must ever be in proportion to industry' (p. 107). In a discussion of the misery generated by the suppression of taxes he makes use of a popular opinion: 'Did not the reformation, itself, otherwise so great a blessing, starve a multitude of poor who were fed by the monasteries?' (IV: 202). Subsequent research after Steuart has shown that Catholic countries such as Spain had a poverty problem too.

The land reformer William Ogilvie (1781) argued that Europe's population was static because of a monopoly ownership of land in every district. He contended that an increase in population would cause a fall in wages to the benefit of the rich, who would spend more on luxuries, depriving the poor of their subsistence. This contradicts Steuart who believed more luxuries meant more employment, which could compensate for the original fall in jobs.

The population debate continued in the nineteenth century, with many of the themes of the previous years and with Malthus, who had drawn so much inspiration from the Scots, used as a starting point for much of their criticism. Alexander Campbell (1796–1870), a journalist, trade union organizer and keen disciple of Robert Owen, argued (1831) that the famous population theory of Malthus was based on the false premise of resource shortage, as an able-bodied labourer in Britain could maintain eighty individuals in comfort and science was at such a stage it could satiate the British with wealth. There was the socialist suspicion that the whole aim of Malthusian doctrine was to control the working classes, restraining their growth by preaching the false doctrine of resource scarcity.

The influential Dugald Stewart, who taught political economy to the young men who wrote on economics for the *Edinburgh Review* at the beginning of the nineteenth century, sought to clarify population theory. He stressed the importance of civil and domestic liberty, in contrast to slavery, as a determinant of population growth. Later he listed the determinants of growth: the age when the parent becomes prolific, the length of pregnancy, frequency of breeding, number of children per family and the period the parent continues to be fertile, factors humans share with animals. Building on the work of Wallace and Malthus he disagreed with the radicalism of William Godwin and argued that marriage is part of the moral and physical order of nature, a father being needed to sustain mother and child at the outset of life. He also examined the determinants of subsistence in terms of soil fertility, industriousness and the choice of food as a staple diet. Stewart had a broader, almost sociological view of the determinants of population growth in terms of the prospects of necessaries for children, being able to maintain rank in society and preferred luxuries. Like Sir James Steuart, Dugald Stewart related the population question to the state of agriculture. He took an interest in the relationship between the size and productivity of a farm, and was intrigued by the idea of an optimal farm: 'The best size of farm is that which affords the greatest proportional produce, for the least proportional expense' (1840 I: 108). He emphasized the importance of a farm being regarded merely in terms of direct subsistence and of producing enough to have a surplus to buy manufactured goods and pay taxes. He thought that agricultural improvements could treble the produce of land but that the possibility of a population crisis was imminent. Echoing Smith, Stewart believed that population growth is the consequence of employment growth: when demand for labour rises more people cultivate the earth; an increased demand for manufactures increases the urban population. He also uses the Smithian idea that a fund of food is needed to maintain the human race. Like Wallace and Smith, Stewart looked at the provision of subsistence through international trade and argued that, in a commercial world, the fear of famine has gone because dearth in one area is compensated by surplus elsewhere. Independently of Malthus, Stewart also established that there is a relationship between a conventional minimum standard of living and the age of marriage.

Chalmers, although viewed as merely a blind disciple of Malthus, thought that an increased supply of food would promote population growth but that the wage fund would be too small to prevent wages falling to subsistence levels (Nisbet 1964). Chalmers had lectured on political economy at Edinburgh to his divinity class during the 1830–31 session, and expanded his thoughts in *On Political Economy* (1832). Like Malthus, he was an advocate of moral restraint, partly because he thought the other 'solutions' of the invisible hand and state control of the economy were inadequate. He lamented the decline in instruction in moral restraint at the parish level, and noted the social unrest resulting from overpopulation and the undermining of Christian parish communities through industrial and commercial expansion. He was also sceptical about bringing further land into cultivation to support a growing population because he considered it too infertile. In his 1833 *Tracts* Chalmers presents the interesting argument that a population can survive a famine and high food prices by cutting down on comforts to release income to purchase necessities. But he fails to see that a poor society with few comforts would not have a reserve of this kind. In his view, cloth is a secondary necessary so if food were scarce less would be spent on cloth. Although this would lead to unemployment in the cloth trade, he argued that this would be compensated for by foreign demand – an optimistic view if the depression were worldwide. Using a more promising psychological approach he says that the population is kept down by influencing the habits of its labourers who, through acquiring a taste for comforts and luxuries, would want to spend less on the necessaries needed by a growing family.

If Chalmers sided with Malthus, Craig certainly did not. In his 1814 work he took an optimistic view of agricultural production. He thought much more improvement was possible in agriculture because more capital can always be invested. He saw other population checks, claiming that higher prices of necessaries tended to prevent marriages and limit population growth while steady corn prices produced habitual enjoyments and fewer marriages. In his 1821 work Craig disagrees with Malthus's view that an increase in food precedes population growth: 'such an increase of food beyond the demand must be purely accidental' (p. 50 footnote). High wages, according to Craig, might have a small impact on population growth. He says both that an increased supply of food is needed to sustain population growth and that agricultural production will not expand unless there is an increase in the number of consumers of it. His idea that, whether postponed or not, marriages could be prolific hits at the core of Malthusian doctrine that later marriages would reduce population growth. Also, he writes,

> Unless there be increasing employment for labourers, and consequently a progressive improvement in their general condition, the people will not increase their numbers merely because they may be fed, more than because they may be lodged, or clothed, or amused...
>
> (pp. 122–3)

In Craig's opinion, if a country has free trade an increased demand for any product could increase demand for labour.

In a wide-ranging assessment of Malthus, Grahame (1816) noted that in rude societies where wealth is more unequally distributed the rich are the most prolific, but in civilized societies it is the poor. Grahame thought that Malthus's population views were morally and politically unsound, and could lead to an increase in licentious celibacy. Grahame insisted that 'necessity is the parent of food' (p. 87), thus, the increasing scarcity of food would prompt more production of sustenance. Grahame also argued that food would not be produced unless it was needed: increased subsistence is the effect not the cause of increased population growth. On marriage he believed that few men would marry without 'some rational ability to support' a family (p. 90). However, he believed that the lower classes will take more risks over the likelihood of having enough to get married; the upper classes are more hesitant because of wanting to maintain a position in society, with their children having the same education and improvement as themselves. Grahame disliked Malthus's proposal to postpone marriages to keep the population down and said it was like denying political freedom. He optimistically thought that giving the poor the freedom to marry would make them more industrious. People are formed by their education not their circumstances and Grahame understood that luxury has a different impact on population according to class. It leads to the working classes multiplying because of increased employment but reduces population growth among the middling classes who try to keep up with fashion and cannot afford children.

Central parts of Malthus's theory came under attack by Samuel Read in 1829, when he repeated many of his arguments of his pamphlet of 1821. He qualified the idea of abstinence from marriage as a panacea for the population problem and also looked at the underlying psychological mechanism determining population growth. He argued that only education and security lead to abstinence because people wait until they are better off to marry. In an advanced society, he maintained, luxury and refinement restrain population growth. In his view it was doubtful if the population was growing faster than either wealth or capital. He also made several attacks on the assertion that there are decreasing returns in agriculture, partly because the use of manure and improved transport can arrest such decline. He thought Britain probably had higher agricultural productivity than the USA despite, as an older country, having extended cultivation further.

In a comprehensive review of population issues Ramsay (1836) argued that where there is a positive check to population it operates on a grand scale, as in Ireland. Where this positive check, the death rate, is greater than the birth rate, few live to maturity. Where there is a preventive check, there are low birth and death rates, more live to maturity and there are more productive labourers as people are better off. He argues, against Malthus, that a man can always produce more than the consumers eat and, therefore, a nation diminishes by reducing the number of labourers.

Another critic of Malthus, Alison, places his theory of population within the stages theory, a very Scottish thing to do. According to this theory, man is indolent and improvident in the savage state: it is the feeling of want in the nomadic stage that causes a change in location and habits. Alison argued that when societies progress subsistence is stored up, enabling the labour of one period to be used as a fund for subsequent times. It is when there is a surplus over subsistence that other sectors, and civilization itself, can emerge: 'what is capital but subsistence stored up, and what is the whole wealth of the world but the accumulation of the surplus produce of the labour of the cultivators of the earth in different ages above what was requisite for their own support?' (1840: 62). He used many arguments *contra* Malthus to prove there was much subsistence. Since 1800 in Great Britain, he contended, agricultural labourers were fewer but the manufacturing population had doubled and been fed because the bounty of nature and the means of increasing food had expanded despite bad seasons in 1837, 1838 and 1839. 'The powers of man over the soil do not diminish as society advances ... they are greatly increased' (p. 48). Merely cultivating meadows and grasslands would, he maintained, produce enough to feed double the present size of the British population. Alison was confident that there was great scope for increasing food supplies, for example, by switching from wheat to potato growing, with the consequence that it is impossible for population growth to reach a limit. If the population cannot keep up with subsistence, the high prices and high wages in agriculture would, he believed, encourage labour to move there and increase production, and the country would switch increasingly from commerce to agriculture. In England, he argued, each agriculturalist supports himself and at least three and half people more. In short, Alison turned Malthus's argument upside down. In his view, there is a cause-and-effect relationship between population and subsistence, with the labour of man providing more than his support: 'this superiority of the powers of production over those of population is a fundamental law of his existence...' (p. 63), and this superiority is constantly increasing, as the history of ancient times proves. There seems to be a mysterious law, he thinks, which means that when the population of one part of the world is increasing, it is stationary or declining in another, and while the demand for labour is crucial to providing for the population, artificial wants and the habit of foresight, encouraging saving, prevent the population from reaching its limit.

Alison makes use of Smith's notion of bettering one's condition and links it to the diffusion of information. Education, he thought, is especially important in modern society but stimulating artificial wants for comforts is more significant than education, which is likely to affect only the few. He argues that what is regarded as a luxury in one age is a comfort in the succeeding period because we want to be better than our predecessors. Instead of living for the day, the desire for betterment will, he believes, lead to a desire for property and such emulation is more likely when there are many landed proprietors in a particular area living on their estates. Population increase, he maintains, is least in the opulent classes, little if at all in the middling classes and most rapid in the lowest. The stability of modern institutions and the limitation of population growth have the same cause: 'The spread of religion, the destruction of slavery, the security of property, the art of printing, the growth of freedom, the rise of the middling ranks, the acquisition of artificial wants...' (1840 I: 299). He wanted all to strive to be richer as money provides a means of storing up property, and the desire to bequeath to successors enables successive generations to improve on the former and embark on greater undertakings. Scotland was in a better position than England to undertake this because savings banks and the availability of banknotes encouraged frugal habits: 'The frugality and foresight which seem to characterize all classes, is the restraint, and the only restraint, which represses the principle of increase within the bounds which the welfare of society requires...' (p. 398). A hierarchy of many ranks enhances, he believed, this desire for betterment because there is the chance of everyone progressing at least a little. Alison noted that in advanced societies where division of labour is much practised an expansion in manufacturing will not be accompanied by the same increase in demand for labour and the impulse to increased population. Instead of poverty restraining population growth, improvidence on the part of the poor can create an excess population. Alison argued, 'It is not by depriving the poor of the means of subsistence, but by giving them the means of enjoyment, that the principles intended for the regulation of their numbers are to be developed' (II: 46) – in other words the poor will always go on having children but the socially ambitious will not. Alison agrees with Malthus that later marriages would curb population growth.

Michael Michie (1997) summarizes what Alison propounded: the population is adapted to each stage of historical development, and by the advanced stage population growth is slower because of the growth of artificial wants; also the increase in agricultural productivity produces a surplus.

Similar to Alison, and unlike Malthus, who regards subsistence as referring only to the agricultural production of a particular country, Burton, in his 1849 book, stated that we have a different view of population if we look at the world as a whole. Burton relies on the psychological argument that the fear of want or of losing caste in society restrains population growth: the enterprising man already knows the folly of early marriages but the idle, improvident man ignores warnings on marriages – the Irish beggar runs no risk of any kind. But he has many arguments which minimize fears that population growth can be excessive: 'Cobbett observed each mouth is born into the world with two hands' (p. 208), thus more population leads to more production. Burton dislikes the idea of checks to population growth and claims that Malthus seems to condone recklessness and cruelty by stating that calamities keep the population down. Burton seems to argue that disease should take its course but that the main object of civilization is to encourage life. It is the duty of government to remove the causes of mortality, he argues, as happened when food, contrary to political economy, was rushed in to Ireland in the famine of 1846. The world is not yet overcrowded.

These later Scottish writers had an impressive array of arguments against the fears of overpopulation raised by Wallace and Malthus, and a more optimistic view of population growth had emerged. Instead of subsistence being the key regulator of population growth, social and psychological forces became crucial.

Population density

The horrors of life in large cities added another dimension to population debates. Wallace (n.d.) thought London had become too large, requiring much provision and transportation. He argued that in cities prices are dearer and dissipation and luxury flourish, unlike the countryside where the air is better and provisions cheaper. In London and Bath and other great cities, he noted, there are many idle servants who could be usefully employed in the country. London should therefore, in his view, be restricted to merchants, tradesmen and those with business there, while manufacturing should be kept to cheap counties.

For Steuart, population density was the consequence and not the cause of urban life. He argued that manufacturing determines where people live, not vice versa, with banks of navigable rivers being the ideal location. He pioneered location theory by studying land use as a series of concentric rings around a city:

> In the center stands the city, surrounded by kitchen-gardens; beyond these lies a belt of fine luxuriant pasture or hay-fields; stretch beyond this, and you find the beginning of what I call operose farming, plowing and sowing; beyond this lie grazing farms for the fattening of cattle; and last of all come the mountainous and large extents of unimproved or ill-improved grounds, where animals are bred.
>
> (*Principles* I: 158)

This was similar to what Johann Heinrich von Thünen (1783–1850) later propounded in *The Isolated State* (1826): a spatial model of a city surrounded by concentric rings of different economic activities to serve the city.

On the other hand, dense populations could have their advantages. Anderson (1782) argues that a country is more powerful if it has a higher population density: denser populations have people united together for mutual protection into a society and there is least waste of labour, even if there are retailers as intermediaries, because agricultural labourers and manufacturers are near each other. Grahame (1816) argued that countries with crowded populations, the consequences of an increase in wealth, avoid famines and have the best quantity and quality of living. In his opinion, a rich country has inequalities of skill and riches but, despite this, there is a more equal consumption.

Emigration

Scotland, a small country with a small population, has long been sensitive to population loss, especially in the eighteenth and nineteenth centuries. Thus, using emigration as a policy tool was inevitably controversial.

Anderson (1785) thought immigration has a two-stage effect on population: an increase in numbers initially then, because the extra people have to be fed, agricultural production rises, causing farmers to have higher profits and then another population increase because they have children from an earlier age. On the other hand, emigration leaves a general languor behind. But, he argues, if the population of the newly settled country has a population growth faster than the home country, then the demand for manufactures will greatly increase employment in the country of origin.

Emigration can cause a cumulative downward spiral in the old country, Anderson noted, as it cuts the population, then the birth rate, and less will be raised in taxation from the depressed population. The higher taxes needed to raise the same tax revenue will, he maintained, further discourage industry and trade. In his detailed analysis of the effects of emigration, Anderson uses the examples of Granada, Antwerp and Amsterdam to prove that emigration causes declines in employment and food. This was in opposition to the views of Richard Price and Benjamin Franklin; they believed that a large outflow would leave more employment and means of subsistence for the remaining population. Anderson used the idea of a cluster of occupations to argue against emigration: when a tailor sets up business in a new place there is a consequent increase in demand for other trades including merchants because of a multiplier operating. He refers to the external economies of scale, whereby several professions gain from a 'number of persons labouring in a compacted body' (p. lxxxiv). Thus every exertion is necessary 'not only to keep our own people at home, but also to entice as many strangers as possible to come and settle among us and thus to augment the strength, the wealth, and prosperity of our people, to the highest possible degree' (p. xcv). The exceptions to the case against emigration would be where a diminished population can still maintain its employment through producing manufactured exports, and where emigrants continue to demand goods from home, accelerating British exports (pp. xcviii–xcix). However, if British emigrants to America had stayed at home, they would have consumed twenty times the amount they imported. Campbell, another opponent of emigration, argued that such an egress of population weakens a people: 'The population, independence and security of all states depend on the greatest number of healthy, active labourers each can support...' (1831: 3). This was mercantilism dressed up in socialist clothes.

But emigration had its supporters. Ogilvie (1781) saw free emigration as the alternative to land reform because migration would bring about higher wages and greater prosperity of the lower ranks, bringing at the end of the process an equilibrium between the conditions of the lower classes in Western Europe and America. Horner (1805) reviewed Lord Selkirk's book for the *Edinburgh Review*. Thomas Douglas, fifth Earl of Selkirk (1771–1820) and a student of Dugald Stewart at Edinburgh University, promoted colonies in Canada for Scottish emigrants. In 1805 he investigated emigration as a solution to the excess population of the Scottish Highlands. Horner noted that in Lord Selkirk's book the property and manners of Highlanders brought about reliance on land, consumption of produce on the spot and the extinction of industry, with the consequence that no surplus was produced.

He also showed that Adam Smith seemed to support emigration because the prelude to agricultural improvement was the fall in the number of small agricultural holdings, as had happened through the introduction of sheep farming, which needed only a few shepherds. The dispossessed, Horner argued, could either move into manufacturing in the Scottish Lowlands or acquire land in America financed by the sale of the smallholder's stock. He saw the complaint that emigration had reduced Britain's military might as unjustified: it was the end to feudalism and low rents, reducing loyalty to clan chiefs in the Highlands, which had stemmed the flow of soldiers. Dispossessed farmers would, he argued, prefer emigration to schemes such as manufacturing and fisheries in the Highlands. But emigration was made more expensive when the Highland Society inspired the Passenger Vessels Act 1803, which stipulated the minimum of food per passenger in the emigrants' ships. According to the Earl of Selkirk, the Highlanders could improve British colonies: Prince Edward Island was a model of what could be done as it had succeeded in both its agriculture and fisheries.

In the post-war depression following the final defeat of Napoleon in 1815 emigration schemes were popular as a means of alleviating unemployment. Craig was sceptical about those schemes because potential emigrants who needed to leave Scotland were too poor to accept the government's offer. Many of them were unused to agricultural work and would not take advantage of settlement abroad. Craig's scepticism was deep mainly because of the psychological costs of moving:

> Mere cheapness of living will not tempt many to abandon their country and their friends, to change all their tastes and habits, and to throw themselves for life among strangers with whom they feel no interest, and from whom they have nothing to expect but the common offices of civility . . . few cases in which expatriation is likely to be attended with even pecuniary advantages.
>
> (1821: 334)

He admitted that, in the case of the Highlands, emigration is an inevitable response to its economic conditions. Suggesting a wave theory of emigration in which the first wave consists of pioneers who report back home and induce further flows, he argued that different parts of the Highlands will send people to settlements where they know the earlier migrants.

Grahame, a supporter of emigration, in his *An Inquiry into the Principle of Population* (1816), saw emigration as the solution to a redundant population in every stage of society until the time (some way off) that the whole habitable earth is populated. Emigration leads, he writes, to the dispersion of technology: there is an increase in productive powers, population, competition and commerce. However, there are barriers to emigration, which he considers at each stage of economic development. In barbaric and hunting societies, he argues, widespread degeneracy means there is no desire to emigrate in order to increase output, while, although pastoral life is well suited to emigration, movement is often provoked by an addiction to war rather than the necessity of obtaining subsistence. He writes that the stage of commerce brings much prosperity because it gives a motive for producing a surplus and less incentive to emigrate while, in advanced settled societies, inequality draws the population together, with the rich gaining nothing by emigration and the poor disinclined to go to dangerous places.

Alison (1840), a great advocate of trade with the colonies, argued that healthy paupers, both men and women, should be sent abroad to British possessions in Royal Navy ships. Burton (1849) sternly argues that emigration is like extending the home territory, with the advantage that migrants, away from relatives, will be forced to abandon idleness. It was especially the 'damaged portions of the people' (p. 340) he wanted out of Scotland. However, he admitted lack of capital could reduce the numbers emigrating.

Large-scale emigration from Scotland in the nineteenth century helped the country to adjust its population size to its resources. Lurking beneath the discussions is some idea of an optimum population. There is, Anderson suggests, no immutable standard for judging how many people can live in a particular place – it cannot be said how necessary the emigration of a surplus population is: 'The population of a nation, therefore, instead of depending on physical causes, which are fixed and permanent, would in this case depend upon political regulations, which are fluctuating, and perpetually subject to change' (1785: xci), noting that political regulations can discourage production and make the rich part of a country into a desert. He observed that even if there were laws against food imports (presumably the Corn Laws) there would still be enough provisions as the increase in the quantity is limitless. In 1799 Anderson gave more detailed arguments for there being sufficient subsistence, and said that agricultural improvements lead to an increase in population. Optimistically, he said the population of a country can never exceed its subsistence, partly because it was part of the divine order that human beings should take up agriculture. Later Burton (1849) thought the population cannot grow too fast if capital, including household possessions, grows faster. Although an optimum population can be defined as one that maximizes output per head, optimality is not a matter of quantity alone. Ferguson perhaps appreciated this more than anyone else in his time. He has, in his *Institutes* (1785), a fuller notion of an optimal population than a mere numerical target. He introduces the notion of the quality of the population, observing that when great numbers are crowded into narrow districts there will be corruption, licentiousness and sedition. The character of the people as a national resource is, he writes, 'their fitness to reap, and to preserve, or to improve the advantages of their constitution, and to support their country in support of their objects' (p. 263).

Smith on population

Contrary to popular opinion, Smith was interested in many dimensions of the population question. He writes in *WN* of the link between population and subsistence growth: 'Every species of animals naturally multiplies in proportion to the means of their subsistence, and no species can ever multiply beyond it' (p. 97) but recognizes that want of subsistence is chiefly a constraint for the lower ranks of people. Smith has a population–wage mechanism – that higher wages increase family size, then the labour supply, leading to lower wages: 'the demand for men, like that for any other commodity, necessarily regulates the production of men' (p. 98). Like Richard Cantillon he thought that population growth was a response to an increase in the demand for labour.

Spengler (1970) was aware of the breadth of Smith's interests in population – population capacity, population growth, levels of living and the spatial distribution of population. Smith thought that colonial powers restricted population growth in their colonies; he was also aware of positive checks to population growth, for example, poverty. Smith, according to Davis (1954), was vague in stating how subsistence was a constraint to population growth. When Smith compared the consumption of the rich to that of their neighbours, the basis of consumption, whether weight, calories or whatever, was unclear. As diets vary so much, the number of people who can be fed is indeterminate. According to Rothschild (1995), the mercantilists saw populousness as a requirement for economic growth but Smith saw it as a consequence, a view aligned to the idea that increased subsistence causes population growth.

Much of the population debate was cloaked in ignorance. Until the Census (or Population) Act 1800 launched the 1801 census for Scotland, as well as for England and Wales, knowledge of population numbers was sporadic and based on private enumerations. Information on food supplies, and on the potential of agriculture to provide more to feed an increasing population, was often based on occasional impressions. But there was an awareness that population was an economic as well as social issue. A growing income needed the extra labour an expanding population could provide: a shortage of people would leave capital and land unexploited. The population, however, could be too large in a given time period and poor in the quality of its health and education. Without explicitly talking about 'an optimal population' – and without making such a measurement and criteria explicit – these writers were all groping to do so.

Property rights and rent

Property rights are much examined in economics because they are fundamental to economic organization, a way of classifying national economies, relevant to economic performance and controversial in producing a new type of income – rent – which reduces the amount of the national product distributed to labour and capital. These rights permit the property owner to use, adapt and even sell such assets. Rent, like private property, can arise from many sources but at its simplest is a payment to an owner for the use of land, buildings or other such articles for a period of time.

Samuel Read, in 1829, argued that all discussions in economics are concerned with justice and ultimately with 'the *possession* or enjoyment, and consequently with the right, to wealth or property' (p. xviii footnote), and that 'the right to wealth or transferable property is acquired solely from the manner in which it is produced or exchanged, or distributed, under the system of the division of labour; that system does in fact consign it, as it were, to its proper owners . . . ' (p. xxi). In a footnote to that page he states 'Political Economy . . . [is] nothing else but the science of what has been called the rights of property.' This strong view does not receive universal assent but it does alert us to the importance of property.

Property rights and rent greatly concerned these Scots. For example, as early as 1698, Andrew Fletcher, in the second of his *Two Discourses concerning the Affairs of Scotland*, wrote that the poor state of Scotland was related to issues of property and rent. He wanted a limit on the ownership of property:

> no man should possess more land than so much as he should cultivate by servants, the whole money, as well as people of this nation, would be presently employed, either in cultivating lands, or in trade and manufactures; that the country would be quickly improved to the greatest height of which the soil is capable, since it would be cultivated by all the rich men of the nation; and that there would still be vast stocks remaining to be employed in trade and manufactures.
>
> (1979: 62)

Rents were so high, Fletcher wrote, that tenants were poorer than their servants and lesser freeholders lacked the capital to develop their lands. He further argued that where paying rents in corn increasingly became the practice, the farm could be ruined by the grounds being kept in tillage; where payment was in cash the landlord might have a variable and unreliable income. With this text, Fletcher started the debate in this period by questioning the extent of property rights and the level of rents.

Origins of property rights

According to the jurisprudential and economics writings of this period, these rights were alleged to have various origins. Simple possession, industrious labour and natural instinct were suggested as justifications for private property.

Lawyers of this time, who laid the foundations of Scots law, had much to say about property. According to conjectural history, a theoretical device of the eighteenth century to discuss various states of affairs by imagining what earlier ages were like, the original community held all things in common. James Dalrymple, Viscount Stair (1619–95), a Scottish judge and staunch supporter of Presbyterianism, having published in 1681 his *Institutions of the Law of Scotland* – virtually founding Scots law – stated that the fruit of the sea and land were common to all mankind but property arose when something was taken and possessed (1693: 166). He went on to say that air, running waters, vast oceans, wild and free creatures, and ways and passages, cannot be appropriated, and to contrast property based on possession with property based on industry. Andrew McDouall, Lord Bankton (1685–1760), in his *An Institute of the Laws of Scotland* (originally produced 1750–53) said that before the Flood all men could use in common the natural product of the ground and animals; after the Flood they brought the fruits of their labour into a common fund, a system that inspired the earliest Christians in Jerusalem. But it was the disadvantages of common ownership, especially 'strife and confusion, and a discouragement to industry' (II: 504) that led to the introduction of private property, expressly or tacitly. 'Property took first place in moveables, which were necessary for subsistence, and thereafter in parts of the ground, possessed with design of appropriation' (p. 505). He said there is the right of disposal of property unless one's judgement is impaired, as is a child's. Interestingly, he acknowledges that private ownership of property is not absolute as its use can be restrained for the public good: 'sumptuary laws are introduced, that people may not exhaust their substance by living profusely . . . upon the like principle, the laws regulating the manufactures of private persons, and prohibiting the export or import of certain commodities, either simply, or on condition of the payment of certain duties to the public . . .' (p. 505). The acquisition of property rights, he wrote, is either by occupancy (first seizure of them), accession, tradition or delivery under the law of nature and nations, or by the civil law; there is also 'industrial accession' through workmanship or industry.

Philosophers could also muse about the nature of property. David Hume turned his attention to property rights, especially in his *Enquiries Concerning Human Understanding and Concerning the Principles of Morals*:

> *What is man's property?* Anything which it is lawful for him, and him alone, to use. *But what rule have we by which we can distinguish these objects?* Here we must have recourse to statutes, customs, precedents, analogies, and a hundred other circumstances; some of which are constant and inflexible, some variable and arbitrary.
>
> (1777: 197; italics in original)

This was a very pragmatic approach: we accept the property rights that have come to be established.

In the opinion of Hardin (2007) Hume regards the rules of property as too artificial to be natural while, according to Taylor (1956), he sees property relations as stabilized by convention, albeit without defining convention. In Hume's view property laws can be changed by human laws and tend to contribute to the public good. Taylor reminds us that although Hume supports the institution of private property in his *Enquiry concerning the Principles of Morals* he regards private property as unjustifiable if there is a state of economic abundance. Property rights, according to Demsetz's view, are an instrument of society and have no place in a solitary Robinson Crusoe world: 'property rights... help a man form those expectations which he can reasonably hold in his dealings with others. These expectations find expression in the laws, customs and mores of a society... property rights convey the right to benefit or harm oneself or others...' (1967: 347). He goes on to write that the 'main allocative function of property rights is the internalization of beneficial and harmful effects' (p. 350), that every right of ownership, whether communal, private or state, is the right to exclude others. Teichgraeber (1978) says that Hume regarded the stability of the possession of goods in society as the single end of justice.

The stage of economic development is linked to the origin of property. Dalrymple (1758), writing about the history of feudal property in Great Britain, argued that before the agricultural stage of development had been reached the more extended intercourse, which leads to affection and the notion of property in land, had not been established. He identified two dimensions to property rights, 'The right of excluding all others from a particular spot of ground is one step in the progress of the idea of property' (p. 77) and the right to transfer property to another. In support of the view that a society has to be fairly advanced before there are private property rights, Sinclair (1795) says that the idea of having lands in common derived from a barbaric state of society and that it is difficult to abolish common land established by custom.

Hume, in *Of Interest*, also uses a stages theory to explain the emergence of private property and a landed class:

> When a people have emerged ever so little from a savage state, and their numbers have encreased beyond the original multitude, there must immediately arise an inequality of property; and while some possess large tracts of land, others are confined within narrow limits, and some are entirely without any landed property. Those who possess more land than they can labour, employ those who possess none, and agree to receive a determinate part of the product. Thus the *landed* interest is immediately established...
>
> (1987: 297–8)

He does not, however, explain why some people have larger estates than others.

A survey of the different origins of property, relying on stages theory, comes from Ferguson. In his *Essay* he clearly links the establishment of property rights to the exercise of power, and notes that in primitive societies the sovereign uses force to convert the people of the country into a property and also has command over what they own for the sovereign's pleasure or profit. Further on in the *Essay* he writes,

> The mechanic and commercial arts took their rise from the love of property, and were encouraged by the prospects of safety and of gain: the literary and liberal arts took their rise from the understanding, the fancy, and the heart. They are mere exercises of the mind in search of its peculiar pleasures and occupations...
>
> (1767: 171)

Power can establish property rights and ensure they are respected. Through respecting private property the last stage of economic development, commerce, is viable.

Ferguson in his *Institutes* (1785) extends his account of the establishment of property rights. In nations with herds, an individual acquires 'an immediate property in cattle, but not in land, a simple form of property based on possession' (p. 31). Then, he writes, he broadens the means of acquiring rights to occupancy, labour, convention and forfeiture. Occupancy means 'no other person can use the same thing without detriment or molestation to the occupier' (p. 198): in other words, the exclusion principle. To explain the origins of an institution is not necessarily to justify its existence but Ferguson argues that because all people have the right to use their talents and faculties they have a right to the fruits of their labour, presumably including their work in clearing and cultivating land.

Samuel Read, in his discussion of property, asserts that land is not wealth until appropriated. Land, human labour and capital are 'the immediate and original sources of wealth and basis for the right to property' (1829: 89). In primitive societies, he argues, only labour is the source of property rights. But, he writes, cultivation of land breeds a sense of property: land is immediately appropriated at the agricultural stage. Only in the desert is there a common and equal right to land as there is no labour, no capital and no improvements.

A difficult issue for the property theorist is human slavery. It was usual for these Scottish writers to deplore the institution of slavery. Dunbar notes that property rights have various origins, including occupancy, but 'The right of mankind to exercise dominion over the inferiour animals has perhaps some limitations. But surely the right of mankind to exercise dominion over their fellow men and to treat them as they treat the animals can be vindicated upon no principle of public utility, nor on any principle recognized by the fundamental laws of human society' (1789–94: 39).

Millar, writing a history of English government (1787), noted that unequal distributions of property lead to the distinction of ranks; in other words, you are what you own. His survey discovered that in Saxon England it was regarded as equitable for the vassal who ploughed and sowed to reap and own what he had obtained through his labour and other inputs, while, in a nomadic society there is common ownership of land leading to a joint reward. However, he contends that improvement establishes property and leads to fixed residence and the desire for pleasures, and that settlement in villages leads to land appropriation as people become weary of disputes over the distribution and management of common property. He argues that the accumulation of property created new motives for action. This summary of Millar indicates how comprehensive his view of property was, showing how, in the course of economic development, the switch from common to private ownership was based on practical matters.

Natural origins of property rights

Property rights can be based on natural instinct, rather than on force or convention. Hutcheson wrote that there is a fifth natural right after the rights to life, to liberty of action, to private judgement and over one's own life:

> Each one has a natural right to the use of such things as are in their nature fitted for the common use of all . . . and has a like right, by any innocent means, to acquire property in such goods as are fit for occupation and property, and have not been occupied by others.
>
> (*System* I: 298)

He distinguishes two types of ownership, common and private, regarding both as having a natural origin. By referring to innocent occupation he rules out acquiring property through force. Smith in his *LJ* (pp. 16–17) closely follows Hutcheson. All have this natural right, he writes, because by nature we are concerned first with supporting ourselves and those dear to us. We therefore have a right to the fruit of our labour unless a public interest overrides it.

Kames develops the natural approach in *Sketches of the history of Man*, explaining that man is by nature a hoarding animal: even bees, sheep and many animals have a sense of property. He then extends the notion of property from hoarding by animals to humans, to justify private property. Custom can reinforce property rights, he argues, and our use of language shows property rights to be natural to us:

> The cattle tamed by an individual, and the field cultivated by him, were held universally to be his own from the beginning. A relation is formed betwixt every man and the fruits of his own labour, the very thing we call property, which he himself is sensible of, and every other is equally sensible. *Yours* and *mine* are terms in all languages . . . the sense of property owes not its existence to society, . . . man by his nature is a hoarding animal and loves to store for his own use.
>
> (1779: 69)

There is a purpose to natural property rights:

> The appetite for property is not bestow'd upon us in vain: it has given birth to many arts: it is highly beneficial by furnishing opportunity for gratifying the most dignified natural affects; for without private property, what place would there be for benevolence or charity? Without private property, there would be no industry; and without industry, men would remain savages for ever.
>
> (1778: 122–3)

The advantage of this natural instinct, he believes, is that it gives us the opportunity to express love for others in benevolence and charity; without having possessions, a person cannot give to others. When money is introduced he argues that the desire for more property increases: far from this being deplorable it is laudable for promoting industry and the arts.

> Money prompts men to be industrious; and the beautiful productions of industry and art, rousing the imagination, excite a violent desire for grand houses, fine gardens, and for everything gay and splendid. Habitual wants multiply . . .
>
> (p. 123)

This sounds less moral than his previous comments but he has an argument in praise of property rights. Rather than private property causing conflict it establishes harmony, for without a sense of property man would be in a state of universal war: 'abstaining from the goods of others is a regulation, without which society cannot subsist' (p. 73).

It was not only Hutcheson and Kames but also Chalmers who wanted to trace property to its natural foundations. Chalmers argued that nature, not justice, is the basis of the idea of property, and that justice enforces those rights rather than creating them. In his *Tracts on Pauperism*, Chalmers writes:

> The desires or notions of property, and even the principles by which it is limited, spring up in the breasts of children, without the slightest apprehension, on their part, of its vast importance to the social economy of the world. It is the provision, not of man, but of God.
>
> (1833b I: 238)

Tracing property rights to God is a grander approach than Kames's. Chalmers says that initially a child regards everything as free to use but a sense of property, which is the work of nature, not of man, emerges.

Contrary to Jean-Jacques Rousseau's view that private property was the cause of all the misery in the world, Alison argues that private property is the natural foundation of the greatest improvement and happiness: 'The desire of acquiring property in the soil, the attachment to a home, and the love of the place of their nativity, are among the strongest feelings of the human breast . . . in the progress of society . . . the first to be developed' (1840 II: 4).

The idea that there are natural foundations to property rights is attractive. It links discussions of property to the basic theme of the Scottish Enlightenment – the nature of man. It also avoids using history or conjectural history to trace the source of rights. The strongest arguments for this approach to property rights are that hoarding is an animal instinct, which none would deny, and that the assumption of private property is present in many languages.

As in many other economic matters, these writers were circling round Smith, who had looked at length at property rights in *LJ*, then in *WN*. Like Hutcheson, Smith believed that property rights are given by nature and that they were essential to promoting individual industry. Elaborately, he mentions the five methods of private appropriation – occupation, tradition, accession, prescription and succession – and places them within the context of the four stages theory of economic development. Property, Smith argues, was initially what a hunter could retain when moving from place to place – clothes and the instruments he used. In some ideas on property overlooked by others, Smith guesses that the origin of private property was when men went to live in cities where the principal persons would divide up the land. According to Lamb (1974), in both his *LJ* and *TMS*, Smith used the idea of the approval of the spectator when discussing occupation as the basis of property rights.

Justifications for private property

Private property rights, long under attack for producing unfairness in society, are variously defended by these Scottish writers. One defence is that property is the reward of labour; another tackles the inequality issue head on by asserting that private property rights confer benefits on society. Property rights are also approved because they arise from the effort of saving or, pragmatically, by sheer force.

To link labour to property rights these Scottish writers used the argument of John Locke's *Second Treatise of Government* (1690): that in acquiring food in the wild the labour of gathering apples or catching animals takes the item away from common property to become the property of the labourer. Locke argues that God did not intend land to be uncultivated but to be given to the industrious and rational. No one, he says, questions that the labour is the labourer's or that the land would have little value without labour.

Hutcheson also linked property rights to labour, in addition to his natural right approach, qualifying: 'the right of property that each one has in the fruits of his own labour ... where no publick interest requires the contrary ...' (*System* I: 320).

He believes both that work has its own reward in property and that such a right is limited to the needs of society. Also, by recognizing the rights of labour as fundamental to engagement in economic activity, he shows the widespread benefits of giving labour its just reward:

> nothing can so effectually excite men to constant patience and diligence in all sorts of useful industry, as hopes of future wealth, ease, and pleasure to themselves, their offspring, and all who are dear to them ... All these hopes are presented to men by securing to every one the fruits of his own labours ...
>
> (p. 321)

Private property could encourage industry and diligence, leading to the promotion of the public good. If it is honest labour, a man is entitled to its product, even if it is more than bare subsistence. As Bowles (1985) reminds us, Hutcheson added the extra criterion of occupation of land to Locke's criterion of having a right to the product of one's labour, seeming to diminish the force of the labour argument. However, Hutcheson is not modifying his labour principle because occupation can involve much labour by the invader or acquirer. Taylor (1956) reminds us that Hutcheson opposed common ownership. He thought common ownership is possible only when property is inexhaustible and not the product of labour. Things not subject to property rights are 'negative community' (*System* I: 330).

Smith endorsed and exalted the relationship between labour and property:

> The property which every man has in his own labour is the foundation of all other property, so is the most sacred and inviolable.
>
> (*WN*: 138)

Foundation, yes, but that still leaves room for other justifications. Winch has the view (1996: 149) that Smith did not entirely follow Locke in stating that property rights originate in labour, although both did agree that government and the defence of property go together.

In an elaboration of the labour approach Ferguson, in his *Principles*, qualifies the idea of property being based on labour by emphasizing the creation of value-added: 'the right of a labourer may extend only to the form, modification, or improvement, he has made, not to the subject or substance which exists independent of his labour' (1792 II: 209). Also, 'Labour constitutes a right to property in the effect, which that labour has produced ... if there be no permanent effect, there is no subject of property' (p. 212). This is, however, a weak property right because the idea of the first occupier owning only the improvement to land and not the land itself is little help in justifying property rights.

Private property inevitably leads to inequality of wealth in society. Hume, in his discussion of property, was happy to accept this outcome:

> Render possessions ever so equal, men's different degrees of art, care and, industry will immediately break that equality. Or if you check these virtues, you reduce society to the most extreme indigence; and instead of preventing want and beggary in a few, render it unavoidable to the whole community ... Perfect equality of possessions, destroying all subordination, weakens extremely the authority of magistracy, and must reduce all power nearly to a level, as well as all property.
>
> (1987: 194)

Thus, he thought that equality could mean poverty all round. Dugald Stewart approved of Hume's view, mentioning that the laws of ancient Rome, which attempted to equalize land distribution, were contrary to natural liberty. Stewart also said there was a practical objection to equality if individuals, by disposing of their holdings, allowed others to accumulate more than an equal share. But he conceded that in a trading republic voluntary equalization of property holdings through a father dividing his state in equal shares between his children would encourage industry. Ferguson warns that if there were equal riches no one would labour for anyone else: 'every one would be reduced to labour for himself' (1772 II: 422). Presumably he is warning of the impossibility of having any substantial-sized business with increasing returns to scale. He sees human beings as progressing from their original state in which poverty and equality were linked. Ferguson further argues that inequality and community spirit can coexist: even in a society of unequal individuals there can still be property set aside for the community in order to provide public revenue, as in the case of Xenophon's proposals for working the silver mines of Athens.

John Millar, in *Letters of Sydney* (1796), examines common ownership to indicate the superiority of private ownership. Although in Sparta there were equal-sized landholdings there are few modern cases of such equalization. During the period of the English Civil War in the mid-seventeenth century there was the belief that Christianity ordered a community of goods; however, the government did not implement this policy because the Levellers were more concerned with a just government than with equality of property. No government, Millar asserts, has the right to produce equality. He imagines levelling as leading to the suspension of labour and the idle squandering their portions, seizing their neighbours' property, annihilating capital and having no funds available to support labourers. Without some people employed in agriculture and manufactures to provide necessaries he predicts people would rob, emigrate or perish.

Craig (1814) thinks that private property rights, the product of habit and experience, are the great motive for individuals to combine into society. He too uses the oldest of arguments, as early as Aristotle, that private property rights increase productivity: if there were equality the poor would reduce their effort and there would be no funds available to employ labour; no one would be temperate and frugal. He knows that primogeniture (the right of the firstborn to succeed to property) is criticized but, nevertheless, he argues that it ensures inequality and allows some to maintain their rank.

Taking up this theme of equality versus inequality, Ramsay (1836) argues that a country with more unequal wealth can raise larger amounts for the state, enabling it to finance fleets and armies, which is why Great Britain had become more powerful than France. Compulsory division of property, he argues, annihilates the aristocracy. He had mixed views on primogeniture: it affords leisure but can cause strife between siblings within families. However, he also argued that people are more enterprising and ambitious in an unequal society. In his later book of 1838 he regards inequality as arising from a mental attitude, the love of distinction: even in the early societies of hunters and shepherds there was great inequality. In his view, the right of property inevitably leads to inequality. The dangers of equality, he says, include creating poverty through dividing property equally at death and the creation of a society based on equality with one taste, one passion and one pursuit, productive of power rather than virtue. Perhaps Ramsay is worrying too much: he notes that there has been no steady progress towards equality, but, rather, convergence then divergence back and forth throughout history in the Roman Empire, France and England.

Considering inequality, Burton (1849) mentions that men are unequal when in a state of nature and later through their mental and physical endowments. Because it is unsafe to interfere with inequalities created by fortune and conduct we let people make fortunes: they provide 'surplus floating capital'. But Burton fails to consider the possibility of the state creating such capital. He does, however, explain how the rich can do good, not by charity wrongly distributed but in other ways. A larger number of small fortunes, rather than a few in the hands of the idle rich, can, he maintains, raise the level of demand. The rich can, he says, be patrons of arts and letters until later mass markets grow up and, while some rich people employ many servants, a pointless vanity, others use their wealth productively, like the Duke of Bridgwater, who built canals.

Property rights have great implications for the whole of society and can be its important justification. In *Letters of Sidney* Millar says that the state of property is the most important influence on 'morals, government, and general welfare of a nation' (1796: 1), although he does not explain these effects in detail.

Private property rights can come under threat when governments use their power to curb the full rights of individuals for the alleged benefit of the community. Craig, in his 1814 work, looking at the practical matter of legislative interference with property rights, conceded one case for interference with private property rights: the compulsory transfer of property to build roads, canals and streets which, although they infringe strict equality, increase public welfare. Moreover, individuals are compensated.

Read devised another argument to justify private property, the saving argument. Wealth, he says, comes from legitimately acquired savings as we have a right to consume, use and bequeath our savings. If there is no inherited wealth, there is no incentive to save and no wealth creation: inviolable property rights are essential to civilization, to agriculture, manufacturing and commerce. He has an idealistic view of property, which ignores the fact that much property was acquired by seizure and yet continues to be regarded as justifiably owned. Burton (1849) also mentions the saving argument, through reminding us that capital arises through saving what is produced by industry and skill.

Pragmatically, private property is justified on the 'might is right' principle. Land is acquired through invasion, colonization and war. Samuel Read faces up to the issue of force:

> All the ways of procuring wealth by voluntary consent of proprietors, whether it be gratuitously delivered up and bestowed, or transferred by treaty and agreement in exchange for a valuable consideration or equivalent, are just and allowable; but all the ways of taking it by force are unjust, and are indeed nothing else but actual robberies, except one, and that is when it is taken by authority of the community to support government, law and justice.
>
> (1829: 90)

This reflects the view that private property can be legitimate but is subject to the power of government, which acts on behalf of the community to exercise power over private individuals.

Suspension of property rights

These writers were aware that terrible crises seem to excuse the suspension of the right to private property to help the community at large. As Kames explains, 'Self-preservation is the strongest of all our principles of action ... to prevent dying of hunger, a man may take food at short-hand without consulting the proprietor ... in a case that can bear no delay, the act is lawful. Similarly two men in a shipwreck fighting for a plank – the person who seizes it has a right based on self-preservation' (1779: 84).

This corresponds to the tradition that private property rights should be suspended to help those in extreme need. Stair comments:

> there is implied in property, an obligation to give, in cases of necessity, to those who have not wherewith to exchange, and cannot otherwise preserve their life, but with the obligation of recompence when they are able; for human necessity doth also infer this.
>
> (1693: 170)

MacCormick, writing in Campbell and Skinner (1982), asserts that Stair is speaking of an enforcement, not a suspension, of justice: the grain owner would be compensated after the siege. Thomas Reid, in his *Active Powers* (1788: 426), wrote that Hume was saying that an equal partition of grain or bread is an act of justice, not a suspension of it.

Read (1829) thought that extraordinary circumstances affect property rights, citing Hume's *Inquiry on Morals* to support the view that justice should be suspended during an emergency. He discusses property rights in a society with many poor people. A right to subsistence from the earth is the right of the unemployed, which he says the law courts recognize by often discharging bread thieves because of their lack of resources; in a besieged city food produced by nature and nature's God can be taken without scruple. He summons Paley to support his belief that in extremity the poor are allowed to appropriate property. Read thought that maintaining property rights against the distressed is contrary to God and that support for the poor can be denied only if impossible. There are two rights – of the poor to have support and of the rich to engross property. However, Read did not appreciate that at a time of distress there are different property rights, not an absence of property rights, otherwise anarchy would occur. When private property is seized some rules have to be devised for its distribution.

Reform of property rights

Many Scottish writers wanted to modify property rights, seeing that the change from common to private ownership could cause inequality and poverty and viewing primogeniture as an ancient property rule of questionable value. In their proposals these critics often overlooked a strand in the literature on property rights from writers as early as Locke and Hutcheson: that the needs of society were considered when asserting private property rights.

A major type of reform of private property rights is to mix them with public rights. By blurring the distinction between what is owned privately, collectively or in common, private property can seem more palatable to its critics. Thomas Reid wrote that 'The State not onely ought to defend the property of its subjects against all who invade it, but also has a Right to Use it in so far as the publick Good Requires' (1990: 75).

As property is subject to the common good, occupation does not confer an absolute right that laws and customs cannot overrule. Those things that can benefit us without becoming private property, such as air, water, the ocean, may not be occupied by individuals (or societies). This leads Reid to the extremely interesting suggestion that perhaps only those things which we actually have to consume may become private property, while things of a 'permanent nature' might be 'left in the Community of Nature or at least remain in a State of positive Communion' (1990: 14). Reid meant to include all land and other real estate in his common ownership. But, in *Active Powers*, Reid praises private property for making us more diligent and therefore socially useful when we seek it. A person can, he argues, be hindered from acquiring private property if it affects the safety and liberty of others – as with private monopolies and possibly wills and entails (restrictions on the use of land). To summarize Thomas Reid, according to Kitagawa (1994), private property was only legitimate if it positively contributes to the common good. Reid agreed with William Ogilvie that God gave man the earth in common occupancy – a property right could not therefore be superseded by a right founded on labour. The most drastic reform would be to get rid of private ownership – and this was in fact the radical approach of Ogilvie. He looked back to an original mythical state of common ownership: 'The earth having been given to mankind in common occupancy, each individual seems to have by nature a right to possess and cultivate an equal share' (1781: 11).

Ogilvie compares this right to the free use of open air and running water. Yet this is mere assertion rather than reasoned argument, as to occupy in common is for an association to take possession: there is no evidence that property started out this way. Ogilvie also argued that the system of property rights needed modernization because it was more suitable for warlike ages, when great groups of men were dependent on their leaders, unlike the modern age, in which now the landlord receives great benefits but makes small contribution to maintaining order or increasing output. Ogilvie, aware of the small chance of land reverting to common ownership, suggested different possibilities for partial land reform: a fixed rent throughout the life of the tenant; a perpetual lease but an increase in rent by a twelfth every thirty years; a perpetual lease with a stated proportion of annual produce paid in the staple commodity with the possibility of revision by a jury at the request of landlord or tenant; all farms freehold but the present rent reserved to the landlord and taxes to new freeholders; a jubilee every fifty years when the freehold is given to the farmer and the average rent of the last seven years to the landlord. He mooted the idea of everyone over the age of twenty without land having the right to claim up to forty acres within his parish. These suggestions show his inventiveness, not his practicality. All of them reduced the power of landlords to the benefit of the tenant, an unrealistic proposal in such a society.

In the spirit of Ogilvie, Dove, mentioning that a few thousands of people had enormous wealth without working while millions barely had the necessaries of life, wanted the land to be open to all. His logic was 'As no individual and no generation is the creator of the substantive, earth, it belongs *equally* to all the existing inhabitants... The object is the *common property* of all; no individual being able to exhibit a title to any particular portion of it' (1850: 383).

This is strictly true but the advantages of private ownership, which might seem a legal fiction, can bring benefits including higher productivity and settled communities. Dove goes on to suggest that rather than achieve equality by the original proprietors of land redistributing their possession, it would be better to make the annual value or rent the nation's common property. Taxing rents from the soil would permit the abolition of all other taxes.

A gradual, and perhaps more painless, way of reforming property rights is to change inheritance laws. Ferguson, in his *Essay* of 1767, admits that the excessive accumulation of wealth in particular hands can be prevented by limiting the increase of private fortunes, prohibiting entails and withholding the right of primogeniture. His argument rests on the fact that these measures are inconsistent with the interests of commerce in giving wider access to wealth: if they ceased there would be greater prosperity.

Without following Ogilvie at his strongest, there can be some redistribution of property. Millar, according to Haakonssen (1985), did not want parliament to redistribute property but he did want abolition of old inheritance laws, permitting a more natural distribution of property. It is an attractive idea as the dead cannot object to the reduction in their property holdings and their descendants are less attached to what they never enjoyed, but there can be an outcry if the rich lose the pleasure of choosing where to bestow their property: the right to alienate is an essential attribute of property. According to Millar's *Letters of Sydney*, what could be done was to alter the rules of legal succession, restrict the making of testaments, and throw the burden of taxes off the poor and middling and onto the rich. He argued that in primitive societies, when property was allegedly held in common, the father is merely an administrator and is succeeded in his work but not his property by his eldest child. Although succession based on consanguinity (being of the same blood) stems from natural feelings there is still scope to attack primogeniture. Millar says it is

> destructive of all energy and activity, it accumulates immense estates which, being uncultivated, are lost to production; it deprives the younger children of that capital which is requisite in all commercial undertakings; it gives them a taste for expences which soon reduce them to beggary; and, by instilling in them early prejudices against the useful professions, it almost precludes the means of their afterwards becoming respectable members of society.
>
> (1796: 59–60)

Primogeniture, he further argued, destroys brotherly affection as younger children live in less style, and testaments are not supported by natural feelings of justice and equity for it is seldom that the neediest or the most deserving inherit. Perhaps primogeniture had an overlooked great benefit: it kept estates and farms large and more efficient. His arguments against entails are strong. In his view, they weaken the property rights of the living, affect cultivation (as they are only life rents there is no power to sell off some land to improve the rest), prevent younger children from receiving capital to succeed in manufacturing or commerce, and lead to frauds and bankruptcies. Read pointed out that laws of entail and other restrictions were unfair in that they prefer one individual to the millions in the population, repress capital value and prevent the best people managing the land. Millar's argument for letting land pass to new owners to do what they will is an attractive idea, especially in a changing society with new uses for land, including building factories. This would not destroy the idea of private ownership but make it more acceptable.

Extensive revisions of property rights were not to Hume's liking. In his essay *Of the Original Contract* he argues that 'as it is evident, that every man loves himself better than any other person, he is naturally impelled to extend his acquisitions as much as possible' (1987: 480) but appreciating that without his restraint society would dissolve. He admitted that much property in durable objects is founded on fraud and injustice. The rules of property are certainly 'uncertain, ambiguous and arbitrary' (p. 482) but little legal solution is possible. Hume was not as imaginative as Ogilvie or Millar.

On balance, supporters of private property outnumbered the drastic reformers who wanted redistribution of land, although several writers were willing to support a modification of private property rights if it was in the public interest.

Rent

The notion and determination of rent were debated in classical economics to ascertain whether rent was a cost of production, a surplus or a monopoly price. Rent, which is a well-known type of payment, becomes a complex concept. This discussion is necessary as factor incomes have to be analysed to see their determinants in relation to final product prices.

Richard Jones, in his *Textbook of Lectures on the Political Economy of Nations* (1852), distinguishes five historical types of rent – labour rent by slave and serf, rent in kind, rent intermediate between those two types of rent, money rent in the pre-capitalist period, and farmer's rent under capitalism as defined by David Ricardo (1772–1823), the London stockjobber turned economist and MP who, in his *On the Principles of Political Economy and Taxation* (1817), attempted to explain how, as the population expanded, so too would the amount of rent of land of different fertilities. This is a difficult classification, which seems to be mainly a history of rent payments, but suggests that rent differs according to its determinants.

Rent was paid in various ways until it settled down to being a money payment due at specified time intervals under a lease. Millar, writing in 1793 on the origin of ranks, mentions the Scottish practice of the tenant paying rent as a share of the crop. The Earl of Selkirk, writing about the Highlands of Scotland, noted that tenants originally paid their rent in military service; later they paid low rents, causing land to have a low value. The 1745 Jacobite rebellion broke down the old system of low rents and the merger of small farms led to agricultural improvement, which made higher rents possible. As Brewer (1998) notes, there was a change in the landlord–tenant relationship in the eighteenth century, from tenants as de facto retainers with low rents to tenants at will with higher rents. This transition, at a time when landlords needed cash to purchase fashionable luxuries, meant that landlords were able to maximize their rents rather than their social control.

A change in the method of paying rent raised the question of what rent is and how it should be justified. Lauderdale justified pure rent in his notes on *WN*, saying that even uncultivated land has some spontaneous production: 'the object of men's desires possesses value independent of any labour being bestowed upon it, and this strictly speaking may be considered as the value of the natural and real rent of land' (1996: 35). When land is improved, he writes, the rent consists of natural rent and profit independent of the labour bestowed, as capital saves labour and is not a deduction from additional labour.

In favour of the payment of rent, Craig (1821) argued that in addition to the profit the landlord receives for the farming stock and implements he has supplied, he obtains rent because land is an essential tool of production. Thus rent is compensation for the services of land and is different from wages and profits. As this is a real service, the proprietor, he says, is entitled to a share of the crop and the rent will be fixed by haggling between landlord and tenant, taking into account the outlays and profits of the tenant. If the rent is too low then the farmer will be indolent and not produce much, or appropriate what should have been the landlord's; if rent is too high the farmer will have a reduced rate of profit. Craig thought it a truism to ascribe rent to a monopoly – no factor could get a return if its supply were unlimited. Much of this reflects Smith's views on rent determination in *WN*, Book I, chapter XI.

Read thought that a landlord's income – rent – was a mixed type of income. In his 1829 book he regarded rent as created partly by capital, which is inseparable from land, and partly by the effect of an increase of population and wealth on land; thus, as he saw it, the capitalist and the general public can have shares of rent. The height of rent depends, he argued, on population density and fertility and levels of prosperity, and it is still best for the income from land to accrue to private individuals. If the government's income was all rents what would it do with this extra revenue? Perhaps it would engage in corrupt patronage.

The remarks of Smith on rent are often cited, partly because his comprehensive approach seemed ambiguous and contradictory. Smith, in *WN*, casually explains the origin of rent, 'As soon as the land of any country has all become private property, the landlords, like all other men, love to reap where they never sowed, and demand a rent even for its natural produce' (p. 67).

In his commentary on the *WN* Buchanan, in 1814, accuses Smith of never explaining why people pay rent and why the landlord alone can reap where he did not sow nor how rent is both the effect of a high price and a component of price.

In *WN* (p. 83) Smith states that rent is the first deduction from the produce of labour under private property and not a residue, but that for rent to exist there has to be a surplus over the costs of replacing stock and providing for the ordinary profits of bringing produce to market. This clearly shows that in matters of distribution the landlord has priority, as he does in society generally. Smith mentions, in a longer explanation of rent, that

> rent may be considered as the produce of those powers of nature, the use of which the landlord lends to the farmer. It is greater or smaller according to the extent of those powers, or in other words, according to the natural or improved fertility of the land. It is work of nature which remains after deducting or compensating every thing which can be regarded as the work of man.
>
> (p. 364)

This is an attempt to provide a very pure idea of rent, appealing to the concept of nature but complicating the idea by referring to improvement. Possibly, rent might be loosely regarded as the profit for carrying out improvements, but there can be rent even on unimproved land, such as the sea shores where kelp is harvested. Smith also looks at the market determination of rent as a price for the use of land, the highest the tenant can afford to pay. As land is usually regarded as fixed in supply, rent, he says, can be considered 'a monopoly price'. But there can, he notes, be market imperfections as the ignorance of the landlord or the tenant of the value of the land can cause a rent to be too high or low. Rent always, he writes, arises on land producing food because there will be both food for the workers to consume and for the payment of profits. Whilst admitting that rent is a component of price he writes that it rises and falls with the price of corn, so that its amount is partly affected by the surplus of revenue after wages and profits have been paid; therefore, 'The rent of a farm . . . must be less when corn is low priced than when it is high' (p. 366).

For rent to have an identity differentiating it from profits and wages there must be a justification. Smith is aware that a landowner farming his own land will receive a mixture of profit and rent as income. As mentioned above, the landlord is paid by the farmer for lending the powers of nature. Human endeavour results in profits and wages but not rent.

Smith appreciates that rent has a role in the allocation of resources. If a differential in rents from different types of land arises then the land would change its use. If there is no margin between the value of produce and the cost of production, as with felling trees, there will be no rent and no motive for employing capital. Smith says that rent is usually a third of the gross produce and is certain and independent of the occasional variations in the output.

In the case of the rent of houses Smith distinguishes the building rent, which is the ordinary profit of building, from the ground rent, which is the surplus above what is sufficient to make a reasonable profit. The rent of land is paid for using something productive, but not so with the rent of a house, which is unproductive. He says: 'The ordinary rent of land is, in many cases, owing to the attention and good management of the landlord' (p. 844), which provides a justification for the payment of rent.

Both property and rent are fuzzy concepts. Property is a complex idea because there are three types of ownership: the landlord owns his land, the capitalist his capital and the labourer his labour despite the landlord being most associated with 'property'. The distribution of income in a sense becomes a power struggle between three types of owner. This will determine how great the amount of rent is once it is separated from profits.

Rent as a surplus

There is some debate, as is often the case in the history of economic thought, about which writer is most likely to have originated a concept or a theory. A good example of this is differential rent theory, a central theory of distribution. According to Brewer (1997), Steuart had some idea of rent as net produce after all costs are paid; Grampp, in his 1976 article, said that Steuart anticipated differential rent theory ten years before Anderson. But there is a difference between intimations of an idea and a careful exposition of it, as surely occurs in Anderson.

Anderson's famous account of the theory of differential rent occurs in his *Inquiry into the Corn Laws; with a view to the New Corn-Bill Proposed for Scotland* (1777). Aware that landowners will take as high a rent for their land as is offered, behaving just like merchants and manufacturers, he tries to explain what will determine rent. In every country, he says, there are different types of soil, distinguished by their fertility. The cost of cultivating the least fertile land will be equal to the selling price of the corn: the more fertile the land the greater the surplus of revenue over cost. If the cost is greater than the selling price of the produce the land will not be cultivated. He argues that because the price of agricultural produce determines rent, and not the other way round, lowering the rent would not reduce the price, which is determined by effective demand for produce and the amount of cultivation up to the point where price equals the cost of cultivating the worst land. In every country there is an effective demand for a certain quantity of grain: demand regulates the price of grain in all cases.

This is one of the earliest expressions in economics of the marginalist principle. Neat as this account of production is, it does not answer the question of whether the landowner obtains the surplus as rent. Profit, rather than rent, could be the surplus, depending on the relative power of the landowner and capitalist. Anderson, writing later in 1799 on the price of grain, notes '*Rent* is, in fact, nothing else than a simple and ingenious contrivance for equalising the profits to be drawn from fields of different degrees of fertility, and of local circumstances, which tend to augment or diminish the expence of culture' (p. 403), which hints at some kind of relationship between fluctuations in rent and in profit.

Surprisingly, Anderson, who seems to have a precise idea of the basis for calculating rent, can ruminate about the extraction of rent as an exercise of self-interest.

> Men... have gradually fallen into the practice of paying rent for land, merely in consequence of a great many practical efforts of the parties concerned each to promote his own interest in the best manner he could, and not from any preconceived idea of any particular plan, far less from any view of either augmenting or diminishing the public welfare.
>
> (p. 419)

He also argues that economic circumstances should relax his rule for establishing rent. Anderson admits, in his *Observations* (1779a), that rents should not be increased in times of scarcity – which contradicts his principle that high produce prices lead to high rents – because farmers will be ruined by high rents when prices fall back. This makes rent a much more complex phenomenon. There are time lags, which prevent a simple relationship between product prices and rent.

Another supporter of the surplus approach, Kames, argued in a work published in 1802 that the rent of a corn farm is the value of the produce minus all the farmer's costs, which is a simpler theory than positing that there are differences in fertility.

Craig challenged in detail the central classical idea that there is an indefinitely regular gradation of cultivation from the most to least productive and a sufficiency of land to supply the increased demand of a larger population, claiming that it was factually wrong. A rise in rent is, he argued, prior to improved and new cultivation. The rise in the price of produce will first increase profits then, at the end of the lease, increase the rent; therefore rent rises when expenses of cultivation fall and vice versa.

The differential rent theory derived from Anderson also came under fire when Read argued that rent is paid on land of uniform quality. Rent will rise if land produces a surplus over maintaining the population and it grows with the growth of villages and towns – the quality of land is irrelevant. Thus, Read follows a surplus approach but not the rigid differential rent version. Buchanan modifies the surplus approach: 'Rent, or the surplus above wages and profit, is the fund out of which the increased expense of production is defrayed...' (1844: 336), but this fund seems, in his view, to be a reserve to pay future costs.

Ramsay (1836) states that rent is the portion of gross produce after replacing fixed capital and wages, and that profits are paid at the ordinary rate. He notes that rent is often confused with interest on capital but gives rent the character of a surplus by saying that it is an extraordinary profit arising from high corn prices. He details the conditions for there to be a surplus: there has to be a limited amount of high quality land, saleable produce from the soil (thus paying to shoot in the Highlands is not paying rent) and low wages. Because, he says, rent is an unnecessary revenue, not needed to ensure cultivation, it is definitely a surplus.

Noting David Ricardo's view of rent as a payment for the use of the original and indestructible power of the soil, De Quincey (1897) claimed it is really the differential powers, not the indestructible powers, which cause rent. But, in fact, his view of rent is very mixed. He thinks it would be better to say that rent is paid for the use of land, the temporary giving up of the rights of landowners, which has no reference to differences in land. We could go further than De Quincey and say that much of rent is paid for the use of space rather than for the use of the power of soil, for example, when land is hired for storage purposes. If there is a contrast between surplus and cost notions of rent then De Quincey is confused. He notes that payment for a house, barns, fences and so forth by the farmer is equal to the interest paid upon the capital the farmer brought into a business, which would suggest that rent is a quasi-cost. There is a difference between an original power and an acquired power. Improvements can either increase productivity or reduce the cost of production, although the latter can be the inverse of an increased power. Gherity (1962) notes that De Quincey could not follow Ricardo on rent theory as he thought there were constant, not diminishing, returns in agriculture. In taking this stance De Quincey abandoned the surplus approach, which states that rent is the surplus over cost on all but marginal land.

A supporter of the differential rent theory, Burton, writes that rent is the 'difference in value between the produce of the more fruitful fields and that of the least productive soil, which the pressure of population drives into cultivation' (1849: 57). Natural advantages, the produce of labour and legal monopoly, Burton argues, create the value of land, and urban land can have high rents despite lack of agriculture.

Smart, late to enter the debate on rent, is a firm follower of the surplus view: 'rent, by its very definition, is a surplus, something that remains when capital has got its interest, the employer his profit, and the workman his wage . . . something that does not enter into the cost of other commodities' (1900: 106).

It is hard to know what he means because all these factors of production, with the possible exception of the employer, will obtain their reward under contracts agreed before production begins. The property owner will not wait until the other factors have obtained their slices of the final revenue and the employer might have to stand back until a profit or loss emerges from economic activity.

A method of determining whether rent is an original income or a surplus suggested by Sinha (2010) examines the consequences of imposing a tax. If it is a necessity then the tax can be passed on, but not if it is a surplus. One can question the validity of this test as a powerful landlord would be able to make an imposition on other factors of production.

Differential rent theory and the surplus approach declined in popularity because of the diminishing importance of agricultural rents and the growth in significance of rents on buildings in an increasingly urbanized society. The idea of relating the amount to different amounts of fertility was irrelevant. Because agricultural improvement was often the outcome of collaboration between and joint investment of landlord and tenant, inevitably the resulting income could be seen as part rent and part profit.

Rent as a cost

Adam Smith, adding another way of looking at the nature of rent, raised the idea of rent as a cost in his concept of a natural price of a good consisting of natural rent, natural profit and natural wages. Rent appeared to be one cost element added to others to determine the final price of a product. Smith was not alone in suggesting a cost approach. It is a strand in rent theory worth pursuing because if rent can be considered a cost it is a necessary payment.

Questioning the 'rent as cost' idea Hume wrote to Smith on 1 April 1776,

'I cannot think that the Rent of Farms makes any part of the Price of the Produce, but that the Price is determined altogether by the Quantity and the Demand' (Smith's *Correspondence* 1977: 186).

Was this the final blow for cost theorists? According to Buckle (1867) – and Buchanan as we have seen – Smith contradicts himself in the *WN* in that he said rent is both a component and the effect of price. Cropsey (1957) is helpful to the consideration of rent as cost, saying that the natural rates of wages, profit and rent are the average rates in a particular neighbourhood. Rent, in his view, is a factor price with its own determinants, which are conventional and based on contract; common wages are based on bargaining. As rent is a monopoly price he argues that it depends on what the farmer can afford to pay.

De Quincey explores the power that gives rise to rent : 'land is a *natural* machine – it is limited – it cannot be reproduced. It will therefore always sell as a power – that is, in relation to the effects which it can produce, not as itself an effect...' (1897: 178).

This view is more on the side of rent as cost than of rent as surplus. We pay factors of production to employ them; their return is to those who use them.

The eighth Duke of Argyll, a fierce anti-Ricardian, wrote extensively on the nature of rent. In his *Essay on the Commercial Principles applicable to Contracts for the Hire of land* (1877) he asserted that land is just another commodity, therefore contracts for its hire are purely economical or commercial. Owners of land can be regarded as monopolists because of having exclusive possession. (Winch (2009) reminds us that 'exclusive possession' was a neglected factor of production, along with mind and ability.) Tenants in Scotland, the Duke believed, can benefit greatly from improving land as the rent is fixed at the outset, but landlords should share in returns to capital investment as they own the productive powers of the soil. His longer work, *The Unseen Foundations of Society* (1893), allowed him to elaborate his views on rent, firmly rejecting the differential theory he rightly traced back to James Anderson, 'the exchangeable value of every article or commodity is always seen to be regulated by the best and the cheapest, and not by the worst or dearest mechanism of production' (p. 348) as the differential theorists said.

All land, he wrote, has rent because it is the price for the exclusive use of land: it is always part of the gross produce. The Duke spelt out the costs arising from the right to have exclusive use of land, including defending it and clearing it. Like Smith he sees that rent reflects costs. To him rent was merely the price of hiring the right to use something owned by someone else. He asks why people hire land and notes many reasons, such as farmers becoming rich enough to have more capital to apply to land, landowners purchasing more land than they can cultivate themselves, and the rise of a social class too poor to acquire, clear and equip land. Firmly he states that rent is a return to the landowner, not a surplus. He rebuts the idea of rent being a surplus through the high prices of grain or similar because rent is both the consequence and cause of prices – the chain of high prices causes higher production, which then raises prices.

> Rent... [is] some price paid for the temporary right of exclusive use over land... depending on the same laws of supply and demand which regulate the hire of every other thing.
>
> (p. 324)

Similarly, wages are paid for the temporary use of labour. He will not go as far as to sáy that the rent determines market prices of produce because product prices are not affected by whether or not rent is charged. The Duke rejected the view that in the progress of society the share of national income going to rent would increase, as would happen if a rising population increases demand, prices and surplus. He states that the rental share was a third in the Middle Ages and perhaps as little as an eighth in the 1890s, and notes that the return to agricultural improvement is less than returns to other investments but that investment goes on as landlords have the incentive of seeing an improved landscape and a more prosperous people.

Price, in his 1893 review of *Unseen Foundations*, reminds us that the Duke minimized the idea of the indestructible powers of the soil and did not like the free gifts of nature to be in common possession. His distinctive approach was to explain that possession should not be a neglected element:

> Possession is a matter involving labour; and the idea that rent may be due to the 'natural' properties of the soil has only arisen because men have failed to discern the 'neglected element' of possession acquired by labour of some kind. It is for the work of exclusive appropriation, originally undertaken and continuously maintained, and for the work also of constant improvement, that rent is paid. 'No rent' land does not exist because, if land will not command a rent for some crop, it will for another, or at any rate for some use or other. The conception of an 'unearned' increment is delusive, for rent is always earned. Here, as in the case of manufacturing industry, the work of the conceiving and enterprising mind is forgotten because it is immaterial in character and does not take a material embodiment.
>
> (p. 269)
>
> The continuous expenditure necessary on landed property, the trouble and exertion involved in original possession, the advantage to the general community of thoroughly enlisting the interest of the owner in improvement, the

> low rate of return yielded in the majority of cases by this improvement, and the incorporation of its results with the soil to such an extent that it is difficult, if not impossible, to distinguish them, are points which merit attention, and may be, and as a matter of fact are often, 'neglected'.
>
> (p. 270)

These long passages are worth quoting because the Duke hit upon the crucial reason for rent, possession. Possession is originally a costly activity and continues to be so. It is as much at the heart of the notion of rent as subsistence is central to wages.

Fetter sums up the debate about rent and regards it as a cost:

> The typical undertaker is supposed to rent his land, to hire his labour, and to borrow his capital. To the undertaker, be he farmer, manufacturer, or merchant, these various costs stand in just the same relation to his production. No one of them is to him a surplus, for he is paying their full value as fixed by competition in the market.
>
> (1901: 434)

Fetter goes on to point out that rent has to enter into the profit and loss account of a farmer. It is not a special case because it is not paid on marginal land: other costs fall to zero on marginal land. If the rent is a competitive one, there must be some product secured for rent even in the case of the marginal unit. He argues that rent is not a surplus above real cost but a regular accruing income, meeting the needs of the money economy. Later Samuelson, in 1977, used a value-added accounting approach in his treatment of rent. Furthermore, in 1992, he says that rent is a cost, not a residual.

To sum up, Tribe neatly wrote 'as for rent it is not the object which is hired but rather the use of an object which is the property of another, the permissible modes of use being specified in the contract' (1978: 24).

Rent or profit?

Much of the debate about the idea of rent concerns whether it is a pure factor income, solely a return to land, or a hybrid income with traces of the returns to other factors of production.

Alexander Wedderburn of St Germains, once a ship's officer transporting bullion from Calcutta to Canton and later a farmer in East Lothian to the east of Edinburgh, published in 1776, three years before his death, *Essay upon the Question What Proportion of the Produce of Arable Land ought to be paid as Rent to the Landlord?* He noted that leases were usually for twenty years and the popular view was that all arable land should produce three rents, for the landlord, for the expense of management and for the farmer. He argued that there would be a greater incentive to improve the land if the lease expired at the death of the tenant but, with improved lands, the duration of leases is less important because output per acre would be less likely to rise over the period of the lease. Where the land is prolific, he wrote, expenses are less than a quarter of revenues, while, with rich land, expenses can be paid and a comfortable living provided for the farmer, who would get 8 or 10 per cent interest on the cost of his farm utensils and would surrender the rest as rent. He noted that if the land is poor then the common practice was to divide the remainder after expenses between the landlord and tenant, and shows that this example reveals that what is profit and what is rent can be a matter of contract or of convention.

The ambiguous nature of rent is noted by Horner (Bourne and Taylor 1994) who argued that when land is improved, rent can be considered part of the profit of stock, an idea inspired by *De la richesse commerciale*. This book, written by historian and economist Jean Charles Leonard de Sismondi (born Simonde in Geneva; 1773–1842), was published in 1803. Craig, as Seligman (1903a) points out, thought that rent and profits are similar and that we should thus refer to the 'rent and profits of fixed capital'. He also argued that land gradually improves and machinery deteriorates through use.

As Fetter (1901) argued, it is difficult to distinguish land from capital. This statement has a strong bearing on the relationship between rent and profit. What is land from the standpoint of society as a whole is capital from the viewpoint of the individual undertaker. As time goes on the improvements to land become more important than the gifts of nature. Thus the return to land is more in the nature of interest (or profit?) than rent. With much truth Cannan (1917) says that it is difficult to say how comprehensive each term for income is when studying the theory of distribution, or to separate one type of income from another.

Thousands of articles are written now about property rights in economics, quite apart from legal texts where property is an essential part of private law. The study of rent has long been a concern of economics as types of income are of major interest to the economist. How property rights are established through the major methods of possession, occupation and labour used to be largely the province of the lawyer but even in the past economic writers had their say on such matters. Rent, which in everyday life seems merely a payment to use someone else's property, becomes a very interesting concept when we ask about its origin and justification. The property rented in the nineteenth century increasingly changed from agricultural land to urban buildings, to some extent paralleling the conceptual change from rent as a surplus to rent as a cost. An analysis of the property market shows that the determination of rent is not entirely different from that of other prices, with demand and supply playing prominent roles.

Profits and wages

This is a very sensitive aspect of economics because levels of profits and wages affect the living standard of all households. In this topic there is the greatest interface between a society and the economy, although the determination of profits and wages is often considered apart from its social context. Profits and wages, if seen as the outcome of a struggle of epic proportions between capital and labour, are determined by the structure of society. The earlier writers, much concerned to root their theories in a general account of human nature, sought a justification for both of them. If viewed as the result of economic forces profits and wages reflect the nature of production. When classical writers dismissed rent as a surplus they were left to consider the relative rewards of production going to profits and wages. Were profits and wages inversely related, or were both capable of simultaneous expansion or contraction? Were wages the essential factor reward and profits, like rent, less essential? Just as there was a crucial linkage between power and the payment of rent, the bargaining power of capitalists and workers was likewise crucial to the determination of profits and wages.

Profits

A difficulty in the study of profits is the obscure boundary between profits and interest, arising from both being returns to capital. One way of distinguishing them is to say that profits are a return to capital, a share in business income, and interest the payment at a pre-agreed rate for the loan of money. Another approach is that profit is the return for using one's own capital and interest is a payment for another person using it, although this is not satisfactory if a business uses outside equity finance. Smith, Sinha (2010) says, regarded profit as the income going to the agent who employs stock (capital), whereas interest is the income to the owner of stock who does not employ it himself. Smith looks at examples of the self-employed: for example, the gardener who cultivates his own land earning rent, profits and wages. He contrasts retailers with rates of profit of up to 50 per cent with wholesalers who obtain only 8 or 10 per cent, but is aware that much of the retailer's profit is actually wages. In a sense the way of speaking of interest and of profit distinguishes them: we say 'interest *on* capital' but the 'profit *of* a business', showing the latter concept to be broader.

Apart from distinguishing it from interest, profit has to be defined to reveal its central characteristic. There are straightforward but vague definitions of profits; for example, Cropsey's (1957) concept that profit, like wages and rent, is a conventional payment based on contract. Hume, in his essay on *Whether the British Government inclines more to an absolute monarchy than to a republic*, refers to servants and tradesmen regarding 'their profits as the product of their own labour' (1987: 48). This is hardly a narrow view of profits as it fails to indicate, in the case of tradesmen, if it is a self-employment income – and it is strange that servants' pay arising from employment should be called profit. He is more precise in his essay *Of National Characters*, stating that people are drawn to particular employments by their views of profit, seeming to use profit in the general sense of being 'gain'. In his *Of Commerce* he narrows the idea further: 'Men must have profits proportionable to their expence and hazard' (1987: 267), suggesting that profit is a reward for undertaking a task and accepting risk.

Profit, in Steuart's view, can be regarded as merely the consequence of the operations of trade. An average profit emerges from the state of demand, which can be affected by the operation of corporations regulating the numbers in a trade. Steuart distinguished positive profit, which 'implies no loss to anybody; it results from an augmentation of labour, industry or ingenuity' from relative profit, which 'implies a loss to somebody; it marks a vibration of the balance of wealth between parties' (*Principles* I: 223) and adds nothing to general capital. He also states that the rate of interest approximates to the rate of profit, as in comparing the foreign trade of two nations.

An unusual way of viewing profit was Lauderdale's comparison of it with the reward to various types of labour. He wrote that in manufacturing there are three types of labour: 'The Labour of the Manufacturer. 2d The Labour of inspection & direction. 3ly The labour performed by Stock or Capital' (1996: 83).

The profit of the master comes from the second and third points. In other words, according to Lauderdale, there is a pot of revenue consisting of profits and wages created through the combined efforts of capital and labour: if capital contributes an increasing amount then more of the revenue will be distributed as profits. The reason he gives for this is that in the cases of both circulating and fixed capital 'the profit is derived from the same circumstance Viz From the operation of the Capital imployed [*sic*] whether fixed or circulating – to supplant a certain portion of labour' (p. 73). Pashkoff (1993) notes that Samuel Read regarded profits as the wage of a superior form of labour, making the relationship between wages and profits a relationship between the wages of inferior and superior labour. We can dispute Pashkoff's view because superintendents often do not own capital necessarily and thus are not entitled to profits. The wages analogy did, however, attract De Quincey, who thought that 'Profits are a mode of wages upon capital; and naturally men must be tempted by higher gains, contingent upon success, in order to compensate greater disadvantages arising to themselves from a particular employment' (p. 270). Perhaps De Quincey is blurring the distinction between profits and wages because the word 'employment' can mean using capital or labouring under the direction of a master. There is a return to the labour argument in Stirling, who argued that the higher profits of the retail trade occur largely because of the 'remuneration for the greater personal exertion of the retail dealer' (1846: 122), a view that is justified only because the self-employed have hybrid incomes, mixing wages and profits.

In *WN* Adam Smith says that profit arises from the accumulation of the stock (capital) that is used to buy materials and subsistence for workers. The value added to materials by the workmen will be divided between wages and profits, which have to be sufficient to exceed what is needed to replace the capital. Smith, according to Cannan (1917), considered only the profits that arise from employing people or buying materials and ignored the value of machinery. Profit as a payment for a type of labour did not appeal to Smith who thought there was something distinct about profit: that it is not a reward for the labour of inspection and direction but proportionate to the value of the stock hazarded. Long before Ricardo, Smith noticed an inverse relationship between wages and profits: for example, that there were lower profit rates in great cities, where the servants are paid more. Hume, like Smith, was not keen on excessively high or excessively low incomes and admired the middling position. In his essay *Of the Middle Station of Life* Hume extols the middle station for giving the fullest opportunity for exercising virtue, towards both superiors and inferiors.

Risk is central to Smith's thinking on profits: he argues that the lowest rate of profit, the clear profit, is sufficient to compensate for the occasional losses to the lender and that this is proportionate to interest, whereas gross profit is not. Giving the example of profits in Bengal received by servants of the East India Company, he argues that the highest rate of profit eats up all rent and reduces wages to bare subsistence levels. (Dwyer (1998) thinks that Smith was against high profits because a rise in the rate of mercantile profit drew capital from the improvement of land, the chief support of all citizens.) If a business is carried on with borrowed money, Smith writes, then the profit rate has to be enough to pay the interest and cover for risk and the trouble of employing capital. Smith argues that the pernicious effect of high profits is to raise product prices more than wages, leading to a fall in real incomes. In *WN* Smith gives five reasons for wage differentials but only two for profit differences – the extent of agreeableness of the employment and the certainty of success. Profits are smaller in cities than in the countryside, he writes, often high in new trades and, unlike rent and wages, low in rich countries and high in poor ones. In his view there is more likelihood of profit rates being equalized than wages. Overall, Smith's survey of profit rates is a conscientious summary of profits in different industries and countries.

Lauderdale thinks it odd that Smith regards interest, but not profits and wages, as a derivative income:

> I can neither earn wages by my Labour or Profit from my Stock, but by employment in the melioration or adapting for use and consumption some raw material, & the reward of this operation must be derived either from the grower, or original proprietor of the raw Material or otherwise from the consumer.
>
> (1996: 29)

Wages and profits are charges that fall on the grower, consumer or both:

> The surplus produce of the Earth is therefore the only original source of Wealth that is of Revenue. – The destiction [*sic*] betwixt Rent as an original source of Revenue, & as the Wages of Labour, profit of Stock & interest of Money is apparent.
>
> (p. 30)

> Net revenue is what remains after defraying the wages of the labour and the profit of Capital imployed [*sic*] . . .
>
> (p. 74)

This suggests that profit is like a cost, not a residual, in the form of net revenue.

To clarify the nature of profit, Ramsay, Seligman (1903b) notes, distinguishes the entrepreneur from the capitalist and gives a comprehensive view of profit: profits of enterprise = salary of the master + insurance for risk + surplus gains. The return to capital, he argues, is determined by the productiveness of industry, not by the competition between owners of capital. He approved of high profits if they arose from high productivity, and not from low wages. Prybyla (1963) points out that Ramsay called entrepreneurs 'masters' and said they were a higher order of labour who were remunerated separately. He distinguishes interest, the net profits of capital, from the profits of the enterprise/master.

Because of the mixed origins of capital the nature of profit is complex. Capital comes from past labour; as Burton (1849) argued, the notion of capital can include education, skill and good character, and a large amount of profit comes from this non-physical capital. The total wage bill, he says, is five times the profits of capitalists: petty retailers can have profits of even 150 per cent but these profits are chiefly wages. Obviously in this case profits are a hybrid income. An industrial labourer, unlike an agricultural labourer, can obtain subsistence only within a complex economy.

De Quincey uses the wages analogy for profits but also links profits to risk. He says that a higher profit is 'no more than insurance upon the general adventure' (1897: 270).

In all these suggestions for defining profit central ideas emerge: profit is a return to the employment of capital, related to the activity of the capitalist, overlapping with wages, and a reward for bearing risk. Read, in his 1829 book, simply states that profit is the reward to capital without labouring oneself. Fortune, accident and risk bring about profit, he says, not hard work. This has the merit of separating profit from wages – the reward for labour – and gives a separate justification for profits.

Profits as a residual

Robert Hamilton in *An Introduction to Merchandize* (1777/79, chapter III, part V) pioneered the residual approach to profits, writes Mepham:

> In all commercial countries there is a fixed rate of interest, and the merchant's gain should only be estimated by the excess of his gross profits above the interest of his stock. The latter may be obtained with little risk or trouble; the former alone is the reward of his industry and the compensation for his hazard. And if the profit of his trade be less than his

> stock would have yielded at common interest, he may properly account it a losing one.
>
> (1983: 49)

Thus interest is a cost of finance and profit a surplus. Smith thought that profits are a residual of a residual, for, after paying rent and replacing capital, wages are paid out of any remaining profit. Smith's idea would be clearer if he distinguished gross from net profit.

The surplus idea can be related to the origins of trade profit. Ferguson, in his *Institutes* (1785), examines how different economic agents gain 'profit'. According to him, the merchant, for example, by supplying the consumer with necessaries and giving the producer an outlet for surpluses has a balance after paying cost and expenses. The profits of trade are mutual, accommodating parties with what they want in return for what they can spare. Just as rent has been thought of as a surplus, profit can be, too, because, he argues, it can only exist because there is a surplus after fixed capital and labour are rewarded.

Read, in his 1829 book, baldly states that profit is the share of wealth belonging to the capitalist after deducting his own wages and rent, but is opposed to the idea of an inverse relationship between profit and wages. It is correct, he says, to speak of profits and rent as 'rates' because they are proportional to a sum, unlike wages, which are represented by the goods they purchase. In his view Smith correctly says that the profit rate is determined by capital scarcity, using as a proxy the interest rate, which was 3 per cent in 1732 but 5 per cent in 1812 when the population was larger.

Ramsay (1836) has a surplus approach, regarding gross profit as the entire surplus going to the master capitalist after paying wages and replacing fixed capital, while De Quincey bluntly states that 'Profits are the leavings of labour' (1897: 254).

Stirling also took a residual approach to profits, regarding them as the 'difference between the value of a product and the cost of its production' (1846: 159).

Why profit is a residual is evident in Smart's description of the process of the distribution of income as profits. An employer sells the good he has produced and 'recoups himself for all the incomes he has advanced during the process, and keeps the balance' (1912: 10). The employer 'makes no fixed charge or salary. Profit is neither a wage nor an interest; it a speculative gain. The attraction of it is the speculation' (p. 157). Risk can lead to profit or loss but Smart is going further to suggest that there is something unexpected about profit.

The residual approach to conceptualizing profit has the attraction of corresponding to reality. However much profit might be estimated in advance, it is often unpredictable. The costs of everything can suddenly change; consumer demand can rise or fall with consequences for unit costs and profits. Unlike wages, profits can be positive or negative (loss).

Justification for profits

Profits meet with the censure of socialists because of the belief that they exist as a consequence of exploiting labour, unjustly transferring income from the industrious to the idle rich suppliers of capital. As labour must obtain wages to exist, why should capital have a return? Justifications of profit include recognizing the work of the person supplying the capital, paying for the saving of labour, enduring privation, being rewarded for introducing a new market or a new process, or obtaining the continuing returns to a continuing capital good.

In his *System* Hutcheson argued that profit is just like the wages of labour. In commerce, for the person employed,

> This additional price of their labours is the just foundation of the ordinary profit of merchants, on which account they justly demand an higher price in selling, than . . . was expended upon the goods . . . there is natural gain in trade, viz, that additional price the labour and attendance the trader adds to the goods.
>
> (II: 63–4)

He sees profit as a payment for the labour of the merchant, as just as a payment to a farmer or an artisan, and, contrary to Aristotle, who denounced the retail trade as leading to unnatural gain, Hutcheson boldly approves of a trader's profit margin. Hume follows Hutcheson in recognizing that merchants perform a useful service. In *Of Interest* he describes merchants, as mentioned in our discussion of self-interest, as 'one of the most useful races of men, who serve as agents between those parts of the state, that are wholly unacquainted , and are ignorant of each other's necessities' (1987: 300).

As intercourse becomes more difficult with an increase in population and industry, it is 'reasonable, that a considerable part of the commodities and labour should belong to the merchant, to whom, in a great measure, they are owing' (p. 300).

Lauderdale explains that since capital saves labour, profits, not wages, are created. In his notes on *WN*, he writes:

> the natural profit of stock or the profit exclusive of competition must be the value of the labour saved by the use of it . . . This is in general however so great that the real profit derived from stock is much under it depending totally upon the degree of competition which the abundance or scarcity of capital creates.
>
> (1996: 27)

> The use of all Capital is not properly as here stated to encrease [*sic*] the productive powers of Labour, but to supplant a portion of Labour that without such Capital would be requisited [*sic*]. This is more obviously the use of fixed Capital . . . It is on this principle that all Capital becomes intitled to a

> profit and the natural profit to which it is intitled is the value of the labour it supplants...
>
> (p. 75)

This view is based partly on the idea that there is a sharing of net revenue between wages and profits, with labour and capital struggling to be rewarded for their relative contributions.

Craig (1814) sides with Lauderdale in linking profit to the saving of labour but also associates profit with parsimony or privation: this can be compared to Nassau Senior's abstinence theory of profit. Privation is both the source of profit and the means of accumulating capital. He also justifies profit as a new addition to value through the employment of capital. Different circumstances give rise to profit and seem to be their justification: there are temporarily high profits when there is a new process or a new market, or a greater risk. To justify mercantile profits Craig, also a supporter of merchants, says that the merchant, using his knowledge of markets, adds value to commodities by removing things from where they are plentiful to where they are scarce, and thus receives profit.

Socialist writers, ever keen to advance the cause of labour, naturally questioned the existence of profit. John Gray's *A Lecture on Human Happiness* (1825) questions the capitalist principle of giving a return to capital while the capital remains intact: 'Can the bee do this? Can the ant do this? No! Neither can man do it without invading the rights of others' (p. 38). This might be strong prose but it is based on a misunderstanding. Capital goods remain intact but produce a stream of products for a long time, justifying profits. There was general agreement among socialist writers that workers are entitled to, and own, the product of their labour, granting them the right to dispose of the product as they please. But the goods produced can either be goods for immediate consumption or capital goods, which will produce incomes for some time to come. Workers can sell these capital goods because they own them but the new owners will receive more than something for the immediate use of the goods – an entitlement to a stream of incomes, profits. It is a paradox that by asserting labour's rights, profits are justified.

Tendency of the rate of profit to fall

It was a commonplace view in classical economics, although there were dissenters, that there was a tendency for the rate of profit to fall, and that a decline in profitability would reduce the incentive to investment and threaten the end of economic growth. Low (1954) says that Hutcheson showed that the diminishing rate of profits was accepted long before the law of diminishing returns. Hume, in saying that there was an inverse relationship between the rate of commercial profits and the quantity of capital productively invested, attempted to justify his belief that the rate of profits would fall. But in *Of Interest* Hume explains that low interest and low profit go together. Writing of merchants with a large amount of capital, he says:

> when they either become tired of business, or leave heirs unwilling or unfit to engage in commerce, a great proportion of these riches naturally seeks an annual and secure revenue. The plenty diminishes the price, and makes the lenders accept of a low interest. This consideration obliges many to keep their stock employed in trade, and rather be content with low profits than dispose of their money at an under-value... (but) when commerce has become extensive, and employs large stocks, there must arise rivalships among the merchants, which diminish the profits of trade, at the same time that they encrease the trade itself. The low profits of merchandize induce the merchants to accept more willingly of a low interest, when they leave off business, and begin to indulge themselves in ease and indolence.
>
> (1987: 302)

This usefully considers the psychological underpinning of the fall in profits and introduces the idea of the 'competition of capitals' as a reason for continued falls. But Hume can see benefits from low profits:

> as low profits arise from the encrease of commerce and industry, they serve in their turn to its farther encrease, by rendering the commodities cheaper, encouraging the consumption, and heightening the industry... interest is the barometer of the state, and its lowness is a sign almost infallible of the flourishing condition of a people.
>
> (p. 303)

Nevertheless the worry about declining profits would not go away.

Smith, in the *WN*, suggests several reasons for a decline in the rate of profit. He says it can be difficult to find new and profitable projects; increasing investment in the wage fund will boost demand for labour, raise wages and lower profits because of their inverse relationship. This increased investment is the basis of his 'mutual competition of capitals' idea, to explain a falling rate of profit in a particular industry, area, market or the economy as a whole. 'When the stocks of many rich merchants are turned into the same trade, their mutual competition naturally tends to lower its profit' (p. 105). But there are, Smith argues, exceptions to this downhill course. Profits can be higher for a long time because the market price is more than the natural price – a manufacturer could have a secret or the market might be distant from the supplier. But, he writes, profits fluctuate so much that often the firms themselves do not even know what their profits are; it is easier to ascertain the rate of interest. Making use of the argument central to differential rent theory and anticipating Ricardo's model of distribution with the example of North American and West Indian colonies, he argues that the most fertile land will be cultivated first but as the colony expands land that is less fertile will be used and profits will fall.

Smith, Ramsay (1836) thought, is wrong to assert that the competition of capitals lowers the rate of profit because competition lowers prices but not the profit rate. This is a strange view as reduced prices and reduced profit margins often go together. Like Ricardo, Ramsay attributes a fall in profits to an expanded population resorting to the use of inferior land. Ramsay could be correct only if land varies widely in quality – something which was questioned.

Ferguson believed competition regulates prices and hence gross profits through the entry of master capitalists to the more profitable branches of industry. Unless few can enter a trade, for example in the cases of army contractors and tax farmers, who have large profits as few are able to undertake the speculation, there is a tendency for profits to move to a common level.

Horner, reviewing Canard's *Principes* for the *Edinburgh Review* of January 1803, had an unusual view of the effect of the competition of capitals on the rate of profit.

> an increased competition lowers the rate of profit... a consequence of an enlarged capital, the amount of profits, upon the whole, is increased... An augmentation of the stock, which is productively invested, is followed by a fall in the rate of profit: only because the actual profits, as now extended, admit of being abridged, without destroying the motive to continue the investment. And this fall of the rate, instead of causing a diminution in the amount of profits, is itself only an effect of these profits having previously been increased, and is, in fact, no more than a return towards their former amount... the reduction (of the rate of profit) can only take place, when the circumstances of the country are such, that the stock of all the capitalists has, upon an average, received a proportionate augmentation. This augmentation arises out of an excess of the annual produce over, which depends upon natural habits of industry and economy...
>
> (1803b: 441)

This argument covers the early stages of a decline in the rate of profit and assumes that the capitalists are not very ambitious, being satisfied with what has become the ordinary rate of return. However, a further decline in the rate as it approaches zero would surely discourage investment.

The outstanding analysis of the alleged tendency of the rate of profit to fall was provided by De Quincey. At the outset of his discussion he thought that it was difficult to establish the true rate of profits because (1) some profits are difficult to identify because they are used to replace capital, (2) what is no more than wages can be falsely called profit on capital, as with Smith's example of a surgeon's honorarium, (a voluntary payment), and (3) it is assumed the average rate of profit is low because of competition but entry or departure from a trade is not always possible. De Quincey dismisses the idea of diminishing returns as the reason for a downward trend in profits because when land is travelling downwards in quality the management of land is travelling upwards through draining, guano, bone dust and spade culture, which raise wages and profits. He uses the rate of interest as a proxy for the profit rate because there can be capital mobility between assets yielding interest and profit-bearing assets to equalize their returns. De Quincey finds further reasons for rejecting the downward tendency thesis. Interest rates can be low because of the high quality of the security – as with Exchequer bills and Scottish bills on long notice – not as a result of the inevitable decline in returns to capital. He concludes that, looking at interest rates as a guide to profit rates, it is clear that they oscillate: there is not the tendency for them to fall. This was a tour de force, demolishing previous arguments for a secular downturn of profits.

Wages

Wages are a payment to labour for giving an amount of time or the product of work to an employer. At a time when so much of production was labour-intensive these writers were inevitably interested in the remuneration of labour. Would most wages be sufficient only to give subsistence to the labourer? Were wage differentials justified? Should there be high or low wages? What did the wage fund explain about wages? What did an analysis of the labour market reveal about wages?

Subsistence and natural wages

The cost of subsistence can be an explanation for basic wages; subsistence wages can be the central factor price, with other wages circling round it. As the cost of subsistence is measurable it is possible to check to see if wages actually correspond to this minimum. Hutcheson does not discuss wages at length: apart from a vague reference to the strength and sagacity of workers he fails, unlike Smith, to provide a theory of wages and wage differentials. But he recognizes in his *System* that bare maintenance is insufficient remuneration and is therefore inherently unjust.

Whether subsistence does determine wages is important because of the belief that wages should refer to the worker's needs. This idea was dismissed by Steuart who, in his opposition to the idea of a link between wages and subsistence, wrote 'the price of a manufacturer's wages is not regulated by the price of his subsistence, but by the price at which his manufacture sells in the market' (*Principles* IV: 157). However, he hints at some recognition of the needs of the worker when setting wages: he recommends that the rate of wages be the average of the wages of the married, sober manufacturer and of the extravagant single person.

In a fine piece of analysis in *WN*, Smith proves that wages and the cost of subsistence did not coincide in Great Britain. The reasons he gives are that in summer wages are higher than in winter despite subsistence being dearer in the latter, fluctuations in wages do not correspond to fluctuations in the price of provisions, regional differences in wages are greater than corresponding differences in provisions, and variations in the prices of labour and of provisions are often in different directions. There were quibbles about Smith's views. Buchanan (1814) questioned Smith's view of the subsistence theory because he failed to see that the great increase in demand for labour came from an increase in the amount of subsistence. This criticism is hardly valid because more demand for labour raises wages and more food reduces its price, thus making wages independent of the cost of subsistence. Another opponent of subsistence theory, in the footsteps of Steuart, was Craig because, as Bruce (1938) reminds us, wages are determined by demand and supply, not by the standard of life. Agreeing with Craig, Read (1829) argued that competing individuals determine the market rate of wages at a particular time; permanent competitors determine the natural/ordinary and average wage rates, which are not based on the cost of subsistence.

The height of wages interested Ramsay (1836), who argued that there is no natural price for labour as workers will strive to get the best wages, however low. Wages are, he wrote, necessary to induce labour and maintain the existence of the labourer: this raises the question of the slippery notion of subsistence. In his view, wages should be enough to sustain a family but the amount of wages should be adjusted to the climate – as people in cold climates need more nourishment. What are necessaries are, he argues, a matter of public opinion: what are considered necessary profits and necessary wages vary from country to country. Consequently, while the subsistence theory was an attempt to provide a floor to the structure of wages, it proved to be too difficult to put into practice.

These Scottish writers also hinted at another objection to the subsistence theory: it confused wages as a payment for work with wages as a welfare payment. Bluntly, Smart ridiculed a popular view of wages:

> ...common as the idea that a man has a claim to a living when it is proved he has worked hard and worked according to his ability...is a mystery to the economist how this idea ever got acceptance.
>
> (1912: 95)

In the real world of markets consumers might not want what a labourer produces, however great his effort and skill, and would certainly be ready to ignore need if a worker's saleable product did not justify a living wage.

Wage differentials

Differentials are a sensitive issue because they raise questions of justice with regard to workers and the efficient management of the labour force. Utopians love equality with no differences in pay between workers, partly because it is thought that need should be the reason, and the only reason, for wages. But differentials are a useful management tool in that they enable employers to raise relative pay to solve the problem of particular labour shortages.

When discussing wage differentials Steuart is interested in the differentiation of money wages in order to equalize real pay. He proposes a survey in Book I of his *Principles* to work out the cost of living in different types of community:

for example, a workhouse and the army. Only a higher cost of living could, in his view, justify city workmen being paid more than their rural counterparts. This is taking us halfway back to the subsistence theory but in the form of differential subsistence costs. Going on to consider other causes of differentials Steuart notes that whereas foreign competition can reduce incomes to the physical necessary level, 'confraternities', supposedly trade unions, of workers such as water carriers, can raise remuneration higher, as can ingenuity. What appear to be the chief determinants of relative pay are skill and productivity (ingenuity and hard labour): 'the free-man will insist upon wages in proportion to the value of his work, when brought to market' (II: 163), not subsistence. He understands that the reasons for differentials would guarantee the permanence of differentials because competition could reduce wages to the lowest level.

Adam Smith stated five circumstances giving rise to wage differentials: the agreeableness or disagreeableness of the employment, the difficulty and expense (or the reverse) of learning the job, the constancy or inconstancy of employment, the amount of trust reposing in the employee, and the probability of expense (pointing to many occupations to confirm this). In addition to these reasons, the 'policy of Europe', which set up apprenticeships, gave workers higher earnings in some trades. However, it was not inevitable that the reasons for wage differentials created permanent differences in pay. Smith did recognize that the working of the market in setting wages was vital: in the case of actors and opera singers the earnings can be high because of the rarity and beauty of their talents, and he admits that extraordinary circumstances will cause demand to fluctuate for different types of labour. Once Smith concedes there is this market determination of wages it is hard for him to think, as it was with Steuart, that wage differentials are permanent. Where Smith is useful is in providing clear testable hypotheses to inspire an empirical labour economics away from value-loaded ideas such as fairness and need. Perhaps the most interesting reason he cites for a wage differential is the cost of training a worker as this introduces the notion of 'human capital' and thus makes wages into a hybrid income with an element of profit, the return to capital.

Another list of reasons for wage differentials is Ferguson's who, according to Craig Smith, wrote in his *Essay* that 'Men are to be estimated, not from what they know but from what they are able to perform; from their skill in adapting materials for the several purposes of life; from vigour and conduct in pursuing the objects of policy, and in finding the expedients of war and national defence' (2006: 101). While this list of reasons is broad enough to embrace the whole range of occupations, Ferguson was, however, aware of educated men treating practical men with disdain, causing wage differentials between white and blue collar workers.

For John Craig, market determination is as crucial to explaining wage differentials as it was a reason for dismissing subsistence wage theory. An engraver can have higher remuneration for a long time because of the years to perfect the art but that differential can be eroded by the number of men who enter the occupation.

Defining wages as the things given or received for labour, Read (1829) relates wages to the personal exertion of body or mind. The whole produce goes to the self-employed; otherwise rent and interest have to be paid first then the rest is divided between the master and workmen who each want to benefit from the other. Like Craig he thinks market determination of wages is important, for different wages are regulated in immediate employment by the number of applicants relative to the extent of the employment. Other reasons for differentials – habits, general character and subsistence – operate, he believes, remotely. He notes that many wage differentials arise from some labour being unproductive and some productive. Given that he thinks productivity is crucial to pay differences, he explains the tragedy of the handloom weavers by saying they put little energy into their work but expected a common share of the most productive nation. In Read's view, labour can become more efficient through greater skill, more and improved capital, and more fertile soil. Burton (1849), too, thought that wages should be dear through higher labour productivity, and noted that the more skilled suffered less from oscillations of trade and that differences in money wages are due to a difference in actual services, obtained by drawing on the mental resources, from which skill and steady energy are thrown into the task. Thus higher wages were justified only through more skill and dexterity. Every neighbourhood, in his view, has average wages, profits and rents, and under good government there is an increasing natural price. Progress, he believed, might take the form of wage, rather than population, growth.

The Scots found the task of explaining the structure of wage differentials quite easy and seized on most of the relevant determinants, although they were still willing to recognize that the wage structure is ultimately flexible, responding to the state of demand in the labour market.

Wage levels

In this period high and low wages were often discussed. Low wages could stimulate workers to be more productive; high wages could increase workers' welfare and make them more fit to labour. Coats (1958) observes that before 1750 most writers agreed that wages should be kept low to keep manufactured exports competitive but that there was a contrary view: that high wages would stimulate effort to the benefit of all.

Hutcheson thought that 'if a people have not acquired an habit of industry, the cheapness of all necessaries of life rather encourages sloth' (*System* I: 318). This expresses the popular view that there is a danger in high real wages, although there is the hope that workers, over time, can become hard-working. Later, Ramsay was cautious about raising wages too much: good wages lead to indulgence in pleasure, not saving, and workers spend money on meat and getting drunk. A way of looking at the consequences of having high wages,

I would argue, is the backward-bending labour supply curve, which shows that raising wages beyond a certain point will lead workers to prefer leisure to work because they are satisfied with their incomes. Carlyle (1867) uses this idea in his *Critical and Miscellaneous Essays* (p. 352).

There are different causes of low wages, including deliberate government policy and technical change. Regarding policy, Dugald Stewart disapproved of the use of immigration as a device to cut wages through increasing labour supply. On the machinery question, that is, the effect on labour of inventing and employing machines, Stewart took the optimistic view there would be only a temporary displacement of workers before the lower product price through using machinery would increase demand and raise the amount of employment. Like Smith he thought that wages vary with the state of the economy, whether it was advancing, stationary or declining.

On the other hand, a high wage policy had many supporters. Steuart, Sen (1957) says, seems to welcome high wages as causing more consumption and circulation but wanted wages to be low in a country dependent on foreign trade. Adam Smith, a champion of high wages, was aware that workers could be lazy: 'Some workmen, indeed, when they can earn in four days what will maintain them through the week, will be idle the other three' (*WN*: 99), but admitted this was not true of all workers. In favour of high wages Smith argued that they encourage industry through making labourers bodily stronger and bettering their condition for the rest of their lives: workers are, he argued, more active, diligent and expeditious. In general Smith was pro high wages, Winch (1985) writes, being concerned with the regulation not of minimum but maximum wages, particularly when overpowerful masters pressed down wages. Smith and Edmund Burke (1729–97), who was born in Dublin and was a famous parliamentarian and orator noted for his philosophical and political thought, especially his opposition to the French Revolution, believed that wages should be the outcome of a free contract between employer and worker and not set by a government that would fail in any attempt to regulate supply and demand.

In practice, Smith admits, in older countries wage levels are low because 'rent and profit eat up wages, and the two superior orders of people oppress the inferior one' (*WN*: 565); in the new colonies wages are high, encouraging population growth. Smith, according to Grampp (1964), was tolerant of the failings of the workman and wanted him well fed, clothed and housed, in contrast to the mercantilist view that low wages encourage industry.

As wages actually paid to workers will be affected by taxation, they can be judged to be high or low pre-tax or post-tax. John Law discussed reducing real wages by taxing food; Hume did so with reservations, arguing in *Of Commerce* that every person should be rewarded according to his/her labour input and that taxes should fall lightly on everyone. Murray (1758) attributed higher wages for day labourers and tradesmen in the previous sixty years to taxes on necessaries, requiring higher wages. Craig (1821) thought any tax on labour would result eventually in higher wages; a tax on necessaries would be passed on in higher wages, but not one on luxuries, which are consumed less by labourers. (The effects of taxation are discussed in Chapter 4.)

The method of wage payment affects the level of wages through changing productivity. Hamilton (1793) believed that a common labourer could triple his wages through a piecework system because greater productivity would finance the higher wages. Steuart in his *Principles* understood this, favouring piece-work wage payments, which encourage the workman to improve his method constantly, rather than time rates. Anderson (1789) defended piecework on the grounds that the alternative, labour paid by the day, approaches slave labour because there is no immediate interest in the quantity of labour performed as when paid by the piece. On the other hand, Smith was concerned that the high wages obtained through piecework would deprive workers of rest.

Wages fund

A distinctive feature of classical economics was the idea that a fund of total wages was needed to finance production. This set a limit on the demand for labour, that is, how many could be employed, and determined the average wage rate for either an individual firm or the economy as a whole. The wages fund doctrine is especially associated with Smith. In *LJ* he writes,

> a poor man with no stock can never begin a manufacture. Before a man can commence farming he must at least have laid in a years provision, because he does not receive the fruits of his labour till the end of the season.
>
> (p. 521)

In *WN* Smith divides the fund into what is paid to workers and what is needed for the employment of masters. More are employed, he writes, when there is a surplus over the cost of maintaining the present landlords and employers, but when the labour force expands there is competition for jobs and the wage rate falls to the lowest level again.

Whatever a person saves from his revenue, Smith says, he adds to his capital, and either employs it himself in maintaining an additional number of productive workers, or in enabling some other person to do so, by a loan. 'Parsimony, and not industry, is the immediate cause of the increase of capital' (*WN*: 337). Thus, saving increases the wages fund, which in turn provides consumer goods for the workers.

Lauderdale, ever keen to dispute with Smith, said in his notes on *WN* that it is wrong of Smith to link the quantity of work to the quantity of capital, as

> the quantity of the Labour performed by Capital and of that performed by the hands of man must in every country be proportionate to the demand, and the demand for all sorts of Labour must be proportioned to the revenue,

> or to what the inhabitants of the Country can annually Command for consumption.
>
> (1996: 64)

> [The number employed is not proportionate to capital but to revenue] for no Capital however extensive can procure more raw material and subsistence than what the produce of the country affords [*sic*] over and above the subsistence of the husbandman and it is this surplus produce which constitutes the Revenue of every country.
>
> (p. 111)

His criticism relies on the distinction between capital, a stock, and revenue, a flow. Lauderdale fails to see that the period of production has to be financed in real or monetary terms. He further fails to analyse the determinants of the demand for labour: if he had, he would have been aware that the demand for labour is based on the ability to pay workers out of circulating capital. There has to be a stock of foodstuffs at the start of the period of production and wages, in a sense, are the running down of a stock of capital.

Lauderdale, according to Paglin (1961), with his scarcity–utility approach to value, regarded wages as income from production and not a cost of production. In his view, there would be high employment earnings because of scarcity, and scarcity of the products of labour, not the wages fund, would determine wages. This sympathetic comment still misses the point; Lauderdale does not understand the nature of the demand for labour, that the wage fund determined demand and scarcity the eventual wages.

Later in the nineteenth century the idea of the wages fund was still respected. For example, the Duke of Argyll, in his *Unseen Foundations* (1893), admits that wages are for the most part paid out of capital and are an advance made in expectation of a return. The fund is not a store of cash but an aggregate of all the causes that determine wages.

If there is a battle between labour and capital, between profits and wages, then there is hope of restoring harmony between these factors of production by recognizing that profits and wages are both earnings of capital and can be distributed in different ways: for example, through a profit-sharing scheme for workers. The Duke of Argyll (1893) recommended that workers become shareholders in large companies in order to appreciate that good dividends are linked to success. This is an interesting suggestion because then the worker would have two returns: the return to the investment in the wages fund, circulating capital, and to the financial capital of the enterprise.

There is little talk about a wages fund today but we can still see it as a useful idea. It deals with an employer's ability to pay and reflects the everyday reality that firms cannot recruit or continue to pay workers if they lack the means to do so. Smith would have been more sophisticated if he had analysed the ability to pay as a general cash flow. If a firm is multi-product, with sales occurring at different times of the year, it will be able to use the revenue from one product to finance the production of others. Smith appreciated that the circulating capital could be financed by borrowing, which gives the fund flexibility and means that the number employed is indeterminate. Building on Smith's ideas, Read (1829) perceptively observes that it is unnecessary for an employer to have a wages fund of his own as he can have loans of money or goods to provide for workers: 'They are often consigned in the shape of a loan from the rich capitalist to the undertaker of a work' (p. 82).

Labour market and wages

It is through the working of a factor market that employers and workers, or, after the advent of trade unions, their representatives, determine wages. Many forces can influence the labour market. De Quincey (1897) stated that there are four elements, all interdependent, which determine wages: (1) the rate of movement in the population, (2) the rate of movement in the national capital, (3) fluctuations in the price of necessaries, especially food, and (4) the traditional standard of living. He regarded population and capital as 'a compound force' determining wages and argued that there could be a rapid increase in wages only if there were rises in the price of necessaries. He seems more concerned with what causes changes in wages than in the determination of their original levels, and ignores the fact that the wage rate in a particular labour market is related to those of other labour markets. In 1799 Anderson, writing on the price of grain, recognized that farm workers' wages had to be proportionate to their possible alternative earnings, an opportunity cost approach.

The outcome of negotiating over employers' offers and workers' acceptances is the determination of the peculiar price of the labour market, a wage rate. Like any market, the labour market can be competitive or have monopoly elements among the buyers (employers) or the sellers (workers). When the market settles down with stable wages it is in a state of equilibrium but it is unlikely that in a large labour market there will be a single wage rate because of the heterogeneity of labour and immobility of many workers.

Smith seems to suggest in *WN* that many wage differences spring from the disequilibrium state of the labour market:

> The price of labour, it must be observed, cannot be ascertained very accurately anywhere, different prices being often paid at the same place and for the same sort of labour, not only according to the different abilities of the workmen, but according to the easiness or hardness of the masters. Where wages are not regulated by law, all that we can pretend to determine is what are the most usual; and experience seems to show that law can never regulate them properly, though it has often pretended to do so.
>
> (p. 95)

There is modernity in this account, making his observations as relevant now as they were over two hundred years ago, with their awareness of the segmented nature of the labour market and the difficulties of implementing pay policies.

Aware of the state of labour markets, in *WN* Smith presents an account of the role of wage and profits in bringing about a local labour market equilibrium.

> THE whole of the advantages and disadvantages of the different employments of labour and stock must, in the same neighbourhood, be either perfectly equal or continually tending to equality. If in the same neighbourhood, there was any employment evidently either more or less advantageous than the rest, so many people would crowd into it in the one case, and so many would desert it in the other, that its advantages would soon return to the level of other employments. This at least would be the case in a society where things were left to follow their natural course, where there was perfect liberty, and where every man was perfectly free both to choose what occupation he thought proper, and to change it as often as he thought proper. Every man's interest would prompt him to seek the advantageous, and to shun the disadvantageous employment.
>
> (*WN*: 116)

This analysis of local markets considers the equalization of wages and of profits. Smith has an idea of gross and net rewards, which he broadly viewed as advantages that are more than monetary payments. Crucial to the working of these markets is that labour and capital are mobile in response to differential gains from employment. But for this equalization to work there must be no government interference with the natural course of things, a free choice of work and continual investment. It is natural, he thinks, to seek gain. His account of the movement to equality/equilibrium is so heavily qualified that its attainment sounds utopian: it is a distant goal coinciding with the triumph of natural liberty. For wages to be fair, Smith argues, the market has to be in a perfect state. This means that, in the absence of monopolistic employers or combinations among workers, labour should be paid at the market rate. Burton (1849) also recommended a free labour market, taking the case of Shotts colliery, west of Edinburgh, which had prospered through free trade instead of regulations since 1837; colliers were previously not allowed to exceed 'a certain day's work' because of the regulation in force.

Smith's analysis of the determination of wages in a labour market culminates in an examination of the process of labour contracts and the nature of wage negotiations.

> What are the common wages of labour depends every where on the contract usually made between those two parties, whose interests are by no means the same. The workmen desire to get as much, the masters to give as little

> as possible. The former are disposed to combine in order to raise, the latter in order to lower the wages of labour.
>
> (*WN*: 83)

But Smith asserts that there is a minimum which cannot be breached too long for the lowest grade of worker – 'the lowest which is consistent with common humanity' (p. 85). Wages will rise, he argues, when there is an increasing demand for workers and employers compete to recruit them. He goes on to say that masters can combine easily but legislation prevents combinations (unions) of workmen. There is, he notes, a tacit agreement among masters to prevent wages rising above the actual rate; and secret collusion to lower wages. Furthermore, in the event of workers joining together in violent protest, the masters will seek help from magistrates because the law is on their side while workers, too poor to accumulate fighting funds, will not be able to strike for long. What Smith acutely recognizes is that wage determination depends on the institutions of the labour market, especially collective forces setting pay.

After it became legal in Britain to establish and run trade unions, writers on economics were interested in whether unions could raise wages – the union wage effect. These Scottish writers generally preferred any way but unionization to achieve higher wages. Burton (1849) showed little enthusiasm for trade unions. He did not support militant trade union action because strikes cause big expenses for the criminal justice system and one strike can cause large secondary layoffs. Education and enlightenment, not trade unions, was, he thought, the answer. He believed that if trade unions created uniform wages there would be a competition in idleness.

Thomas S. Cree, a Glasgow industrialist born in 1837, with robust free market opinions and respected enough in his writing to receive a Doctor of Laws degree from Glasgow University, discussed wage determination under collective bargaining and contrasted it with market determination. In his *A Criticism of the Theory of Trades' Unions* (1892) he argued that trade unions destroy the haggling which occurs in a market and lack a principle for fixing the proper remuneration of labour:

> the true economical wage is the wage necessary to attract a sufficient number of men able to do the work properly . . . the real reserve price put upon their labour by the men in the trade who are in the strongest position for bargaining . . .
>
> (p. 18)

He was a believer in the wages fund doctrine, arguing that wages are paid out of capital not produce by using the illustration of a whaler who returns without a catch. Wages cannot go on increasing at the expense of profits, he explained, as capital is needed to carry on a business and pay expenses:

> in fixing prices or wages, *laissez-faire* is the true economical policy. Even to meet the increasing size of manufacturing concerns, combination of workmen is a mistake. With one side uncombined, the true price will readily be reached, through a number of hirings.
>
> (p. 32)

An employer has to offer at least the lowest current rate to get workers. However, there is 'no duty to pay a certain rate, no such thing as a just or unjust wage, apart from the competition rate' (p. 42).

This polemic in favour of free labour markets was against the growing unionization of the labour force. The politics of the time approved of the creation and work of strong independent trade unions; it would be almost another hundred years before legislation curbed the power of unions.

Conclusion

Wages can be regarded as a residual income or a payment, which takes priority in the distribution of income. In *WN* Smith sees rent as the first deduction from the produce of labour; profit is the second. This is to some extent a reasonable social account in that it reflects the ranks of society, which had the landlords at the top. According to Read, the fund from which market wages are derived was the residual or surplus of the product, after rent and interest had been deducted (Pashkoff 1993).

In classical economics wages and profits were supposedly inversely related – one could only rise at the expense of the other – but Scottish writers challenged this. Seligman (1903a) notes that Craig, in opposition to Ricardo, stated that high profits and high wages often go together. Ramsay, Prybyla (1963) says, modified the inverse profits–wages relationship by saying if productivity increases and the labour supply is constant both real wages and profits will rise.

Rent, profits and wages arise from peculiar relationships. The landlord and tenant agree on rent; the capitalist and the customer ultimately on profits; the employer and worker on wages. All of these relationships are essentially based on power: the stronger partner will gain at the expense of the other. But this raises the further question: what determines power? Resources can be crucial, for example, when the employer has funds to resist a strike or when workers are forced by economic necessity to take the wages offered. Power is also a consequence of the state of a market. If it is a buyer's market then generally prices will be pushed down, and the reverse for a seller's market. Samuels recognizes that there is a model of power in *WN*: 'Market order is achieved only within the structure of power' (1977: 177). Who has a prior claim and who is fated to receive a surplus as a reward will, therefore, vary. Rent and profits, according to Samuels, are the principal contestants for the surplus; but others contested this view.

Profits and wages have many linkages when they face each other as competitors for the shares of output as they are both factor rewards and are overlapping in their natures. Labour contains an element of human capital, suggesting that wages are not entirely distinguishable from profits, and profits were often thought to be a payment for a special type of labour: superintendence. The earlier insistence that profits and wages are inversely related, with one increasing only at the expense of the other, was challenged: Smith admits that they could rise or fall together. We have to conclude then that whatever happens neither wages nor profits are essential payments, at least in the short run. There are many cases of labourers being paid virtually nothing and firms can easily change from making a profit to suffering a loss. What is important is to analyse the market for labour and the determinants of a firm's profit and not rely on generalizations.

Poverty

The existence of poverty in Scotland, and remedies to cure it, excited the comments and proposals of writers from Fletcher and Hutcheson to Smart. How much poverty was there? It can be measured only in an indirect way: looking at those in receipt of benefits and those migrating from their homes in a desperate search for food give us hints; the extreme 'measure' of poverty is mortality rates, which soared in Scottish cities in the nineteenth century. However, all these indicators fail to provide the full story.

The widespread poverty in Scotland in the early eighteenth century at the outset of our inquiry is summed up by Whatley:

> Living standards . . . were low for the bulk of the population, more so in the country than the towns, although regional and local variations as well as enormous differences between the circumstances of one household and another confound confident generalisations. Poverty, resulting from old age, illness, unemployment, or other personal disasters, including debts, rent arrears, a midwife's fee or funeral expenses, was crippling whether located in town or in a rural township. Uncertainty prevailed at all levels, although desperation was most strongly felt among the landless and itinerant poor who flitted from town to town in search of a livelihood . . .
>
> (2000: 76)

There was enough visible poverty in the nineteenth century, especially in Scottish cities and towns after a large part of the population transferred from the countryside, to prompt members of the medical and religious professions, as well as anyone concerned with law and order, to devise new schemes or to advocate the termination of existing policies. Scotland lacked the Poor Laws of England but looked to them in policy debates. This was the old idea of borrowing ideas from abroad to initiate a new approach. Scots saw no reason for the state to bear the whole burden of helping the poor: churches and charitable societies could either fill in the gaps left by the state or go further and provide a new solution to poverty. Given that the poor were to be helped, a point which was to be challenged by writers such as Craig, how could an efficient system of administration, which would avoid fraud, not encourage subsidized laziness among the poor and not be unfair between different classes of the poor, be devised? The poverty problem could be seen as the consequence of excess population – to take Alison as an example – or of the state of the economy, as when Smith related wage levels to whether an economy was expanding, contracting or stationary.

After looking at the causes of poverty we examine a variety of specific proposals to relieve poverty – slavery, employment schemes, cheaper food, emigration, land redistribution and savings banks – before entering the great debate between providing for the poor through the Poor Laws or through charity and contemplating the possibility of a new national welfare programme.

Causes

The causes operated at different levels: the overall economic condition of the country can be blamed for the poverty of many individuals, or the individuals themselves can behave in a way that will keep them at the bottom of the income distribution, or legislation can contribute to worsening a problem it seeks to remedy.

John McFarlan (1740–88), minister of the Canongate Kirk, Edinburgh, published his *Inquiries concerning the Poor* (1782) after fifteen years of ministry in that slum area. Given the roughness of the poor area where he served, it is not surprising that he mentioned drunkenness and debauchery as causes of poverty but, more importantly, he used the popular eighteenth-century approach of linking poverty to the stages of economic development. Briefly, prominent writers, especially Hume, Kames and Smith, posited a succession of phases through which an economy could progress in its economic development (this is discussed in greater detail in Chapter 6). The most primitive stage is of hunters and gatherers, followed by nomadic shepherds who gradually settle to provide an agricultural stage; the final stage is commerce and manufacturing. What McFarlan cleverly did was to ask if there was a type of poverty peculiar to each stage. In a barbarous primitive nation he thought no one was poor, presumably because everyone had to be self-sufficient. Life in a society of shepherds was not one of private property with one person having resources at the expense of others but was hospitable enough to avoid the creation of a poor section of the population. In the agricultural stage, instead of self-sufficiency, many in the population would depend on the few. He thought that then slavery would emerge, with the fortunate effect that workers would have no problem with subsistence because masters would be obliged to feed them even if sick or old. But in the stage of commerce and manufacturing, the stage Scotland had reached by the mid-eighteenth century, a poverty problem would occur even in the presence of great prosperity and luxury, partly because the economy was subject to cyclical fluctuations. Commercial societies with professional armies would, for example, have extra poverty because soldiers' pay would be low and their employment reduced in peacetime.

In his survey of economic conditions over the centuries Playfair (1807) mentioned the changing incidence of poverty. He noted that when a nation becomes rich, the proportion that are poor increases both in capital cities and throughout the nation; however, he argues that this does not matter as much as the figures might indicate. Bringing in a psychological dimension he, like Smith, points out that there is more humiliation in one's own home village than in anonymous towns. Fluctuations in wealth could, he argued, occur in different ways. Wealth could fall because the wealth of the business seldom goes beyond the second generation and almost never beyond the third, while the death of unproductive labourers before their children can maintain themselves could cause poverty because the parents had no wealth to pass on. He was also interested in the phases of economic development, arguing that over time the productive classes become poorer, the middle classes disappear and industry becomes more concentrated. When wealth increases societies that are less hospitable and more socially divisive are created, resulting in less mutual support for the poor. Underneath this statistical work, Playfair, according to Grossman (1948), is distinguishing two types of poverty: that of the lame, sick, infirm, aged and orphaned and that caused by the general wealth increasing: this is in a sense a contrast between micro- and macroeconomic explanations.

The causes of poverty could be general as a result of a bad harvest. Sinclair (182-) mentions severe famines in Scotland in 1698–99, after scanty crops for seven years, 1740–41 and 1782–83 – during the latter even the peas in store for the navy were brought to market. But a calamity could have good effects in the reduction in intemperance and vice and the introduction of new varieties of oats, despite the evil consequences of a decrease in population, an increased number of poor and the impaired health of the working classes.

In other writers more causes are identified, including the personal characteristics of the poor. Craig, in his 1814 book, thought some causes of poverty unavoidable, especially mental and physical defects from birth, and old age; he also contended that ignorance and weakness of character are causes. Poverty, in his view, can occur because the potential for productiveness is ignored. Burton, in pointing out that there is no limit to available productiveness, writes: 'the cause of the poverty of the poor is, that they produce little' (1849: 41). In rich, industrious countries such as Britain 'there is a sort of ceaseless warfare between the two classes – those who work and have, and those who would have without working' (p. 310). In hotter countries, he believed there is indolence because people can consume without producing much. Optimistically, Burton asserts that in Britain the industrious do not object to the indolent poor because the mixed racial origins of the population make them more tolerant of other people.

In the nineteenth century a new cause of poverty emerged – immigration. Ireland suffered a cataclysmic drop in food supplies through potato blight in the mid-1840s. Scotland, Ireland's immediate neighbour, was soon to take in many starving migrants. In the 1841 population census 4.8 per cent of the Scottish population had been born in Ireland; in 1851, this rose to 7.2 per cent. De Quincey (1897) argued that the effects of migrant Irish paupers in England and Scotland could not be checked by new laws. The ruin, he argues, was twofold: Irish competition in the labour market degrades wages, and the poor Irish are a charge to English and Scots funds. Further, Irish children compete with English adult workmen, several of them doing the work of one man. However, De Quincey fails to debate both the pros and cons of immigration. The Irish contributed to the building of the Scottish infrastructure crucial to the expansion of the nineteenth-century Scottish economy, while the labour force of important heavy manual industries vital to Scottish industrialization, such as coal mining, was largely Irish.

Specific solutions: slavery

It is sensible to get the bad news out of the way first. That is true of anti-poverty policies of this period. What resembled slavery was actually suggested by two of these Scots, Fletcher and Hutcheson. Sadly, enslaving human beings and often treating them like the lowest animals has persisted from ancient times to the present day. Of course slaves can be treated kindly to extract the best work from them but they can still yearn for the freedom to do something else and be in another place.

If the times seem dangerous there is a temptation to propose extreme remedies. Andrew Fletcher of Saltoun (*c.*1653–1715), also known as 'the Patriot', was an early writer on the poverty question and is associated with the slavery approach. What incited him to devise a scheme to solve the poverty problem of his day was his awareness of 200,000 vagabonds (an estimate later disputed) roaming the countryside. According to Fletcher, these people murdered, robbed, rioted at public meetings such as weddings and begged from poor tenants who could ill afford to be charitable. Fletcher thought that the way to solve this threat to public order was to insist that landowners adopted, in a sense, these unfortunates and tie them to their land. This was a brave proposal, which, he immediately appreciated, would be criticized as 'slavery'.

In the second of his *Two Discourses concerning the Affairs of Scotland* (1698) Fletcher argued that it is necessary to provide for the poor everywhere. He traced the problem of poverty to the freeing of slaves who professed Christianity in the time of Emperor Constantine: it was inevitable they would be poor as they lacked estates or professional education. Furthermore, under slavery, slaves and their families had been provided with meat, clothes and lodging. Hospitals and almshouses, he then argued, had to be built for idle and lazy people who increased the population to the cost of the nation. To make the revival of a form of slavery palatable Fletcher distinguishes the slave who is absolutely subject to the will of another from one who has certain limitations necessary for the sake of the commonwealth. He wanted every master of a family to employ the indigent, allowing them no possessions and having the power to sell them. However, he saw such 'slaves' as being under the protection of the law, not liable to mutilation, torture or being killed. If a master granted them freedom he would then be required to give them the means to subsist, otherwise, Fletcher argued, they would revert to being vagabonds. According to Fletcher's argument, every man of sufficient estate should take some of these vagabonds and employ them in various occupations – hedging, ditching or a mechanical art; this would be the priority in landlords' expenditure, taking precedence over indulgence in luxuries.

A strict system of control over workers was not new to Scotland: Fletcher points to the precedent in the Scottish Acts of 1579 and 1597, which gave persons of sufficient estate the right to take the child of any beggar, train him for service and oblige him to serve for life. In a collection of Fletcher's pamphlets (1997) the editor, Robertson, praises Fletcher for his clarity in distinguishing personal slavery, which is being enslaved to a tyrant with complete arbitrary power, from political slavery. But a careful inspection of Fletcher's scheme reveals the objectionable aspects of the institution of slavery – being under control, being an object of trade and being denied many human rights, including the right to own simple possessions. Fletcher's scheme would have been stronger if he had proved that slavery was better than other options. Later, Dugald Stewart regarded this early proposal as a return to villainage (being a feudal serf) and suggested, as an alternative for alleviating poverty, the encouragement of manufacturing and commerce to provide a fund to sustain an increasing population.

But Fletcher was not alone in this tough approach to the poor. Francis Hutcheson conceded strong powers to the state – to compel each person to work to prevent them being a burden on the industrious, and to insist on parents educating their children to allow them eventually to support themselves. Hutcheson wants to sternly enforce the work ethic, exempting no one from the duty 'to follow some profession or business subservient to some common good' (*System* II: 113). If exhortation were not enough, he argued, another remedy for persistent vagrants and the vice-ridden who ruin themselves and families was needed – slavery. Terence Hutchison noted the paradox that 'The great ancestor of economic liberalism, Francis Hutcheson himself, laid it down at this period that sloth should be punished by temporary servitude at least' (1953: 61).

In a sense Fletcher and Hutcheson were merely reflecting support for an institution acceptable in their times. Workers engaged in Scottish coalmining and salt-making, bound to their employers under legislation dating back to 1606, could leave their employers only with written permission in order to prevent labour being poached through the offer of higher wages. This legislation was partially repealed in 1775 then completely in 1799 to end this 'state of slavery or bondage, bound to the Collieries and Salt-works where they work for life, transferable with the Collieries and Salt-works, when their original masters have no further use of them', to quote the 1775 Act. But obeying the spirit of the times is no excuse for a thinker who wants lasting praise.

Specific solutions: employment schemes

Scottish writers in the eighteenth century shared the ideas of contemporary mercantilist policies towards helping the poor, especially with regard to employment. There is a simple logic in saying that you solve unemployment by providing jobs in government employment or in the private sector by government subsidy. In extreme cases the employment offered could be of little worth other than giving the jobless some activity to appear to justify an income. Early in the period David Black, in his *Essay upon industry and trade* (1706), saw the provision of employment for the poor as an important task of burghs. He wanted vagabonds, beggars and the idle to be set to the manufacture of coarse wool for home industry. He also argued that towns should encourage shipping, navigation, artificers and mechanics. Lindsay (1736) also argued that the poor should be employed to increase the nation's wealth as idleness caused the poor to resort to theft, robbery or begging to provide for their maintenance. His harsh proposals would put young people in a charity workhouse from the age of four or five, where they would be taught to weave, receive no wages and, at the age of twenty-five, be dismissed with a suit of clothes and a loom. He argued that once the unemployed portion of the poor had been provided with a livelihood, help to the aged and infirm would be affordable. This attempt to deal with idleness from a person's earliest years reflected the eighteenth-century view that pauper children should be trained for servile occupations in order to preserve social and occupational hierarchies. Johnston (1946) mentions that from 1617 children, with their parents' consent, could be bound by the kirk session to an employer to the age of thirty. Pauper children could also be despatched to work in the mills of the early nineteenth century.

Sinclair, believing that 'It is a duty incumbent upon every political society to provide for such unhappy individuals belonging to it, as from the poverty of their situation, from sickness, want of employment, and the various unavoidable misfortunes to which human nature is liable, are unable to maintain themselves...' (1790: 211–12), had specific proposals. He suggested that a commissioner for the management of the poor would be appointed to obtain income from managing turnpike roads and the cultivation of royal forests, and that the poor would make and repair roads and labour in the fields, even growing tobacco again in Britain.

Critics of direct employment measures, for example Robert Wallace, worried that workhouses would encourage idleness, wanted such schemes to be downgraded to occasional employment. Many schemes to help the poor were deemed pointless. Craig (1814), too, was sceptical of public relief, questioning the idea that work should be provided for all willing to undertake it, something a government could not do by legislation as it is the demand for labour that regulates labour. He also raised the perennial concern that more work in the public sector is at the expense of less in the private, the 'crowding-out' problem:

> The establishment of public manufactures can have no tendency to increase the demand. Those who apply at the workhouses may indeed get employment, but, to exactly the same extent, other labourers must be thrown idle.
>
> (II: 317)

He went on to discourage support for these schemes because to provide employment schemes for workers with redundant skills is a waste of national capital, deadening ingenuity and discouraging movement to new types of employment. But he would concede public works schemes as a temporary measure, for the state benefits from executing major investments such as roads, canals and harbours. These schemes could help only the able-bodied poor; those unable to work still needed some other type of help.

Specific solutions: cheaper food

The poor could be given food instead of employment. If poor people are starving then a response to their condition is simply to provide food freely or at affordable prices. Steuart looked cautiously at this cheap food policy. He notes that it is difficult to identify the 'poor' as it means something different for each class: we have an indeterminate policy if we are ignorant of who they are and how much to bestow upon them. Speaking as the owner of Lanarkshire estates he noted that in his area the poor were less obvious because they stay at home. In 1769 Steuart suggested a plan to bring down the price of subsistence universally but only when the lower classes were in distress; at other times they should buy at dear prices for there was no case for keeping food prices below what the poorest manufacturer could pay. In his dissertation on grain he notes the difference between 'the poor who by their industry feed themselves' and 'the poor who are gratuitously fed by others' (1783: 39). The first category can take care of themselves and are useful to the state; the second is a charge patiently borne by others on the principle of humanity. Dugald Stewart disputed Steuart's opinion that the floor to the prices of necessaries is determined by the means of the lower orders because of the existence of poor relief, which increases purchasing power. But he admitted that rising food prices, caused by increased demand for food from increasing human and horse populations, was a problem. As the crisis of the poor was a lack of sustenance, he approved of legislation to provide relief by the dispensing of potatoes, rice or soup at public kitchens but not of tea, alcohol and opium, which made for poor nourishment.

Craig thought that any compulsory fund should be confined to providing basic subsistence, especially in emergencies, and should certainly not be on a generous scale: subsistence but below that of workers independent of parish support. In the absence of public works schemes, he argued that money and provisions should be given to the unemployed but relief should stop when the demand for labour revived. But he warned that distributing money in times of scarcity and distress leads to increased prices and further poverty. He had a different version of the cheap food policy – importing food. Lower prices at home would, he thought, be counterbalanced for the farmer by bounties, which would attract new capital to the trade and retain experienced hands.

With both employment and food distribution schemes there is the ever present consequence of interfering with markets. Providing new jobs can be at the expense of existing jobs unless there is an overall increase in the demand for labour. Reducing the price of food for the poor also has its difficulties as the paupers might resell the food, providing unfair competition with regular food supplies. If farmers were ordered to provide some food more cheaply they could easily run into financial problems through selling below cost; if a government subsidy helped them with their costs they had an incentive to be inefficient.

Specific solutions: land redistribution

The starving poor could be rescued from their plight by receiving the gift of land to cultivate the provisions they needed. Taking land from existing owners would obviously challenge private property rights but, as argued above, the public interest has long been a reason for modifying such rights. Hutcheson hinted at this – great inequalities of wealth will grant disproportionate power to individuals and threaten the state as a whole:

> there should be such Agrarian laws as will prevent any immoderate increase of wealth in the hands of a few, which could support a force superior to the whole body.
>
> (*System* II: 248)

He needed to provide strong reasons to justify something as drastic as taking land from current landowners and trace the effects of doing so.

Attention to the land issue is prominent in Ogilvie (1781), in his proposals to help the poor. The cultivation of the soil open to everyone through land reform would, he argued, make poverty disappear as, with their own land at last, the poor would have food. Like many a utopian Ogilvie did not appreciate that there is no proof that the poor would be any good at agriculture and produce a reasonable livelihood.

As Scotland lacked the laws and the willingness of government to provide more than the barest of necessities, with the consequence that at least a tenth of the population, some 250,000, were in total destitution despite the fact that the abundance of resources, including fertile land, could maintain a population a hundred times larger, a drastic land solution was suggested by Archibald Alison (1840). He argued in favour of a wider distribution of land, making it easy for the 'lower orders' to possess small parcels of land. He had precedents for this, citing various examples of English aristocrats – Lord Winchelsea, Lord Grosvenor and the Duke of Marlborough – who had offered small portions of land to the poor and thus avoided the distribution of poor relief and created a need for more livestock. His proposals reflect the fact that, in early societies, relieving the poor was not a problem because people were bound to the land and were the responsibility of proprietors. But with the industrialization and urbanization of Scotland in the nineteenth century land redistribution could soon become an irrelevance. In the anonymity of large cities there would be too many to be helped by charity or the gift of land, and the idea of turning back the clock and persuading the urbanized masses to return to the fields was unrealistic.

Specific solutions: emigration

If there are difficulties in creating employment or in providing food a population can afford, reducing a population through emigration would spread existing employment and food supplies. But emigration is an expensive activity, particularly because of the need to travel large distances. Movement to nearby European countries would do little to help the Scottish poor because many neighbouring areas had excess population too. North America became the most important destination but it was thousands of miles away.

In his *Observations* (1805) the Earl of Selkirk, a strong supporter of emigration, dismissed economic development as an inferior solution to poverty – public works like the Caledonian Canal would, he argued, temporarily halt emigration only during the period of construction. He was concerned that it would be mainly tenants who would emigrate because of the high cost of the passage to North America; cotters (minor tenants), who might have no rights over land, would move to the manufacturing towns of southern Scotland. To combat this, he thought that a grant to would-be migrants could be a one-off expense to help the poor rather than a permanent requirement to maintain them. Scotland, he thought, would not suffer through emigration as the initial reduction in population would provide greater subsistence for those who remain; later, natural increase of the population would replace the population that had left.

Archibald Alison was also a fervent advocate of emigration to British colonies and the USA, expanding Selkirk's analysis and observing that in some years of the 1830s over 70,000 emigrated from Britain. He saw the dynamic potential for Scotland of such movement:

> If, by the removal of some hundred thousand of the more destitute of the people, more employment is left for those who remain behind, their wages will rise, their habits will improve, the standard of comfort to which they are habituated will be elevated; and population will gradually but certainly be brought under its real limitations, the prudential considerations and acquired wants of individuals.
>
> (1840 II: 404)

Thus, according to Alison, emigration would be more than a temporary solution to overpopulation and the resultant poverty, and a means of bringing future population growth under control.

However, like the Earl of Selkirk, Alison was concerned that the best people with some capital tended to emigrate rather than the poorest in the community, who needed public and private subsidization of their migration. Emigration has always been attractive to the fittest and most enterprising, thus stripping a country of its most talented.

Nevertheless, emigration could be regarded as the only remaining solution after the failure of other approaches. Burton's contribution to the *Westminster Review*, reprinted in *Poor Laws and Pauperism* (1841), follows up his long-standing interest in the poor. He detailed how severe the problem was. The rundown state of the Highlands forced vagrants down to the central belt of Scotland, with the consequence that the private charity houses of refuge for the destitute in Edinburgh and Glasgow were becoming overwhelmed. Begging had to be permitted to keep many people alive. A drastic solution was needed to replace the contemporary response to poverty: home schemes had failed so emigration should be tried.

Specific solutions: savings banks

Henry Duncan viewed the need for savings banks (mentioned in Chapter 3) within the context of helping the poor. This was probably the most durable of private sector proposals. In his view, a well-designed institution would encourage young people to curb their frivolous expenditures and foster a spirit of self-reliance to insure against diseases and old age. His savings idea was founded on his view of the Scottish character, especially the fact that many Scots feared becoming a burden on the parish. Looking at Duncan's proposals without proper actuarial calculations it is difficult to assess the contribution of such schemes to alleviating poverty. Presumably not much could be accumulated for rainy day expenditures by workers earning the low wages of the time. Consequently, savings at best could only supplement a reliable, comprehensive scheme.

Specific solutions: the Chalmers parish method

Thomas Chalmers wrote often and vigorously on the problem of poverty in Scotland, and in his own Glasgow parish of St John's he implemented a plan for alleviating it. It was the most famous of Scottish anti-poverty schemes. In *The Christian and the Civic Economy* (1821) he argued that, as a general principle, the withdrawal of government from an activity improves it because commerce is elevated and the best of human nature asserts itself: pauperism is cured by resurrecting providential habits. Daringly, he asserted his belief that the moral regimen of a country parish could be introduced into a large city because there is the same relationship between a church minister and people and a possible balance between the wealthy and the poor in a large city:

> It is the resort of the annuitants, and landed proprietors, and members of the law, and other learned professions who give impulse to a great amount of domestic industry, by their expenditure; and, on inquiring into the sources of maintenance and employment for the labouring classes there, it will be found that they are chiefly engaged in the immediate service of ministering to the wants and luxuries of the higher classes of the city. This brings the two extreme orders of society into that sort of relationship which is highly favourable to the general blandness and tranquillity of the whole population.
>
> (I: 27)

This was an early example of the idea of income trickling down from the rich to the poor, through the former's demand creating paid employment. Such an inequality of incomes immediately makes a charitable redistribution to relieve poverty possible. In his devolution of poverty management, Chalmers wanted to organize relief at the lowest geographical unit, the district, where a deacon or church elder could get to know fully the resources and needs of each household. He saw legislation as preventing 'fountains of charity' (p. 55) from operating. He identified these fountains as the habits and economies of the people, the kindness of relatives, and the sympathy of the wealthy and of the poor for each other. He wanted saving to be encouraged to allow a workman to afford to negotiate for higher pay and withstand recessions. The 'economy of high wages' appealed to him: higher wages by encouraging greater productivity paid for themselves.

In his *Tracts on Pauperism* (1833b) Chalmers lamented the increase in the expense of helping paupers under compulsory schemes and the lack of vigilance of undermanagers when there is a common fund. He thought he had a better scheme. In his parish church he was able to run up a surplus of income over expenditure sufficient for a contingency fund. The careful work of church deacons, who considered each plea for aid, had prevented an increase in the number of paupers, although that could have been because strict rules discouraged applicants. In Chalmers' *On the power, wisdom and goodness of God* (1833a) he argued that it is wrong to say that everyone has a right to the means of subsistence; nature provides for the destitute through human compassion. Compulsory poor rates, he argued, would reduce net rents, leave land uncultivated and increase rural unemployment; thus the amount of subsistence of the poor would fall. This view of Chalmers' is perhaps too pessimistic because a high demand for agricultural produce with consequential price increases would make the poor rates affordable.

In Chalmers' diaries for 1811–13, Mary Furgol discovered that he thought 'people should be encouraged to be as independent as possible, that if relief were given, it should be minimal, and that it must at all costs be made obvious that no regular official relief system could be automatically depended upon in the event of a simple plea for help' (Cheyne 1985: 124). This is a useful summary of his stance.

A retired Lord of Session (Scottish judge), David Monypenny of Pitmilly, born 1769, published support for Chalmers in his *Remarks on the Poor Laws* (1834). He thought that Chalmers had dealt with the greatest problem of poverty relief, that of administrating a voluntary scheme, as over two hundred parishes had imposed a compulsory assessment, far in excess of what was supposed to be an exception. It was impossible, in Monypenny's view, to have the coexistence of compulsion and voluntary collection: compulsion should end or private charity would disappear. He thought that Chalmers had shown that even in the poorest city the voluntary system could apply because the duty of charity is an imperative for all. Archibald Alison (1840) had tepid praise for Chalmers, believing he succeeded in his parish experiment in Glasgow because he attracted enthusiastic religious folk from other parishes. Burton thought Chalmers' Glasgow scheme was possible only because there were respectable citizens to act as deacons, and witheringly dismissed the Chalmers plan as 'a pet scheme, in short, of the aristocracy of Glasgow' (1849: 23). He thought that a new system for helping the Scottish poor was needed – one which the country could afford and which would be based on companionship, benevolence and kindness. Ironically, this was, in a sense, what Chalmers wanted, but Burton failed to devise a detailed practical scheme. Nevertheless, in a boost to Chalmers and others who advocated church schemes, Grahame (1816) admitted that charity is widespread and permanent only when inspired by religion.

Poor Laws or charity

Instead of local schemes varying from place to place there is the alternative of a national scheme established by legislation. Scotland had laws concerning the poor between 1535 and 1929. In Scotland begging outside the parish of one's birth was illegal from 1535. In 1579 a fundamental statute close to English legislation was enacted, making parishes responsible for keeping a record of their poor, and in 1597 beggars had to take common works employment. The next century developed the law. In 1692 magistrates were ordered to establish correction houses or workhouses while an act of 1698 permitted magistrates to force vagabonds into suitable work. Eventually the system settled down with the Poor Law (Scotland) Act 1845 unifying the system of relief through setting up a central Board of Supervision, which could raise local taxes to help the poor. Gradually, outdoor relief was replaced by help through the workhouse. Furthermore, in Scotland, unlike in England, the poor could appeal if denied relief as the rules for the system were formulated centrally but the administration was local. An example of local poor relief at Kirkcaldy in 1742, mentioned by Fay (1956), was an employment scheme that provided lint for the poor to spin into yarn.

In the early nineteenth century, Mitchison (1974) states that Scotland's relief of the poor was praised for being low cost and limited. Even a House of Lords committee in 1817 mentioned the 'admirable' practice of Scotland. Cage commented that 'perhaps the most important characteristic of the old Scottish poor law was its flexibility and diversity' (1975: 118). The Scots disapproved of the English law for giving the able-bodied unemployed the right to relief, violating the Scottish Act of 1661, which excluded from help persons in 'anie way able to gain their living'. Flexibility came through allowing local discretion, originally by parish churches but increasingly by heritors (landed proprietors), who had the right because of legal cases of 1751–52 to administer voluntary money: during the bad harvests of 1799–1800 some parishes did aid the able-bodied. Landowners, however, had a waning interest in helping the poor: when faced with the choice of paying for schools or for the poor, they preferred to support education, a more predictable expense.

The poor were entitled to half the voluntary collections at church doors; money was also available from other fundraising. Being responsible for helping the poor enhanced the churches' role in society, and gave them good cause for opposing the Poor Laws. The Free Church minister Dr Thomas Guthrie (1803–73) wanted no Poor Laws as they challenged Scottish virtues; his fellow minister Chalmers went as far as to suggest that landowners should not obey the Poor Law. Voluntary subscriptions at the church door, Burton (1841) pointed out, avoided regular assessment, but the number of assessed parishes for a poor rate by the kirk session and heritors rose from ninety-three in 1798 to 200 in 1820. By the 1830s half of the expenditure on poor relief came from assessment; the rest was from charitable sources, including church door collections. In Scotland maintenance of the poor was done on the cheap, costing a fifth of what it cost in England, but how adequate the provision for the aged and infirm was in either Scotland or England is difficult to measure.

Not much was changed by the Poor Law (Scotland) Act 1845. According to Wright (1953) the entire poor relief system continued to rely on self-help. Parochial boards with tax-raising powers could provide relief outdoors in the form of small weekly cash payments or in poorhouses. Five years' residence in parishes was needed to obtain help.

> The paucity of official relief in Scotland was taken for granted and counteracted by mutual help and much philanthropic endeavour. After 1845 the Scots pauper had a much improved lot for ten years, with increased funds available for his relief. The distinctive poor law system did ensure that, for Scottish workers, wages were not kept low by concealed subsidies (grants in aid). By tradition wages were left free to reflect the supply and demand for labour related to bargaining power.
>
> (p. 15)

Checkland (1980) took a stronger view of the 1845 Act, arguing that it changed poor relief from a voluntary to a compulsory system. A major aspect of the

Act was the option of the poor entering a workhouse to get relief. Whether workhouses were a suitable solution had been questioned by E. Jones in *Observations on the Scheme before parliament* (1776), cited by Coats (1960). Agriculture was then the first object in every nation but it could not be taught in poorhouses, which were, Jones thought, more suitable for manufacturing towns. This is an odd view as the simple crafts of workhouses could be practised in any type of area. Stewart, also commenting on workhouses, preferred the poor to work at home because workhouses had high running costs and low productivity due to the fact that persons were deprived of their liberty. However, he did argue that workhouses were justifiable where the poor could not get better residence.

Using workhouses was regarded as an incompetent solution to poverty. Craig mentioned that the extravagance of the Poor Law overseers caused waste of public money; he wanted them elected annually and backed up by inspectors to check applicants for relief. John McFarlan and Lord Kames, too, regarded maladministration as the great problem of the Poor Laws – Kames noted that the cost of maintenance in a poorhouse was double that in a private house. The dissolute and idle should not, in their view, be given charity, and the fact that charity has been given to the undeserving poor has multiplied their numbers. Kames, according to Coats (1960), argued that a man's natural impulse to action is discouraged by the Poor Laws. Writing about the English Poor Law with relevance to Scotland, Kames in his *Sketches* said, 'What a confused jumble do they make, when they attempt to mend the laws of nature! Leave nature to her own operations; she understands them the best' (1778 II: 10).

Hamilton (1822) thought that managers of a fund are apt to be profuse in their distribution when there is compulsory assessment, attracting immigrants from the country. But, where affluent persons have not given voluntarily, he still approved of compulsory assessment.

The workhouse policy affected the labour market. Lauderdale, in his notes on *WN*, says that the general tendency was to let masters reduce wages to their low point when food was plentiful and cheap. Consequently, in a year of scarcity when food prices are high wages are too low, requiring an increase of the poor rates to help those with deficient incomes. More, he argues, is thus paid in poor rates than the rate dictated by the price of maintenance.

The search for principles for founding a welfare system occurred in Scottish writers' analysis of both the English and Scottish laws. Although Thomas Carlyle was chiefly an observer of the effects of English Poor Laws what he said had application to Scotland. Given his gospel of work he was inevitably wary of any incomes in the form of welfare benefits rather than wages. In *Chartism* he sternly refers to 'this law of no work no recompense ... Work is the mission of man in this Earth' (1840: 20). He also stated that 'He that can work is a born king of something; is in communion with nature, is master of a thing or things, is a priest and king of Nature so far' (p. 23), but grudgingly admitted that the new Poor Law, which provided relief only within workhouses, did give 'a protection of the thrifty labourer against the thriftless and dissolute...' (p. 21). He summed up the new Poor Law as '*laissez faire, laissez passer*'. Carlyle always found it easier to denounce wrongs than to provide solutions to the problems of his day.

In *Past and Present* (1843) Carlyle wrote: 'A Poor-Law, any and every Poor-Law... is but a temporary measure; an anodyne, not a remedy. Rich and Poor, when once the naked facts of their condition have come into collision, cannot long subsist together on a mere Poor-Law' (p. 3), thus showing sympathy for the poor without wrecking the underlying economic mechanisms of society. As the Cambridge economist Alfred Marshall, in his *Principles of Economics* (1890), was to recognize, much of the problem of poverty is the result of the ill-functioning of the labour market. Carlyle called for fair wages, a change in distribution:

> the world has been rushing on with such fiery animation to get work and evermore work done, it has had no time to think of dividing the wages; and has merely left them to be scrambled for by the Law of the Stronger, Law of Supply-and-demand, law of Laissez-faire, and other idle Laws and Un-laws. (1843: 27)

> Let inventive men cease to spend their existence incessantly contriving how cotton can be made cheaper; and try to invent a little how cotton at its present cheapness could be somewhat justlier divided among us... (p. 229)

His suggestion that workers have an interest, a joint interest with their employers, in their enterprises did not go as far as a profit-sharing scheme. Carlyle in *Chartism*, according to Welch, attacked the new Poor Law for the utilitarian assumption that the working poor are things. Carlyle approved of abolishing the old Poor Law, which was 'a bounty on unthrift, idleness, bastardy and beer-drinking' (Welch 2006: 384) and did not protect the industrious and frugal worker. In *Chartism* Carlyle saw that the Poor Law could be the first step to benefiting the labouring class through making all classes work and the higher class give more guidance to the lower classes.

Any perceived deficiency in the Poor Laws was always an excuse for advocating total reliance on voluntary charity. This was linked to the alleged superior morality of being charitable. In his *System*, Hutcheson, according to Coats (1960), argued that making charity a legal requirement would abate the beauty of giving. The principles to be followed in charitable giving are

> First, that it be not hurtful to the morals of the object... by encouraging them in sloth, meanness of temper, or any vicious dispositions; and again, that it be not so immoderate as to exhaust its own foundation ...or

> incapacitate the donor for other offices of life toward those whom he may be more sacredly obliged to support.
>
> (*System* I: 306)

Charity could never be a total solution. Dugald Stewart was astounded that in England, where there were benefit clubs and friendly societies, a seventh of the population in 1776 was still in receipt of parochial relief. He noted that voluntary charity provides much of the relief of the poor and the rich do not shirk their duty. He also supported the idea of friendly societies (societies that build up funds to provide the members with benefits to cover death, sickness and unemployment) as they encourage industry and economy. In a summary, Milgate and Stimson (1996) report that Dugald Stewart thought the Poor Laws were an example of multiplying the objects of the law unnecessarily and that self-help was better.

Craig, an advocate of the voluntarist approach, asserted that the poor have no *claim* to property. What they receive in help should, he argued, be left to the feelings and conscience of the individual. In his view government help has bad effects as the poor are discouraged from labour by pensions, sickness and unemployment pay, and one of the consequences is that marriages are contracted without regard for the cost of maintaining any offspring. His view was so extreme, he could write,

> There is but one effectual way of impressing upon their minds the possibility of their being abandoned to the extremity of want, and that is by the example of others gradually perishing without relief.
>
> (1814: 293–4)

However, voluntary charity is alarming if misdirected and inappropriate: it is hard to know how much is being given to a beggar and, if too much is given there is the risk of turning begging into a trade. Burton reports that street begging was so well organized that there were warehouses for the sale and hire of impostors' dresses and children could be hired to accompany beggars for a day or a week. His article on vagrancy in the *Edinburgh Review*, October 1842, mentions agricultural labourers who gave up jobs of seven shillings per week to earn twenty to thirty-five as vagrants. Not all charity had to cease: he says there is a case for the rich helping on particular occasions when there are unavoidable calamities. Distributing all superfluous wealth to the poor would, however, he argues, create more destitution and destroy the inducement of the industrious to accumulate.

Underpinning the voluntary approach was the belief that to solve the poverty problem it was essential to understand human nature. The personal characteristics of the poor were seen as a crucial contributor to the existence of poverty if they had brought their wretchedness on themselves and had in their own hands the chance of becoming prosperous. In other words, they had a moral duty to work. Passages from the Bible were cited by supporters of this view in the debate. Grahame (1816), in his work on population, notes that Malthus quotes St Paul's stern injunction that a man who doesn't work should not eat. However, Grahame says that the injunction applies only to teachers of Christianity; other texts insist on giving to the necessitous, for example, Deuteronomy 15:11 and Matthew 35:31.

Given human nature, in McFarlan's view the poor had to be disciplined not helped. He wanted strict control of the poor, emphasizing the role of the police and even downgrading the importance of charity. An excess of alms-giving would, according to him, increase the numbers of the poor because if one helps a beggar, others are encouraged to beg. He also thought workhouses were worthless; in his plan, strict policing of poor areas through inspectors visiting the poor in their homes would discover the real character of the poor. Persons of poor character would be given little, and there would be a house of correction in every town or large parish to prevent vagrancy, idleness and vice.

However, some writers held a less pessimistic view of human nature. As Archibald Alison argued (1840), the growth of artificial wants is essential to progress and civilization. The middling and upper classes, by learning the pleasures of intellectual cultivation and refined taste, rise above the brutish habits of the lower classes; therefore, it is crucial to change the habits of the poor, to encourage artificial wants, supremely the pleasure of possessing property, which requires self-control and the avoidance of ruinous desires. It was not only acquisition of land, but deposits in savings banks, which were advocated to improve habits.

Linked to poverty was population increase, which could be caused by neglecting moral principles. Malthus had popularized 'moral restraint' in the form of postponing marriage, behaviour within everyone's scope and sure to lead to increased family prosperity. Hamilton (1822), similarly, was not keen to help healthy employed men with large families and insufficient wages and wanted imprudent marriage to be avoided. Able unemployed men must, he thought, seek different work if in a declining occupation, but if there is a low general demand for labour then gentlemen of landed property may offer jobs on moderate terms. No charity should, in his view, be given to mothers of illegitimate children beyond the first child. Grahame, dissenting from this view, wanted to promote marriage among the poor as children could increase family income.

Human nature often responds to incentives. As Dugald Stewart argued, property ownership could be that incentive:

> ...the happy effects which the possession of property, however trifling, has on the character and habits of the lower orders...Whatever circumstance stimulates an individual to look forward to a distant futurity, cultivates his habits of self-command and advances him in the scale of moral beings; removing him from the condition of those savages who hunt or fish when they are hungry, and eat and sleep till they hunt or fish again.
>
> (1840 II: 323)

But was this realistic given the low wages of the time? Would landowners sell their property? Not likely.

Another powerful disincentive to improving human character is possibly inequality. Millar, in *Letters of Sidney*, outlines the widespread ill effects of inequality: few would care about defending their country despite there being trade wars and the possibility of the growth of monopolies; more would be spent on the criminal justice system because of fraud and dishonesty; more on guarding of property and more on police officers and prisons. With such a starting point, Millar argues that his proposals on taxation and property would permit that

> the great body of the people, relieved from the pressure of taxes, and acquiring some little property by succession would be enabled to educate their children and might view an independent and comfortable provision in their old age as easily attainable by industry and economy, increasing and husbanding those little fortunes which they had inherited from their relations.
>
> (1796: 92)

There would be sufficient 'motives to exertion' from increasing enjoyments, security from the fickleness of fortune and establishing one's family at least at an equal rank. Millar detailed the many benefits of reducing inequality. With more equality the rich would be less exposed to indolence and vice and more knowledge would be diffused, leading to higher productivity and the greater chance of a genius being discovered in literature and the fine arts. In his essay *Of Commerce* David Hume wrote: 'a too great disproportion among the citizens weakens any state. Every person, if possible, ought to enjoy the fruits of his labour, in a full possession of all the necessaries, and many of the conveniences of life. No one can doubt but such equality is most suitable to human nature' (1987: 265). Hume, according to Brewer (1997), thought that growth would equalize incomes as the poor would gain more in happiness than the rich would lose and thus natural forces in the economy could obliterate poverty. Hume's view is very modern for he suggests a painless way to achieve more equality, a gradual way, in which all would gain and no one lose because there would be a general increase in incomes.

Given so many onslaughts on the Poor Laws it is surprising to find their supporters. But Grahame (1816) questioned the abolition of the Poor Laws, realizing that administrative errors have to be distinguished from the system itself. His social argument for such legislation was that the rich and the poor both benefit from Poor Laws because they create bonds between them: the rich, who benefit from the laws to preserve inequalities, private property and the division of labour, have a moral obligation to provide charity and be virtuous.

As a last resort, because of the unreliable help provided by private charity, the Poor Laws are acceptable as the only means left to provide enough benefit although they could still be reformed. That was the attitude of William

Pulteney Alison (1790–1859), an Edinburgh University graduate and follower of Dugald Stewart's ideas, who rose to the grand heights of the medical profession as president of the Royal College of Physicians, Edinburgh, and professor of the Institutes of Medicine at Edinburgh University. He used his experience of treating Edinburgh's population to demonstrate that poverty was the main cause of the high mortality rates of Edinburgh and Glasgow but recognized private charity could not be the whole answer. Fervently, he argued that private charity, being partial and uncertain, varies according to the accident of residence and whims of the rich, unlike the uniformity of the Poor Law. In a crisis it was not enough, as in treating the epidemic fever of Edinburgh and Glasgow. There could, therefore, he argued, be both public and private provision, as was the case in England, which had the largest compulsory scheme of poor relief in the world. He dismissed the view that Scotland needed less poverty relief per head than England because Scotland has a better behaved and industrious population, mentioning the drunkenness and early improvident marriages in large Scottish towns. The answer, he thought, was establishing a workhouse on English lines in every considerable Scottish town to provide for about 4,000 paupers: this would solve vagrancy and extend relief to the able-bodied. He also wanted the £140,000 spent on poor relief in Scotland to be gradually increased to £800,000. William Alison's views were much in keeping with the philosophy of the age: that the poor had to be taken off the streets and given supervised work.

His brother, Archibald Alison, believed that, with a proper system of Poor Laws population problems would diminish, because the population would not sink to a low level of degradation and become trapped in poverty. In England, Archibald Alison asserted, the Poor Laws contributed to the middle and lower classes being more comfortable than anywhere in the world, avoiding redundancy of population, reckless habits and improvident conduct. He would accept Poor Laws if they were reformed according to four principles. First, provision would be offered to all persons with a particular type of need, irrespective of birth or residence. Second, help should be adapted to the needs of an individual, taking age into account, and offered to the able-bodied in local public works schemes. Third, a redundant population would be reduced by publicly funded emigration schemes. Fourth, local law courts, not landowners, would set the poor rate. He approved of the English principle of granting relief only to those inside workhouses but would exempt the old and the married suffering from the casualties of life. Perhaps Archibald Alison tried too hard to tidy up the system. Every proposal he made was expensive and unlikely to meet the approval of the penny-pinching governments of his day.

A new national approach

So much of the discussion of poor relief focused on the poor rate, a local tax, and needed to be considered within the whole context of public finance. Sinclair

(1790) proposed to help the poor under existing taxation, through dividing the revenue raised into two parts to pay a bounty upon exported manufactures and

> annually distributing the other [part] among such of the married poor as have families to maintain, in the proportion to the number of their children, and giving small annuities to those who, after a life spent in laborious industry, are unable, from sickness or age, to maintain themselves; that thus the situation of that valuable class of men might be rendered as comfortable as the imperfection of human nature will allow.
>
> (p. 128)

This was only a partial scheme, excluding the unmarried and the feckless.

Craig (1814) asserted that public funds should not be based on voluntary contributions but on equal payments not proportionate to wealth and income, and levied weekly to make it easier for labourers to pay them. Private charity would have only a supplementary role: it could mitigate calamity in special cases, for example, families struggling hard to avoid being paupers, or the diseased and aged who need more than the public provision.

Samuel Read was remarkably prescient in devising a national scheme so early in the nineteenth century. The poor had their champion in him. In his 1829 book he expressed his strong views on the entitlement of the poor to help and what form that help should take. His proposals, probably the most radical of the time, went far beyond the Poor Laws. With good management, he argued, the unemployed can be kept on half the amount of ordinary wages. The aged, infirm and orphans should be supported liberally; others sparingly. But instead of parish relief, he argued that a national scheme financed by a general tax on all classes but administered by parishes was needed. This would provide for all in want and suppress public begging.

To justify his proposal he argued that a compulsory legal scheme forces the uncharitable to contribute and is more certain than a voluntary scheme to distribute benefits. He believed that in a civilized society all in want have the right to support, including the unemployed, who should get free aid or paid employment. With traces of the earlier analysis of poverty within the context of the stages of development, he points out that an unemployed man in modern society is in a worse state than a savage, who could procure subsistence for himself because goods are produced by nature. Therefore, he contended that the unemployed have the right to subsistence from the earth, and that society is at war with him if it refuses support.

He found important precedents for helping the poor: law courts, for example, often discharged stealers of bread. He also uses the previously cited argument for the suspension of property rights in times of distress: in a besieged city, for example, food can be taken without scruple because extraordinary circumstances affect property rights. However, as mentioned in Chapter 5, Read does not appreciate that at a time of distress there are different property rights, not an absence of property rights, otherwise there would be anarchy.

Another supporter of a national scheme, Smart (1900), discussed the poor rate in his book on taxation. Because the relief of the poor, like defence, is a national service, he contended that it should not be financed by a local poor rate. He argued that, in practical terms, it is impossible to levy a local income tax, and a property tax hits problems of valuation. It thus seems that by the end of the nineteenth century there were useful guidelines for founding a modern welfare state.

Smith on poverty

Smith wanted a labour market approach to helping the poor. He had noted that Scotland, through lacking England's Act of Settlement, which insisted on paupers returning to their place of birth, had freer labour mobility and similar wages in nearby places. But there is more to Smith's attitude to the poor than the idea that labour mobility would solve the poverty problem, always a dubious proposal when an economy is so depressed that there are no prosperous places crying out for more labour. He engaged with the principal issues, including the 'slavery' approach to coping with the poor. In *LJ* he regards colliers and salters as 'the only vestiges of slavery which remain amongst us' (p. 191) and shows they are different from ancient slaves because they are paid like labourers, have their own property, are not sold separately from the sale of the work and can marry and practise a religion freely. Their wages, he argued, would fall if their employment were open to free competition. But, on economic grounds, Smith soon dismisses slavery as a bad institution because slaves work less than freemen and are more careless in production than if they provided for themselves.

Before McFarlan, Smith used the stages theory, which holds that in the age of hunters the population exists at the minimum level of income, while in the commercial stage prosperity extends to many, but not all, the lowest members of society. To Smith 'poverty' was very complex. Considering it several times in a writing career spanning three decades he had an opportunity to develop his views and not merely repeat simple ideas. In his *TMS* poverty causes psychic pain, that is, the concealment of being poor through shame, rather than primarily economic distress. In *LJ* Smith says there is an institutional approach to poverty in that law and government are instruments of the rich to oppress the poor. In *WN* he sees real poverty as not obtaining the necessities of life with one's wages. This attitude to poverty, a concentration on the labour market, is sensible, for even today the income of the majority of households is wages: improve them and living standards will rise.

At times one wonders if Smith deeply cared about the poor. In *TMS* he writes:

> The mere want of fortune, mere poverty, excites little compassion. Its complaints are too apt to be the objects rather of contempt than of fellow-feeling. We despise a beggar; and, though his importunities may

> extort an alms from us, he is scarce ever the object of any serious commiseration.
>
> (p. 144)

However, he does believe that a fall from riches to poverty causes distress to the sufferer and evokes sympathy: we support those who originally were well-off but not those who have been poor for some time. Further on, Smith complacently writes:

> The rich only select from the heap what is most precious and agreeable. They consume little more than the poor, and in spite of their natural selfishness and rapacity, though they mean only their own conveniency, though the sole end which they propose ... be the gratification of their own vain and insatiable desires, they divide with the poor the produce of all their improvements. They are led by an invisible hand to make nearly the same distribution of the necessaries of life, which would have been made, had the earth been divided into equal portions among all its inhabitants, and thus without, intending it, without knowing it, advance the interest of the society, and afford means to the multiplication of the species ... In what constitutes the real happiness of human life, they [those who do not own land] are in no respect inferior to those who would seem so much above them. In ease of body and peace of mind, all the different ranks of life are nearly upon a level, and the beggar, who suns himself by the side of the highway, possesses that security which kings are fighting for.
>
> (pp. 184–5)

This sounds implausible and almost a suggestion that there is material equality in society; however, Smith is concentrating his attention on the distribution of the *necessaries* of life and not of all income. Given the fact that many would be living on farms, paid in kind, and with simple tastes, the poor and the rich would consume similar amounts of basic goods. This passage also looks at poverty from a psychological rather than material standpoint. To be convincing Smith should have justified his view that the poor are contented.

Smith's views can hardly be regarded as any foundation for policy measures as strong as the Poor Laws but he was concerned with the poverty of workers, if not of the unemployed or infirm. He uses a reciprocity argument that it is equitable that those who provide food, clothing and lodging for the population should themselves have tolerable subsistence. Grandly, he expressed the view that 'No society can surely be flourishing and happy, of which the far greater part of the members are poor and miserable' (*WN*: 96) without proposing many remedies.

In *WN* Smith suggested modest redistribution to help the poor: carriages of luxury would have higher tolls than carts for necessaries – 'the vanity of the rich is made to contribute in a very easy manner to the relief of the poor'

(p. 725), a suggestion reflecting the popular contemporary view that luxuries should be taxed highly and necessaries little. In his public finance proposals Smith certainly did not recommend high levels of expenditures: he thought public expenditure was not for the sake of improving society so should be self-financing. He gave examples of self-funding, including the fact that taxes on the Turkey Company paid for British diplomatic representation in that country. Education, he pointed out, did not need great public funding, although, even for the poor, education would not be entirely free as scholars would pay fees to provide an income for the schoolmasters. His suggestion of a self-financing approach to help the poor through trade protection was surprising for an advocate of free trade; however, he thought tariffs should be reduced gradually to maintain employment and that a bounty on corn exports is wrong if corn prices rise to the detriment of the poor.

According to Rothschild (1992) Smith was considered a friend of the poor. Six times in his chapter on wages he uses the expression 'the labouring poor', and argued in favour of a liberal reward for labour. She also notes (1995) that Smith does not care about the fecklessness and indolence attributed to the poor: let them enjoy a few days' relaxation per week or indulge themselves after hard work. Smith was more humane, Conniff (1987) observed, than Burke on poor relief, although they shared the view that wages should arise from a free contract. It seems then that Smith had sympathy for the poor but was not the most active of their helpers. Smith in *TMS*, according to Coats, argued that 'the peace and order of society is of more importance than even the relief of the miserable' (1960: 42).

Concluding remarks

Poverty is a perennial problem – 'the poor we have always with us' as the Gospels say. The problem will not go away, because people grow old, get sick and are subject to fluctuations in a national economy. Thus the provision of appropriate welfare is a crucial and perpetual issue of social and economic policy and, indeed, what was discussed in the writers cited still enters modern debates. Why bother at all with the poor? Briskly, Nicholson gives his answer: 'Poor relief is ostensibly for the benefit of the individuals concerned; but as a matter of public policy it confers common benefits in the prevention of crime and in the satisfaction of a sense of justice or of charity' (1893–1901 III: 373). Thus welfare benefits are based on an appeal to compassion or on prudence to prevent the poor revolting and seizing the property of the rich.

There were limits to the self-help of people in need of help. The poor could not or would not save in a precautionary way, so who should help and why? Only members of the population with surplus income could provide aid voluntarily through charity or compulsorily through some form of taxation. It needs strong persuasion to get people to give away their income: the idle rich often hate the idle poor and express those feelings through avoiding charity – hence the criticism that voluntary schemes would be unable to generate enough income. It was easier raising funds to help the sick and aged than generating the means to pay the unemployed, which meant that a private solution to helping the poor was unlikely to be comprehensive. There was always the suspicion that some claimants were dishonest and work-shy, giving critics of poor relief a reason for giving only what was legally required. Moreover, if a government scheme were adopted, at what level would it be administered? Local institutions existed but were difficult to finance if there were not a suitable mixture of rich and poor in the same locality, to make redistribution possible. A national scheme had a better chance of financial success, but was slow in coming. Against this background, it is to the credit of Samuel Read that he drew up realistic proposals.

Condition of the Economy

6

Economic growth

Scottish writers, whether mercantilist or classical, were in favour of economic growth. There was an awareness that through economic growth material success would increase welfare for all, including the poor; they rarely mentioned the negative impacts of growth – apart from the few references that economic growth, by diverting resources from the production of basic food to luxuries, reduces subsistence and population growth. If growth is desirable it is important to investigate its causes and to explain the mechanisms that would work the wonder of pulling an economy out of stagnation. The supply of factors of production might be enlarged, and their productivity improved, through increases in population and saving. Or the route to faster economic growth could be by pursuing a strategy, especially by improving the allocation of resources from unproductive to productive activities, by increasing specialization through the division of labour, or by attending to incentive mechanisms.

Adam Smith showed, in the very title of his economics magnum opus *An Inquiry into the Nature and Causes of the Wealth of Nations*, that economic growth was his central theme. In several senses he set the agenda for investigating economic growth. At the outset he contrasted the division of labour with the ratio of productive to unproductive labour as the major causes of growth. Furthermore, his many economic investigations, including his examination of the effects of institutions on economic welfare and government policy, were conducted in the hope of promoting economic expansion.

General observations about growth

Before dealing with the grand themes of economic growth, especially the division of labour and incentive mechanisms, there are minor issues relative to economic growth that we need to look at. These include the diversity of the national economy, the use of existing wealth, and the climate – all possible factors in the growth process.

Like many backward economies, Scotland, at the start of the eighteenth century, was a specialized economy. Rossner sums up the state of Scotland during the period 1700–60 as 'an open yet small, low-level-stable-state economy' (2008: 301), with 80 per cent of its population employed in agriculture. The obvious response to this was to recommend that Scotland diversify its economic activities. Steuart seized on what has been, for many countries, the major means of economic growth there: the migration of workers from low productivity agriculture to the higher productive industries of the city. He warned against the dangers of a stagnant agricultural sector not producing a surplus: 'this will produce a wonderful simplicity of manners, (but) will ruin the system of modern policy…' (*Principles* I: 105). He recognized that some countries need large agricultural labour forces as a source of soldiers, but argued that wherever possible labour should move to industry and obtain its food through trading manufactured goods. The conditions for growth in the manufacturing sector were clearly stated: 'ready sale, the regulated price of work, and certain profit resulting from industry' (p. 204). Steuart thought the diversification of the economy into industry was helped by the change from slavery to freemen, permitting wage payment according to the amount of work produced and thus creating an incentive to increase productivity. He instructs the statesman: 'to preserve a trading state from decline, the greatest care must be taken, to support a perfect balance between the hands employed in work and the demand for their labour' (p. 242).

At the outset of the take-off into growth the existing stock of wealth is important. Ferguson, in his *Institutes*, asserted that 'Wealth is a national resource because it may be employed in maintaining useful or serviceable men, and in supplying the exigencies of state' (1785: 264).

He appreciated both the old mercantilist idea of wealth as an idle hoard of money kept as a reserve and the classical view that wealth stimulates economic activity. For him, the state of a nation's wealth is not estimated from the state of its 'coffers, granaries or warehouses at a particular time', in other words what it has hoarded, but from 'the fertility of its lands, from the numbers, frugality, industry, and skill of its people' (p. 273).

Not only the level but the distribution of wealth counted. In Great Britain there is greater diffusion of wealth, he notes, and this has meant greater economic growth than in other countries:

> a proper distribution of wealth insures the increase of opulence, by sustaining a regular progressive demand in the home market, and still more effectually, by affording to those whose habits are likely to create a desire of supplanting labour, the power of executing it.
>
> (pp. 349–50)

Thus wealth had to be in the right hands. Ferguson hints at some redistribution to the poor, who would increase the demand – a stable demand – for necessaries, and to savers financing capital accumulation.

As wealth can expand or diminish, economic growth and economic decline can be analysed together. Playfair, in his *An Inquiry into the Permanent Causes of the Decline and Fall of Powerful and Wealthy Nations* (1807), surveys the factors producing decline, or negative growth. Wealth vanishes, he writes, if a commercial nation becomes corrupt and luxurious: there is higher expenditure and more taxation, loss of trade, neglect of industry, and a growing preference for trade over manufacturing, as in Holland. As he was also interested in wealth distribution he observes that because of an unequal division of wealth there is no hope and no exertion: families live on the interest of money instead of engaging in manufactures or commerce.

Apart from its endowment of wealth, a country embarking on growth has to cope with its climate. Scotland has a distinctive climate as a northern country and is obviously not able to do much about this. Hume follows Montesquieu in linking climate and economic growth. A sharp distinction is made between the torpor of the tropics and the vigour of temperate climes where the production of essential clothing and housing launches an economy on a growth trajectory. But Hume avoids taking the effects of climate too far. In his essay *Of National Characters* he writes: 'nor do I think, that men owe any thing of their temper or genius to the air, food or climate' (1987: 200). In China he finds that there is the greatest uniformity of character despite great variations in air and climate throughout that vast country.

Productive and unproductive labour

The distinction between productive and unproductive labour, Smith thought, was second only to the division of labour as a cause of economic growth. Productive labour creates value-added through the goods it produces. Smith explains that in manufacturing, unlike in menial service, labour adds to the costs of materials, the worker's maintenance and the master's profits. On the other hand, unproductive labour is not realized in 'any permanent subject, or vendible commodity, which endures after that labour is past, and for which an equal quantity of labour could afterwards be procured'. (*WN*: 330). Explaining the crucial role of parsimony, or thrift, he writes:

> Capitals are increased by parsimony, and diminished by prodigality and misconduct... Whatever a person saves from his revenue he adds to his capital, and either employs it himself in maintaining an additional number of productive hands, or enables some other person to do so, by lending it to him for an interest, that is, for a share of the profits... Parsimony, and not industry, is the immediate cause of the increase of capital.
>
> (p. 337)

The whole point of this saving is, he argues, to provide consumer goods for others, either through accumulating a wages fund to employ workers directly, or indirectly through lending savings to other employers. (The possibility of savings being hoarded and not invested is not contemplated.) Savings, in Smith's view, create circulating, not fixed, capital, which is productive because it increases the demand for labour.

In his application of the productive and unproductive labour distinction Smith fervently objected to the Physiocratic view, propounded in France in the mid-eighteenth century, that manufacturing is sterile. He did that to be consistent: in his view farm workers have no greater power than manufacturers to increase annual produce without saving because the same rules apply. A trading and manufacturing nation, he states, is not less productive than an agricultural one because it can trade manufactured goods for rude produce suitable for the wage fund. Smith also added a surprising addition to his classification of productive industries – retailing – because of its usefulness in breaking up bulky items or transporting them.

This central distinction between productive and unproductive labour provoked a semantic debate, within which 'productive' was not always defined very clearly. It is easy to find examples that would ridicule the distinction. Cannan (1917) noted Smith's inconsistencies. Smith, in *WN*, Book I, includes the output of actors and musicians in annual output, despite saying they were unproductive labour.

Dugald Stewart preferred to call labour 'effective', rather than productive, and provides many test examples of labour on the borderline between productive and unproductive, generally preferring the Physiocratic view that agriculture is productive and manufacturing not, instead of Smith's criteria for 'productive', that is, being vendible and durable.

Lauderdale, in his *Inquiry*, finds the equating of the unproductive with the failure to provide a permanent product and the condemnation of services analytically unsound. He is keen to assert that the same labour can be productive or unproductive according to the use. A cook making a tart for immediate consumption is called unproductive in Smith's schema but not if the tart is made for sale in a pastry cook's shop:

> it is impossible to discern why that should not be considered as wealth which tends to the satisfaction of man's immediate desires, as well as that which is stocked and stored up for the satisfaction of his future desire…
>
> (1804a: 152)

The usefulness of many services, in Lauderdale's view, is enough to label them productive: for example, law and medicine are services useful to the nation. Chalmers (1832) thought that the distinction between productive and unproductive labour is mischievous and has discouraged occupations conducive to well-being. Because a clergyman does not produce something tangible he is called unproductive. (Chalmers was a clergyman!) Whatever labour is to my enjoyment, he says, is productive. There are, he argues, many anomalies in the productive/unproductive distinction – a gunsmith is productive but a soldier is unproductive, a confectioner is productive but a domestic cook is unproductive, an instrument maker is productive but a musician is unproductive.

A very broad view of labour can also be found in Burton: 'Whatever society pays for, and ought to pay for, may fairly be considered as productive labour for the present purpose; for though there are no tangible objects created by it, yet it contributes in the end to the increase of production. Whatever tends to organise and civilise mankind is thus productive' (1849: 51), including judges and teachers.

The arts were used to provide illustrations of unproductive labour. An artist can produce wealth in the fundamental sense of adding to the cost of raw materials the value of his maintenance, in other words covering his expenses. Actors and musicians, by entertaining foreigners, can bring in subsistence from abroad. Sir Walter Scott in the introductory epistle to the Revd Dr Dryasdust in his *The Fortunes of Nigel* (1822) firmly asserted that

> a successful author is a productive labourer, and that his works constitute as effectual a part of the public wealth as that which is created by any other manufacture. If a new commodity, having an actually intrinsic and commercial value, be the result of the operation, why are the author's bales of books to be esteemed a less profitable part of the public stock than the goods of any other manufacturer?
>
> (p. 14)

Interestingly, he makes services appear productive because they contribute to producing a physical product. His argument could therefore not be extended to performing actors and musicians.

Smith engaged in a pointless exercise if the distinction between productive and unproductive labour is so difficult to make as to render it useless. Samuel Read wrote that 'Productive labour is that which is directly employed in the production of wealth or vendible property, and of which the effects remain apparent after the labour itself is past, fixed and realized in some material object or commodity' (1829: 35).

This is in accord with the idea of 'productive' meaning adding to the wage fund. Read admits that unproductive labour is concerned with what is perishable and ceases to be visible but is necessary to the production of wealth: for example, it includes the police who protect society, including producers. There cannot be an excess of unproductive labour as their wages are voluntarily given, he argues, and private prudence will determine the number of servants. He finds both productive and unproductive labour necessary and industrious: productive labourers include merchants and those who direct labour; non-labourers, including landholders and capitalists, can cause happiness. Both public debt and public salaries increase the non-labouring classes.

In support of Smith, Buchanan, in his 1814 commentary on *WN*, argues that if we deny Smith's distinction between productive and unproductive labour we deny the distinction between capital producing revenue and capital used for immediate consumption, between consumption goods and capital goods. A worker is thus productive if he reproduces his maintenance as happens when he adds to the wages fund. Among the commentators on Smith's distinction, Fleischacker (2004) argues that productive labour produces necessities and unproductive labour luxuries. We would starve if farmers went on strike but not if lawyers and entertainers did. This interesting suggestion is debatable. Farmers do produce luxuries that are not relevant to life and death but, as real incomes rise, the wage fund will proportionately include more luxuries. Also, given the division of labour all occupations are interdependent and important as they contribute to overall output. If the occupations were useless they would wither away and the practitioners find themselves unable to sell their output. But Hill (1999) is right in saying that the connection between the two distinctions productive/unproductive and goods/services amounts to productive meaning producing something *capable* of increasing the *stock* of material wealth.

Craig (1814) argued that the distinction between productive and unproductive labour should rest on the actual duration of the product, a point in agreement with Lauderdale and also in accord with Smith, who wrote that productive labour produces something permanent. The productive class can be identified: as 'whenever it affords a profit, or, in other words, produces more the means of enjoyment than it consumes...' (II: 97) it agrees with the central interpretation of productive labour because that labour contributes goods to the real wage fund. Craig includes within the unproductive category the expenditure of wealth on pleasures and comforts of the proprietor and thinks merchants transfer rather than produce the means of enjoyment. To justify these views Craig needed to link types of labour to value: if he appreciated the breadth of the goods and services regarded as valuable he would have been less confident in calling any labour unproductive.

Sinclair (1823) looked in detail at the productive/unproductive distinction by identifying different occupational groups. He has eleven productive classes, including agricultural labour and the literary class; eleven useful or indirectly productive, including the political, revenue, legal, clerical, medical, innkeeper and servant classes; and five useless or unproductive classes, including the insane, confined debtors, infirm poor, adults living on charity, vagrants and criminals. He says that productive classes add to national wealth and capital; the indirectly productive, by their demand, promote reproduction by the productive classes. This version of the distinction, although not dealing with the goods/services distinction, broadens the idea: to be productive is to create value-added. This is true to modern definitions of the gross domestic product as the sum of value-added in each industry.

The participants in the debate over the productiveness of labour repeated some central ideas – that to be productive means creating value-added, producing something which is capital-like, and having a saleable output for, for the most part, a physical good. Why the debate is important at all is because labour productivity is a central determinant of economic growth. What Smith was saying is that productive labour produces something for the wages fund, the prerequisite for production. Thus the size of next year's annual produce depends on the ratio of this year's productive to unproductive labour. If only Smith had asked the question 'productive of what?' and answered 'productive of additions to the wages fund' much confusion would have been avoided.

Division of labour

The division of labour is central to Smith's account of economic growth. At the outset of the *WN* Smith states that economic welfare, which he considers to be income per head, or the annual produce of labour divided by the number of consumers in a nation, is determined by two factors, 'the skill, dexterity and judgment with which its labour is generally applied' and to a lesser extent the proportion of useful labour. The division of labour increases workers' skill and dexterity in their particular jobs. This division can be of two forms, both having the effect of increasing productivity: occupational division is the distribution of the labour force among different occupations to create specialization; subdivision of labour splits up a job into its component parts. Read, in 1829, noted that the occupational division of labour is like the subdivision of labour in a particular occupation. Conversely, subdivision is a form of occupational division of labour because it creates a host of new narrow occupations.

Social life made the division of labour into a cooperative form of production based on free labour. Samuel von Pufendorf (1632–94), the German jurist who was to inspire Hutcheson, in his *De Officio* (II: 89) pointed out that we have great comforts through the aid of others (Skinner 1995: 170). Hutcheson builds his economics on his realization that absolute solitude, which would make birth and sustenance impossible, is not mankind's natural state. To obtain the necessaries of life cooperation is important: there has to be a division of labour:

> 'tis well known that the produce of the labours of any given number, twenty, for instance, in providing the necessaries or conveniences of life, shall be much greater by assigning to one, a certain sort of work of one kind, in which he will soon acquire skill and dexterity, and to another assigning work of a different kind, than if each one of the twenty were obliged to employ himself, by turns, in all the different sorts of labour requisite for his subsistence, without sufficient dexterity in any.
>
> (*System* I: 288)

The division of labour has beneficial consequences, not just social but economic, through producing greater skill, dexterity, productivity and invention. Through the division of labour a complete range of produce is available for barter, and outside of manufacturing it is necessary for labourers to cooperate for defence and infrastructure projects such as cultivating forests, draining marshes or enclosing land.

Division of labour was not as central to Steuart's analysis as it was to Smith's but there are scattered allusions to the principle. He clearly believed in the advantages of the occupational division of labour: 'experience shows, that it is better for a man to apply close to one trade, than to turn himself to several' (*Principles* I: 101). This was very much the productivity argument of the ancient Greek writers Plato and Xenophon. Not that Steuart claimed to be original. He acknowledged important precursors such as Xenophon, Mandeville, Hume and Montesquieu.

In *LJ* Smith makes the transition from the idea of the division of labour as a form of cooperation, mentioning humans' constant need for the assistance of others, to the division of labour as a technique of production. He mentions all the different occupations needed to provide food and other goods, being acutely aware of the vast occupational division of labour. Most arts and sciences, he says, have been invented and improved to supply the great wants of mankind, that is, food, clothing and lodging: it is a mark of civilization if these are well provided. Without contradicting the social origins of the division of labour principle he writes: 'This division of work is not however the effect of any human policy, but is the necessary consequence of a naturall disposition altogether peculiar to men, viz the disposition to truck, barter, and exchange' (p. 347). He argues that even the savage, through seeing that a surplus product can be disposed of through barter and trucking, will separate trades. Although the natural argument is used, it is not a difference in men's abilities that counts although they share the same basic propensity; he argues that the philosopher and porter are different in genius but not because of an original difference between them and, because they are engaged in exchange, the philosopher and the porter benefit each other. From considering occupational division of labour he then considers subdivision of labour, a fitting version of the concept for the age of commerce and manufacturing. He takes the case of pin-making, an example already used in the French *Encyclopédie*, appearing to confine the principle to manufacturing. In his pin-making example, when twenty men practise division of labour, compared with a solitary workman carrying out all operations, per capita output rises from twenty to 4,800 pins. 'Agriculture however does not admit of this separation of employment in the same degree as the manufactures of wool or lint or iron work' (p. 342), mainly because farm occupations change with the seasons. But he contradicts this view of the division of labour and of agriculture through giving examples of agricultural invention, such as the milling of corn and cog-wheels to improve winches, and says that 'It was probably a farmer who first invented the plow' (p. 346). Smith claimed that it was division of labour that led to inventions, yet there appeared to be invention in agriculture, the sector which was supposed to lack division of labour. In saying that in agriculture subdivision of labour is not easily done he uses the bad example of contrasting different agricultural occupations such as grazier and corn farmer, rather than sub-occupations. Smith's dogmatic view that the division of labour occurs in manufacturing but not agriculture ignores the fact that a large market for agricultural produce in each season could make division possible. Contra Smith, Alison (1840) says there is division of labour in agriculture to produce a given amount of subsistence: in the nineteenth century fewer men were needed be achieve this, thus causing a decline in the rural population.

Smith writes of the occupational division of labour, 'It is not from the benevolence of the butcher, the brewer, or the baker, that we expect our dinner, but from their regard to their own interest' (*WN*: 26–7). In other words, it is worthwhile for these different producers to specialize and by doing so they produce a larger and better product to the benefit of the public at large.

The great advantage of the subdivision of labour is that 'The price of the work will here be less, the publick will be far better supplied, and the artisan will be far better rewarded... The price of labour comes to be dear while at the same time work is cheap' (*LJ*: 343). On the plus side for the worker the division of labour allowed him/her to have higher wages through economic growth. Smith, when looking at the various conditions of the labourer, classifies economies according to whether they are growing, stationary or declining: 'The progressive state is in reality the chearful and the hearty state to all the different orders of society. The stationary is dull; the declining, melancholy' (*WN*: 99). There are two beneficiaries of the adoption of the division of labour method – the consumer who can buy more at a lower price and the labourer who obtains higher wages – but Smith does not explain why the productivity gains will be passed on in higher wages and not in enhanced profits. He explains how there is a productivity gain through outlining the advantages of the division of work: increased dexterity of workmen, saving of time lost in passing from one type of work to another, and the invention of machines (although he admits inventions can come from machine makers rather than machine users); this is a repeat of what he lists in *LJ* as the three effects of the division of labour, all causes of increased productivity. In stating in the *WN* that it is the certainty of being able to exchange one's surplus produce that encourages occupational specialization, he can make the extent of the market the essential condition for a division of labour. Small markets in small places cannot absorb the large output from practising the division of labour, but an international market can.

A contemporary of Smith, Ferguson, dealt with the division of labour in his *Principles* (1792), aware of the occupational division of labour without spelling out the productivity implications of the principle:

> In the progress or result of commercial arts, employments are adapted to all varieties of disposition, capacity, or genius. There are different tasks to suit different types of man.
>
> (I: 250)

This is an interesting suggestion: because there is a diversity of persons it is good to have a variety of occupations. A consequence of this is that a person should stick to his original occupation:

> There is a calling in the rude ages of mankind, in which every individual is bred from infancy, and of which he cannot remit the practice, without extreme danger; that of penetration and sagacity, respecting the friend with whom he is to cooperate, or the enemy of whom he is to beware.
>
> (p. 251)

Unfairly, Hamowy (1968) records, Smith accused Ferguson of plagiarizing him by using the concept of division of labour, despite the term having a wide circulation. Not only was it unfair, it was a mistake, because Ferguson has a different treatment of the concept. Also, very differently from Smith, Ferguson in his *Essay* is prepared to relate the division of labour to different abilities:

> Persons who are occupied with different subjects, who act in different scenes, generally appear to have different talents, or at least to have the same faculties variously formed, and suited to different purposes.
>
> (1767: 26)

He is undecided whether occupations are based on different talents or not and does not seem to care. A variety of reasons can, in his view, explain occupational choice:

> The accidents which distribute the means of subsistence unequally, inclination, and favourable opportunities, assign the different occupations of men; and a sense of utility leads them, without end, to subdivide their professions.
>
> (p. 180)

Ferguson has a different account of the benefits of the division of labour from Smith, saying that specialization will improve the quality of work, and that there are economies of scale reducing expenses, and increasing profits and output:

> The artist finds, that the more he can confine his attention to a particular part of any work, his productions are the more perfect, and grow under his hands in the greater quantities. Every undertaker in manufacture finds, that the more he can subdivide the tasks of his workmen, and the more hands he can employ on separate articles, the more are his expences diminished, and his profits increased. The consumer too requires, in every kind of commodity, a workmanship more perfect than hands employed on a variety of subjects can produce; and the progress of commerce is but a continued subdivision of the mechanical arts... Every individual is distinguished by his calling, and has a place to which he is fitted... By the separation of arts and professions, the sources of wealth are laid open; every species of material is wrought up to the greatest perfection, and every commodity is produced in the greatest abundance.
>
> (p. 181)

Millar also relates the division of labour to human diversity:

> In every polished nation the labour and application of the people is usually so divided, as to produce an endless variety of characters in those who follow different trades and professions. The soldier, the clergyman, the taylor, the farmer, the smith, the shopkeeper; all those who earn a livelihood by the exercise of separate employments, whether liberal or mechanical, are led by the different objects in which they are conversant, to contract something peculiar in their behaviour and turn of thinking.
>
> (1787: 31)

That human characteristics will affect the ultimate occupational distribution of labour is a testable hypothesis but is questionable because the state of the labour market often fails to provide job opportunities to suit everyone: possessing musical talent, for example, is no guarantee of a musical career.

Marx commented that 'Adam Smith said nothing at all new about the division of labour. What characterizes him as the quintessential political economist of the period of manufacture is rather the stress he lays on it' (1867: 468, note 19), which was at most grudging praise for Smith's recognition of the emerging industrial age. There are many willing to see in the division of labour principle a force for good, both improving workers and improving society. Kames argued that specialization is fruitful for the whole of society:

> The general good is an object too remote to be the sole impulsive motive to action. It is better ordered that in most instances individuals should have a limited aim, what they can readily accomplish. To every man is assigned his own task; and if every man do his duty, the general good will be promoted much more effectually, than if it were the aim in every single action.
>
> (1779: 64)

Smith, in West's view (1964), argues that the division of labour changes men's characters from being lazy to being dextrous. Smith thus was an environmental determinist believing that men are formed by their employments. Swingewood (1970) says Smith and Ferguson went beyond looking at the economic significance of the division of labour to considering the social aspects of it. As Hill (2007) observes, Smith thought, the division of labour could enhance social solidarity because it transformed the quality and means of interdependence as well as increasing personal and private independence.

Criticisms of the division of labour principle

The division of labour principle was severely criticized for its mental effects. In *WN* Smith points out that through the division of labour employment becomes confined to a few very simple operations with the effect that

> The man whose whole life is spent in performing a few simple operations, of which the effects too are, perhaps, always the same, or very nearly the same, has no occasion to exert his understanding, or to exercise his invention in finding out expedients for removing difficulties which never occur. He naturally loses, therefore, the habit of such exertion, and generally becomes as stupid and ignorant as it is possible for a human creature to become.
>
> (pp. 781–2)

The worker thus is incapable of rational conversation or generous sentiment and just judgement, has less physical vigour and is unlikely to make a good soldier. As there can be division of labour in manufacturing, but not agriculture, as Smith believed, the change from rural to urban employment supposedly dulls the brain. This is pure romanticism. The expression 'village idiot' is well known: who has ever spoken of the 'city idiot'? To counter the degrading effects of the division of labour Smith recommends the establishment, at small public expense, of parish schools to teach reading, writing and accounting. The public would give small premiums and badges for distinction to encourage the children.

Millar, according to West (1964), says in his *An historical review of the English government* that if the subdivision of labour makes tasks too narrow the worker has few ideas and has to work twice as hard. Kames, according to Hemingway (1989), said that the division of labour under flourishing manufacturing made individuals ignorant and unsociable, although the principle did not affect painting and sculpture, which required skill and invention to a high degree. Kames, too, was aware of the mixed effects, even mental, of the division of labour:

> Constant application . . . to a single operation . . . excludes all thought and invention: in such a train of life, the operator becomes dull and stupid, like a beast of burden.
>
> (1778 I: 194)

Smith, in predicting that the repetitive tasks undertaken in a specialized manufacturing process would dull the brain, takes up an odd position, for earlier in the *WN* he stated that an effect of the division of labour was the invention of machines, which presumably needs much mental effort: 'When one is employed constantly on one thing his mind will naturally be employed in devising the most proper means of improving it' (p. 346). He could have resolved this paradox by stating that as innate intelligence varies greatly from person to person a particular situation will produce different effects according to the initial intellectual endowment of the worker. But he cannot do this because of his conviction that natural abilities differ little. In *WN* he asserts that the difference in natural talent is less important than habit, custom and education. Skinner (1998) puts Smith's example of the philosopher and the porter, different in training but not in intelligence, into a wider philosophical context. David Hume in *Of the Original Contract* wrote, 'how nearly equal all men are in their bodily force, and even in their mental powers and faculties, till cultivated by education ... ' (1987: 467–8), and in his *Enquiries Concerning Human Understanding* (1777 VII: 7) wrote, 'there is a great uniformity among the actions of men ... human nature remains still the same'. But such venerable authorities can be wrong and should definitely not be followed without evidence.

We can, however, like Ferguson note the advantages of repetitive work, as he applauds tedious occupations:

> Reflection and fancy are subject to err; but a habit of moving the hand, or the foot, is independent of either. Manufactures, accordingly, prosper most, where the mind is least consulted, and where the workshop may, without any great effort of imagination, be considered as an engine, the parts of which are men.
>
> (1767: 182–3)

Smith and his supporters failed to appreciate that people can like boring occupations that allow them to leave their creativity for their leisure hours. T. S. Eliot, the poet, worked at commercial correspondence for a bank during the day and wrote at night. Miners chipped away at coal seams in their working hours but played in bands and debated in miners' institutes in their leisure time. Repetitive jobs are very restful and allow a worker to build up mental reserves, which can be engaged in other activities after the day has ended. Nicholson put it well in his *Principles*:

> It must not be forgotten also that the monotony of work involves less mental strain, and leaves the worker, with reasonable hours of labour, energy and inclination for self-culture.
>
> (1893–1901 I: 120)

The very fact that there was so much campaigning in the nineteenth century for a shorter working day to permit more leisure was recognition of the fact that workers were capable of using their spare time usefully.

If not on mental grounds, the division of labour principle can be attacked for its social ill effects. Ferguson, as Lamb (1973) tells us, complained in his *Essay* that the division of labour, by separating professions, broke the bands of society and withdrew individuals from the common sense of occupation in which the sentiments of heart and mind are most happily employed. Ferguson, Hill (2007) states, could have been the first person to criticize commercialization because of its alienating effects. Other attacks on the principle – this time, according to Stimson (2004), for being founded on avarice – came from Godwin in his *Enquiry into Political Justice*. The natural propensity to truck, barter and exchange is, he wrote, a manifestation of a 'truckling and servile act'. Thomas Reid, reports Kitagawa (1994), while he praised occupational specialization, claimed its bad effects included the possibility of riot and dissipation among manufacturers.

Dugald Stewart, although much interested in economic growth, refuted exaggerated claims for the division of labour. At the outset of his *Lectures on Political Economy* he admits that the division of labour could simultaneously achieve high wages and a competitive industry but thought Smith was wrong on the technical effects of the division of labour. Perceptively, Stewart noted that in mechanical matters the division of labour had a limited effect but that specialization in the intellectual arts confers benefits for centuries. There is not much to be gained by increased dexterity as there is a limit to the increase in rapidity of manual acts yet the saving in time by concentrating on one operation is as true of intellectual as of physical activities. Stewart regarded the introduction and improvement of machinery as the cause of civilization but did not expect invention to be a by-product of the subdivision of labour. Although division of labour does provide an analysis of work in its component parts it is the employer or observer who sees this analysis, not the workman: many inventors have never been workmen. Further, Stewart questions the possibility of the division of labour being the primary cause of increased productivity though says Smith was not in error but his argument was 'partial and incomplete' (1840 I: 326). Stewart says there are other important causes of economy of labour and time such as chemical processes used in bleaching and distilling and an improved transport system. Lauderdale in his 1804 reply to Brougham's criticisms of the *Inquiry* in the *Edinburgh Review* argued,

> only in the early stages even of manufacturing industry, any advantage can possibly appear to be derived from the division of labour; for in the progress of our manufactures, the benefit of some of our most important chemical discoveries obviously arises from combining, under one process, the formation of things of very different descriptions; and the perfection of the application of capital in supplanting labour, universally consists in the number of different processes that are executed in the same moment.
>
> (1804b: 58)

General superintendence and management, also, can bring about increases in labour productivity, Stewart reminds us. Smith neglected the organization of production and it is hard to find a theory of the firm in the *WN*. Although division of labour could extend to relationships between firms Smith does not examine competition in this sense, according to Tribe (1978). Winch (1997) makes the point that Smith omits to say who managed the pin workshop and invested in the machinery. Entrepreneurs were indistinct from those who invest capital.

Perhaps Smith made too much of the division of labour principle. Horner, in his notes on *WN*, points out that the division of labour is not the only cause of an improvement in the effective powers of human industry. Different manufactures should be considered relative to climate and soil. Hilton (1988) suggests that Smith's pin-making example of the division of labour was as much concerned with motives – why people divide their labour – as with the effects of the division of labour on the community.

Capital

Capital accumulation, rather than productive labour or the division of labour, is also a determinant of economic growth. Brewer (1999), in asserting that the central role of capital accumulation is absent from both Ferguson and Smith in their treatment of economic growth, is making a point more concerned with fixed capital than circulating. Basic to the idea of productive labour was that it produced capital in the form of the wages fund. There must be capital accumulation both to build up the wage fund, necessary to have division of labour, and to invest in human capital in the form of training to make workers more dextrous (although Smith claimed it was division of labour itself that caused dexterity). Smith says that accumulation of circulating capital has to precede the division of labour because workers have to be maintained and materials and tools purchased before the sale of the product. Different industries have different ratios of circulating to fixed capital, thus making Smith's account of capital more relevant in some industries than others.

Smith's comments on capital were disputed. Buchanan, in his 1814 commentary on *WN*, thought it wrong of Smith to say that there is a limit to the employment of capital, because an increase in capital leads to an increase in expenditure; in other words, there is a multiplier at work. If there is no limit to the increase in expenditure there is no limit to its employment. Cannan (1917), says that Smith is wrong to assert that the division of labour necessitates a great accumulation of stock. The isolated man needs as much as a man in a group. He would need more stock and not one but two years of food in case of the failure of a crop. The isolated worker also needs a greater diversity of tools than the specialized labourer practising the division of labour. But Cannan cannot refute the idea that employment is based on a firm's ability to pay, which necessitates circulating capital.

Repeatedly, Lauderdale argues the importance of capital:

> That man uses capital in the form of machinery to supplant labour, is one of the peculiarities and distinguishing features of his character. If it was not for this singular faculty, his efforts to provide for his wants, like those of the other animals, would be bounded by what his hands, his teeth, and his feet, could enable him to accomplish.
>
> (1804b: 162)

A great deal of what the Austrian economist Eugen von Boehm-Bawerk (1851–1914) wrote about capital and roundabout methods of production is anticipated by Lauderdale, who uses the example of a man preparing land with a spade accomplishing as much in a day as fifty men using their fingernails – this simple capital tool has supplanted the labour of forty-nine men. A plough would supplant even more. It is justified, Lauderdale notes, to increase one's capital in order to extend lands or to use an invention to supplant labour, but otherwise curtailing expenditure in order to accumulate capital is to be deplored as production is discouraged, then diminished. To improve the cultivation of land more capital is required but there cannot be an unlimited application of capital, given present knowledge, because no further produce will result.

In discussing the division of labour Lauderdale, in his comments on Smith, argues that machinery proceeds from division of labour in the earliest of societies and increases agricultural productivity, but that division of labour is more important to the nice execution of refined manufactures. Increased manual dexterity is less important than the replacement of labour by capital. Smith was keen to link the division of labour principle to human propensities; Lauderdale argues that creating capital goods is an inherent human characteristic – we are essentially toolmakers:

> That it is to the characteristic faculty which man possesses, from the earliest period of his existence, of applying mechanical principles to the construction of tools and machines, calculated to perform and supplant labour, and to his powers of using capital for the same purpose, in all his commercial relations, as well as in every transaction which requires the exertion of labour, that he owes the ease and wonderful rapidity with which labour is executed; and, consequently, that extended opulence which expands itself throughout civilized society.
>
> (1804b: 297)

Lauderdale not only emphasizes capital accumulation in the growth process but in the related matter of the role of demand. By doing so he takes a more dynamic view of the division of labour.

> The advanced price, in consequence of an extension of demand, operates not alone as an encouragement to exertion in those who manufacture the commodity; for it creates a necessity of abridging the consumption of some less pressing object of desire, in order that the goods which were appropriated to acquire it, may be applied to pay the advanced price of the commodity. Whatever, therefore, fixes or determines the proportion of demand that exists for different articles of wealth in any society, must regulate the distribution of its industry.
>
> (1804b: 306–7)

He analyses the determinants of demand. There is a basic desire for food but as incomes and effectual demand grow luxuries are within the reach of a consumer. Possibly the distribution of wealth regulates the commodity structure of demand, the direction of industry and the progress of population. If Great Britain were divided into small properties each with an annual income of £100 then the pattern of consumption would be simpler as many manufactures would not be affordable. Firmly, he says 'great inequality of fortune, by impoverishing the lower orders, has everywhere been the principal impediment to the increase of public wealth' (1804b: 345).

Lauderdale, in his notes on *WN*, complains that at the outset Smith did not have a third source of economic growth, capital supplanting labour. Believing that the division of labour was applicable to all industries, Lauderdale says improved agriculture increased real incomes of workmen, which increased consumer expenditure. Dogmatically, in opposition to Smith, Lauderdale asserts that saving does not increase national wealth:

> the effects of parsimony [saving] must be hostile to reproduction. It must occasion a failure of demand for the articles of annual produce proportioned to the value saved both reducing the value of existing consumer goods and the produce of the ensuing year. Saving can increase the wealth of the saver at the expence of other members of society. The great mass of wealth in a community can alone be increased from the source from whence all capital and riches sprung that is by an increase of production and it is an extended demand arising from expenditure – not a diminution of demand (which must be the consequence of deprivation of expence) by which this is to be obtained.
>
> (1996: 91)

Lauderdale might be congratulated for understanding that levels of demand have to be taken into account but he does not see, as Smith certainly did, that capital accumulation has to be financed through savings. Lacking a national accounting framework Lauderdale got into a muddle over the role of saving. To show his alternative view of economic growth he reiterates that there are two ways of augmenting capital: either through additional exertions to create more capital goods or by taking labour from the production of consumer goods to put towards the production of capital goods.

Less clear is Lauderdale's distinction between national wealth and individual riches. He argues that the former is not the sum of the latter and that, whereas national wealth grows with abundance, individual riches are enhanced by scarcity. This odd view arises from not using the idea of total revenue: price multiplied by quantity. If the same prices prevail throughout a national economy then national wealth will be simply the sum of individual riches. Whether or not the total revenue of individuals increases when there is more scarcity depends on the nature of the demand curve facing them: an individual's total revenue could be greater with a larger stock at lower prices. The motivation for this odd distinction seems to be to warn of the dangers to a national economy of excessive saving. However, in the course of discussing changes in prices driven by scarcity he notes that a consumer's reaction is different in the case of necessaries, where consumption will continue, but it will not for other goods. He considers how a rise in the price of sugar will affect the effective demand for other goods, such as meat, and bring their prices down. Lauderdale seems to be hinting at a general equilibrium approach to pricing, or at least is describing a price structure.

Lauderdale, in his *Inquiry* of 1804a, pointed out that supplanting labour with capital reduces product prices in a growing economy. More importantly, Lauderdale, as Cole (1956) mentions, in his idea of capital supplanting labour, suggests that the principle of substitution is based on varying elasticity. Lauderdale assumed that there were unused resources in society and that the demand for capital is derived from consumer demand and limited by the state of technique. He concentrates on capital as a physical stock rather than a fund. Ahmad (2007) suggests that Lauderdale's substitution theory could distinguish him from his predecessors and that it anticipates the modern use of isoquants – those curves that show the different combinations of two factors of production that produce the same quantity of output. Lauderdale was opposed to Smith's insistence that saving is the means of creating wealth and, as Corry (1962) points out, was more interested in growth economics than short-run Keynesian problems and thought the capital stock could be so large that full employment output would exceed demand. Fetter (1945) tells us that Lauderdale believed that only industry could increase capital but fell into the basic error in his treatment of savings of looking at present, not past, results of savings. Thus, there is a mixed reaction to Lauderdale who, at least, could drag economic growth theorizing out of the division of labour debate to make us discuss the roles of capital and savings, which are still central to growth theory.

Playfair, a pioneer in the presentation of statistical data, who studied nations' prosperity over the long period of three thousand years, put capital accumulation in context. Growth, as he saw it, sometimes requires capital accumulation and sometimes other stimuli, such as proximity to the sea – as with Mediterranean countries (northern countries instead took to manufacturing and fishing when unable to transport heavy goods great distances) or crucial inventions (the magnetic needle for navigation, the printing press and gunpowder), the habits of industry, the availability of credit, the example of the commerce of the East and the progress of agriculture and manufactures. Playfair, according to Grossman (1948), identifies three stages of capital accumulation – less capital available than can be invested, sufficient capital and more capital, which can be profitably invested.

A final word on the role of capital comes in Burton who asserts: 'the effect of capital on production ... is merely the effect of accelerated production, for capital is past labour laid by to assist in increasing the impetus of future – the limit of wealth is never deficiency of consumers but of producers and productive power. Every addition to capital gives to labour either additional employment or additional remuneration, [and] enriches the country of the labouring class' (1849: 42), and that 'the human being has unsupplied desires or demands' (p. 44). Burton is neatly contrasting the roles of consumption and production and is emphasizing that production is more important without seeing, as Lauderdale did, that without actual or expected consumption production would not occur. Burton reveals his elevated view of human nature 'that man, not only collectively, but individually, was placed here rather to increase than to consume the objects of human desire that he sees around him...' (p. 48). In other words, the point of being human is economic growth.

Incentives

The principal cause of economic growth, if not the division of labour, is incentive mechanisms, much mentioned in the Scottish school. The incentives could be the joy of activity or work itself, receiving the fruit of one's labour, profit, obtaining luxuries or gaining the benefits of an unequal society. In a sense the division of labour is the physical mechanism to promote economic growth and incentives the mental means.

In his *System* Hutcheson is interested in incentives:

> nothing can so effectually excite men to constant patience and diligence in all sorts of useful industry, as the hopes of future wealth, ease, and pleasure to themselves, their offspring, and all who are dear to them... All these hopes are presented to men by securing to every one the fruits of his own labours that he may enjoy them, or dispose of them as he pleases... If goods procured, or improved by the industrious lye in common for the use of all, the worst of men have the generous and industrious for their slaves. The most benevolent temper must decline supporting the slothful in idleness...
>
> (I: 321)

Prospective gain, obtaining a proper reward for one's labour and having private property, are identified by him as incentives. He also muses on a political route to incentivizing a population:

> a wise political constitution could compel all men to bear their part in labour, and then make a wisely proportioned distribution of all that was acquired, according to the indigence, or merit of citizens.
>
> (p. 322)

But then he doubts this approach because just treatment is not guaranteed if everything depends on the pleasure of the magistrate conducting the distribution.

David Hume makes incentive mechanisms fundamental to his explanation of the growth process. He argues in *The Stoic* that 'The great end of all human industry is the attainment of happiness' (1987: 148), a happiness obtained through activity: 'vigorous industry gives pleasure to the pursuit even of the most worthless prey . . . Begin by curing yourself of this lethargic indolence; the task is not difficult: You need but taste the sweets of honest labour' (pp. 149–50). More strongly, on the theme of labour as an end in itself, he writes in *The Sceptic*: 'a life of pleasure cannot support itself so long as one of business, but is much more subject to satiety and disgust . . . Business and action fill up all the great vacancies in human life' (1987: 167). Whereas Smith regards labour as disutility, producing toil and trouble, Hume links labour to utility. He writes: 'the happiest disposition of mind is the *virtuous*; or, in other words, that which leads to action and employment' (p. 168). Joy through work is his belief. In *Of Refinement in the Arts* he notes 'In times when industry and the arts flourish, men are kept in perpetual occupation, and enjoy, as their reward, the occupation itself, as well as those pleasures which are the fruit of their labour. The mind acquires new vigour, both satisfies its natural appetites, and prevents the growth of unnatural ones, which commonly spring up, when nourished by ease and idleness' (1987: 270). In *Of Interest* he mentions 'There is no craving or demand of the human mind more constant and insatiable than that for exercise and employment; and this desire seems the foundation of most of our passions and pursuits . . .' (1987: 300).

As well as work as its own incentive, the restlessness of humans can be a motivation. Hume in *Of Money* argues that with increased refinement men are not

> content with what can be raised in their neighbourhood, there is more exchange and commerce of all kinds, and more money enters into that exchange. The tradesmen will not be paid in corn; because they want something more than barely to eat . . . The landlord lives in the capital, or in a foreign country; and demands his rent in gold and silver, which can easily be transported to him.
>
> (1987: 291)

Hume argues in *Of Commerce* that landowners and farmers redouble their efforts when a nation abounds in manufactures and mechanic arts. The production of luxuries, he notes in that essay, adds to the happiness of the state. But the labour producing such goods could instead, he argues, be employed in the army and navy; he thus presents a choice between the happiness of the subject and the greatness of the state.

Another great incentive is profit. Hume in *Of Interest* wrote:

> if the employment you give him be lucrative, especially if the profit be attached to every particular exertion of industry, he has gain so often in his eye, that he acquires, by degrees, a passion for it and knows no such pleasure as that of seeing the daily encrease of his fortune. And this is the reason why trade encreases frugality, and why, among merchants, there is the same overplus of misers above prodigals, as, among the possessors of land, there is the contrary.
>
> (1987: 301)

Steuart was a supporter of Hume's position and traces the consequences of it as 'a taste for superfluity in those who have an equivalent to give for it. This taste will produce demand and this again will become the main spring of the whole operation' (*Principles* I: 192).

Adam Smith, although making the division of labour and productive labour the major explanations of economic growth, does look at other possible determinants. In *TMS* he raises the issue of incentive mechanisms and asks: 'What is the reward most proper for encouraging industry, prudence, and circumspection? Success in every sort of business . . . Wealth and external honours are their proper recompense, and the recompense which they can seldom fail of acquiring . . .' (p. 166). This is a very materialistic view but not more so than Hume's.

Ferguson, in his *Essay*, supports the Humean position that activity itself can be the incentive:

> it is a blessing to meet with incentives to action, whether in the desire of pleasure, or the aversion to pain. His activity is of more importance than the very pleasure he seeks, and languor a greater evil than the suffering he shuns.
>
> (1767: 43)

We can see in Ferguson that incentives are essential for the functioning of the exchange economy and the minimal state (see previous section on self-interest and later discussion of natural liberty):

> men are tempted to labour, and to practise lucrative arts, by motives of interest. Secure to the workman the fruit of his labour, give him the prospects of independence or freedom, the public has found a faithful minister in the acquisition of wealth and a faithful steward in hoarding what he has gained. The statesman in this, as in the case of population itself, can do little more than avoid doing mischief.
>
> (p. 143)

This is a clear expression of the idea that the economic mechanism has to be supported by suitable politics, with the state keeping out of the way. The policy for a prosperous population with liberty is

> to secure to the family the means of its subsistence and settlement; to protect the industrious in the pursuit of his occupation; to reconcile the restrictions of police, and the social affections of mankind, with their separate and interested pursuits . . . The object of commerce is to make the individual rich; the more he gains for himself the more he augments the wealth of his country . . . When the refined politician would lend an active hand, he only multiplies interruptions and grounds of complaint; when the merchant forgets his own interest to lay plans for his country, the period of vision and chimera is near, and the solid basis of commerce withdrawn. He might be

> told, perhaps, that while he pursues his advantage, and gives no cause of complaint, the interest of commerce is safe.
>
> (p. 144)

There has to be something, in other words, to motivate greater effort. The existence of luxury goods could, Ferguson contends, be the temptation to spur workers to greater endeavour. Luxury, however, often associated with decadence, was a controversial route to economic improvement.

Ferguson in his *Essay* (p. 244) writes that luxury can be variously described as

> our panegyric of polished ages, the parent of arts, the support of commerce, and the minister of national greatness, and of opulence. It is, in our censure of degenerate manners, the source of corruption, and the presage of national declension and ruin. It is admired, and it is blamed; it is treated as ornamental and useful; and it is proscribed as a vice . . . When . . . luxury is made an article of national lustre and felicity, we only think of it as an innocent consequence of unequal distribution of wealth, and as a method by which different ranks are rendered mutually dependent, and mutually useful. The poor are made to practise arts, and the rich to reward them. The public itself is made a gainer by what seems to waste its stock, and it receives a perpetual increase of wealth, from the influence of those growing appetites, and delicate tastes, which seem to menace consumption and ruin.
>
> (pp. 245–6)

He thinks it difficult to use luxury as an indicator of morality:

> We must look for the characters of men in the qualities of the mind, not in the species of their food, or in the mode of their apparel . . . The use of morality on this subject, is not to limit men to any particular species of lodging, diet, or cloaths, but to prevent their considering these conveniences as the principal objects of human life.
>
> (p. 247)

Ferguson was daring in not siding fully with censorious moralists and in pointing out the economic benefits of luxury. The pursuit of luxury is an aspect of an incentive mechanism but not the entire driving force of economic advancement.

Luxury can be a driving force in an economy but not a universal remedy for stagnation. Wallace (n.d.) doubted if luxury would lead to agricultural improvement and thought instead it might be its hindrance. If small farms were consolidated into larger units, he argued, rich farmers would be encouraged to have children who live in idleness and greater luxury, spending heavily on the building and furnishing of palaces and pleasure grounds. Women of fashion, moreover, are idle and decrease the labour supply. Instead of luxury as an incentive mechanism, Wallace employs the psychological argument that to make Highlanders industrious some hard-working tradesmen and manufacturers should be sent among them as example of industry, encouraging them to take up honest labour. The sight of the great profits of labour, and of the affluence and abundance with which it supplies the labourer, would naturally produce a love of those profits, and a desire for that affluence and abundance (1753: 160). This is a practical application of Hume's belief that the prospect of gain will be a powerful incentive.

Incentive mechanisms were approved by later writers. Craig has a straightforward view that as society develops each person is induced by remuneration to practise his expertise. At last public works are undertaken in which all concur, including roads, bridges, harbours: 'The sole purpose of society being to combine the efforts of individuals so as to produce the greatest happiness to all...' (1814 I: 123).

He also links inequality to incentives. General good can, he writes, result from inequalities in riches – workmanlike habits, suitable education, the performance of unpleasant task and the stimulus to inventive genius – but complete equality of comfort and social rank would lead to poverty and ignorance. In Craig's view, the aristocracy enfeeble and corrupt but the middle classes, through necessity, practise economy and provide for their children. He also thought that individuals will be most strenuous in their efforts when the field is open and entitlement is according to talents. He also writes that the circumstances of the times stimulate exertions and create talents, as in the case of the English Civil Wars, despite 'the austerity of the Puritans, the degrading profligacy of the court of Charles the Second'. In his view, 'The desire of bettering their condition, which, unless when withered by oppression, is the most vigorous and persevering passion of the human heart' (p. 75), a view which takes us back to Smith.

Read (1829) curiously regarded the object of all improvement as the increase of the non-labouring class, thus making inequality a major element in the growth process. He agrees with David Hume's view, in his essay *Of Avarice*, that the desire of gain is always operative and in every person. Later, in 1849, Burton reasoned that ownership is a stimulus to labour, the corollary of labour producing property rights.

Not all of these writers went along with the idea of the potency of incentives as the way to economic growth. Playfair is sceptical about the efficacy of incentive mechanisms because tastes are acquired when young and persist through life; businessmen cannot take up amusement and a poor country has the same degree of industry from generation to generation. He argues, 'Without rent and taxes there are only three things that excite the exertion of man: – Necessity, arising from natural wants; a love of pleasure; or, a love of accumulation' (1807: 236) – not excluding incentives as these loves are a desire for various gains.

Afterword

These writers failed to reach a consensus on the causes of economic growth. In a crude sense, comparing the division of labour and the distinction between productive and unproductive labour, vital for the creation of circulating capital, is a contrast between the rival influences of labour and capital. Curiously, Smith regarded the division of labour as more important, perhaps reflecting the labour intensity of contemporary technology.

An important critic of Smith, Lauderdale, both presented a fierce challenge to Smith and vigorously produced another theory. Lauderdale in his *Inquiry* took a very different line from Adam Smith on the causes of economic growth, deriding the division of labour as an important factor, showing the difficulties of distinguishing productive from unproductive labour, and emphasizing capital accumulation at an appropriate rate as more important.

We see in Bowles (1986) that Smith used a priori reasoning to explain economic growth: the natural progress of opulence was based on the natural inclinations of mankind. (When it came to incentives human nature was centre stage.) Agriculture is the leading sector because it can employ the most productive labour for a given capital. Myint (1977) thought that Smith uses a balanced growth approach when attributing the origin of manufactures to agricultural improvements. He also argued that foreign commerce develops a taste for manufactures, a very Humean opinion. However, Rashid (1987) reminds us that Smith thought manufacturing, where division of labour is practised, the main source of labour productivity. Today, with manufacturing in decline in so many countries, Smith still has relevance by taking the division of labour principle from its original manufacturing home to every industry through emphasizing the many advantages of specialization. As Samuels (1977) notes, Smith's view of economic growth was narrowly materialistic. However, in the *WN*, Dwyer (1998) reminds us, Smith was concerned that economic growth, if too rapid, would encourage excessive self-interest and gain.

In a country as poor as Scotland was in 1700 there was a choice: grow or perish. The growth path was advocated with passion by many of these writers; something had to be done to stop shrinking incomes and the loss of population. Just as there are techniques for making particular objects there are mechanisms for getting an economy to grow, such as a release of native energy or a deliberate strategy. Government expenditure or exhortation could help, but what was really needed was an understanding of the growth process. Division of labour was extensively examined as a way to ensure a surge in productivity but the crucial role of incentives in changing an indolent into an industrious people is more fundamental.

Economic development

Economic development can be distinguished from economic growth. Development consists of those gradual improvements, often small in themselves, that cumulatively make substantial changes in a society; economic growth is a greater and more fundamental expansion. To achieve economic development there is a choice between change wrought through government intervention and natural progress.

There was an acute awareness of the backwardness of Scotland relative to England, inevitably making economic development a major issue discussed in the years leading to the Union of 1707. Would a union impede or accelerate improvement? Anyone wanting to promote economic development chose the likely winners – the industries with the greatest potential – and an appropriate strategy for them. Fisheries, wool and linen manufactures were repeatedly mentioned then as the key industries for economic development, and always lurking in the background was foreign trade, because through exports Scotland would be able to benefit from the purchasing power of richer countries.

Seton in *The Interest of Scotland* (1700) claimed that the union would improve Scotland in four ways. Equal access to the world would increase trade; the poor would not be a burden to the nation because of increased employment in manufacturing and fisheries; Highlanders would turn from ancient customs and language towards virtue and industry; and courtiers would be balanced by commoners throughout Great Britain. In his *Scotland's Great Advantages* Seton was keen to emphasize the role of fisheries in economic development: 'our Seas are stored with variety of excellent Fishes . . . The catching them might Imploy and Inrich many Thousands who live very Idle and Miserable' (1706: 5). In *Some Thoughts* (1705) he argued that the joint company for fisheries established in 1661 had failed because the proprietors had withdrawn their shares, not because fishing was to be avoided. Scotland still had advantages; it could outflank the Dutch, who travel to more distant fishing grounds, by producing 90 per cent cheaper and catching more fish. Therefore, Seton thought that Scottish shipping could increase and the poor could be employed in the industry. He also argued that if foreign salt were imported duty-free, fisheries would do even better. Seton did not want only to promote fisheries but the wool industry, saying that boroughs should advance the wool industry by encouraging weavers, dyers and dextrous dressers of wool. To improve the quality of wool he suggested that there should be inspectors of woollen goods in every shire. Generally, he saw a considerable role for government in economic development but questioned the worth of the societies and monopolies established in the reign of King Charles II, for they had spoilt the exporting of linen and woollen goods through discouraging smaller businesses in order to obtain a higher profit for the privileged firms.

David Black in *Essay upon industry and trade* (1706) argued that industry and trade are interdependent and that unnecessary luxuries such as tobacco, tea and coffee, prominent in trade, drain away money which could be used to finance industry. He wanted to use Scotland's competent labour force to promote the favoured industries: fisheries and woollen. Fishing would do well through government support in the form of drawbacks from taxation and the cessation of duties on salt and other necessary materials: this would be a help at a small cost relative to the value of fish obtained. Local governments should buy busses (two- or three-masted vessels used in fishing) and equip them, to encourage the poor to be seafarers. Aware that it could be hard for fishing to thrive under public management he repeated that the nation would benefit whatever the circumstances of catching the fish. Very much in favour of having a woollen industry, he wanted the banning of raw wool exports and other raw materials such as hemp and fur, to encourage Scottish manufactures. This shows his great belief in the amount of value-added in manufacture but, he maintains, the rate of return to capital in agriculture could be greater than in manufacturing. Black took the debate on development forward in several ways. He realized the importance of education, lamenting the fact that lairds' education lacks vocational relevance, and that mechanics in Scotland have little education. Using the analogy of Holland to generate policy proposals he suggested that measures to stimulate development could include low taxes on trade, representation of merchants on great councils, low interest, more self-financing of business, domestic manufacturing of Scotland's own raw materials and employment for its poor.

In contrast to Black, Clerk found that the breadth of the terms of the union gave hope. In his *Letter to a friend* (1706b) work he was pleased that the amount of customs on foreign trade and liquor excises would be £80,000 above current tax receipts, giving the government improved finances. Also, as Scotland had suffered from English action against the Darien Company, the compensation offered should be accepted. The promotion of the herring industry was, Clerk thought, enough to justify the union of Scotland and England. He believed that Scottish herring would replace the Scandinavian exports to England, gaining increased returns to capital and more investment. Through the removal of the tariff barrier to English markets the Scottish linen industry would improve. More strongly than many of his contemporaries Clerk advanced the case for using the Equivalent – the sum granted under the Act of Union to erect public works – not only to encourage fishing and manufactures but to build harbours, new towns and churches, as well as supporting the poor. Rather like Sir William Petty in the seventeenth century and John Maynard Keynes in the twentieth century, Clerk even countenanced absurd projects for the sake of boosting employment:

> For tho' all the *Equivalents* were spent on levelling our Mountains and other as ridiculous Works, yet being spent among ourselves, they answer their chief Design; and many thousands of poor People, Work-men and Tradesmen, will thereby get Employments . . .
>
> (1706b: 34)

These Scottish proposals had varying degrees of ingenuity but all had a haphazard quality as they were not linked together into an overall strategy.

Government schemes

There is a crucial relationship between economic development and the functions exercised by a government as law and order make economic development possible. As Smith wrote,

> Commerce and manufactures can seldom flourish long in any state which does not enjoy a regular administration of justice, in which the people do not feel themselves secure in the possession of their property, in which the faith of contracts is not supported by law, and in which the authority of the state is not supposed to be regularly employed in enforcing the payment of debts from all those who are able to pay.
>
> (*WN*: 910)

In my view, anarchy and insecurity of property lead a nation to regress to the agricultural stage, and without property rights there is no incentive to do more work than is necessary to obtain food. Bowles (1986) mentions that the security of property, brought about by law and order, would encourage manufacturing.

David Hume, in his essay *Of the Rise of Arts and Sciences*, argues that there must be a free government as a prerequisite for improvement. He notes that the establishment of law has to come before other developments: 'From law arises security; From security curiosity: And from curiosity knowledge' (1987: 118).

Apart from providing a framework of law and order some of these writers wanted governments to be active in trade and industrial policies. Trade was an early candidate for government attention. George Ridpath (d. 1726), a journalist who was a fierce Presbyterian and an inventor of a method of shorthand, recommended Scotland becoming a free port, possibly with the Crown imposing a tax on land, to reap the advantages of foreign free ports: 'Commerce is Encouraged by easie Imports, by lowering the Interest of Money, by promoting Home Manufactures, and taking care to imploy their Subjects' (1702: 111). A full, if vague, agenda.

Setting up a trade council was a popular policy. Paterson, in his *Proposals and reasons for constituting a council of trade in Scotland by the celebrated John Law* (1751), noted that since the Union of Crowns in 1603 Scotland had lost over a third of its people and 53 per cent of its other value. To recoup the losses from that union he proposed regulating home and foreign trade and refunding the Indian and African companies, and recommended the establishment of a council of trade with a president appointed by the king and twelve members chosen by the nobility and MPs. It would be funded by a levy on a fortieth of the value of all lands, rents, houses, money and goods, and by a fortieth of manufactures, and a twentieth of sums sought in legal actions would contribute; overall, the council would be able to borrow up to £1 million. The council, he explained, would adjust tariff policy by removing all duties on Scottish exports and doubling the duty on imported foreign liquors and commodities. Also, in order to maintain the corn price within a set narrow range, a Corn Law would establish granaries to receive a tenth of corn output. Allied to these policies would, he suggested, be a reduction of the rate of interest to 3 per cent in order to help fisheries and permit projects with lower returns to be undertaken. Although lower interest rates would increase the value of land and raise rental incomes, they would also reduce the incomes of widows and orphans; however, he thought that such an ill effect would be worthwhile for the sake of the nation. What he was suggesting was very modern: a development agency to subsidize new industries through grants and cheaper finance, and a tidying up of the tariff structure of trade.

The linen industry also had its fervent supporters. Lindsay (1736) argued that it was Scotland's staple commodity and needed encouragement through the abolition of petty duties to free up the trade, and greater allocations of public funds to improve the quality of linen. He too advocated support for fisheries, especially by small busses, which could catch shoals of herring coming into Scottish firths; fisheries, as he saw it, provide a nursery for seamen and provide onshore employment for carpenters, coopers and others.

Sponsorship of the wool industry also featured in contemporary pamphlets. Melvill (1734) proposed that the £14,000 of government grants for encouraging the manufacturing of coarse wool should be split into £10,000 for interest-free loans to weavers, repayable after ten years, and £4,000 to provide for two inspectors of the industry. With good workmen and the cheaper cost of living of Scotland, competition with the English in the production of broadcloth from coarse wool would succeed but young Scots should, he suggested, train in Norwich to improve their skills. In favour of promoting the woollen rather than the linen industry he argued that linen was not the staple industry of Scotland because Scotland imports flax but produces its own wool: home production would create value-added in manufacturing. Murray, too, was a fervent advocate of promoting the wool industry. He argued in 1775 that Scotland had many advantages. The distance from farm to manufacturer in Scotland was on average only fourteen miles – compared to eighty miles in England – and Scotland had cheaper costs of living and wages, and advantages in fuel and the supply of water. Sheep, in Murray's opinion, are superior to cattle as they provide both food and clothing. Through manufacturing its own woollen goods Scotland could save at least £500,000 annually but the country needed a superior breed of sheep and more participation of women in the industry, using them as bookkeepers. To further this economic development, he proposed that public funds should be diverted from the linen industry, sheep imported from Spain, houses given to English woollen workers to help them settle in Scotland, and goods sold in Canongate Hall.

Particular schemes attracted particular criticisms. The Earl of Selkirk had little patience with the popular proposals for development of his day. Long leases as a route to agricultural improvement were not as good, in his opinion, as the proprietor paying for improvements and giving the occupier an allowance for any work done. Promoting manufacturing in the Highlands he also thought objectionable because of its small scale, the lack of adult dexterity in the labour force and poor transport. Fishery schemes, which included the built-in incentive of offering land to fishermen with a rising rent to encourage more productive fishing, were, he thought, better.

The principle of giving state aid to industry was an important part of the Act of Union, especially in Article XV:

> XV. Whereas Scotland will become liable to customs and excise duties which will be applicable to the payment of England's existing National Debt, and whereas the yield of these duties will increase and a portion of the increase will be applied to the same end, Scotland is to receive as an 'Equivalent': (1) a lump sum of £398,085, 10s. and (2) the increase in Scotland's customs and excise revenue for the first seven years after the Union, and thereafter such part of the increase as would be required for the debt. This 'Equivalent' is to be devoted to (a) recompensing those who lost through the standardising of the coinage, (b) payment of the capital (with interest) advanced for the Company of Scotland (which is to be dissolved), (c) the payment of the public debts of the Scottish Crown, and (d) payment of £2000 yearly for seven years to encourage the wool manufacture and thereafter to promote fisheries and other 'manufactures and improvements'.

Campbell (1964) explains that the Equivalent granted by the government of Great Britain, was the capitalized value of the existing revenue yield to help service the English national debt. In addition a later compensation scheme, the Arising Equivalent under the Annexing Acts of 1752 and 1774, beginning with the annexation of over fifty estates forfeited in 1747 after the Jacobite rebellion against the Hanoverian Crown, swelled the public coffers. In practice the Equivalent was not a success for Scotland. Money went to Scottish aristocrats and officials, and was not spent on economic projects. The revenue from these grants and from the increased tax on linen exports, the salt tax and the malt tax also produced too little. What did bring economic success after 1707 was access to London capital markets and fiscal benefits such as bounties (subsidies), especially on the export of fish and meat, and, from 1727, funds for economic development, especially for the linen industry, through the Board of Trustees for Manufactures and Fisheries.

Adequate finance from public bodies was not the sole precondition of development. Durie (Devine 1978) refers to the direct investment by landowners, lawyers, trade credit and loans provided by banks in the form of cash credits. Help came to the linen industry through, variously, the provision of working capital for raw materials, work in progress and stock awaiting transport, and fixed capital, especially for the stage of bleaching and finishing; the growing of flax was subsidized and prizes were offered. Over half of the Board's support for the linen industry was spent on regulation to maintain quality through cloth stamp masters and yarn inspectors, and the encouragement of flax cultivation. In his 1979 study of the Scottish linen industry Durie praised the Board of Trustees for being more active and diligent in dealing with industrial problems than its Irish counterpart and the Annexed Estates Commission. It raised standards of production through its network of stamp masters checking the quality of output. But it is hard to measure how efficient the Board was in managing its funds.

Despite Smith writing in the *WN* against the mercantilists who strongly supported government intervention in industry, according to Sinclair (1790), he sees a case for introducing industry where it is unknown: for example, introducing fisheries into northern Scotland. In addition, he thought that bounties would permit the extension of Scottish agriculture.

It can be argued that, at so early a date, Scotland was fortunate in having the Board of Trustees. It provided an institutional basis for government-promoted development but it did lack imagination in what to promote: wool and fish would hardly take the country into the modern age. There was a dearth of industrial visionaries in the eighteenth century, unaware of the huge heavy industries soon to emerge, which would make Scotland into a serious industrial power.

The natural laissez-faire approach

Using natural forces to bring about development was the alternative to relying on government schemes. Smith sponsored natural liberty and repeatedly said that development arises from the division of labour, and through following the rules of justice:

> The security which the laws in Great Britain give to every man that he shall enjoy the fruits of his own labour, is alone sufficient to make any country flourish ... The natural effort of every individual to better his own condition, when suffered to exert itself with freedom and security, is so powerful a principle, that it is alone, and without any assistance, not only capable of carrying on the society to wealth and prosperity, but of surmounting a hundred impertinent obstructions with which the folly of human laws too often incumbers its operations ...
>
> (*WN*: 540)

Thus law and order and little else are, in Smith's view, important for economic development.

In the eighteenth century, an age of small government, some writers wanted anyone but the state to effect economic development. Hume, for example, was laissez-faire in his beliefs and believed in natural forces. He thought there was an inherent tendency, as he says in his *The Rise and Progress of the Arts and Sciences*, for countries to progress to a peak before decline, because natural and artificial bodies have their limits. He partly explains this by saying that young scientists get discouraged and glory departs from science.

Smith mentioned many non-governmental mechanisms to promote development. His novel idea in *TMS* was that the industry of mankind is in continual motion because of a deception based on our confusing frivolous desires with the regular and harmonious movement of the system, machine or economy. This deception prompts the cultivation of the ground, the building of houses, the founding of cities and inventions; it leads to more labour, the redoubling of natural fertility and the maintenance of many more inhabitants. This psychological theory has its attraction especially when applied to investment theories based on expectations and other mental phenomena.

A more specific mechanism was within the property market, which possessed a power for improvement. In *LJ* Smith writes, 'When land is in commerce and frequently changes hands it is most likely to be well managed; those who have raised a fortune by trade or otherwise have generally money besides what they lay out' (p. 70); owners of old family estates seldom have any money. Smith in *WN* noted that long leases had been introduced into Scotland in 1449 but their beneficial influence was diminished because the heirs of entails were not allowed to lease for long periods, often no more than a year. Thus, he argued, when there is a major change in society there will be a spontaneously improved economic management. However, the agricultural reformer William Ogilvie fervently believed in long leases to encourage development and population growth, suggesting the addition of five years to a lease for the birth of the first child and three years for each sibling, and leases for life, or alternate lives. Ogilvie accused many forms of government action of being barriers to development: bans on the exportation of corn, restraints upon inland commerce and the regulations of fairs. Restrictions to protect woollen manufacturers, he noted, had the unfortunate effect of depressing the price of wool.

John Millar, in his *An historical view of the English government*, clearly uses the natural approach:

> Upon the whole, there is good reason to conclude, that the mercantile people are the best judges of their own interest, and that, by pursuing those lines of trade which they find most beneficial to themselves, they are likely to produce, in most cases, the greatest benefit to the public. The administrators of government can seldom, from their own knowledge, be sufficiently qualified to judge in matters of this kind: and they are likely to be directed by persons who have an interest to mislead them. They have, therefore, frequently contributed more to hurt, than to improve the commercial machine, by their tampering; and their interpositions, besides loading the public with immediate expence, from the bounties bestowed upon the favourite branches of trade.
>
> (1787 IV: 109)

The inferiority of government in matters of commerce seems to spring, he thinks, from a deficiency of information and a lack of judgement. Possibly this was true of government then but it not always true of government because civil servants can build up experience and collect information more extensively than any single business.

A strong endorsement for the natural approach came from Dugald Stewart, who thought that as there is no limit to our wants there is no limit to our improvement. In a primitive society, he notes there is little chance of intellectual improvement because labour is entirely absorbed in obtaining subsistence. But he agreed with Smith's view that there is an order of progress in economic development of first agriculture then manufactures then foreign commerce. He sees the opposite in France, which, by mercantilist intervention in industry before the founding of the Physiocratic agrarian system, damaged the national economy. True to a libertarian view of economic policy, Stewart said that the only stimulus a statesman can give to industry is a decrease in the rate of interest, presumably by allowing free determination of the interest rate, or a lower rate under the usury laws. This would not direct the distribution of capital and would stimulate all parts of the economy.

The mechanisms of the market economy in themselves can create the conditions for economic development. Anderson, prominent among the promoters of economic development in eighteenth-century Scotland, based his views on extensive surveys. For him, development would start with the creation of markets, not government schemes:

> the most effectual mode of exciting industrious exertions among mankind, is to place them in such circumstances as enable them to find a ready market for the several articles that their industry can obtain, or their ingenuity discover, and then to leave individuals under very few restrictions, to find out the way in which they can most benefit themselves by their several exertions.
>
> (1785: xx)

A lack of markets would, in his view, lead to poverty and indolence; the increase in the number and size of market towns facilitates communication between economic agents; therefore, a dispersed population is the enemy of progress.

> A steady market for all the products of labour, and exertions of genius, must be ever within reach, before a spirit of industry can arise among mankind; and such a market can only be found in a large town, occupied by a numerous people.
>
> (p. xxxvii)

However, Anderson admits that such a happy state of affairs is rare, as men like to dictate rules for others' conduct.

Improved communication comes not only from establishing markets but from advances in transport. Anderson's *The Bee*, 13 July 1791, argued that the first great national improvement, the foundation of other improvements in commerce, agriculture and manufactures, was roads. He cites the case of the important journeys between Glasgow and Edinburgh, which took up to a week in the 1760s but were reduced to six to eight hours in the course of thirty years. New roads, in his opinion, lead to increased consumption and lower prices, and the inhabitants of towns become more active and more industrious. On 23 January 1793 in the same publication he observed that canals between inland towns facilitate commerce: not all canals have to be connected to the sea. There is, however, the question of who pays for the construction and maintenance of transport networks.

Underlying economic motivations can bring about development: as with economic growth, incentive mechanisms cannot be ignored. Craig mentioned in his 1814 book the inducements to invest in an industry – the search for the highest profit and the nature of the trade, which would preferably be more respectable and less hazardous, or a continuation of a previous pattern of investment. He makes a clear distinction between a trade that is to the interest of an individual and one benefiting the state, which is concerned with the aggregate interests of all inhabitants: this is why a government should, in his view, never order the employment of capital in a particular way; that is, to the interest of an individual. In modern Europe it is a mistake, he thought, to overthrow the natural distribution of capital in favour of speculations affording no revenue to the people. He does think, however, that a government can influence an industry: it can grant a bounty if there is deficient profit in a promising industry but in general it is wrong to help unprofitable firms. Ultimately, he thought that individuals and the state have the same concern: to employ capital where it yields most profit. In his view, a government should be cautious in helping the investment of fixed capital; it is better to encourage investment in circulating capital because it can easily be withdrawn and reinvested.

Prizes as a stimulus to development

It seems optimistic to expect unaided natural forces to achieve desired economic development: some stimulus is needed, especially to change a traditional society used to the old methods of old industries. But most proposed stimuli take us back to the grants and subsidies route to development. However, prize schemes did exist: for example, linen weavers from various parts of Scotland competed for the prize of a loom awarded by the Board of Trustees.

Although a supporter of development through public subsidy, Lindsay also championed the idea of prizes to improve the industry. Anderson (1785) in his advocacy of a woollen industry for the Highlands suggested a prize system run by a new society to improve the breeding of sheep and quality of wool through overcoming a local obstacle to developing the industry: sheep had to be housed at night because of attacks by foxes and eagles but taking them indoors affects the quality of wool. The prizes he suggested were at least five shillings for the head of a fox or eagle.

The great agricultural improver Sir John Sinclair, writing in wartime, argued that the peace and quiet of Scotland's country agricultural improvement could be partly advanced by a system of prizes. He proposed that the European powers and the USA agree to provide a reward, a prize of at least £1,000, for a useful discovery in Rural Economy, Medicine or the Useful Arts.

In his advice to the gentleman farmer, Kames writes that it is important for a landowner to promote emulation and industry through a board for improving agriculture, similar to those already set up for fisheries and manufactures. This might sound like another example of the statist approach but it goes beyond government intervention to consider the prize approach for stimulating change. He wants the board to appoint an inspector to monitor the progress on improvements under its direction and award a few silver medals for the best conducted farms, to arouse emulation and promote industry. It would also publish details of useful inventions and give premiums in the form of ploughs, harrows and carts to farms likely to benefit from the board's instructions.

Prizes have long been used to encourage academic and sporting achievement; Smith thought premiums and badges would encourage the acquisition of basic education and, in more recent times, prizes have been offered to stimulate entrepreneurship. Prizes are attractive in that they cost less than subsidization, are a one-off help rather than a permanent support and provide relatively inexpensive publicity for a particular activity. But there is always the objection that they have a narrow influence, affecting only a few individuals rather than large groups of the population, unless prizes create a climate of competition with all-round benefits.

Stages of economic development

In the eighteenth century a popular way of analysing social and economic change was the study of the stage-by-stage changes in societies and national economies until they reached the climax of commerce and manufacturing. This movement was not abrupt but a gradual transition, a step-by-step improvement. The Scots were not the first to think of civilization passing through a succession of ages. Hesiod, writing about 700 BC, uses the stages of gold, silver, bronze and iron ages to trace decline; this was, however, unlike the Scots who showed each stage to be better than the previous: Montesquieu was a closer precursor of the Scottish writers. Swingewood sums up: 'The Scots . . . classified societies as savage, barbaric and polished (Ferguson, Robertson) or as hunting, pastoral, agricultural (Smith, Millar) in terms of their prevailing mode of production' (1970: 168), reminding us of the variants of stages theory.

David Hume often returned to a stages theory. In the essay *Of Commerce* he contrasts the savage state of hunting and fishing and the modern state where most of the population are husbandmen (farm workers) or manufacturers. In *Of Refinement in the Arts* he says that the advance of industry brings sophistication. Hume, Low (1952) suggests, has two distinct phases in his theory of development: the self-supporting family with tradition fixing its consumption patterns, and the next phase when foreign trade, or some other outside agent, leads to ambition in economic affairs prompted by a desire for luxuries, leading to a continuous future expansion and development.

Smith's four-stage theory is the most quoted of all the Scottish versions of stages theory. In *LJ* he mentions the four ages of hunters, shepherds, agriculture and commerce in his consideration of the acquisition of property by occupation. In *WN* Smith again employs the stages theory in his discussion of defence. The two most primitive stages of hunters and shepherds require, he writes, everyone to be a warrior, but in the agriculture stage and under commerce and manufacturing it is best to have a professional army, applying the principle of the division of labour to assert the distinctness of military occupations. Brewer (1998) says Smith thought progress from one stage to another was easy and automatic – all that was needed was peace and security. Smith was, moreover, not concerned to explain how progress happened but why it was slow.

Ogilvie (1781) argued that the European system of landed property had progressed through three stages: first, the domestic where cultivation is under a sympathetic clan chief, then the feudal with attachment to a lord, and finally the commercial stage where cultivators lack security and the landlord squeezes industry out of them.

The various users of the stages theory compete for the title of the best expounder. Smith, Ferguson and Millar all have their supporters. Bowles (1984) and Dwyer (1998) regarded Millar as superior to the rest because of his analysis of both the advance and decline of societies and his comparison of eighteenth-century Britain with fifteenth-century Italy.

It is an interesting anthropological exercise to describe the nature of human society at different stages of its development, but more difficult to explain the force that effects change, that is, why societies are not stuck at the same stage of development for ever. In *Of Eloquence* Hume asserts: 'There is certainly something accidental in the first rise and the progress of the arts in any nation' (1987: 106). Men, according to Smith, and perhaps in an echo of Hume's view, naturally move from one stage to another. Dwyer (1998) shows that Millar followed on from Smith who, obsessed with agricultural improvement, argued that an agricultural revolution could occur only when former pasture land became scarce enough to push up the price of animal flesh. Then livestock, he argued, could produce manure used in intensive agriculture, generating profit, which stimulates the luxury trade and makes the markets more important in society.

There can be logic in progressing from one stage to another; as Kim (2009) notes, agriculture has to precede manufactures and commerce in order to provide raw materials and food for the workforce. Both Hume and Steuart, Brewer (1997) says, thought that changes in taste, which were increasingly sophisticated, were crucial to development.

It is also important to consider, as Rosenberg (1968) urges, the economic surplus generated at each stage of economic development. In the final stage, the tastes of upper classes are important in switching their consumption from services, especially servants, to manufactures.

A charming description in Kames of the development of an economy towards agriculture is that

> Plenty of food procured by hunting and fishing, promotes population: but as consumption of food increases with population, wild animals, sorely persecuted, become not only more rare but more shy. Men, thus pinched for food, are excited to try other means for supplying their wants. A fawn, a kid, or a lamb, taken alive and tamed for amusement, suggested probably flocks and herds, and introduced the shepherd-state.
>
> (1778: 90)

These are, Kames acknowledges, slow changes. Because of the hoarding principle men multiply their flocks and herds but this theory is not a worldwide phenomenon because there is no evidence of a hunter or shepherd state in the torrid zone, the belt of the earth between the tropics, where people pick their food from trees. Kames, in his 1796 edition of his *Sketches of the history of Man*, argued that the shepherd stage, then agriculture, is friendly to the population because with a permanent division of land the production of food expands in proportion to the number of consumers.

The stages are linked to institutional change. Like Hume, Smith saw the growth of commerce and manufactures, in the last stage, as producing political and institutional structures. Ferguson, Hill (1997) writes, thought that progress meant going through stages based on the social structure, the levels of government and proficiency in the arts. Hodgson (1870d), writing in an industrial age, asserted that when industry expands it is necessary to have security of property to suppress violence and fraud and to settle disputes. But law and order require taxation and more government institutions – gone were the days when the lord provided justice and policing for free. For Hodgson the highest stage of progress is when credit is introduced, as well as insurance; in other words, commerce with a modern financial sector.

Economic development came slowly in Scotland. From 1750, in southern Scotland, improvement occurred in manufacturing centres and in those rural areas supplying an urban labour market. Interestingly, women did well. In the late eighteenth century women and children experienced a greater increase in their standard of living and employment than men did, especially in the rural textile industry where previously only men were paid (Gibson and Smout 1995).

Concluding remarks

The state of the Scottish economy was repeatedly discussed as a major issue at the time of the debates that led to the Union of Parliaments in 1707. Initially, the government interventionist approach, particularly with regard to the linen industry, was adopted because of the finance provided for it under the Equivalent. But the economic philosophy of the times – that natural processes were to be left alone to achieve the desired improvement – later developed, not least in the writing of Adam Smith.

The period 1700–1900 was a long age of improvement in Great Britain, not excluding Scotland. Farmers changed their methods, manufacturers took up inventions, new towns and cities were built, living standards for many rose and there were substantial advances in the arts and sciences. In Scotland, for those ambitious to achieve, improvement strategies were available. Industries thought to have potential, like fishing and textiles, could be selected for financial support, or there could be faith in innate entrepreneurial ability to effect great change. Underlying all discussions on development is an ideological stance, which needs examining.

7 Economic Ideology

In Scotland, writings on economics sprang from an interest in philosophy. Philosophy gave Scottish writers an interest in systems and the clarification of concepts; furthermore, if they adopted a creed or an ideology, the treatment of a wide range of economic issues could be unified around a central theme. In earlier centuries theology would have provided a framework for the economic theorizing of these Scots; but by the eighteenth century references to the deity were peripheral in economic analyses. In the Scottish Enlightenment God was not central to the new thinking of the age; Nature was much more important.

Smith never spoke of 'capitalism', but his key theme, natural liberty, contained many elements of what was later labelled capitalism – profit-seeking behaviour, running businesses free of government control, and freedom in investment and pricing decisions. Perhaps there was no need to mention capitalism itself. Winch (1985) says that the traditional order was regarded for a long time as equivalent to the capitalist order. Macfie (1971) explains that 'The system of natural liberty in such a society of individuals, with built-in safeguards, secures, as well as is possible between men, justice, their economic welfare, and their happiness' (p. 599). What this liberty was needs some untangling. It could be linked to the Enlightenment interest in human nature or merely mean what life is like when nothing is done to meddle with basic economic mechanisms.

At the core of the concept of natural liberty is the idea of spontaneity, especially in the allocation of resources; socialism is less easy to describe because in its growth as a creed in the nineteenth century it meant different things. It could be the product of a political revolution or a process of gradual change, something local or national. By 1900 it had many organizational expressions, including utopias, cooperatives, trade unions and a planned economy. But central to much of socialism was the importance of labour for determining value, and the nature of income distribution possible through new types of economic organization.

Natural liberty

In discussions of natural liberty there is a choice between attributing it to natural laws and regarding it merely as a default position, a kind of negative liberty with few restraints on individual action.

The hidden nature of natural liberty is such that 'Things not so intended, such as the larger benefits of the system of natural liberty, are instinctually unseen and remain perennially unseen unless continually highlighted by the culture... most people are very slow to appreciate the abstract merits of natural liberty' (Klein 2009: 268). This is an echo of previous discussions of the invisible hand.

In a survey of natural law Bittermann (1940a) says that Locke regarded the law of nature as reason and the will of God. Hutcheson thought that natural laws are the rules of conduct which tended to promote the greatest happiness and the perfection of mankind most effectually. In a further article (1940b), Bittermann explains that in the eighteenth century there were two meanings of 'nature' – the totality, or part, of phenomena, or the action of Providence or God. 'Natural law' is an expression occasionally used in the *TMS* but not in the *WN* where Smith refers to the natural order, or the natural course of things such as profits or trade; 'natural' seems, in his view, to be the result of economic or political conditions, not a matter of history but of human relations in the absence of government, an analytic device. Hume thought that phenomena, not knowledge of the Deity, showed an order or a plan in nature.

Francis Hutcheson's inaugural lecture of 1730 at Glasgow University, *On the Natural Sociability of Mankind*, is relevant to the idea of a system of natural liberty. At the outset he considers the nature of man. Although he says we naturally desire things for ourselves and others there is a conflict between different desires: 'aversion from work and a taste for pleasures often get the better of an ambition to get rich' (2006: 198). While seeking profit we can, he says, also be benevolent. Social life is natural to man because we need the help of others, but we have greater desires, desires which make things more sublime, such as honour.

Utilitarianism, the distinct contribution of Hutcheson to economics, is linked to natural liberty. He pioneered this long before the more famous Jeremy Bentham in his *Introduction to the Principles of Morals and Legislation* (1789) referred to the greatest happiness for the greatest number as a policy goal. In his *An Inquiry into the Original of our Ideas of Beauty and Virtue* (written in 1725), Hutcheson employs that idea, and states the greatest happiness principle in his *System* as:

> When the soul is calm and attentive to the constitution and powers of other beings, their natural actions and capacities of happiness and misery, and when the selfish appetites and passions and desires are asleep, 'tis alleged that there is a calm impulse of the soul to desire the greatest

> happiness and perfection of the largest system within the compass of its knowledge.
>
> (I: 10)

The principle becomes the basic assumption of quantifiable pleasure and pain analysis: 'Duration and number are applicable to every perception or action of the mind... It is from some complex modes of figure and motion that pleasure is perceived' (p. 6); later he writes of comparing pleasures by intenseness and duration. He goes on to assert that the two 'calm natural determinations of the will' are 'an invariable constant impulse toward one's perfection and happiness of the highest kind' (p. 9) and 'toward the universal happiness of others' (pp. 9–10). Pursuing greatest happiness does, he believes, require a special mental effort as selfish passions of hunger, thirst and lust are in conflict with benevolent impulses such as pity, condolence and gratitude. He is aware that self-love will rule over benevolence unless 'one is aware of the high pleasures of self-approbation' (p. 44) or God rewards goodwill towards others. Hutcheson argues that we have a natural moral sense to approve certain things, to have benevolent affections, and that, in general, pursuing the happiness principle is a prudent policy: 'We must live in society, and by the aid of others, whose happiness, or misery, whose pleasures, or pains, we cannot avoid observing' (p. 109). No doubt to the horror of Calvinist contemporaries, he argues that there is no ultimate ill will or malice in human nature and that as soon as we observe others we are morally improved by them. Robustly, he asserts:

> there is a natural subserviency of the private or selfish affections, while they are kept within certain bounds, not only to the good of the individual, but to that of the system...
>
> (p. 149)

Believing that a state of love, goodwill and bounty is seen to be preferable to every man and an excess of selfishness causes misery and moral evils, he underpins this view by asserting that we have natural compassion and God has planted a high standard of virtue in our hearts: 'the course of life which GOD and NATURE recommends to us as most lovely and most conducive to the true happiness of the agent, is that which is intended for the general good of mankind...' (p. 227).

What Hutcheson is doing is to tell us over and again that you can trust human beings when left alone to be good and do good because, based on the conviction that there is a natural desire to seek happiness for all, benevolence is inherent to their nature. This is his strong case for the free society and economy.

The sentiments expressed by Ferguson in his *Essay* were in the spirit of Hutcheson:

> The interests of society and its members are easily reconciled. If the individual owes every degree of consideration to the public, he receives in

> paying that very consideration, the greatest happiness of which his nature is capable; they are the most happy men whose hearts are engaged to the community, in which they find every object of generosity and zeal...
>
> (1767: 58)

Here Ferguson reminds us that the virtuous acts of considering others bring us a reward, our happiness. To be generous and community-minded is the recommended way to live, doing more than following one's nature but doing it voluntarily and not under any compulsion.

Natural liberty, as Lindsay also argued, is inseparable from self (or private) interest; thus linking private interest to the public good in economic matters. He asserted that a commonwealth flourishes only 'where every Individual finds his Account in his own Business, and by promoting his own Interest he so far advances that of the Publick' (1736: 40). Natural liberty is not an aspect of actions but the system that connects all of them.

David Hume supports natural liberty – within limits – in his essay *Of Polygamy and Divorces*, writing: 'the heart of man naturally delights in liberty, and hates every thing to which it is confined; it is also true, on the other, that the heart of man naturally submits to necessity, and soon loses an inclination, when there appears an absolute impossibility of gratifying it... what is man but a heap of contradictions?' (1987: 188). Hume is vague about what 'necessity' is, perhaps meaning that we have little scope for action and therefore liberty does not mean much. Hume, Goldsmith (1988) asserts, is a natural law theorist because he thought rules of justice and regular government are necessary for society.

Natural liberty is, I would argue, inherent in individuals and has powerful and beneficial consequences for economic life. In Anderson's *The Bee* (13 July 1791) politicians are told not to dream of compulsory laws or expensive premiums to make people industrious:

> All that is wanted is to remove those bars that prevent individuals from being able to benefit themselves from their exertions; this being done, they will soon avail themselves of their native powers, with an infinitely greater degree of energy than ever could have been otherwise conceived possible.
>
> (p. 14)

This regards the notion of natural liberty as a default position. 'Native powers' are not linked to the attainment of happiness but to the releasing of an immense amount of human energy.

Not only does this kind of liberty bring energy but the best employment of wealth. Ferguson elaborates on this in his *Principles*,

> states may rate their prosperity, ... by that wealth which, in consistence with public service, they are enabled to leave in the hands of the industrious citizen. In his hands it is employed to its best uses, the rearing of a family, the

> establishment of manufacture, the purchase of materials and other articles, in the outlay of a lucrative and prosperous trade.
>
> (1792 II: 421)

Again, following natural liberty is seen as virtuous and compatible with public service. Because private interest is the great principle of the accumulation of wealth, everything susceptible of improvement, Ferguson argues, should be in private hands.

Even Steuart, noted for his keenness on government action, could make comments compatible with support for the idea of natural liberty. Sen (1957) notes that Steuart thought a few springs move and regulate the world; natural liberty can be the consequence of an internal natural force.

In *WN*, when discussing the Physiocratic system in a crucial passage, Smith uses the analogy of the human body to contrast two ways of conducting a national economy:

> Some speculative physicians seem to have imagined that the health of the human body could be preserved only by a certain precise regimen of diet and exercise... But the healthful state of the human body, it would seem, contains in itself some unknown principle of preservation, capable either of preventing or of correcting, in many respects, the bad effects even of a very faulty regimen... in the political body, the natural effort which every man is continually making to better his own condition is a principle of preservation capable of preventing and correcting, in many respects, the bad effects of a political economy, in some degree, both partial and oppressive. Such a political economy, though it no doubt retards more or less, is not always capable of stopping altogether the natural progress of a nation towards wealth and prosperity, and still less of making it go backwards. If a nation could not prosper without the enjoyment of perfect liberty and perfect justice, there is not in the world a nation which could ever have prospered. In the political body, however, the wisdom of nature has fortunately made ample provision for remedying many of the bad effects of the folly and injustice of man, in the same manner as it has done in the natural body for remedying those of his sloth and intemperance.
>
> (pp. 673–4)

Remedies, presumably in the form of economic policies, are, in this view, unnecessary, because nature cures itself. Francis Horner, writing in his journal (1 December 1800) of Adam Smith, says, 'As a system, his work is evidently imperfect; and yet it has so much the air of a system, and a reader becomes so fond of every analogy and arrangement, by which a specious appearance of system is made out...' (Horner 1843 I: 126). He could have been kinder to Smith by emphasizing the principle of preservation.

In his essay on the *History of Astronomy* (1980) Smith wrote that every system of philosophy was created by human psychology and could be replaced by new ones. His new system seems to be linked to vitalism. Smith, in trying to utilize a contemporary medical theory, was following the tradition of the medical men who took up economics. The great mercantilist Sir William Petty spoke of healthy and sick bodies when analysing an economy such as Ireland's and the leading Physiocrat, Quesnay, was aware of the principle of the circulation of the blood when he invented his *tableau économique*, a primitive input–output table.

An explanation of Smith's view of natural liberty as a natural force is suggested by Packham (2002), who links the concept to the new vitalist physiology of the Edinburgh Medical School used in the mid-eighteenth century. Smith's friend, William Cullen, applied this new science to the study of the nervous system; Smith himself in his *History of the Ancient Physics* refers to the vital principle which animates the life of both plants and animals. Like the vitalists, Smith described the system as harmonious, integrated and mutually beneficial. Samuels backs this up in his view that 'Smith's simple and obvious system of natural liberty was a shrewd method of harnessing and releasing the human propensities deemed favourable to the creation of opulence and good order and suppressing the unfavourable one' (1977: 196). Also, Thomson (1965) says that Smith regarded nature as an active force and resembles Darwin in his picture of harmony and progress where artificial restraints do not impede natural human propensities. The vitalist approach has hints of Physiocracy, which emphasized the power of nature – if unrestrained, this power, it was believed, would drive the economy forward. Smith, Nagao (2007) notes, declared that the system of natural liberty is the true system of political economy in his discussion of Physiocracy.

In the background of these discussions of natural liberty – but without daring to speak its name – was always the Physiocratic idea of laissez-faire. Nicholson, however, in an article of 1885 does equate natural liberty with laissez-faire and argues that self-interest, not force, public opinion or enthusiasm, is the best way to extract human labour. He further claimed that rewards according to sacrifice and effort coincides with notions of equity in most civilized communities. In recognition of the globalization of the day he regarded government interference as impossible where there is international mobility of capital and labour, and an international division of labour. Under natural liberty, he concluded, all classes in Britain increased their prosperity.

As discussed in the chapter on the functions of government, people, Smith thought, should follow their own interest subject only to the rules of justice, while the sovereign's only concerns are to be defence, justice and public works. If other systems vanish, 'the obvious and simple system of natural liberty establishes itself of its own accord' (*WN*: 687).

Smith's views on interferences to natural liberty are strong, especially when they affected the allocation of resources through directing or diverting capital from where it would naturally go. In *LJ* he takes the example of a bounty, which he argues encourages people to crowd into a trade merely to benefit from the subsidy, unlike 'When things are left to their naturall course, according as the demand is, the quantity made is greater or less in each commodity' (p. 365). The awful consequence of interference is a disequilibrium brought about through excess supply. Smith notices the accompanying reduction in economic welfare: in 'the giving bounties for one commodity, and the discouraging another, diminishes the concurrence of opulence and hurts the natural state of commerce' (1766: 529).

Smith puts his system on a pedestal: it is something to be admired. In *TMS*, Smith writes that

> the perfection of police, the extension of trade and manufactures, are noble and magnificent objects. The contemplation of them pleases us... They make part of the great system of government, and the wheels of the political machine seem to move with more harmony and ease by means of them. We take pleasure in beholding the perfection of so beautiful and grand a system, and we are uneasy till we remove any obstruction that can in the least disturb or encumber the regularity of its motions.
>
> (p. 185)

Intellectual and aesthetic pleasure resulting from contemplating a system creates a reverence that makes the beholder determined to remove anything which will detract from it. All Smith wants is for us to keep our hands off a system that can work well on its own; it is conceited, in his view, for people in government to imagine they have a superior wisdom, which will cause interventions:

> Some general, and even systematical, idea of the perfection of policy and law, may no doubt be necessary for directing the views of the statesman. But to insist upon establishing, and upon establishing all at once, and in spite of all opposition, every thing which that idea may seem to require, must often be the highest degree of arrogance. It is to fancy himself the only wise and worthy man in the commonwealth...
>
> (p. 234)

Perhaps Smith is objecting to permanent economic policies and conceding the need for state remedies only in emergencies.

It is clear from *WN* what Smith thinks the arrogance of the statesman might do. Inequalities in wages and profits can, he argued, be caused by the policy of Europe. He details the legislation interfering with the natural course of business: wage regulation, which reduces wages; obstructing the movement of labour (as under the Act of Settlement) and of capital between different employments and places; and restraint of competition by privileged corporations, especially through apprenticeships, which restrict entry to a trade. Schemes of registration, in his view, contribute to the working of closed corporations:

> People of the same trade seldom meet together, even for merriment and diversion, but the conversation ends in a conspiracy against the publick, or in some contrivance to raise prices.
>
> (p. 145)

Instead of corporations regulating a trade, Smith argues that firms should be effectively disciplined by their customers.

Smith's originality, according to Viner, was

> his detailed and elaborate application to the wilderness of economic phenomena of the underlying concept of a co-ordinated and mutually interdependent system of cause and effect relationships which philosophers and theologians had already applied to the world in general.
>
> (1927: 198)

These words are kind because Smith does not clearly set out these relationships, and it is questionable how original he was. Viner says that Smith derived his natural liberty ideas from the Roman jus naturale of Grotius and Pufendorf and the Renaissance emphasis on the individual, the naturalistic philosophy of Shaftesbury, Locke, Hume and Hutcheson, the optimistic theism of the Scottish philosophers and the empiricism of Montesquieu.

Despite an impressive intellectual inheritance Smith prefers to look at examples of natural liberty without really examining it as a concept: Smith's argument for a natural order is inferred from specific data, not deduced from generalizations about the universe in general. But it was a principle with great force. By allowing the free establishment and operation of markets the average person would, he believed, see an improvement in economic welfare. In his *TMS* Smith, as Cohen (1989) notes, wants a few powerful mechanisms to order human society, in order to transform self-interested action into something of public benefit. Herbener (1987) says that the pillars which integrate *TMS* and *WN* are impartial spectators, self-command and humanity (simultaneously), virtues and general rules of conduct. Smith, Thomson (1965) reports, writes that systems are like machines. In both the *TMS* and the *WN* 'the structure of the system is constituted by an equilibrium between the individual and society' (1965: 226). This view makes sense because competition is the opposite of the state monopolies so abhorrent to Smith.

There is an important connection between natural liberty and competition. Grampp (1964) notes that in Smith's *LJ* the natural order is the competitive market; it is not related to the pursuit of ordered social relations as in the *TMS*. Winch (1997) observes that, in Book III of *TMS*, Smith wrote that liberty meant free markets and civil liberties; he thus equated competition with perfect liberty because it matches natural justice and expediency.

What then is the 'harmony' of his system? In the *WN*, according to Viner (1927), there is a sort of average or statistical harmony which shows that natural processes can be beneficial in general but not in all individual cases. Viner says that natural liberty can be extended in four ways: by freedom in the choice of occupations, in trade in land, and in internal trade or international trade. But he gathers together departures from harmony noted in the *WN*: (1) masters and workmen dispute over wages, (2) the public conflicts with masters and workmen and apprentices over apprenticeships, (3) high profits of merchants and manufacturers disadvantage the public, (4) merchants and manufacturers have opposite interests to farmers' and landlords' and the general public's, (5) resources are misallocated because the chance of success in risky ventures is overestimated, (6) the private sector does not maintain roads adequately, (7) the division of labour has bad effects on workers, and (8) in old countries rent and profits squeeze wages. This list is long enough to chip away the idea of harmony to little more than a vague suggestion. But in all the above instances Viner is exposing the bad effects the system might have without attacking the system itself.

Did Smith exaggerate the importance of the restrictions on liberty he identified? In general, Buchanan thought it rare for legislation to advance society, preferring 'the spontaneous product of individual prudence' (1844: 317). Giving as a confirmatory example bank regulation in the United States, which he says shows the futility of stringent state control, he argues that natural liberty is a way of avoiding pointless interference in the national economy; his stance does not, however, prevent him criticizing Smith's analysis of natural liberty in his commentary on *WN* (1814). Buchanan thought Smith overrated the power of the corporations – they had to be responsive to the state of trade, and combinations of traders could break down through individual traders selling when it suited them. The market itself can, Buchanan argued, breed collusion because combinations of either masters or servants can arise through scarcity of labour or of work. Buchanan says Smith is wrong to say that workmanship is worse in the towns than in the suburbs because of corporations: there are enough free men to have competition with corporations. Apprenticeships, the object of Smith's fierce criticism, were, Buchanan pointed out, based on voluntary contract, with legislation merely enforcing them. He argues further that if a trade fails, a workman is in trouble not because of the apprenticeship laws but because the division of labour has made him too specialized. Other critics of Smith, including Sir Frederick Eden, said Smith overrated the effect of the law of settlement on labour mobility as young people find it easy to change their residence. He further argued that, unlike Smith's view, it was not only merchants who opposed the public interest; landlords and all orders of society are warped by their own partial views. Land law seems to have been handled too roughly by Smith, who, in Buchanan's opinion, exaggerates its effects: laws on primogeniture, perpetuities or entails applied to only a small proportion of land.

Later writers interpreted natural liberty as particular types of freedom, or tried to reinforce general principles. Dugald Stewart, Rothschild (1992) reports, thought the notion of freedom in political economy is freedom of trade and industry, free circulation of labour and of stock, plus free competition between individual citizens. He thought both liberty and equality are inimical to property. Craig in a sense reverts to Hutcheson's theme of linking the powerful themes of happiness and liberty:

> Each man's happiness being entrusted to his own care, no other person, merely with a view to his advantage, can control his conduct. If we see our neighbour running head long into misery, we may warn him of his danger, and advise him to change his course; but we can have no pretence for forcing him to adopt our opinions, and to walk in that track which we inform him leads to happiness.
>
> (1814 I: 328)

In other words, control over individuals can be informative, even educative, which is much milder than ordering someone's actions. Freedom is so important that we do not impose anything but advice on other people.

Natural liberty can be the reason for general optimism. According to Chalmers, as the spontaneous workings of human nature, not public policy, provide for us, there is no need to be anxious about population or capital and rush to advocate government policies because there are 'self-regulating interests… Interests which result with so much certainty from the checks and the principles that nature has already instituted, as to supersede all public or patriotic regulation in regard to either of them' (1833a II: 45–6). Chalmers says that in an economy there is a law of oscillation like that in the planetary system: there is no deficiency of capital because of our appetite for gain, and capital suits itself to the needs of the country through changes in prices and profits. Hilton, quoted in Waterman (1991), sums up Chalmers as a moral paternalist and economic individualist who supported laissez-faire.

Natural liberty was highly praised by Burton who argued that organization comes from the natural tyranny of men, taking as an example the sumptuary laws designed to protect people from extravagance and ruin. 'Each withdrawal of interference is a symptom that the light of civilization has enabled the human ruler to see his own weakness contrasted with the Divine goodness and strength' (1849: 250). What the legislature should do, he writes, follows from the fundamental roles of the minimal state: security, and the protection from injury to life and reputation. Further interference cannot be effective, he argued; for example, the requirement for a ten-hour day is deceptive if a man has to work twelve hours to obtain sufficient food. Attempting to improve the conditions of a trade is impossible – it would be better, in Burton's opinion, for parents to keep their children from the trade, thereby causing a labour shortage and higher wages. True to his libertarian principles he asserted that conventional habit and public opinion were better than legislation.

The Duke of Argyll described society as an organism with 'its own natural laws of life and growth' (1893), its 'unseen foundations', which he summed up as a claim of a right to possession of certain things, and obligations of good faith in all transactions. He argued for the existence of natural laws in man's constitution and the divine government of the whole system. He also attempted to explain the idea of natural liberty by contrasting property and monopoly, lamenting that the concepts are often confused: property is the result of individual freedom but monopoly is a restraint on freedom, the privileged access to what others own (p. 532). A guild monopoly is based, he writes, on loyalty to one's mates and not to human freedom and the nation's welfare (539).

Recent commentators have explored many interpretations of Smith's great scheme – natural liberty. Smith, as Goldsmith (1988) notes, rejected ideas of an original state of nature and an original contract in favour of tracing development through four stages. Fitzgibbons (1995) suggests that whereas Hume wanted a system of commerce, Smith wanted a system of nature. Smith, Rosenberg (1960) tells us, was not simply laissez-faire in his attitudes: he had an elaborate conception of conflicting forces that compel human action and was aware of the effects of different kinds of institutional arrangements on human action and welfare. The desire for wealth is, in Smith's view, counterbalanced by the desire for indolent and easy living. A great diversity of interest is summed up by Rosenberg in the expression 'the general interest'. The environment Smith proposed was, Herbener (1987) says, capitalism based on a system of just property in a society of contract. There would, according to Smith, be non-violent voluntary exchange, limited government and a largely spontaneously ordered society where individuals interact within a system of natural law.

Natural liberty appeared to have won the hearts of a succession of economic writers from Hutcheson onwards. This put them at odds with other developments in society, particularly as parliament passed more and more laws affecting property and the running of business. Perhaps what the Scots were storing up for future generations were strongly argued principles, which would inspire people tired of interfering governments.

Socialism

Socialism is a diffuse and confusing idea because its varieties are so great. In a lecture at Oxford in 1894, Nicholson identified many types of socialist. At the core of the idea of socialism is a system that intends to provide a new type of society based on equal treatment of all members of the community. The community can be a small group, with only enough people to run a farm or a factory, or as extensive as a whole country. Socialism can be an economic organization, or a political entity exercising degrees of social control, with totalitarianism as the extreme.

In the opinion of Young (1983), Scotland failed to produce a major socialist thinker because the intelligentsia of the Scottish Enlightenment imposed English traditions and industrialization on the Scots, preventing the emergence of Scottish intellectual leaders of the working-class movement. The Scottish Marxists could not understand why capitalism ruled with absolute sway in Scotland. But a closer examination of the Scottish literature shows that several strands of socialist thinking were discussed, even by the leading intellects of the Enlightenment.

It would be amazing to describe Smith as a leading founder of socialism because of his strong support for natural liberty but he did inspire many later writers on socialism. He has a concern for the poor, a dislike of high profits, a labour theory of value and an awareness of the possible mental deterioration associated with the division of labour, which inspired many utopian communities to avoid occupational specialization.

The case for state action

The grandest schemes of socialism encompass the comprehensive and coordinated working of the whole state. Steuart admits in his *Principles* that there is less of a case for individuals to follow their inclinations now that we have formed trading nations, and riveted together a multitude of reciprocal dependences, which tie the members of them together. People discover the advantages of living in a well-ordered society and will accept a measure of control.

Steuart had a vision of a balanced economy. In his *Principles* he presents the balance as natural or coming from government. From his mercantilist forebears Steuart could be expected to place the balance of trade in a central place in his thought but he went further, using 'balance' in different ways including the balance between work and demand, between the classes and between parts of a country. A balance in accounting is a familiar notion in economics but we can also have a balance in a watch and a balance for weighing. Steuart seems often to use the watch analogy: he says, in the context of how demand encourages farm production, 'The demander must have an equivalent to give; it is this equivalent which is the spring of the whole machine; for without this the farmer will not produce any surplus...' (I: 134). Again, 'a taste for superfluity...will produce demand and this gain will become the main spring of the whole operation' (p. 192). When discussing countercyclical policy, Steuart uses 'balance' as something like a pair of scales: a statesman has to load the lighter side of the balance to counteract competition. He maintains that it is possible to have a more or less stable equilibrium: 'the balance of work and demand, and that of population and agriculture, can be kept in a gentle vibration, by alternate augmentations' (p. 315). He hints at a full employment macroeconomic equilibrium.

Within a country the 'equal balance' between work and demand should, he writes, be promoted by the statesman, even if it means stimulating the demand for luxury at home until workers are given more useful employment. This balance is crucial to economic prosperity:

> When it [the balance of work and demand] vibrates in moderation, then industry and trade go on prosperously, and are in harmony with each other; because both parties gain. The industrious man is recompensed in

> proportion to his ingenuity; the intrinsic value of goods does not vary, nor deceive the merchant; profits on both sides fluctuate according to demand, but never get time to consolidate with, and swell the real value, and never altogether disappear, and starve the workman.
>
> (p. 241)

This is an idyllic picture, which almost sounds utopian. It is the task of the statesman to maintain this happy state of affairs; the point of maintaining the balance between work and demand is not 'to enrich the state, but... to preserve every member of it in health and vigour' (p. 288). However, this requires much government action.

The 'even balance' can be achieved through a variety of policies; for example, by levying taxes not so much to pay interest but to increase the circulation of money throughout the economy. At the heart of employment policy would be the collection of data to enable the statesman to 'prevent anyone from rising above, or sinking below that standard which is best proportioned to the demand made for their particular industry...' (p. 99). His 'balance of work and demand' (p. 203), presumably the goods supplied by work and demand for them, would, Steuart writes, be constantly examined by merchants who have the crucial role in the Steuartian economy of fixing and stabilizing prices. In his industrial policy Steuart, like his French exemplars of the seventeenth century, was unashamedly keen to intervene in manufacturing, avoiding laissez-faire principles. It seems an invasion of natural liberty mattered little to him because intervention was beneficial: 'the duty of every statesman to make his people happy and flourishing' (IV: 171).

There can, in Steuart's view, be a balanced society with a harmony between the classes. He had a notion of a perfect state of affairs 'when every class in general, and every individual in particular, is made to be aiding and assisting to the community, in proportion to the assistance he receives from it' (I: 101); a society based, in other words, on a tacit understanding of mutual services. In a rich country there has to be, he argued, a 'just balance' between the Crown and the wealthy. Discussing public credit he says it is important to preserve a balance between the moneyed interest and the landlords:

> The firm establishment of public credit tends greatly to introduce these reciprocal sentiments of good-will among the two great classes of a people and thereby to preserve a balance between them. The monied interest wish to promote the prosperity of the landlords; the landlords, the solidity of credit; and the well-being of both depends upon the success of trade and industry.
>
> (IV: 98)

This is a rejection of the popular contemporary view that the emergence of a new class with its power based on money through the creation of the national debt is regrettable. Within society Steuart wants a balance in tax burden between groups on the ability-to-pay principle: 'in imposing land taxes... the load of all impositions may be equally distributed upon every class of a people who enjoys superfluity, and upon no other' (p. 100). He also considers another class relationship – between farmers and free hands – who produce, respectively, two types of good: food and luxuries (a broad class of good – anything not necessary as food, clothing, housing or protection from injury). It is the task of the statesman to create 'reciprocal wants... in order to bind the society together' (I: 46). In the absence of money and luxurious arts 'consumption and produce becoming equally balanced, the inhabitants will increase no more, or at least very precariously...' (p. 49).

Within a nation there is the relationship between rich and poor, a balance of wealth between subjects, which creates a circulation of wealth:

> The desires of the rich, and the means of gratifying them, make them call for the services of the poor: the necessities of the poor, and their desire of becoming rich, make them cheerfully answer the summons; they submit to the hardest labour, [...] for the sake of an equivalent in money.
>
> (II: 39)

Consumption therefore makes the balance tip, changing the relative proportion of riches between individuals.

Steuart noted that there is also a geographical balance between parts of a country, especially between cities and the country. Cities, he wrote, although associated with poor health and debauchery, have the advantages of increasing the overall level of productivity of the whole population, making taxation possible and increasing land values. As labour rushes to the cities, Steuart noticed that agricultural labour becomes scarce and its wages increase but balance is restored by the continuing growth of the cities, which both demand even the most distant agricultural produce and build the necessary roads. This geographical balance is also, he argued, an industrial balance between industries that satisfy basic needs and those based on newly created wants. In a primitive economy once basic needs are satisfied there is no need to work further; in advanced economies the balance between subsistence and demand has to be maintained, for example as in Holland, which keeps food prices low and constant to the benefit of the lower classes.

In my view, this is an amazing array of balances, enough to bind the whole economy and society together. It follows the socialist principles of providing universal benefit from economic activity through integrating many activities but it needs more to achieve its goals than a suggestion of an economic policy here and there.

After Steuart there is no Scottish writer with such an integrated and broad vision of an economy relying on government to keep it in balance. But later there were a few suggestions for ensuring all the balances mentioned. Economic libertarianism did not completely rule economic thought but traces of the idea of a controlled economy remained. Craig, for example, in pursuit of the good of the nation would permit extensive legislation. He wrote:

> Regulations enforced by the community, from views of public advantage, are very various and important...all laws of police, laws for forming and repairing roads, bridges and canals, by which citizens are forced to relinquish their property for a just equivalent; regulations of trade; every kind of test or exclusion from office on account of opinions held to be dangerous to the public safety; the collection of the revenue, the commission of the requisite authority and power to public functionaries and, in general, whatever institutions, or regulations, are demanded by the exigencies of the state...statutes must be promulgated, declaring explicitly what is considered as necessary for the good of the nation.
>
> (1814 I: 321–2)

However, most of these proposals at best provided a framework for economic action and required no government expenditure – the population at large would carry out the government's wishes at their own expense.

A staunch defender of strong government, Carlyle greatly loathed laissez-faire principles: 'a government of the under classes by the upper on a principle of *Let alone* is no longer possible in England in these days...The Working Classes cannot any longer go on without government; without being *actually* guided and governed...' (1840: 49). Also, he wrote:

> the right of the ignorant man to be guided by the wiser, to be, gently or forcibly, held in the true course by him, is the indisputablest...Society struggles towards perfection by enforcing and accomplishing it more and more.
>
> (p. 52)

If not entirely Steuart's full dream of the balanced economy it is a nudge in that direction.

Utopias

Utopias, those ideal communities that correspond to a set of noble principles, have a long ancestry dating back to Plato's *Republic* and Sir Thomas More's *Utopia* of 1516. Several Scottish writers had mixed proposals of their own. In a simple way, Wallace's anonymously published *Various Prospects of Mankind, Nature and Providence* sets out the utopian conditions that would presumably maximize population growth:

> As the complete culture of the earth requires vigorous endeavours, idleness must be banished, universal industry must be introduced and preserved. Labour must be properly and equitably distributed; every one must be

> obliged to do his part and the earth must be cultivated by the united labours of all its inhabitants acting in concert, and carrying on a joint design.
> (1761: 26–7)

Wallace suggests a perfect constitution in which a council would assign employment, all males would have a comprehensive education in agriculture, and marriage would be the norm for all adults.

> That there should be no private property. That every one should work for the public, and be supported by the public. That all should be on a level and that the fruits of every one's labour should be common for the comfortable subsistence of all members of the society. And, lastly, that every one should be obliged to do something, yet none should be burdened with severe labour.
> (p. 46)

These are put forward as the fundamental maxims of society and include the popular items for a visionary's list of no private property or private employment, equality, work for the common good and easy community obligations. But to establish such a perfect government would require a revolution in an existing society or the foundation of a new society on uncultivated territory. Although Wallace admits that utopianism is attractive to him, he realizes that it is pointless because the population would expand greatly in such a community but be constrained by the subsistence available: 'the earth could not nourish them for ever, unless either its fertility could be continually augmented, or by some secret in nature . . .' (p. 115).

His sad conclusion is that a perfect government creates a catastrophe. Wallace, Church of Scotland minister as he was, had to wrestle with the problem of nature destroying what was the ideal and concluded that nature has built-in constraints. Malthus used *Various Prospects* to comment that when Wallace argued that equality would be destroyed by the force of population he 'did not seem to be aware that any difficulty would arise from this cause till the whole earth had been cultivated like a garden, and was incapable of any further increase of produce' (1989 I: 306). The whole basis for Malthus taking up his pen, he admitted in the first edition of his *Essay on Population*, was to attack Godwin and other idealists for not appreciating the consequences of their ideas. In Wallace, Malthus had a teacher who convincingly explained that human perfection was impossible because the principle of subsistence checking population growth could not be ignored.

David Hume, in his essay *Idea of a Perfect Commonwealth*, considered James Harrington's *Commonwealth of Oceana* (1656) to be 'the only valuable model of a commonwealth, that has yet been offered to the public' (1987: 514), but his interest was political not economic. Hume's central concern seems to be the working of the legislature and executive. Although willing to concede that a magistrate could attempt some innovations for the public good, he conservatively wanted change only if it were consistent with preserving the constitution.

An insight into Hume's stance is provided by Wolin (1954), who thinks that Hume, aware of the revolutions of the seventeenth century, preferred the informal communal arrangements of English society. A carefully devised utopia would not appeal to Hume, who linked morals to the passions, not reason, and did not want to undermine the immutable values of natural law.

The land reformer William Ogilvie, naturally given to the utopian ideal, argued that land was originally in common ownership and that the greatest happiness would be promoted when everyone had an equal share of the soil. There were two major routes to effecting such a change in ownership in his opinion – reforming existing land ownership and establishing a new settlement. The latter would be easier if uninhabited land abroad was colonized, but he also thought a new type of settlement would be possible in an older country – it would be 'the joint property of the whole community in the whole soil' (1781: 62). Citizens who were at least 21 years old would claim up to forty acres anywhere in their parish, unless prevented by other laws; a special board would finance the purchase of estates; and landowners could be given a premium for setting up at least 200 farms with a size of twenty to forty acres. Strangely, he denied being a utopian and stated he was merely extrapolating from agrarian experience. It is hard to believe that agriculture would flourish under this system and that there would be enthusiasm to take up small farms.

As Nagao (2003) notes, Thomas Reid, in his essay *Some considerations on the utopian system*, used familiar assumptions for his version of socialism by regarding labour as the origin of national wealth and the market as an inefficient method of allocation. An economic system controlled by a central authority would, he declared, be better and more efficient than a system of self-interest. To achieve this new system he wanted the abolition of private property and the direct control of labour. Later, in his *Practical Ethics*, Thomas Reid suggested communal ownership, believing that the acquisition of private property caused divisions in society: all should work for the state, he wrote, and have no private property. To reinforce this new type of society moral training would be part of education and a new incentive – public honours for moral exertion – be introduced.

The idea of utopianism never seemed to catch on, perhaps because it was too prescriptive, and Smith and his friends were right in saying that the desire for liberty is a basic human trait which would never tolerate an economic organization so rigidly and firmly constructed. Nagao shrewdly observes: 'a vision of utopia was not a plan to change an existing government according to it, but a reference point from which a philosopher could see a society critically' (2007: 17).

Cooperatives

Instead of the all-embracing idealism of a utopia or an adversarial trade union movement the cooperative approach represented a way of advancing the claims of labour and improving the lot of the working classes.

In *A New View of Society*, 1813–16 (1970), Robert Owen described his famous community, still visited by tourists today, at New Lanark near Glasgow. His father-in-law David Dale started a cotton manufactory in 1784 on uncultivated, unpopulated land. A village with low-rent houses to induce families to come to work at the mill was built, as was a large house for five hundred children from Edinburgh workhouses; a system of education was put in place there and the children were subjected to less onerous labour to stop them running away.

This community had some idealistic features. It aimed to be the vehicle for forming human character through the strict training of children in good habits from their earliest years. Vice was curbed by checking drunkenness, lying and disputes. To discourage drinking, increased excise duties on spirits were imposed and the number of shops selling alcohol reduced.

Owen had the foresight in constructing an experimental community to relate it to the wider labour market. He wanted increased knowledge of the condition of labour through the quarterly collection in every locality of the average price of manual labour, and of the numbers receiving parish support or who were unemployed or partially employed. To cure unemployment he proposed spending the money currently supporting the unemployed on public works such as the making and repairing of roads, work on canals, harbours, docks, shipbuilding and materials for the navy.

His scheme was cooperation on mildly socialist lines. Like other socialists he was anti-Malthusian, believing that an intelligent and industrious people can create more food. But he was not keen on workers' rights: no trade unions were to challenge the authority of the owner and certainly there was no profit-sharing. What was attractive to the visitors, many from overseas, was the discipline and training of the workforce. Marx put his finger on the heart of Owen's philosophy at New Lanark – it was a new method of production:

> Robert Owen, who was the father of the co-operative factories and stores, . . . in no way shared the illusions of his followers about the field of effectiveness of these isolated elements of transformation, not only made the factory system in practice the sole foundation of his experiments, but also declared that system to be theoretically the point of departure for the social revolution.
>
> (1867: 635 footnote 46)

Haworth (1976) also comments that New Lanark was more an experiment in factory management than the creation of an ideal community. Owen wanted the greatest happiness for the greatest number and assumed that full employment and good housing would accomplish it. He was an environmental determinist who disliked committees and democracy, preferring his own strong direction, and thought people could be trained to be good.

Owen's *A Further Development of the Plan for the Relief of the Manufacturing and Labouring Poor* 1817 (1970) was bolder and more socialistic. He wanted mixed agricultural and manufacturing communities of 500 to 1,500 people, large enough to be viable, sharing income and expenditure. In this heaven men would work cheerfully for themselves and for the public good, free from a system of remuneration by the day or by the piece of work. Without onerous effort they would acquire necessaries and comforts abundantly and without disputes. It would be possible to find competent managers working without compensation and living on the same terms as the others. Curiously, he suggested that outside investors should be encouraged, offering them a return of 5 per cent, in a sense departing from the mutuality at the basis of a socialist cooperative and creating a capitalist firm. As a sop to his socialist supporters he attacked individualism for restricting the food supply. Under cooperation he believed existing resources could increase the food supply to allow at least a quadrupling of the population with a tenfold increase in comfort.

With all the exquisite detail beloved of socialist reformers Owen, in his *Report to the County of Lanark* (1820), elaborates on his cooperative schemes. Rejecting the principles of minute subdivision of labour and the pursuit of private interest he recommended associations of men, women and children with a minimum of 300 and maximum of 2,000. On land of 800 to 1,500 acres he suggested that buildings should be erected around four sides of a square, or parallelogram; they would have private sleeping and sitting rooms for adults, general sleeping apartments for the children, storerooms, an inn for strangers and an infirmary: 'these establishments... founded by landowners and capitalists, public companies, parishes, or counties, will be under the direction of the individuals whom these powers may appoint to superintend them... Those formed by the middle and working classes, upon a complete reciprocity of interests, should be governed by themselves,... by a committee of all the members of the association between certain ages – for instance between thirty-five and forty-five...' (1970: 255).

These versions of communal schemes were detailed enough to encourage the foundation of Owenite communities; he himself wasted his fortune on two short-lived cooperatives in Indiana and in Hampshire. The difficulties of making a community function are great. The kind of person who wants to enrol will often have no relevant agricultural and industrial experience and be reluctant to accept authority from a committee or anyone, while idealists do not often become effective producers.

Campbell, writing in 1831, with his experience of the Glasgow Friends of Truth Co-operative Union, noted that the five hundred societies of his organization in Great Britain and Ireland had the same objects of joint ownership of land and equipment, housing for workers and the elderly, and educational establishments. In these cooperatives an individual could earn one to ten thousand shares and obtain interest at 5 per cent quarterly, but the shares would be cheap enough to allow even the poor to participate. In return for work, members could have a credit in the accounts or cash to spend at the cooperative's shop. (Campbell was also a socialist who opposed heavy taxation, arguing that taxes lessen consumption, throw workers out of employment and can lead to wage reductions.) Giving workers a stake in the capital of the cooperative was sensible because they would have an interest in its financial success and not just demand higher and higher wages to the point where even depreciation could not be financed.

Cooperation was possible without setting up cooperatives. Hodgson was a supporter of one type of cooperation, observing that capital and labour are inevitably allied and mutually indispensable. Cooperation essentially has a pacific aim of creating harmony between labour and capital. A form of cooperation in this weaker sense is the division of labour, which means that many people doing different things collaborate to a common end. In 1877 Hodgson examined institutionalized cooperation in the form of cooperative societies, which enable the whole world to be increasingly engaged in collaborative activity. Consumer cooperatives reduce the waste of too many shops, prevent fraud and forgery, encourage saving and provide facilities for recreation and instruction. In the nineteenth century cooperation and competition were regarded as stark alternatives but Hodgson said they could coexist through quality competition between cooperatives. Later Smart (1912) took a broad view of self-interest, which incorporated cooperation, by saying that we have to consider the wants and wishes of others. By this cooperation we allow millions of people to survive.

Cooperatives could have gone the way of grand utopias but they survived in Scotland and England perhaps because of their more limited objectives and simple technology. Consumer cooperatives were linked into a respectable retail chain, and simple producer cooperatives in low technology industries such as boot and shoe manufacture had a long life. The benefits in both producer and consumer cooperatives are distributed to workers and consumers, not to shareholders, perhaps part of the reason for their success.

National economic planning

Steuart was a pioneer of the idea of national economic planning but in a gradualist way, arguing that changes in policy should be made slowly by a skilful hand. There are many references in his *Principles* to plans. He wants plans for enclosing thousands of acres with hedges and ditches, a plan for granaries, a plan for bringing down the price of subsistence, a plan to bring down the price of subsistence universally, a plan to stabilize oatmeal prices, a planned canal for national improvement, a plan to build many public roads. Later in his life, in 1783, Steuart argued for a plan that would base the intervention price for corn on the best information gained by consulting farmers: this would avoid any price instability, which would affect supply, prices, ability to pay rent and the pattern of farm production. He showed how the plan would be executed in detail: all corporations, communities, employers and municipalities would be ordered to draw up lists of their inhabitants, and granaries would be set up to store eight bushels of wheat for every resident of an area. The granary plan would be gradually introduced, to ensure an appropriate level of stock, through farmers presenting their new grain to the granary in return for receipts; what they had deposited would circulate like currency. Grain would be issued only to those on the lists but markets would be opened to sell small quantities to the poor. What could be planned for a basic commodity like corn could be applied, he believed, to the rest of the economy until a national economic plan was created.

A national economic plan was carefully described in the writings of John Gray, an Edinburgh printer and newspaper pioneer (*c.*1799–1883), and publisher of a succession of newspapers including the *North British Advertiser*. In 1825, the year he started his lucrative career, he published his *A Lecture on Human Happiness*, which revealed his early socialist ideas and pointed towards his idea of planning. He used a more concrete idea than utility, stating that the attainment of happiness results from satisfying all animal and intellectual wants. Lamenting the fact that the labouring classes were getting only one-fifth of the produce of their labour, he proposed a restructuring of the labour force and cooperation. To achieve this, Gray recommended that the unproductive classes be reduced through sacking half of the civil service, maintaining the army only for defensive purposes, teaching people to live in peace to render lawyers unnecessary, and dismissing two-thirds of shopkeepers as they waste time in decorating their shop windows and waiting for customers. (It is amusing to read of suggestions from a socialist amounting to ruthless efficiency; today socialists are more likely to protect employment at all cost.) He abhorred competition built on the principle of market-determined production set on making a profit because, in the absence of competition, wealth would be accessible to all. With the prospect of unlimited employment for all and a fivefold increase in income he predicted that the productive classes would want to join Owenite communities. Owen disliked Gray's ideas, accusing him of providing no explanation for his system of production, exchange and distribution, a system which risked promoting idleness because of the principle of equal distribution, and which was a step too far for Owen.

The more ambitious *Social System* showed Gray's determination to change the nature of the social system:

> what we chiefly want is a controlling and directing power by which the various parts of our commercial system may be so fitted and adapted to each other as to produce a harmonious instead of an incongruous whole... (1831: 5)

Given the assumption that production is the cause of demand he wanted a National Chamber of Commerce to combine capitals, and direct and control cultivation, manufacturing and trade. Workers and owners of capital would, he thought, volunteer, not be forced: the incentive for a capitalist to join a commercial association would be payment for the use of buildings and capital surrendered and a salary for managing the works. To promote these reforms

Gray advocated the use of the press, the appointment of a committee to inquire into the state of the country and the publication of a prospectus to attract capital from individual owners of business. A system of national warehouses would collect producers' output for distribution to retailers who would sell at prices covering material cost, wages and a gross profit margin to pay other expenses and permit rapid accumulation of capital. In this paradise

> the Chamber of Commerce . . . having the means of ascertaining, at all times the actual stock of any kind of goods on hand, would always be able to say at once where production should proceed more rapidly, where at its usual pace, and where also it should be retarded.
>
> (p. 45)

When unsold stocks built up, capital and labour would, he argued, be switched to other production; redundant workers would be paid their usual wages. Fiat money issued by standard banks would be used to pay wages and salaries.

In his proposals Gray was a pioneer of macroeconomic management:

> Effectual demand . . . the desire to possess any thing, combined with the ability to give an equivalent for it – is the only thing wanting to cause houses to be built, clothes to be manufactured, and food to be produced in quantities without any known or comprehensible limit.
>
> (p. 195)

In a curious description of planning he thought a plan was necessary for every part of the economy but that the '*aggregate of parts*' would be under divine rather than human governance (pp. 331–2), which is perhaps an extreme version of the invisible hand idea. Gray compared the population of his time to 'an ungoverned regiment of soldiers, who are told to march in line; but as there is no one to give the word of command, there can be no simultaneous movement . . . If . . . a due proportion of money makers included, producers were to move on simultaneously, there could be no over-production' (p. 279). Through his social system he felt there would be the means to demand all these things. The benefits of this social system would be considerable as the manufacturer would have 'no market to seek, no customers to higgle with, no bad debts to fear, no pecuniary considerations to harass, no commercial perplexities to annoy him . . . a liberal salary as his reward' (p. 51).

Beneath the surface of Gray's reasoning lurks Say's law of markets, that is, that everyone as a producer would create demand for others' produce. The basis of employment follows, Gray says, the principle 'PRODUCTION NATURALLY THE CAUSE OF DEMAND, SHALL BE SO PRACTICALLY . . . Supply and Demand are exchangeable terms. Supply is Demand and Demand is Supply' (1848: 245). He summons in support James Mill and McCulloch, supporters of Say. Gray wants it to be easy to sell the produce of labour at a fair profit as his system links production and demand. Anticipating the command economies of the twentieth century he opposed unions of workers or employers and thought strikes would be pointless: no one would gain because there would be no spare profits to finance higher wages.

Gray praises his system as consistent with individual competition in occupations, private accumulation of capital, and all types of government and religion. He claimed it was a voluntary system but it is hard to imagine many would join his scheme, as some capitalists and workers would see their remuneration much diminished. It could be pioneered within a sector but Gray wanted integrated national production. What is praiseworthy about this plan is the attempt to suggest a coordinating mechanism in the warehouse system and a method of adjusting production plans.

Trade unions

Socialism in Britain and the trade union movement marched hand in hand in the nineteenth century. How much Scotland was affected by laws against combinations (trade unions) is difficult to judge. Gray (1928) painstakingly examines the issue. There was an ambiguity in the idea of combination as it could be combinations of master craftsmen or of their journeymen but the legislation seemed to be aimed against wage earners. It was possible for workmen to combine to seek a court order, as when Edinburgh compositors combined in 1804 to fix piecework prices for the local printing trade. The Combination Acts of 1799 and 1800 forbad societies for the purpose of political reform and made interference with commerce and trade illegal, but not a single prosecution in Scotland was conducted under them: they were abolished in 1824 but after a spate of strikes the Act of 1825 restored the common law of conspiracy with regard to trade union action. It was not until 1875 that criminal sanctions against unions were removed. Marwick (1935) mentions early unions in weaving and cotton spinning; by 1840 unionization of carpenters, masons and coalminers had started. In the latter half of the century, when new manufactures grew up outside the incorporated bodies, employers either combined together to resist workers or relied on the labour market to replace troublesome workers rather than use the common law. In 1897 the Scottish Trades Unions Congress was founded to coordinate the working of over a hundred Scottish unions: the unions became a serious force in the Scottish economy.

What did the Scottish economics writers think of this new labour market development? Craig (1814) was an early supporter of the freedom of trade unions to function. There should be, he advocated, a repeal of laws oppressing the working classes – game laws, laws relating to apprenticeships, corporations and settlements restricting movement and the employment of labour. The same civil rights should apply irrespective of rank and wealth, it being wrong to regard society as divided into the rich and the poor perpetually arrayed against each other, as 'society consists of insensible gradations, rising from the lowest to the highest station' (p. 198). He seemed to be proclaiming a move towards egalitarianism through identifying the interests of the majority with the interests of society. Joseph Hume, the Radical MP who flirted with socialism was, according to Grampp (1976), best known for obtaining the repeal of the Combination Laws in 1824. George Combe (1788–1858), more famous for his establishment of phrenology, the study of the significance of bumps on the skull, approved of the remedies popular with trade unions for the ills of contemporary society in his *The Constitution of Man*, first published in 1828. He supported union demands for shortening working hours, arguing that machinery and science would produce more and more goods with less labour needed. Also, if shops closed no later than eight o'clock in the evening workers would have time for self-improvement.

In the nineteenth century the opponents of trade unionism seemed to harden their views as the century moved to its close. A severe critic of unions, Cree, in his *A Criticism of the Theory of Trades' Unions* (1892), presented many objections to their conduct. Whilst approving of the betterment of working men he attacked the means adopted to achieve this and argued that employers must be able to dismiss workers in order to carry on a business. As for the popular union demand to limit hours of work, Cree thought it ignored the different power of work from man to man and would lead to falls in wages. Unions, he thought, were anti-competitive, restricting labour supply to raise wages despite the consequent unemployment, to the detriment of workers, and causing the flight of capital abroad through fear of unions. Workers as sellers of their labour have no more right, he wrote, than other sellers to combine. It was, he thought, not merely in industry but in society at large that unions could be criticized for creating hatred between persons as well as between labour and capital. His *Evils of Collective Bargaining* (1898) is also negative about trade unions. Workers under individual bargaining are not at a disadvantage as they can go from employer to employer. Cree thought that trade unions were a bad deal for workers because the benefits received were small given the premia paid. Despite talking about the 'just wage' the idea is, in his opinion, little more than a request for more pay. He accused collective bargaining of preventing market clearing, reducing the product of labour through strikes and lockouts, and destroying good relations between employers and employees. Again, he complains about the methods of unions: the limitation of the number of apprentices, demarcation of work causing low productivity, and the setting of a minimum wage for a normal day. What results from unionism, he says, is the unemployment of old, weak men who cannot do enough to earn a wage under the 'common rule' principle. Because of the anti-women employment rule adopted by some unions, as in printing, unions increased total wages through insisting that men, who had higher wages than women, were employed. (There are echoes here of Chalmers who, in Book III of *The Christian and the Civic Economy of Large Towns* (1821), had argued that wages could be raised above the 'fair market price of labour' only by excluding from the competition in the labour market a certain number of their own body, who would become outcasts.) Cree could only see trade unions at their worst, and believed that the working class's lot could only be improved by thrift or an increase in general production. However, non-unionized employment was not heaven. In a democratic society there should be freedom of association to tackle low pay and poor working conditions.

It was the nature of trade unionism, not the growth of state socialism, which concerned the Duke of Argyll. He admitted that labour has the right to form trade unions to allow them to press for higher wages and that they could withhold their services (1893), but did not agree that they had the right to dictate how members should work. Trade unions would, in his view, benefit everyone by effecting stable employment conditions by minimizing labour unrest, which discouraged investment. He supported the Factory Acts because men and women are, in a sense, productive machines: there is a loss if they are damaged. The Duke, like Cree, was concerned with unions challenging the right to manage but thought there was a limit to managerial freedom.

Assessments of socialism

Socialism in its different forms provoked much antagonism. Theoretical and practical objections were raised against it. Burton in his *Political and Social Economy* (1849) described the inventions of Claude Henri de Rouvroy, Comte de Saint-Simon, and other socialists as hollow and fallacious, especially proposals to organize society by artificial means, to regulate industry, to divide the produce of labour equally or in another arbitrary way and to divide the general fund produced by labour according to their own views not through competition. Idealistic schemes did not appeal to him as he wanted property to be tolerated and families to retain their rights, with parents rearing their own children. Looking at Louis Blanc's proposed national workshops he complained it would be a tyranny with as many state officers as workmen. Socialism, in his view, poisons the propensity to seek advantage for oneself and one's offspring. The socialists of the time apparently failed to explain how society ensures that each does his social duty in the absence of strict control – such as everyone being treated as a soldier – because Burton mentions there is a shortage of people fit to direct/superintend industrial enterprise, which would, he argues, make socialism practically impossible. All socialist schemes are, he concluded, attempts to rearrange what the Deity has arranged in the natural order. This was quite a catalogue of accusations!

In contrast to the growing contemporary admiration for Marx in socialist circles, Hodgson's successor as professor of political economy at Edinburgh University in 1880, Shield Nicholson, was, as Steedman (2004) notes, very anti-Marxist. Nicholson called Marx the Mad Mullah of Socialists and thought that the cure for Marxism was to get rid of its causes, including the growth of industrial trusts. In his view, Marx underemployed the role of demand and had no idea of the services of commerce. Nicholson extended his attack on socialism with strong libertarian arguments. In a lecture at the British Association's meeting in Oxford in 1894 he brushed aside the idea that altruism had become greater at the end of the century, mentioning that it was a period of increasing militarism, as well as of industrial strife. He disliked the idea of attributing all reforms to socialism: reform is the antithesis of the revolutionary desire of socialists to tear up the contract basic to society. His specific criticisms of socialism were many: it suppressed animal instincts, led to harmful taxation, ruined land and capital, repressed exchange, instituted a system of forced labour, suppressed new opinions, ended competition and imposed on government tasks beyond its ability such as the regulation of wages and employment. Aware of the great problem of analysing socialism, with its varied and shifting meanings, he identified the Christian socialist, the agnostic socialist preaching the religion of humanity, the social democrat, the utilitarian socialist, the labour socialist who wants a living wage, the revolutionary socialist and the Fabian socialist preaching gradualism. At the end of the first volume of his *Principles* (1893–1901) Nicholson reviews socialism and attacks optimistic views on the benefits of increasing government control. He points out that control often leads to natural decay and that to say that circumstances are different now and more suitable for advancing noble aims ignores how many worthwhile schemes have failed in the past, including Christian socialist endeavours. Nicholson was attempting too much in putting together diverse types of socialism for his analysis rather than weighing up the pros and cons of each.

Robert Flint (1838–1910) wrote an assessment of socialism, covering over five hundred pages. He was born near Dumfries, educated at Glasgow University, was professor of moral philosophy at St Andrews University (1864–76), where one of his duties was the teaching of political economy, and then professor of divinity at Edinburgh University until 1903. He ranged over many subjects in his work, including the philosophy of history and theism. At the outset of *Socialism* (1894) he admitted sympathetically that ' Socialism has its deepest and strongest root in a desire for the welfare of the masses who toil hard and gain little' (p. 10) and 'Socialism . . . as I understand it, is any theory of social organisation which sacrifices the legitimate liberties of individuals to the will or interests of the community' (p. 17). The strengths of socialism are, he writes, its belief in the brotherhood of man, and its attack on war and on the oppression of the poor. But he witheringly notes that as early societies had primitive socialism it would be foolish to try to restore it: it is unnatural for both adults and societies to restore their childhood. Every land and every age had some communism, he wrote, but in large countries it could flourish only if a nation were divided into thousands of small communities. In his own times, depressed times, Flint observed that it was the unemployed not the working men who took up socialism.

What he disliked in socialism was the emphasis on class conflict, egalitarianism and workers' rights. He questioned the idea of class conflict because there are 'insensible gradations' of the classes despite a gap between the extremes of the very rich and the very poor. The promotion of equality, the core of much socialist thought, did not appeal to him because he saw nothing unjust about the inequality of wealth. He attacked the socialist list of the basic rights to live, to labour and to have the entire produce of labour. The first right would, he argued, cause property to be seized to provide a livelihood, and society would be required to support its members without any contractual duty to do so. There is a right to be a free labourer but not a right to work, for then the state would have to supply jobs and appropriate private capital to do so. The right to receive the full produce of labour would destroy the return to capital thus necessitating that the labourer own capital, land and the means of production.

Flint reported that in the 1890s popular communism advocated state control, and recommended the abolition of most private property and common ownership of capital – a kind of collectivism and social despotism. He argued against the view that labour is the sole source of wealth and thus robbed if some of the national income was distributed as rent and profits, and against the labour theory of value: value was not seen as the product of the operation of several factors of production. Flint reminds us that labour can be valueless, making it impossible for it to be the substance of value; the manufacturer is entitled to be paid for the use of his building, machinery and materials.

Flint did have an alternative to the socialism of his day. Instead of the conflict between capital and labour he argued there could be harmony between the classes and that the capitalist needs labourers to be his friends and should seek to improve their lot. Labour, he thought, can improve its lot under both competition and cooperation but not on its own: 'Competition, as the term is used in economics, implies self-love, a regard to one's own interest; altruism is not the immediate source of any merely business transaction' (p. 122). It is, however, difficult to see how this harmony would be established. Flint thought profit-sharing was undesirable unless there was sufficient trust within an enterprise, and that workers would prefer wages, which are more certain than profits, as the latter can fluctuate. He noted that without socialism, in seventy years of competition between industrialist and capitalist, pauperism had grown at a slower rate than population or wealth.

Flint quotes Frederic Harrison, a prolific late Victorian essayist, 'There is no case on record of a body of workmen creating a new market, or founding an original enterprise' (p. 112). Flint wanted to bring socialism down to earth and defeat its ideology empirically. He identified the ways in which socialism would curb human progress through restricting liberty and increasing public interference. Because the opposite of competition is not cooperation but compulsion, work would be assigned by a socialist authority. But an equal distribution of produce is impossible because men differ in ability and produce output of varying quality. Even Saint-Simon's principle of distribution according to ability is not, he argued, an alternative to present ways of sharing revenue because ability is measured by the value of what workers do. Wages are not slavery but the consequences of a contract. Socialists, Flint thinks, are better at criticizing evil than proposing remedies and socialism, he forecast, would lead to a reduction in the amount of capital: once the rich had been bought out they would not be allowed to provide any further investments. A socialist system would also be inefficient because of the expense of employing many officials and inspectors: 'The whole tendency of Collectivism is to replace a resistible capitalism by an irresistible officialism...' (p. 272). He argued that a nation has no better title to land than has an individual. Although Flint seemed as hard as his name he did think that employers should provide old age pensions; it would be wrong, however, to give charity to the idle and drunken. He also thought that state education increased the national welfare. 'The great bulk of human misery is due not to social arrangements but to personal vices' (p. 379).

It thus seems that the various socialist schemes of these two hundred years met with little approval at the end of period covered by this book. But the intellectual seeds bore fruit in the twentieth century as different schemes of cooperation flourished and national economic planning was practised in many countries. What were identified as the difficulties of socialism, especially its egalitarianism and bureaucratic methods, were so forcefully described by the Scottish writers that they perhaps contributed to the milder forms of socialism which came to be practised in Britain.

8 Conclusions

This book has aimed to present the ideas of a remarkable group of men at the dawn of modern economics who, over the course of two centuries, discussed in depth the principal themes of economics still central to the subject today. Prompted by the changes in Scotland's economy in trade, monetary and fiscal matters, they had to make sense of basic economic mechanisms. Related to those immediate concerns were issues of population, poverty and distribution of income, which greatly affected economic welfare. Underlying specific economic issues were questions of the determinants of economic growth and development and the ideological framework for judging economic policy.

Something as matter-of-fact and everyday as trade was given an exalted position because it was thought it could bring economic dynamism and civilization to Scotland. It was tempting to continue in the narrow protectionist way of keeping Scotland sealed from the outside world or to break out into free trade, and while the Scots could produce champions of trade liberalization in Hume and Smith, they could never give up the protectionist temptation. Two economic doctrines were used to attack the protectionism of the mercantilism: the price-specie flow mechanism and the notion of a convergence between rich and poor countries. Both were able to provoke major economic debates but neither developed into watertight theories in that period. To their credit these Scots, in an age of empire, did not accept colonization as pure gain.

International trade is a form of exchange that itself is a fundamental economic mechanism. With characteristic thoroughness the Scots wanted to discover the psychology beneath exchange and opted for self-interest, which they proved to be a benevolent, not selfish, motive. Given there is exchange what happens? They provided an early analysis of equilibrium in markets and stood back to assess the commercial society exchange had created. Exchange, of course, needs prices and in value theory the ingenuity of these writers was prolific. Objective and subjective approaches, cost versus utility as a basis of value, the creation of demand and supply analysis, the linking of aesthetic theory to value theory and the introduction of Austrian economics to consolidate value theory are all in their writing.

Money as an institution threw up many inquiries. The relationship of money to prices in the quantity theory and the question of whether money was active or passive concerned them, but perhaps they were better at setting the agenda for monetary debates than for settling them. Inspired by the banking innovations of their day many of them heartily embraced a change to a paper currency in a world that was experimenting with new types of bank.

Aware of the change in the political firmament, through Scotland losing its parliament and separate running of its economic affairs, the role for government inevitably excited their interest. Their debates were crucial in deciding upon the level and distribution of public expenditure. Most of these Scots opted for a state with only minimal functions, even after industrialization and urbanization threw up problems that seemed to have only a public sector solution. They saw that a government could be given powers to order the population to follow state objectives and not increase public expenditure in every case. No one went as far as to sugges abolishing the state roles of defence and law and order, which is possible; a writer like Steuart proposed so many economic policies that the state appeared to be a dormant giant capable at any time of bursting into a host of new activities. Once the state was grudgingly allowed to function in some ways, the financing of the implementation of those policies had to be decided. Taxation was the only way but this did not prevent discussion of which taxes should be imposed, whether the tax burden was too high, whether tax rates should be set at a level which reduced tax revenues and the scope for simplification, and other reforms of the tax system. These writers unified their discussion of tax through drawing up canons, or principles, of taxation, which have never departed from public finance debates. Taxation was rarely enough to cover government expenditure so there was the inevitable accumulation of a national debt. Hume was not the only economics writer to deplore the existence of that debt but such writers existed in an intellectual community which could see that debt as finance could improve a country. Anxiety over the large debt did, however, lead to schemes to redeem it. They did more than list repayment methods, also considering the macroeconomic consequences of reducing debt.

Population was a grand theme of Scottish economics, reaching its theoretical peak in Wallace's works, which inspired the more famous English economist Malthus. However, so vigorous was the Scots writers' criticism of Malthus that it seems that their pioneering work in demography had been in vain. With much thoroughness the economic welfare of the population through the distribution of rent, profits and wages was analysed. Older theories, apart from the wages fund theory, were found not to be durable as, undermining these theories, was the growth of market analysis as the basis of economic power in society. The extreme issue for economic welfare is the response to poverty. Numerous schemes abounded but so did the overriding issue of whether Poor Laws or private charity would solve the problem. A visionary, Samuel Read, provided a viable national insurance scheme not dissimilar from the systems of modern states.

Beyond the particularity of individual economic theories and economic policies are the fundamental issues of economic growth and development and the ideological assumptions of these writers. Although the division of labour was preached by Smith as the principal key to economic growth, it had its critics and was not as important as capital accumulation in increasing the productivity of labour and the use of incentive mechanisms. Economic development could occur naturally (possibly encouraged by prizes) or be induced by government grants which, in the case of Scotland, were readily available.

What is more difficult to explain is the economic ideology of the Scottish writers. Natural liberty sounds good as a slogan but it is little more than freedom from restraint unless it is linked to natural forces. Nineteenth-century socialists, whether in trade unions or political parties, relied on Marx as a mentor, neglecting the rich discussions in Scottish economics of utopias, economic planning and cooperation.

The examination of so many economic matters raises the question of whether there was a unifying theme in Scottish economists' works. It is too much to expect agreement between so many talented and imaginative writers and think of them as merely precursors or disciples of the most famous, Adam Smith, but there are recurrences of two themes: the first, what is natural; the second, what is justifiable. Natural exchange, natural prices, natural liberty, natural property rights are just part of a long list of natural entities. But the view that economics is only watching what occurs and not influencing it was not universally accepted. These writers liked to tease a problem apart and get to the conceptual roots. The justification for many things, especially rent, profits, wages and interest, had to be settled, perhaps because at heart these Scots were benevolent people who wanted to see that economic welfare was not neglected.

A modern message from all these debates is obvious, partly because many of these concerns are perpetual. Discussions of the national debt, economic growth and development, the role of taxation, the extent to which a government should be interventionist, population growth, the relief of poverty, the distribution of the national income and the control of banks have their roots in these Scottish debates. But what did these Scots achieve in their writings? How does Smith compare with the rest? He was often treated as a yardstick and often enters into these debates (although not always with acknowledgement). The ambiguities of his views show how concerned he was to attempt to be comprehensive in his treatment of every topic. There are many exceptions to his central opinions, making it difficult to apply simple labels to him such as free trader, arch opponent of state intervention, unsympathetic to the poor. All these descriptions fail to recognize the breadth and mixture of his opinions.

Opening ancient graves can be surprising. But bringing back these past figures has shown the wide and vigorous opinions of these writers. How they argued! There were the pioneers who put forward ideas now more often attributed to Smith, and the later writers who criticized and qualified what he had written.

The eighteenth century is regarded as the golden age of Scottish economics, but in the next century the fertility of Scottish economics did not decline. Soon after 1800 Lauderdale, Horner, Playfair, Craig and Read wrote vigorously on the subject. Later still, Jenkin, Nicholson and Smart showed that the flame of Scottish economics had not been extinguished.

Appendix: Biographical sketches of the major Scottish writers

Francis Hutcheson (1694–1746) was educated at Glasgow University and taught by Gershom Carmichael, succeeding him as professor of moral philosophy in 1730 after a period as a Presbyterian minister in his native Ireland. His philosophical writings covered aesthetics and ethics, in which his utilitarianism and economic thought were revealed. He was an educational innovator in changing from lecturing in Latin to English. His first publication, *Inquiry into the Original of our Ideas of Beauty and Virtue*, 1725 (1738), relied on the idea of an internal sense of aesthetics and morality. Much of his economics is elaborated in his posthumous *A System of Moral Philosophy* (1755). Adam Smith was his pupil and successor but one.

Robert Wallace (1697–1771) is chiefly known as a pioneer in population theory, rightly recognized by Malthus as his precursor. Like his father, Wallace was a Church of Scotland minister and educated at Edinburgh University. A minister in Edinburgh from 1733 he took a deep interest in church patronage and general affairs, and as moderator (leader) of the church from 1742 to 1746 he followed a middle way in church politics. He participated in the intellectual life of the Scottish Enlightenment through the Philosophical Society, where he met David Hume and engaged in a debate on the size of the population in ancient times.

Thomas Reid (1710–96) learned his classics, philosophy and mathematics as a student at Marischal College, Aberdeen, then turned to divinity. Like his father he became a Church of Scotland minister. He taught mathematics as regent of King's College, Aberdeen, in 1751 and participated in the Aberdeen Philosophical Society where he expressed his first interest in political economy. His *Inquiry into the Human Mind on the Principles of Common Sense* (1764) established him as a leader of a philosophical school in opposition to Hume. Taking over from Adam Smith as Professor of Moral Philosophy at Glasgow (1764–81), he included more philosophy in his lectures than his predecessor but did not abandon politics and economics.

David Hume (1711–76) was in his day a famous historian but is now chiefly regarded as a leading empirical philosopher, also famed for his contributions to economics. He was at the very centre of the Enlightenment, as a close friend of Adam Smith, and keen participant in Edinburgh intellectual clubs. Born in Berwickshire to a landowner, educated at Edinburgh University where he acquired the basis of his classical, philosophical and scientific knowledge, he trained for a while in the law before a short sojourn in Bristol as a clerk to a sugar merchant. His three years in France enabled him to write his first philosophical work, *A treatise of human nature* (1739); his later enquiries into human understanding and morals were better received. In 1748 he went to Vienna and Turin on a diplomatic mission led by General St Clair; he was secretary to the British ambassador to Paris from 1763 to 1765. Local political factions and the opposition of the clergy, including Francis Hutcheson, and his atheistical opinions prevented him from election to chairs at either Edinburgh or Glasgow Universities. His first successful publication was his *Political Discourses* (1752), which contains his principal contribution to economics in nine essays. Appointment as Keeper of the Advocates Library in 1752 gave him the opportunity to amass the materials that resulted in *The History of England,* published in separate volumes in 1754–62 (1778); he resigned in 1757 to be succeeded by Adam Ferguson. His writings made him a rich and contented man. He was a founder of the classical school of economics.

Sir James Steuart, later Steuart Denham (**1711–80**), was the son of a baronet with estates near Edinburgh and Glasgow. He was educated at Edinburgh University and admitted as an advocate to the Scottish bar. In a visit to France and Italy in 1739 he established his connections with exiled Jacobites who wanted the restoration of the Stuarts, ousted in 1688, to the British throne. When Prince Edward Stewart led his Jacobite rebels into Edinburgh in 1745 Steuart became his secretary and soon ambassador to Paris. In fourteen years of exile in France, Netherlands, Germany and Italy he was able to amass materials for *An inquiry into the principles of political economy* of 1767, which soon was much cited in Britain and in Germany. Through his wife's energetic advocacy he received a royal pardon for his support of the Jacobite cause and returned to his estates and continued to write on economics. Although not central to Edinburgh intellectual life, Steuart was acquainted with Hume and Smith.

Adam Ferguson (**1723–1816**) was the son of a Church of Scotland minister in Perthshire. Educated at St Andrews and Edinburgh Universities, where he knew from an early age leaders of the Scottish Enlightenment, including Hugh Blair and William Robertson, he later became acquainted with David Hume and Adam Smith. Before he had finished his divinity studies, in 1745 he was appointed chaplain with the Black Watch regiment, a post that enabled him to use his knowledge of Gaelic, and he continued in army life for nine years. In 1757, in succession to David Hume, he was keeper of the Advocates Library for a year then for another year tutor to the sons of the future prime minister, the Earl of Bute. In 1759 he was elected Professor of Pneumatics and Moral Philosophy at Edinburgh University. He acquired wide fame through his *Essay on the History of Civil Society* (1767), while his *Institutes of Moral Philosophy for the Use of Students of the College of Edinburgh*, 1769 (1785), was also widely successful. As professor he was able to take leave to tutor the Earl of Chesterfield on a grand tour of Europe; he was also part of a diplomatic mission to Washington in 1778 to negotiate an agreement between the new nation and Britain. In 1785 Dugald Stewart succeeded to his chair.

Adam Smith (**1723–90**) is always worthy of a whole book of biography but he appears here as only one of dozens of Scottish economics writers. He was brought up in Kirkcaldy, across the Firth of Forth from Edinburgh, and educated in the burgh school before going to Glasgow College (later University) at the age of thirteen to continue with his classical and mathematical studies and to explore moral and natural philosophy. He was greatly influenced by Francis Hutcheson. He was awarded a Snell Exhibition to Balliol College, Oxford (1740–46), intended to equip him for a career as an Anglican priest – a career he never pursued. Having experienced classroom teaching at Glasgow he did not take easily to the freedom of private study, but read so extensively in French and other literature that he was able, on Lord Kames's recommendation, to lecture in Edinburgh from 1748 to 1751 on rhetoric and belles-lettres to young advocates. In 1751 he returned to Glasgow to take up the post of professor of logic then of moral philosophy in 1752. The publication of his *Theory of Moral Sentiments* (1759), an essay in ethics built on the principles of sympathy and the impartial spectator, led to his appointment as travelling tutor to the young Duke of Buccleuch and in 1764 the abandonment of his Glasgow chair. The grand tour to France and Switzerland enabled Smith to meet the French economists of the day, including Quesnay and Turgot. On his return to Scotland in 1766 he began the long haul of collecting materials and writing *The Wealth of Nations* (1776), a comprehensive exposition of economics founded on the principle of natural liberty. The discovery in 1895 of student lecture notes of his *Lectures in Jurisprudence* helps us to understand the foundations of his economic thinking. In 1778 he took up residence in Edinburgh for his appointment as commissioner of customs and the salt tax (also his father's occupation). His writing is a joy to read, perhaps because of its lively verbal style: his physical weakness required it be dictated.

John Millar (1735–1801) was educated at Glasgow University, where he attended Adam Smith's lectures. Uncle of John Craig, he became tutor to Lord Kames's children. He practised as an advocate at the Scottish bar for a year before he was appointed to the Regius Chair of Civil Law at Glasgow in 1761. He ventured far from his task of teaching Roman law to consider moral philosophy and sociology. Hume and Smith greatly influenced his thinking; but he was opposed to Thomas Reid's appointment at Glasgow, because of his criticism of Hume. He was a supporter of Charles James Fox, of American independence and, initially, of the French Revolution.

James Anderson (1739–1808) was born in Edinburgh and studied chemistry at the university. He married a major Aberdeenshire heiress and took to agricultural improvement at Monkshill. He wrote prolifically on agriculture, economic development and the principal economic debates of the day, including the Corn Laws. In 1783 he moved to Edinburgh, founding, and writing much of, a weekly paper, *The Bee*, 1791–94.

Dugald Stewart (1753–1828) was the son of Matthew Stewart, Professor of Mathematics at Edinburgh University. At Edinburgh and Glasgow Universities Dugald was taught by Hugh Blair, Adam Ferguson and Thomas Reid. In 1772 he took over his father's Edinburgh University teaching and in 1778 Adam Ferguson's; he was appointed Professor of Mathematics in 1778 and was Professor of Moral Philosophy from 1785 to 1820. In 1800 he introduced a separate course on political economy which was taken by the Whigs, including Francis Horner and Henry Brougham, who wrote for the *Edinburgh Review*. His voluminous works range over mental and moral philosophy, aesthetics, economics and biographies of Smith, Reid and William Robertson the historian. He was influenced by the thinking of Isaac Newton and Thomas Reid. One of the best connected of economic writers of the period, his acquaintances ranged from illustrious predecessors such as Adam Smith to emerging writers including the Earl of Lauderdale.

Sir John Sinclair (1754–1835) was educated at Edinburgh High School, Edinburgh, and Glasgow and Oxford Universities, and then called to the Scottish and English bars without practising as a lawyer. He inherited extensive estates in Caithness in 1770 and entered parliament in 1780 for his county, which had a seat in alternate elections preventing him from sitting continuously in the House of Commons. A European tour in 1785 after his wife's death gave him a lifelong interest in agricultural improvement. Pitt financed the Board of Agriculture and in 1793 rewarded Sinclair with its presidency for organizing the use of exchequer bills to maintain the credit of Lancashire manufacturers. The Board promoted field drainage, improved farm equipment and roads. Sinclair's expenditure on the Board contributed to his bankruptcy in 1811. In 1790 he persuaded the Church of Scotland to establish a statistical account of Scotland, twenty-one volumes in all, based on submissions from parish ministers. In his numerous books and pamphlets he ranged from agriculture to the study of public finance and the monetary issues of the day.

Lauderdale (James Maitland, eighth Earl of) (1759–1839) had an extensive education at Edinburgh University, Trinity College, Oxford, and Glasgow University, the latter under John Millar. Although called to the Scottish bar, in 1780 he took up politics as Member of Parliament for Newport and became a supporter of Charles James Fox. He succeeded to the earldom in 1789 and became a Scottish representative peer in 1790 but was deselected in 1796 for his radical views, and was brought back to the Lords in 1806 with the British peerage of Baron Lauderdale of Thirlestane. Out of parliament he wrote many economics pamphlets and his *Inquiry* (1804a), his principal economics work. By the early 1820s he had abandoned his radical stance in politics and opposed parliamentary reform.

Thomas Chalmers (1780–1847) was educated at St Andrews University, which he entered at the age of eleven. He continued to be interested chiefly in mathematics and natural philosophy even when he became a parish minister. But a religious conversion in 1810 when ill with consumption set him on a trajectory which was to make him a leading Scottish intellectual and church leader of his day. His first book was on economics, *An Enquiry into the Extent and Stability of Natural Resources* (1808), which demonstrated his interest in trade and population issues. He continued to write on economics, especially on poverty, and tried an experiment in voluntary help for the poor when he was minister of St John's, Glasgow. He also wrote on astronomy and divinity. In 1843, when the Free Church split off from the Church of Scotland, he became its leader.

Joseph Shield Nicholson (1850–1927) was educated at King's College, London, and Cambridge University; he was appointed Professor of Political Economy at Edinburgh University in succession to W. B. Hodgson in 1880. In the forty-five years he held the chair he wrote on money, trade, socialism and public finance, produced a three-volume *Principles of Political Economy* (1893–1901) and published three novels. A popular lecturer, he faithfully expounded the ideas of his mentor, Adam Smith.

William Smart (1853–1915) initially followed his father's footsteps, taking employment with a Glasgow thread mill; but he obtained a first class degree in philosophy at Glasgow University in 1882 and left business life in 1884. Soon he was lecturing on political economy at Glasgow, then Dundee. In 1892 he was the first person to lecture exclusively on economics at Glasgow University, and became the incumbent of its first chair in the subject in 1896. After early interests in socialism and women's wages he turned to the Austrian theory of value, but retained an interest in social issues, especially housing and the Poor Law.

Bibliography

Primary sources

Alison, Archibald (1840) *The Principles of Population and their connection with human happiness*. Edinburgh: William Blackwood; London: Thomas Cadell.

Alison, Archibald (1847) *Free Trade and Fettered Currency*. Edinburgh and London: William Blackwood & Sons.

Alison, Archibald (1850) *Essays Political, Historical and Miscellaneous*. Edinburgh and London: William Blackwood & Sons.

Alison, William Pulteney (1840) *Observations on the Management of the Poor in Scotland and its effects on the health of the great towns*. Edinburgh: William Blackwood & Sons; London: Thomas Cadell.

Anderson, Adam (1787) *An historical and chronological deduction of the origin of commerce from the earliest accounts*. London: J. Walter.

Anderson, James (1777) *An Inquiry into the Corn Laws: with a view to the New Corn-Bill Proposed for Scotland*. Edinburgh: Mundell.

Anderson, James (1779a) *Observations on the means of exciting a spirit of national industry; chiefly intended to promote the agriculture, commerce, manufactures and fisheries of Scotland in a series of letters to a friend written in 1775*. Dublin: S. Price and others.

Anderson, James (1779b) *An inquiry into the causes that have hitherto retarded the advancement of agriculture in Europe, with hints for removing the circumstances that have chiefly obstructed its progress*. Edinburgh: Charles Elliott; London: Thomas Cadell.

Anderson, James (1782) *The Interest of Great Britain with regard to the American Colonies considered to which is added An Appendix containing the outlines of a plan for general pacification*. London: T. Cadell.

Anderson, James (1785) *An Account of the Present State of the Hebrides and the Western Coasts of Scotland*. Edinburgh: C. Elliott; London: G. Robinson.

Anderson, James (1789) *Observations on Slavery; particularly with a view to its effects on the British Colonies in the West Indies*. Manchester: J. Harrop.

Anderson, James (1791–94) *The Bee or Literary Weekly Intelligencer*. Edinburgh: Mundell & Son.

Anderson, James (1792) *Observations on the effects of the coal duty upon the remote and thinly populated coasts of Britain, tending to show if it were there removed the prosperity of the country promoted, and the account of the revenue augmented to an astonishing degree*. Edinburgh: printed for the author.

Anderson, James (1799) *Recreations in Agriculture, Natural History, Arts and Miscellaneous Literature, volume I*. London: James Wallas and R. H. Evans.

Anon (1705) *An Essay for Promoting of Trade and Increasing the Coin of the Nation: In a letter from a Gentleman in the Country to his Friend at Edinburgh, a Member of Parliament*. Edinburgh.

Argyll, eighth Duke of, George Campbell Douglas (1877) *Essay on the Commercial Principles applicable to Contracts for the Hire of land*. London: Cassell, Pether & Galpin.

Argyll, eighth Duke of, George Campbell Douglas (1893) *The unseen Foundations of Society: An examination of the fallacies and failures of economic science due to neglected elements*. London: John Murray.

Bankton, Lord: see McDouall, Andrew.

Bell, Benjamin (1797) *Observations on the assessment of tolls as public revenue*. Edinburgh: Mudie & Sons.

Bell, Benjamin (1799) *Three essays on taxation of income*. London: T. Cadell & W. Davies.

Black, David (1706) *Essay upon industry and trade, showing the necessity of the one, the conveniency and usefulness of the other, and the advantages of both*. Edinburgh: James Watson.

Black, William (1706a) *Answer to a letter concerning trade sent from several Scots gentlemen that are merchants in England to their countrymen who are merchants in Scotland*. Edinburgh.

Black, William (1706b) *Some considerations in relation to trade*.

Black, William (1707) *Some overtures and cautions in relation to trade and taxes, humbly offered to the parliament, by a well wisher to his country*. Edinburgh.

Blair, Hugh (1825) *Lectures on Rhetoric and Belles Lettres*. 14th edn, London: T. Cadell et al.

Brougham, Henry (1803) *An Inquiry into the Colonial Policy of the European Powers*. Edinburgh: E. Balfour, Manners & Miller, and Archibald Constable.

Buchanan, David (1814) *Adam Smith's* An Inquiry into the nature and causes of the Wealth of Nations *with notes and additional volume by David Buchanan*. Edinburgh: Waugh and Innes.

Buchanan, David (1844) *Inquiry into the Taxation and Commercial Policy of Great Britain; with observations on the principles of currency, and of exchangeable value*. Edinburgh: William Tait.

Burton, John Hill (1841) *Poor Laws and Pauperism in Scotland*. Edinburgh: Adam & Charles Black.

Burton, John Hill (1849) *Political and Social Economy: its Practical Implications*. Edinburgh: William and Robert Chambers.

Campbell, Alexander (1831) *An address on the progress of the cooperative system*.

Carlyle, Thomas ([1829] 1899) 'Signs of the times', *Edinburgh Review*, in *Critical and Miscellaneous Essays*, vol. II. London: Chapman & Hall.

Carlyle, Thomas ([1831a] 1899) 'Characteristics', *Edinburgh Review*, in *Critical and Miscellaneous Essays*, vol. III. London: Chapman & Hall.

Carlyle, Thomas ([1831b] 1904) *Sartor Resartus*. London: Chapman & Hall.

Carlyle, Thomas (1840) *Chartism*. 2nd edn, London: James Fraser.

Carlyle, Thomas ([1843] 1899) *Past and Present*. London: Chapman & Hall.

Carlyle, Thomas ([1850] 1899) The Present Time *and* The New Downing Street *in Latter-Day Pamphlets*. London: Chapman & Hall.

Carlyle, Thomas ([1867] 1899) 'Shooting Niagara: and after', *Macmillan's Magazine*, in *Critical and Miscellaneous Essays*, vol. V. London: Chapman & Hall.

Chalmers, Thomas (1808) *An Enquiry into the Extent and Stability of National Resources*. Edinburgh: Oliphant and Brown.

Chalmers, Thomas (1821) *The Christian and Civic Economy*. Glasgow: Chalmers & Collins.

Chalmers, Thomas ([1832] 1856) *On Political Economy in connexion with the moral state and prospects of society*. Edinburgh: Thomas Constable.

Chalmers, Thomas (1833a) *On the power, wisdom and goodness of God as manifested in the adaptation of external nature to the moral and intellectual constitution of man*. London: William Pickering.

Chalmers, Thomas (1833b) *Tracts on Pauperism*. Glasgow: William Collins.

Chamberlen, Hugh (1705) *Proposal For a Land Credit, presented to the Parliament, By the Committee, to whom it was referred to be Considered*. Edinburgh.

Clerk, Sir John (1705) *The circumstances of Scotland consider'd, with respect to the present scarcity of money: together with some proposals for supplying the defect thereof and rectifying the balance of trade*. Edinburgh: James Watson.

Clerk, Sir John (1706a) *An essay upon the XV Article of the Treaty of Union, wherein the difficulties that arise upon the equivalents, are fully cleared and explained*. Edinburgh.

Clerk, Sir John (1706b) *Letter to a friend, giving an account how the Treaty of Union has been affected here*. Edinburgh.

Combe, George ([1828] 1836) *The Constitution of Man considered in relation to external objects*. 4th edn, Edinburgh: William and Robert Chambers.

Craig, John (1814) *Elements of Political Science*. Edinburgh: William Blackwood.

Craig, John (1821) *Remarks on Some Fundamental Questions in Political Economy Illustrated by A brief Inquiry into the Commercial State of Britain since the year 1815*. Edinburgh: Archibald Constable.

Cree, T. S. (1892) *A Criticism of the Theory of Trades' Unions*. 3rd edn with appendices, Glasgow: Bell & Bain.

Cree, T. S. (1898): *Evils of Collective Bargaining*. 2nd edn, Glasgow: Bell & Bain.

Dalrymple, John (1758) *An essay towards a general history of feudal property in Great Britain*. London.

Dalrymple, John (1782) *Facts and their consequences, submitted to the public at large, but more particularly to that of the finance minister*. 4th edn, London: J. Stockdale.

Dalrymple, John (1783a) *State of the public debts, as they will stand on the 5th of January, 1783*. 5th edn, London: J. Stockdale.

Dalrymple, John (1783b) *An argument to prove that it is the indispensable duty of the creditors of the public to insist that the Government do forthwith bring forward the consideration of the nation*. 3rd edn, London: J. Stockdale.

Dalrymple, John (1783c) *An attempt to balance the income and expenditure of the State: with some reflections on the nature and tendency of the late political struggles for power*. London: J. Stockdale.

Dalrymple, John (1784) *An address to, and expostulation with the public*. 2nd edn, London: John Stockdale.

De Quincey, Thomas ([1897] 1970) *Political Economy and Politics*, vol. IX of *Collected Writings*, ed. David Masson. New York: Augustus M. Kelly.

Dirom, Alexander (1796) *An Inquiry into the Corn Laws and Corn Trade of Great Britain, and their influence on the prosperity of the kingdom, with suggestions for the improvement of the Corn Laws*. Edinburgh: William Creech.

Dove, Patrick (1850) *The Science of Politics*, part I. London: Johnstone & Hunter.

Dove, Patrick (1854) *The Science of Politics*, part II. London: Johnstone & Hunter.

Dunbar, James (1789–94) *Institutes of Moral Philosophy*, edited from the Aberdeen University MS 3107/5/2/6 with an introduction in Japanese by Hiroshi Mizuta. Hitosubashi University Centre for Historical Social Science Literature. Study series no. 35.

Duncan, Henry (1816) *An essay on the nature and advantages of parish banks for the savings of the industrious*. 2nd edn, Edinburgh: Oliphant, Waugh & Innes.

Elibank, Baron: see Murray, Patrick.

Ferguson, Adam ([1767] 1966) *An Essay on the History of Civil Society*. Edinburgh: Edinburgh University Press.

Ferguson, Adam (1785) *Institutes of Moral Philosophy*. 3rd enl. edn, Edinburgh: John Bell & William Creech.

Ferguson, Adam (1792) *Principles of moral and political science*. London: A. Strahan & T. Cadell; Edinburgh: W. Creech.

Fletcher of Saltoun, Andrew (1979) *Selected Political Writings and Speeches*, ed. David Daiches. Edinburgh: Scottish Academic Press.

Fletcher of Saltoun, Andrew (1997) *Political Works*, ed. John Robertson. Cambridge: Cambridge University Press.

Flint, Robert (1894) *Socialism*. London: Isbister & Co.

Forbes of Culloden, Duncan (1730) *Considerations on the state of the nation, as it is affected by the excessive use of foreign spirits*. Edinburgh.

Forbes of Culloden, Duncan (1744) *Some Considerations on the Present State of Scotland: In a Letter of the Commissioners and Trustees for Improving Fisheries and Manufactures*. Edinburgh: W. Sands, A. Murray & J. Cochran.

Geddes, Patrick (1885) *An Analysis of the Principles of Economics (Part I)*. London and Edinburgh: Williams & Norgate.

Gerard, Alexander ([1759] 1780) *An Essay on Taste, to which is now added Part Fourth, of the Standard of Taste*. 3rd edn, Edinburgh: J. Bell & W. Creech.

Grahame, James (1816) *An Inquiry into the Principle of Population*. Edinburgh: Archibald Constable.

Grahame, James (1817) *Defence of Usury Laws, and Considerations on the Probable Consequences of their Projected Repeal*. 2nd edn, Edinburgh: Archibald Constable.

Gray, John (1831) *The Social System: A Treatise on the Principle of Exchange*. Edinburgh: William Tait.

Gray, John (1848) *Lectures on the Nature and Use of Money, delivered before the members of the Edinburgh Philosophical Institution during the months of February and March 1848*. Edinburgh: Adam & Charles Black.

Hamilton, Andrew (1793) *An inquiry into the principles of taxation, chiefly applicable to articles of immediate consumption*. 2nd edn, Edinburgh: Peter Hill.

Hamilton, Robert (1814) *An Inquiry concerning the rise and progress, the redemption and present state, and the management of the National Debt of Great Britain*. 2nd edn, Edinburgh: Oliphant, Waugh & Innes.

Hamilton, Robert (1822) *An address to the Inhabitants of Aberdeen on the management of the poor*. Aberdeen: D. Chalmers and Co.

Hodges, James (1703) *A letter from Mr Hodges at London to a member of the parliament of Scotland*. Edinburgh.

Hodges, James (1705) *Considerations and Proposals for Supplying the present Scarcity of Money, and Advancing Trade*. Edinburgh.

Hodges, James (1706) *Essay upon the union*. London.

Hodgson, W. B. (1860) *Two lectures on the Conditions of Health and Wealth educationally considered*. Edinburgh: James Gordon.

Hodgson, W. B. (1870a) *Competition*. London: W. W. Head.

Hodgson, W. B. (1870b) *Turgot: His Life, Times and Opinions*. London: Trubner & Co.

Hodgson, W. B. (1870c) *The true scope of economic science: A lecture delivered March 1st, 1870*. London: W. W. Head.

Hodgson, W. B. (1870d) *On the importance of the study of economic science as a branch of education for all classes: A lecture delivered at the Royal Institution of Great Britain in 1854*. 3rd edn, London: N. Trubner & Co; Edinburgh: W. P. Nimmo & Co.

Hodgson, W. B. (1871) *Inaugural Address, 3 November 1871*. Edinburgh: Edmonston & Douglas.

Hodgson, W. B. (1877) *The Inaugural Address delivered at the opening of the Eighth Annual Co-operative Congress Glasgow 1876*. Manchester: Cooperative Printing Society.

Horner, Francis (1802a) 'Irvine's Emigration from the Highlands', *Edinburgh Review*, no. I (October), pp. 61–3.

Horner, Francis (1802b) 'The Utility of Country Banks', *Edinburgh Review*, no. I (October), pp. 106–8.

Horner, Francis (1802c) 'Thornton on the Paper Credit of Great Britain', *Edinburgh Review*, no. I (October), pp. 172–201.

Horner, Francis (1803a) 'Lord King's Thoughts on the Restriction of Payments in Specie at the Banks of England and Ireland', *Edinburgh Review*, no. IV (July), pp. 402–21.

Horner, Francis (1803b) 'Canard's *Principes d'Economie Politique*', *Edinburgh Review*, no. II (January), pp. 431–50.

Horner, Francis (1804) 'Observations upon the Bounty upon Exported Corn', *Edinburgh Review*, no. IX (October), pp. 190–208

Horner, Francis (1805) 'Lord Selkirk on Emigration', *Edinburgh Review*, no. XIII (October), pp. 185–202.

Horner, Leonard (ed.) (1843) *Memoirs and Correspondence of Francis Horner, MP*, 2 vols. London: John Murray.

Howe, P. P., Waller, A. R., Glover, A. and Thornton, J. (eds) (1930–34) *The complete works of William Hazlitt*, 21 vols. London: J. M. Dent & Sons.

Hume, David ([1739] 1978) *A Treatise of Human Nature*. Oxford: Clarendon Press.

Hume, David ([1777] 1975) *Enquiries Concerning Human Understanding and Concerning the Principles of Morals*. Oxford: Clarendon Press.

Hume, David ([1778] 1938) *The History of England from the Invasion of Julius Caesar to the Revolution in 1688*. Indianapolis: Liberty Fund.

Hume, David (1987) *Essays, Moral, Political and Literary*. Indianapolis: Liberty Fund.

Hume, Joseph (1812) *A copy of a letter addressed to the Right Honourable the Chancellor of the Exchequer and the substance of a speech of Mr Joseph Hume, on the third reading of the Bill (Friday, July 21, 1812) for preventing frauds and abuses in the frame-work knitting manufacture, and in the payment of persons employed therein*. London: J. Stockdale.

Anon [Hume, Joseph] (1816) *Thoughts on the new coinage, with reflections on money and coins, and a new system of coins and weights on a simple and uniform principle*. London: J. J. Stockdale.

Hume, Joseph (1839) *On the Bank of England; and State of the Currency: The Speech of Joseph Hume, Esq, MP in the House of Commons, on the 8th of July 1839*. Hansard Parliamentary Debates.

Hutcheson, Francis (1738) *An Inquiry into the Original of our Ideas of Beauty and Virtue*. 4th edn, London: D. Midwinter et al.

Hutcheson, Francis (1755) *A System of Moral Philosophy in Three Books*. Glasgow: A. Foulis; London: A. Millar and T. Longman.

Hutcheson, Francis (2006) *Logic, Metaphysics, and the Natural Sociability of Mankind*, ed. James Moore and Michael Silverthorne. Indianapolis: Liberty Fund.

Jenkin, Fleeming (1887) *Paper Literary, Scientific, &c by the late Fleeming Jenkin, FRS LLD*, ed. S. Colvin and J. A. Ewing, vol. II. London: Longman, Green.

Johnston, Thomas (1946) *A History of the Working Classes in Scotland*. 4th edn, Glasgow: Unity Publishing.

Kames, Lord, Henry Home (1758) *Historical law-tracts*. Edinburgh: A. Millar; London: A. Kincaid & J. Bell.

Kames, Lord, Henry Home (1774, 1778 and 1796) *Sketches of the history of Man: Considerably improved in a second edition*. 4 vols. Edinburgh: W. Strahan and W. Creech; London: T. Cadell; Basil: J. J. Tourneisen.

Kames, Lord, Henry Home (1779) *Essays on the Principles of Morality and Natural Religion: corrected and improved, in a third edition. Several essays added concerning the proof of a deity*. Edinburgh: John Bell; London: John Murray.

Kames, Lord, Henry Home (1802) *The Gentleman Farmer: being an attempt to improve agriculture, by subjecting it to the test of rational principles*. 5th edn, Edinburgh: Bell & Bradfute.

Keith, George Skene (1792) *Tracts on the Corn Laws of Great Britain*. Edinburgh: and London: J. Murray and C. Eliot.

Lauderdale, Earl of (1797) *Thoughts on Finance, suggested by the measures of the present session*. 2nd edn, London: G. G. and J. Robinson.

Lauderdale, Earl of (1798) *A Letter on the present measures of Finance in which the Bill now depending in Parliament is particularly considered*. London: J. Debrett, and G. G. and J. Robinson.

Lauderdale, Earl of (1804a) *An Inquiry into the Nature and Origin of Public Wealth, and into the Means and Causes of its Increase*. Edinburgh: Archibald Constable.

Lauderdale, Earl of (1804b) 'Observations by the Earl of Lauderdale on the Review of his Inquiry into the Nature and Origin of Public Wealth', *Edinburgh Review*, no.VIII.

Lauderdale, Earl of (1805a) *Hints to the Manufacturers of Great Britain, on the Consequences of the Irish Union; and the system since pursued, of borrowing in England for the service of Ireland*. Edinburgh: Archibald Constable & Co., etc.

Lauderdale, Earl of (1805b) *Thoughts on the Alarming State of the Circulation and on the means of redressing the Pecuniary Grievances in Ireland*. Edinburgh: A. Constable & Co., etc.

Lauderdale, Earl of (1812) *The Depreciation of the Paper Currency of Great Britain proved*. London: Longman, Hurst, Rees, Orme & Brown, and J. Budd; Edinburgh: Constable & Co.

Lauderdale, Earl of (1814) *A Letter on the Corn Laws*. Edinburgh: Constable & Co., etc.

Lauderdale, Earl of (1819) *Protest entered in the Journals of the House of Lords against the Second Reading of a Bill entitled An Act to continue the Restrictions contained in several Acts, on Payments in Cash by the Bank of England . . . and to provide for the gradual Resumption of such Payments, and to permit the Exportation of Gold and Silver*. London: C. H. Reynell.

Lauderdale, Earl of (1829) *Three Letters to the Duke of Wellington on the Fourth Report of the Select Committee of the House of Commons, appointed in 1828 to enquire into the public income and expenditure of the United Kingdom, in which the nature and tendency of a sinking fund is investigated, and the fallacy of the reasoning by which it has been recommended to public favour is explained*. London: John Murray.

Lauderdale, Earl of (1996) *Lauderdale's Notes on Adam Smith's Wealth of Nations*, ed. Chuhei Sugiyama. London and New York: Routledge.

Law, John (1705) *Money and Trade Considered: With a Proposal for Supplying the Nation with Money*. Edinburgh: Andrew Anderson.

Law, John (1751) *Proposals and reasons for constituting a Council of Trade in Scotland first published at Edinburgh 1700*. Glasgow: Rob and Foulis.

Lindsay, Patrick (1736) *The interest of Scotland considered with regard to its police in imploying of the poor, its agriculture, its trade, its manufactures and fisheries*. Edinburgh.

Locke, John ([1690] 1980) *Second Treatise of Government*. Indianapolis: Liberty Fund.

McCulloch, J. R. (1816) *An Essay on the question of Reducing the interest of the National Debt in which the justice and expediency of that measure are fully established*. Edinburgh: David Brown and Adam Black.

McCulloch, J. R. ([1863] 1975) *A Treatise on the Principles and Practical Influence of Taxation and the Funding System*, ed. D. P. O'Brien. 3rd edn, Edinburgh and London: Scottish Academic Press.

McDouall, Andrew ([1750–53] 1993) *An Institute of the Laws of Scotland in Civil Rights*. Edinburgh: The Stair Society.

McFarlan, John (1782) *Inquiries concerning the Poor*. Edinburgh: J. Dickson.

Malthus, T. R. ([1795] 1989) *An Essay on the Principle of Population*, 2 vols, ed. Patricia James. Cambridge: Cambridge University Press for the Royal Economic Society.

Mautner, Thomas (ed.) (1993) *Francis Hutcheson: Two Texts on Human Nature*. Cambridge: Cambridge University Press.

Melon, Jean-François (1734) *Essai politique sur le commerce*.

Melvill, Thomas (1734) *The True Caledonian, addressed to the people of Scotland*. Edinburgh: P. Matthie.

Millar, John ([1787] 1803) *An historical view of the English government from the settlement of the Saxons in Britain to the accession of the House of Stewart*. London: Strahan & Cadell.

Millar, John (1793) *The origin of the distinction of ranks; or, an inquiry into the circumstances which give rise to influence and authority in the different members of society*. Basil: J. J. Tourneisen.

Millar, John (1796) *Letters of Sidney on inequality of property: To which is added a treatise of the effects of war on commercial prosperity*. Edinburgh.

Miller, Hugh (1844) *A Word of Warning on Sir Robert Peel's Scotch currency scheme*. Edinburgh: J. Johnstone.

Monypenny, David (1834) *Remarks on the Poor Laws*. Edinburgh: Thomas Clark.

Murphy, Antoin E. (1994) *John Law's 'Essay on a Land Bank'*. Dublin: Aeon Publishing.

Murray, Patrick (1758) *Thoughts on Money, Circulation and Paper Currency*. Edinburgh: Hamilton, Balfour, Neill.

Murray, Patrick (1775) *Eight sets of queries... upon the subject of wool and woollen manufactures*. London and Edinburgh: William Creech.

Nicholson, J. Shield (1885) 'A plea for orthodox political economy', *National Review*, vol. VI, pp. 553–63.

Nicholson, J. Shield (1893–1901) *Principles of Political Economy*. London: Adam & Charles Black.

Nicholson, J. Shield (1894) *Historical Progress and Ideal Socialism: An evening discourse delivered to the British Association at Oxford in the Sheldonian Theatre 13 August 1894*. London: Adam & Charles Black.

Nicholson, J. Shield (1895) *A Treatise on Money and Essays on Monetary Problems*. 3rd edn, London: Adam & Charles Black

Nicholson, J. Shield (1903) *The Tariff Question with special reference to wages and employment*. London: Adam & Charles Black.

Nicholson, J. Shield (1909) *A Project of Empire: A critical study of the economics of imperialism, with special reference to the ideas of Adam Smith*. London: Macmillan.

Nicholson, J. Shield (1917) *War Finance*. London: P. S. King & Son.

Nicholson, J. Shield (1920) *The Revival of Marxism*. London: John Murray.

Ogilvie, William (1781) *An essay on the right of property in land, with respect to its foundation in the law of nature: its present Establishment by the Municipal laws of Europe and the Regulations by which it might be rendered more beneficial to the lower Ranks of Mankind*. London: J. Walter.

Oswald of Dunnikier, James (1750) 'Letter to David Hume', in James Fieser (2003) *Early Responses to Hume's Moral, Literary and Political Writings*, vol. I. Bristol: Thoemmes Press, pp. 21–32.

Owen, Robert ([1820] 1970) *A New View of Society and Other Writings*. Harmondsworth, Middlesex: Penguin Books.

Paterson, William (1751) *Proposals and reasons for constituting a council of trade in Scotland by the celebrated John Law*. Glasgow: Rob and Foulis.

Playfair, William (1787) *An Essay on the National Debt, with copper plate charts for comparing annuities with perpetual loans*. London: J. Debrett and J. Robinson.

Playfair, William (1793) *The History of Jacobinism, its crimes, cruelties and perfidies: comprising an inquiry into the manner of disseminating, under the appearance of philosophy and virtue, principles which are equally subversive of order, virtue, religion, liberty and happiness*. London: John Stockdale.

Playfair, William (1794) *Peace with the Jacobins Impossible*. London: John Stockdale.

Playfair, William (1797) *Letter to Sir W Pulteney, Bart. MP on the establishment of Another Public Bank in London*. London: printed for the author and sold by Crosby.

Playfair, William (1801) *The Statistical Breviary; showing on a principle entirely new, the resources of every state and kingdom in Europe ... to which is added a similar exhibition of the ruling powers of Hindoostan*. London: J. Wallis, etc.

Playfair, William (1807) *An Inquiry into the Permanent Causes of the Decline and Fall of Powerful and Wealthy Nations illustrated by four engraved charts designed to show how the prosperity of the British Empire may be prolonged*. 2nd edn, London: Greenland and Norris.

Playfair, William (1809) *Introduction to An Inquiry into the nature and causes of the Wealth of Nations*. 11th edn, London: T. Cadell & W. Davies.

Playfair, William (1813–14) *Political Portraits in this New Era*. London: C. Chapple.

Playfair, William (1814) *A letter to the Right Honourable and Honourable lords and Commons of Great Britain on the advantages of apprenticeships*. London: Sherwood, Neely and Jones.

Ramsay, George (1836) *An Essay on the Distribution of Wealth*. Edinburgh: Adam & Charles Black.

Ramsay, George (1838) *Political Discourses*. Edinburgh: Adam & Charles Black.

Read, Samuel (1816) *On Money and the Bank Restriction Laws*. Edinburgh.

Read, Samuel (1818) *The problem solved of the explication of a plan, of a safe, steady, and secure government paper currency and legal tender*. Edinburgh: Macredie, Skelly & Co.

Read, Samuel (1819) *Exposure of Certain Plagiarisms of JR Macculloch, Esq.* Edinburgh: Macredie, Skelly.

Read, Samuel (1821) 'Some Considerations stated, relative to the Adjustment of Debts, Public and Private, contracted during the late Depreciation of the Currency', *Farmers' Magazine*, vol. 22, pp. 291–302.

Read, Samuel (1829) *An Inquiry into the Natural Grounds of Right to Vendible Property, or Wealth*. Edinburgh: Oliver & Boyd.

Reid, Thomas (1788) *Essays on the intellectual and active powers of man*. Dublin: P. Byrne and J. Milliken.

Reid, Thomas (1990) *Practical Ethics: Being Lectures and Papers on Natural Religion, Self-Government, Natural Jurisprudence, and the Law of Nations*, ed. with intro. and commentary by Knud Haakonssen. Princeton: Princeton University Press.

Scott, Sir Walter (1822) *The Fortunes of Nigel*. Edinburgh: Archibald Constable.

Scott, Sir Walter ([1826] 1972) *Thoughts on the Proposed Change of Currency*. Shannon, Ireland: Irish University Press.

Selkirk, Earl of, Thomas Douglas (1805) *Observations on the Present State of the Highlands of Scotland with a view of the causes and probable consequences of emigration*. London: Longman, Hurst, Rees & Orme.

Seton, William (1700) *The Interest of Scotland in Three Essays*. London: A. Baldwin.

Seton, William (1705) *Some thoughts on ways and means for making this nation a gainer in foreign commerce, and for supplying the present scarcity of money*. Edinburgh: James Watson.

Seton, William (1706) *Scotland's Great Advantages by an union with England shown in a letter from the country*. Edinburgh.

Sinclair, Sir John (1790) *The History of the Public Revenue of the British Empire*. 2nd edn, London: T. Cadell.

Sinclair, Sir John (1791) *Address to the Landed Interest on the Corn Bill now defending in parliament*. London: T. Cadell.

Sinclair, Sir John (1795) *Address to the Members of the Board of Agriculture on the Cultivation and Improvement of the Waste Lands of this kingdom*. London.

Sinclair, Sir John (1796) *Account of the Origin of the Board of Agriculture and Its Progress for Three Years after its Establishment*. London: printed by W. Bulmer and Co.

Sinclair, Sir John (1797) *Letters written to the Governor and Directors of the Bank of England in September 1796 on the pecuniary distresses of the country and the means of preventing them with some additional observations on the same subject, and the means of speedily re-establishing the public and commercial credit of the country*. London: W. Bulmer and Co.

Sinclair, Sir John (1799) *The speech of Sir John Sinclair Bart MP on the bill for imposing a tax upon income in that debate on that bill on Friday the 14th December 1798*. London: J. Debrett.

Sinclair, Sir John (1810a) *Remarks on a pamphlet intitled 'The Question concerning the Depreciation of the Currency Stated and Examined' by William Huskisson, Esq. MP together with several political maxims regarding coin and paper currency, intending to explain the real nature, and advantages, of the present system*. London: T. Cadell & W. Davies, etc.

Sinclair, Sir John (1810b) *Observations on the Report of the Bullion Committee*. 2nd edn, London: T. Cadell & W. Davies, etc.

Sinclair, Sir John (1811?) *The speech of Sir John Sinclair, Bart. On the subject of the Bullion Report in the House of Commons, on Wednesday, the 10th of May, 1811*. London: R. McMillan.

Sinclair, Sir John (1819) *Thoughts on the Paper Circulation; with some remarks on the speech of the Earl of Liverpool, in the House of Peers, on the report of the Bank Committee; and a plan for re-establishing the financial circumstances of the country*. Edinburgh: Archibald Constable, etc.

Sinclair, Sir John (182-) *On the famines, or severe scarcities with which Scotland has been much afflicted, and the means of remedying such calamities*.

Sinclair, Sir John (1822) *Address to the owners and occupiers of land in Great Britain and Ireland; pointing out the effectual means for remedying the agricultural distresses of the country*. Edinburgh: Archibald Constable, etc.

Sinclair, Sir John (1823) *Analysis of the Statistical Account of Scotland*. London: Abernethy & Walker.

Sinclair, Sir John (183-) *On the Corn Laws; the improvements; the improvements of which they are susceptible; and the necessity of adhering to the present system, but remedying its defects*.

Sinclair, Sir John (1833) *On the Necessity of preserving the Corn Laws and resisting 'with spirit and energy' any attempt to repeal them*.

Sinclair, Sir John (1834) *On the necessity of a total repeal of the malt tax, and, the practicability of the measure, By a conversion of 'THE DEAD WEIGHT', to the amount from four to five Millions sterling, from temporary, into 'Perpetual Annuities'*. Edinburgh.

Smart, William ([1891] 1910) *An introduction to the theory of value: On the lines of Menger, Wieser and Böhm-Bawerk*. London: Macmillan and Co.

Smart, William (1895) *Studies in Economics*. London and New York: Macmillan.

Smart, William (1900) 'The Taxation of Land Values with reference to the London County Council Resolutions and the Glasgow Bill'. Read to the Scottish Society of Economics, Edinburgh, 25 October 1899.

Smart, William (1912) *The Distribution of Income*. 2nd edn, London: Macmillan.

Smart, William (1916) *Second Thoughts of an Economist*. London: Macmillan.

Smith, Adam ([1759] 1976) *The Theory of Moral Sentiments*, ed. D. D. Raphael and A. L. Macfie. Indianapolis: Liberty Fund.

Smith, Adam ([1776] 1976) *An Inquiry into the Nature and Causes of the Wealth of Nations*, ed. R. H. Campbell and A. S. Skinner. Indianapolis: Liberty Fund.

Smith, Adam (1884) *An Inquiry into the Nature and Causes of the Wealth of Nations: With an Introductory Essay and Notes by Joseph Shield Nicholson*. London: T. Nelson & Sons.

Smith, Adam ([1762] 1978) *Lectures on Jurisprudence*, ed. R. L. Meek, D. D. Raphael and P. G. Stein. Indianapolis: Liberty Fund.

Smith, Adam (1980) *Essays on Philosophical Subjects*, ed. W. P. D. Wightman and J. C. Bryce. Indianapolis: Liberty Fund.

Stair, Viscount: see Dalrymple, James.

Steuart, Sir James ([1767] 1998) *An inquiry into the principles of political oeconomy*, ed. Andrew S. Skinner, Noboro Kobayashi and Hiroshi Mizuta. London: Pickering & Chatto.

Steuart, Sir James (1769) *Considerations of the interest of the County of Lanark*. Glasgow: Robert Duncan.

Steuart, Sir James (1772) *The principles of money applied to the present state of the coin of Bengal, being an inquiry into the methods to be used for correcting the defects of the present currency*. 2nd edn, London.

Steuart, Sir James (1783) *A Dissertation on the Policy of Grain, With a view to a PLAN for preventing Scarcity, or Exorbitant Prices in the Common Markets of England*. London: W. Strahan & P. Cadell.

Stewart, Dugald (1840) *Lectures on Political Economy*, ed. Sir William Hamilton. Edinburgh: Thomas Constable.

Stewart, Dugald (1854–60) *The Collected Works of Dugald Stewart*, ed. Sir William Hamilton. Edinburgh: Thomas Constable.

Stewart, Dugald (1858) 'Account of the Life and Writings of Adam Smith, LLD' and 'Account of the Life and Times of Thomas Reid, DD', in Sir William Hamilton (ed.), *The Collected Works of Dugald Stewart*. Edinburgh: Thomas Constable.

Stirling, Patrick James (1846) *The Philosophy of Trade; or, Outlines of a Theory of Profits and Prices, including an Examination of the Principles which determine the relative value of corn, labour, and currency*. Edinburgh: Oliver & Boyd.

Wallace, Robert (n.d.) 'Of the Prices and Dearth of Provisions'. Edinburgh University, Laing Manuscript Collection, La.II.620.

Wallace, Robert (1753) *A Dissertation on the Numbers of Mankind in Antient and Modern Times*. Edinburgh: G. Hamilton & J. Balfour.

Wallace, Robert (1758) *Characteristics of the Present Political State of Great Britain*. 2nd edn, London: A. Millar.

Wallace, Robert (1761) *Various Prospects of Mankind, Nature and Providence*. London: A. Millar.

Wedderburn of St Germains, Alexander (1776) *An Essay upon the Question What Proportion of the Produce of Arable Land ought to be paid as Rent to the Landlord?* Edinburgh: Balfour & Smellie.

Secondary sources

Ahmad, S. (2007) 'On the Bicentennial of the Other "Inquiry": Lauderdale's', *Journal of the History of Economic Thought*, vol. 29 (1), pp. 85–100.

Anderson, Gary M. (1988) 'Mr Smith and the Preachers: The Economics of Religion in the Wealth of Nations', *Journal of Political Economy*, vol. 96, pp. 1066–88.

Andriopoulos, Stefan (1999) 'The Invisible Hand: Supernatural Agency in Political Economy and the Gothic Novel', *ELH*, vol. 66, pp. 739–58.

Arnon, Arie (1987) 'Banking Between the Invisible and Visible Hands: A Reinterpretation of Ricardo's Place within the Classical School', *Oxford Economic Papers*, vol. 39, pp. 268–81.

Berdell, John F. (1998) 'Adam Smith and the Ambiguity of Nations', *Review of Social Economy*, vol. 56 (2), pp. 175–89.

Berry, C. J. (2006) 'Hume and the Customary Causes of Industry, Knowledge, and Humanity', *History of Political Economy*, vol. 38, pp. 291–317.

Beveridge, Craig and Turnbull, Ronald (1997) *Scotland after Enlightenment: Image and Tradition in Modern Scottish Culture*. Edinburgh: Polygon.

Bittermann, Henry J. (1940a) 'Adam Smith's Empiricism and the Law of Nature: I', *Journal of Political Economy*, vol. 48, pp. 487–520.

Bittermann, Henry J. (1940b) 'Adam Smith's Empiricism and the Law of Nature: II', *Journal of Political Economy*, vol. 48, pp. 703–34.

Blunt, Anthony (1940) *Artistic Theory in Italy, 1450–1600*. Oxford and London: Clarendon Press.

Bourne, Kenneth and Taylor, William Banks (eds) (1994) *The Horner Papers: Selections from the Letters and Miscellaneous Writings of Francis Horner, MP, 1795–1817*. Edinburgh: Edinburgh University Press.

Bowles, Paul (1984) 'John Millar, the Four Stages Theory, and Women's Position in Society', *History of Political Economy*, vol. 16 (4), pp. 619–38.

Bowles, Paul (1985) 'The Origin of Property and the Development of Scottish Historical Science', *Journal of the History of Ideas*, vol. 46, pp. 197–209.

Bowles, Paul (1986) 'Adam Smith and the "Natural Progress of Opulence"', *Economica*, NS, vol. 53, pp. 109–18.

Brewer, Anthony (1997) 'An Eighteenth-Century View of Economic Development: Hume and Steuart', *European Journal of the History of Economic Thought*, vol. 4, pp. 1–22.

Brewer, Anthony (1998) 'Luxury and Economic Development: David Hume and Adam Smith', *Scottish Journal of Political Economy*, vol. 45, pp. 78–98.

Brewer, Anthony (1999) 'Adam Ferguson, Adam Smith, and the Concept of Economic Growth', *History of Political Economy*, vol. 31, pp. 237–54.

Briones, Ignacio and Rockoff, Hugh (2005) 'Do Economists Reach a Conclusion on Free-Banking Episodes?' *Economic Journal Watch*, vol. 2, pp. 279–324.

Brown, Stewart J. (1982) *Thomas Chalmers and the Godly Commonwealth in Scotland*. Oxford: Oxford University Press.

Brownlie, A. D. and Lloyd Prichard, M. F. (1963) 'Professor Fleeming Jenkin, 1833–85 Pioneer in Engineering and Political Economy', *Oxford Economic Papers*, NS, vol. 15, pp. 204–16.

Bruce, Thor W. (1938) 'The Economic Theories of John Craig, A Forgotten English Economist', *Quarterly Journal of Economics*, vol. 52 (4), pp. 697–707.

Buchanan, James M. (1976) 'The Justice of Natural Liberty', *Journal of Legal Studies*, vol. 5, pp. 1–16.

Buckle, H. T. (1861) *History of Civilization in England*, vol. 3. London: Parker, Son and Boum.

Cage, R. A. (1975) 'The Making of the Old Scottish Poor Law', *Past and Present*, no. 69, pp. 113–18.

Campbell, R. H. (1964) 'The Anglo-Scottish Union of 1707. II. The Economic Consequences', *Economic History Review*, NS, vol. 16, pp. 468–77.

Campbell, R. H. and Skinner, Andrew S. (1982) *The Origins and Nature of the Scottish Enlightenment*. Edinburgh: John Donald.

Cannan, Edwin (1917) *A History of the Theories of Production and Distribution in English Political Economy from 1776 to 1848*. 3rd edn, London: Staples Press.

Carstairs, A. M. (1955) 'Some Economic Aspects of the Union of Parliaments', *Scottish Journal of Political Economy*, vol. 2 (3), pp. 64–77.

Cesarano, Filippo (1998) 'Hume's Specie-Flow Mechanism and Classical Monetary Theory: An Alternative Interpretation', *Journal of International Economics*, vol. 45, pp. 173–86.

Chancellor, Valerie (1986) *The Political Life of Joseph Hume 1777–1855: The Scot Who Was for Over 30 Years a Radical Leader in the House of Commons*. London: Bennett Lodge.

Checkland, Olive (1980) *Philanthropy in Victorian Scotland: Social Welfare and the Voluntary Principle*. Edinburgh: John Donald.

Checkland, S. G. (1956) 'David Hume: Writings on Economics', *Economic History Review*, NS, vol. 9, pp. 386–8.

Checkland, S. G. (1975) *Scottish Banking: A History, 1695–1973*. Glasgow and London: Collins.

Cheyne, A. C. (ed.) (1985) *The Practical and the Pious. Essays on Thomas Chalmers (1780–1847)*. Edinburgh: The Saint Andrew Press.

Coats, A. W. (1958) 'Changing Attitudes to Labour in the Mid-Eighteenth Century', *Economic History Review*, NS, vol. 1, pp. 35–51.

Coats, A. W. (1960) 'Economic Thought and Poor Law Policy in the Eighteenth Century', *Economic History Review*, NS, vol. 13 (1), pp. 39–51.

Cohen, Edward S. (1989) 'Justice and Political Economy in Commercial Society: Adam Smith's "Science of a Legislator"', *Journal of Politics*, vol. 51 (1), pp. 50–72.

Cole, Arthur H. (1958) 'Puzzles of the "Wealth of Nations"', *Canadian Journal of Economics and Political Science*, vol. 24, pp. 1–8.

Cole, A. V. (1956) 'Lord Lauderdale and his "Inquiry"', *Scottish Journal of Political Economy*, vol. 3 (2), pp. 5–25.

Conniff, James (1987) 'Burke on Political Economy: The Nature and Extent of State Authority', *Review of Politics*, vol. 49, pp. 490–514.

Corry, B. A. (1962) *Money, Saving and Investment in English Economics 1800–50*. London: Macmillan & Co.

Costigan-Eaves, Patricia and Macdonald-Ross, Michael (1990) 'William Playfair (1759–1823)', *Statistical Science*, vol. 5, pp. 318–26.

Cropsey, Joseph (1957) *Polity and Economy: An Interpretation of the Principles of Adam Smith*. The Hague: Martinus Nijhoff.

Davie, George (1991) *The Scottish Enlightenment and Other Essays*. Edinburgh: Polygon.

Davie, George (1994) *A Passion for Ideas: Essays on the Scottish Enlightenment*, vol. II. Edinburgh: Polygon.

Davis, G. F. (2003) 'Philosophical Psychology and Economic Psychology in David Hume and Adam Smith', *History of Political Economy*, vol. 35, pp. 269–304.

Davis, Joseph S. (1954) 'Adam Smith and the Human Stomach', *Quarterly Journal of Economics*, vol. 68, pp. 275–86.

Deans, Robert H. and Deans, Janet S. (1987) 'J Shield Nicholson's Project of Empire: the Edinburgh Economist Evolved from a Free Trader into a Premier Apologist for Imperialism', *American Journal of Economics and Sociology*, vol. 46 (3), pp. 319–40.

Demsetz, Harold (1967) 'Toward a Theory of Property Rights', *American Economic Review, Papers and Proceedings*, vol. 57, pp. 347–59.

Devine, T. M. (ed.) (1978) *Lairds and Improvement in the Scotland of the Enlightenment*. Strathclyde: Strathclyde University.

Dickson, W. K. (1932) *David Hume and the Advocates' Library*. Edinburgh: W. Green.

Dome, Takuo (1998) 'Adam Smith's theory of Tax Incidence: An Interpretation of His Natural-Price System', *Cambridge Journal of Economics*, vol. 22, pp. 79–89.

Dow, Alexander, Dow, Sheila and Hutton, Alan (1997) 'The Scottish Political Economy Tradition and Modern Economics', *Scottish Journal of Political Economy*, vol. 44, pp. 368–83.

Dow, Alexander, Dow, Sheila and Hutton, Alan (2000) 'Applied Economics in a Political Economy Tradition: The Case of Scotland from the 1890s to the 1950s', *History of Political Economy*, vol. 32, supplement, pp. 177–98.

Durie, Alastair J. (1979) *The Scottish Linen Industry in the Eighteenth Century*. Edinburgh: John Donald.

Dwyer, John (1998) *The Age of Passions: An Interpretation of Adam Smith and Scottish Enlightenment Culture*. East Linton, East Lothian: Tuckwell Press.

Eagly, Robert V. (1961) 'Sir James Steuart and the "Aspiration Effect" ', *Economica*, NS, vol. 28, pp. 53–61.

Eagly, Robert V. (1970) 'Adam Smith and the Specie-Flow Doctrine', *Scottish Journal of Political Economy*, vol. 17 (1), pp. 61–8.

Elmslie, Bruce Truitt (1995) 'Retrospectives: The Convergence Debate between David Hume and Josiah Tucker', *Journal of Economic Perspectives*, vol. 9, pp. 207–16.

Evensky, Jerry (2001) 'Adam Smith's Lost Legacy', *Southern Economic Journal*, vol. 67 (3), pp. 497–517.

Fay, C. R. (1956) *Adam Smith and the Scotland of His Day*. Cambridge: Cambridge University Press.

Ferguson, Niall (2001) *The Cash Nexus: Money and Power in the Modern World 1700–2000*. London: Penguin Books.

Fetter, Frank Albert (1901) 'The Passing of the Old Rent Concept', *Quarterly Journal of Economics*, vol. 15 (3), pp. 416–55.

Fetter, Frank Albert (1945) 'Lauderdale's Oversaving Theory', *American Economic Review*, vol. 35, pp. 263–83.

Fisher, Irving (1894) 'The Mechanics of Bimetallism', *Economic Journal*, vol. 4, pp. 527–37.

Fitzgibbons, Athol (1995) *Adam Smith's System of Liberty, Wealth and Virtue: The Moral and Political Foundations of the Wealth of Nations*. Oxford: Clarendon Press.

Fleischacker, Samuel (2004) *On Adam Smith's Wealth of Nations: A Philosophical Companion*. Princeton and Oxford: Princeton University Press.

Flinn, Michael (ed.) (1977) *Scottish Population History from the 17th Century to the 1930s*. Cambridge: Cambridge University Press.

Forbes, Duncan (1954) 'Scientific Whiggism: Adam Smith and John Millar', *Cambridge Journal*, vol. 7 (August), pp. 643–70.

Friedman, Milton (1990) 'Bimetallism Revisited', *Journal of Economic Perspectives*, vol. 4, pp. 85–104.

Gee, Alec (1998) 'James Anderson, Development Economist: A Cautionary Tale', *Manchester School*, vol. 66, pp. 581–606.

Gherity, James A. (1962) 'Thomas De Quincey and Ricardian Orthodoxy', *Economica*, NS, vol. 29, pp. 269–74.

Gibson, A. J. S. and Smout, T. C. (1995) *Prices, Food and Wages in Scotland 1550–1780*. Cambridge: Cambridge University Press.

Gilbert, Geoffrey (1997) 'Adam Smith on the Nature and Causes of Poverty', *Review of Social Economy*, vol. 55, pp. 273–91.

Goldsmith, M. M. (1988) 'Regulating Anew the Moral and Political Sentiments of Mankind: Bernard Mandeville and the Scottish Enlightenment', *Journal of the History of Ideas*, vol. 49, pp. 587–606.

Grampp, William D. (1948) 'Adam Smith and the Economic Man', *Journal of Political Economy*, vol. 56, pp. 315–36.

Grampp, William D. (1976) 'Scots, Jews, and Subversives among the Dismal Scientists', *Journal of Economics History*, vol. 36, pp. 543–71.

Grampp, William D. (2000) 'What Did Smith Mean by the Invisible Hand?' *Journal of Political Economy*, vol. 108, pp. 441–65.

Gray, J. L. (1928) 'The Law of Combination in Scotland', *Economica*, no. 24, pp. 332–50.

Groenewegen, Peter (2001) 'Thomas Carlyle, "The Dismal Science", and the Contemporary Political Economy of Slavery', *History of Economics Review*, vol. 34, pp. 74–95.

Grossman, Henryk (1943) 'The Evolutionist Revolt against Classical Economics: In England – James Steuart, Richard Jones, Karl Marx', *Journal of Political Economy*, vol. 51 (6), pp. 506–22.

Grossman, Henryk (1948) 'W. Playfair, the Earliest Theorist of Capitalist Development', *Economic History Review*, vol. 18, pp. 65–83.

Haakonssen, Knud (1985) 'John Millar and the Science of a Legislator', *The Juridical Review*, part 1 (June), pp. 41–68.

Haakonssen, Knud (1986–87) 'Reid's Politics: A Natural Law Theory', *Reid Studies*, no. 1, pp. 10–27.

Halberstadt, William H. (1971) 'A Problem in Hume's Aesthetics', *Journal of Aesthetics and Art Criticism*, vol. 30, pp. 209–14.

Hamowy, Ronald (1968) 'Adam Smith, Adam Ferguson, and the Division of Labour', *Economica*, NS, vol. 35, pp. 249–59.

Hardin, Russell (2007) *David Hume: Moral and Political Theorist*. Oxford: Oxford University Press.

Harlen, Christine Margerum (1999) 'A Reappraisal of Classical Economic Nationalism and Economic Liberalism', *International Studies Quarterly*, vol. 43, pp. 733–44.

Haworth, A. (1976) 'Planning and Philosophy: The Case of Owenism and the Owenite Communities', *Urban Studies*, vol. 13, pp. 147–53.

Helleiner, Eric (2002) 'Economic Nationalism as a Challenge to Economic Liberalism? Lessons from the 19th Century', *International Studies Quarterly*, vol. 46, pp. 307–29.

Hemingway, Andrew (1989) 'The "Sociology" of Taste in the Scottish Enlightenment', *Oxford Art Journal*, vol. 12 (2), pp. 3–35.

Herbener, Jeffery (1987) 'An Integration of *The Wealth of Nations* and *The Theory of Moral Sentiments*', *Journal of Libertarian Studies*, vol. 8, pp. 275–88.

Hicks, Sir John (1967) *Critical Essays in Monetary Theory*. Oxford: Clarendon Press.

Hill, L. (1997) 'Adam Ferguson and the Paradox of Progress and Decline', *History of Political Thought*, vol. 18, pp. 677–706.

Hill, L. (2007) 'Adam Smith, Adam Ferguson and Karl Marx on the Division of Labour', *Journal of Classical Sociology*, vol. 7, pp. 339–66.

Hill, Peter (1999) 'Tangibles, Intangibles and Services: A New Taxonomy for the Classification of Output', *Canadian Journal of Economics*, vol. 32, pp. 426–46.

Hilton, Boyd (1988) *The Age of Atonement: The Influence of Evangelicalism on Social and Economic Thought, 1795–1865*. Oxford: Clarendon Press.

Hipple, Walter J., Jr (1955) 'The Aesthetics of Dugald Stewart: Culmination of a Tradition', *Journal of Aesthetics and Art Criticism*, vol. 14, pp. 77–96.

Hoh-Cheung and Mui, Lorna H. (1961) 'William Pitt and the Enforcement of the Commutation Act, 1784–88', *English Historical Review*, vol. 76, pp. 447–65.

Hollander, J. H. (1895) 'The Concept of Marginal Rent', *Quarterly Journal of Economics*, vol. 9, pp. 175–87.

Hollander, J. H. (1896) 'Adam Smith and James Anderson', *Annals of the American Academy of Political and Social Science*, vol. 7, pp. 85–8.

Hollander, J. H. (1911) 'The Development of the Theory of Money from Adam Smith to David Ricardo', *Quarterly Journal of Economics*, vol. 25, pp. 429–70.

Hollander, Jacob H. (1927) 'Adam Smith 1776–1926', *Journal of Political Economy*, vol. 35, pp. 153–97.

Hook, Andrew and Sher, Richard B. (eds) (1993) *The Glasgow Enlightenment.* East Linton, East Lothian: Tuckwell Press.

Huch, Ronald K. and Ziegler, Paul R. (1985) *Joseph Hume: The People's MP.* Philadelphia: American Philosophical Society.

Humphrey, Thomas M. (1999) 'Mercantilists and Classicals: Insights from Doctrinal History', *Federal Reserve Bank of Richmond Economic Quarterly*, vol. 85 (2), pp. 55–82.

Hundert, E. J. (1974) 'The Achievement Motive in Hume's Political Economy', *Journal of the History of Ideas*, vol. 35, pp. 139–43.

Hutchison, T. W. (1953) 'Berkeley's Querist and Its Place in the Economic Thought of the Eighteenth Century', *British Journal for the Philosophy of Science*, vol. 4, pp. 52–77.

Ignatieff, Michael (1983) 'John Millar and Individualism', in I. Hont and M. Ignatieff, *Wealth and Virtue: The Shaping of Political Economy in the Scottish Enlightenment.* Cambridge: Cambridge University Press, pp. 317–43.

Insh, George Pratt (1932) *The Company of Scotland Trading to Africa and the Indies.* London and New York: Charles Scribner's Sons.

Jevons, W. Stanley ([1871] 1970) *The Theory of Political Economy.* Harmondsworth, Middlesex: Penguin Books.

Jones, Peter (1976) 'Hume's Aesthetics Reassessed', *Philosophical Quarterly*, vol. 26, pp. 48–62.

Kauder, E. (1953) 'Genesis of the Marginal Utility Theory: From Aristotle to the End of the Eighteenth Century', *Economic Journal*, vol. 63 (3), pp. 638–50.

Keith, Theodora (1909) 'The Economic Causes for the Scottish Union', *English Historical Review*, vol. 24, pp. 44–60.

Kennedy, Gavin (2009) 'Adam Smith and the Invisible Hand: From Metaphor to Myth', *Econ Journal Watch*, vol. 6 (2), pp. 239–63.

Keynes, John Maynard (1936) *The General Theory of Employment Interest and Money.* London: Macmillan.

Kim, Kwangsu (2009) 'Adam Smith's Theory of Economic History and Economic Development', *European Journal History of Economic Thought*, vol. 16, pp. 41–64.

Kitagawa, Kurtis G. (1994) 'Not Without the Highest Justice: The Origins and Development of Thomas Reid's Political Thought'. Ph D thesis. Edinburgh: University of Edinburgh.

Klein, Daniel B. (2009) 'In Adam Smith's Invisible Hands: Comment on Gavin Kennedy', *Econ Journal Watch*, vol. 6 (2), pp. 264–79.

Kobayashi, Noburu (1967) *James Steuart and Friedrich List.* Tokyo: The Science Council of Japan.

Laidler, David (1981) 'Adam Smith as a Monetary Economist', *Canadian Journal of Economics*, vol. 14, pp. 185–200.

Laidler, D. (1984) 'Misconceptions about the Real-Bills Doctrine: A Comment on Sargent and Wallace', *Journal of Political Economy*, vol. 92 (1), pp. 149–55.

Lamb, Robert (1973) 'Adam Smith's Concept of Alienation', *Oxford Economic Papers*, vol. 25, pp. 275–85.

Lamb, Robert (1974) 'Adam Smith's System: Sympathy not Self-Interest', *Journal of the History of Ideas*, vol. 35 (4), pp. 671–82.

Lehmann, William C. (1971) *Henry Home, Lord Kames, and the Scottish Enlightenment: A Study in National Character and in the History of Ideas*. The Hague: Martinus Nijhoff.

Leslie, T. E. Cliffe (1870) 'The Political Economy of Adam Smith', *Fortnightly Review*, vol. 8 (1 November), pp. 549–63.

Lindgren, J. Ralph (1969) 'Adam Smith's Theory of Inquiry', *Journal of Political Economy*, vol. 77, pp. 897–915.

Locke, John (1953) *Two Treatises of Government*, ed. Peter Laslett. 2nd edn, Cambridge: Cambridge University Press.

Low, J. M. (1952) 'An Eighteenth Century Controversy in the Theory of Economic Progress', *Manchester School*, vol. 20 (3), pp. 311–30.

Low, J. M. (1954) 'The Rate of Interest: British Opinion in the Eighteenth Century', *Manchester School*, vol. 22 (2), pp. 115–38.

Lucas, Robert E., Jr (1996) 'Nobel Lecture: Monetary Neutrality', *Journal of Political Economy*, vol. 104 (4), pp. 661–82.

Luehrs, Robert B. (1987) 'Population and Utopia in the Thought of Robert Wallace', *Eighteenth-Century Studies*, vol. 20 (3), pp. 313–35.

Macfie, A. L. (1959) 'Adam Smith's Moral Sentiments as Foundation for His Wealth of Nations', *Oxford Economic Papers*, NS, vol. 3, pp. 209–28.

Macfie, A. L. (1971) 'The Invisible Hand of Jupiter', *Journal of the History of Ideas*, vol. 32, pp. 595–9.

Macleod, Alistair M. (2007) 'Invisible Hand Arguments: Milton Friedman and Adam Smith', *Journal of Scottish Philosophy*, vol. 5 (2), pp. 103–17.

Malek, James S. (1972) 'Adam Smith's Contribution to Eighteenth-Century British Aesthetics', *Journal of Aesthetics and Art Criticism*, vol. 31, pp. 49–54.

Marshall, Alfred ([1890] 1959) *Principles of Economics, Part I*. London: Macmillan.

Marshall, M. G. (1998) 'Scottish Economic Thought and the High Wage Economy: Hume, Smith and McCulloch on Wages and Work Motivation', *Scottish Journal of Political Economy*, vol. 45, pp. 309–28.

Marshall, M. G. (2000) 'Luxury, Economic Development and Work Motivation: David Hume, Adam Smith and J. R. McCulloch', *History of Political Economy*, vol. 32, pp. 631–48.

Marwick, W. H. (1935) 'Early Trade Unionism in Scotland', *Economic History Review*, vol. 5 (2), pp. 87–95.

Marx, Karl ([1867] 1976) *Capital: A Critique of Political Economy*. Harmondsworth, Middlesex: Penguin Books.

Mason, John W. (1980) 'Political Economy and the Response to Socialism in Britain, 1870–1914', *Historical Journal*, vol. 23, pp. 565–87.

Mayer, T. (1980) 'David Hume and Monetarism', *Quarterly Journal of Economics*, vol. 95, pp. 89–101.

Meek, Ronald L. (1956) *Studies in the Labour Theory of Value*. London: Lawrence & Wishart.

Meek, Ronald L. and Skinner, Andrew S. (1973) 'The Development of Adam Smith's Ideas on the Division of Labour', *Economic Journal*, vol. 83, pp. 1094–116.

Mepham, Michael J. (1983) 'Robert Hamilton's Contribution to Accounting', *Accounting Review*, vol. 58, pp. 43–57.

Michael, Emily (1984) 'Francis Hutcheson on Aesthetic Perception and Aesthetic Pleasure', *British Journal of Aesthetics*, vol. 24, pp. 241–55.

Michie, Michael (1997) *An Enlightenment Tory in Victorian Scotland: The Career of Sir Archibald Alison*. Montreal and Kingston: McGill-Queen's University Press.

Milgate, M. and Stimson, S. C. (1996) 'The Figure of Smith: Dugald Stewart and the Propagation of Smithian Economics', *European Journal of the History of Economic Thought*, vol. 3, pp. 225–53.

Mill, J. S. (1845) 'De Quincey's Logic of Political Economy', *Westminster Review*, vol. 43, pp. 319–31.

Mill, J. S. ([1848] 1917) *Principles of Political Economy with Some of their Applications to Social Philosophy*. London: Longmans, Green & Co.

Milne, Maurice (1995) 'Archibald Alison: Conservative Controversialist', *Albion: A Quarterly Journal Concerned with British Studies*, vol. 27, pp. 419–43.

Mitchison, Rosalind (1974) 'The Making of the Old Scottish Poor Law', *Past and Present*, no. 63, pp. 58–93.

Mizuta, Hiroshi and Sugiyama, Chuhei (1993) *Adam Smith: International Perspectives*. Basingstoke: St Martin's Press.

Moore, Gregory (2000) 'Nicholson versus Ingram on the History of Political Economy and a Charge of Plagiarism', *Journal of the History of Economic Thought*, vol. 22, pp. 433–60.

Mullett, Charles F. (1968–9) 'A Village Aristotle and the Harmony of Interests: James Anderson (1739–1808) of Monks Hill', *Journal of British Studies*, vol. 8, pp. 94–118.

Murphy, Antoin E. (2003) 'Paper Credit and the Multi-Personae Mr Henry Thornton', *European Journal of the History of Economic Thought*, vol. 10 (3), pp. 429–53.

Myers, Milton L. (1967) 'Division of Labour as a Principle of Social Cohesion', *Canadian Journal of Economics and Political Science*, vol. 33, pp. 432–40.

Myint, H. (1977) 'Adam Smith's Theory of International Trade in the Perspective of Economic Development', *Economica*, NS, vol. 44, pp. 231–48.

Nagao, Shinichi (2003) 'The Political Economy of Thomas Reid', *Journal of Scottish Philosophy*, vol. 1, pp. 21–33.

Nagao, Shinichi (ed.) (2007) *Politics and Society in Scottish Thought*. Exeter: Imprint Academic.

Nakano, Takeshi (2006) ' "Let your science be human": Hume's Economic Methodology', *Cambridge Journal of Economics*, vol. 30, pp. 687–700.

Naldi, Nerio (1993) 'Gershom Carmichael on "Demand" and "Difficulty of Acquiring": Some evidence from the First Edition of Carmichael's Commentary to Pufendorf's De Officio', *Scottish Journal of Political Economy*, vol. 40, pp. 456–70.

Nisbet, J. W. (1964) 'Thomas Chalmers and the Economic Order', *Scottish Journal of Political Economy*, vol. 9 (2), pp. 151–7.

Norton, David Fate (1985) 'Hutcheson's Moral Realism', *Journal of the History of Philosophy*, vol. 23, pp. 397–418.

O'Brien, D. P. (1966) 'J. R. McCulloch and the Theory of Value', *Scottish Journal of Political Economy*, vol. 13 (3), pp. 332–51.

O'Brien, Patrick K. (1988) 'The Political Economy of British Taxation, 1660–1815', *Economic History Review*, NS, vol. 41, pp. 1–32.

Packham, Catherine (2002) 'The Physiology of Political Economy: Vitalism and Adam Smith's Wealth of Nations', *Journal of the History of Ideas*, vol. 63 (3), pp. 465–81.

Paganelli, Maria Pia (2009) 'David Hume on Monetary Policy: A Retrospective Approach', *Journal of Scottish Philosophy*, vol. 7 (1), pp. 65–85.

Paglin, Morton (1946) 'Fetter on Lauderdale', *American Economic Review*, vol. 36 (3), pp. 391–3.

Paglin, Morton (1961) *Malthus and Lauderdale: The Anti-Ricardian Tradition*. New York: Augustus M. Kelley.

Pashkoff, Susan (1993) 'Two Contributions to the Decline of Ricardian Economics: Samuel Read and George Poulett Scrope', *Contributions to Political Economy*, vol. 12 (1), pp. 47–69.

Perlman, Morris (1995) *The Transfer of Technology: Change of Paradigm or Change of Packaging? The Case of Fleeming Jenkin*. London: LSE Centre for the Philosophy of the Natural and Social Sciences.

Pesciarelli, Enzo (1999) 'Aspects of the Influence of Francis Hutcheson on Adam Smith', *History of Political Economy*, vol. 31, pp. 525–45.

Petersen, Dean James (1994) 'Political Economy in Transition: From Classical Humanism to Commercial Society – Robert Wallace of Edinburgh'. Ph D thesis. Urbana-Champaign, University of Illinois and Ann Arbor, MI, University Microfilms International.

Petrella, F. (1968) 'Adam Smith's Rejection of Hume's Price-Specie-Flow Mechanism: A Minor Mystery Resolved', *Southern Economic Journal*, vol. 34, pp. 365–74.

Prendergast, Renee (1987) 'James Anderson's Political Economy – His Influence on Smith and Malthus', *Scottish Journal of Political Economy*, vol. 34 (4), pp. 388–409.

Price L. L. (1893) 'The Unseen Foundations of Society', *Economic Journal*, vol. 3, pp. 264–71.

Prybyla, Jan S. (1963) 'The Economic Writings of George Ramsay, 1800–71', *Scottish Journal of Political Economy*, vol. 10 (3), pp. 305–21.

Rae, John (1834) *Statement of some new principles on the subject of political economy: exposing the fallacies of the system of free trade, and of some other doctrines maintained in the 'Wealth of Nations'*, Boston: Hilliard, Gray.

Rashid, Salim (1987) 'Political Economy as Moral Philosophy: Dugald Stewart of Edinburgh', *Australian Economic Papers*, vol. 26, pp. 145–56.

Rashid, Salim (1994) 'The Intellectual Standards of Adam Smith's Day', *Journal of Libertarian Studies*, vol. 11, pp. 107–16.

Recktenwald, Horst Claus (1978) 'An Adam Smith Renaissance Anno 1976? The Bicentenary Output – A Reappraisal of his Scholarship', *Journal of Economic Literature*, vol. 16, pp. 56–83.

Redman, Deborah A. (1993) 'Adam Smith and Isaac Newton', *Scottish Journal of Political Economy*, vol. 40 (2), pp. 210–30.

Reilly, E. F. (1940) 'The Use of the Elasticity Concept in Economic Theory: With Special Reference to Some Economic Effects of a Commodity Tax', *Canadian Journal of Economic and Political Science*, vol. 6 (1), pp. 39–55.

Robbins, David O. (1942) 'The Aesthetics of Thomas Reid', *Journal of Aesthetics and Art Criticism*, vol. 2, pp. 30–41.

Roberts, R. O. (1945) 'Thomas Chalmers on the Public Debt', *Economica*, NS, vol. 12, pp. 111–16.

Roberts, T. A. (1973) *The Concept of Benevolence: Aspects of Eighteenth Century Moral Philosophy*. London and Basingstoke: Macmillan.

Robertson, John (1997) 'The Enlightenment above National Context: Political Economy in Eighteenth-Century Scotland and Naples', *Historical Journal*, vol. 40, pp. 667–97.

Rosenberg, Nathan (1960) 'Some Institutional Aspects of the Wealth of Nations', *Journal of Political Economy*, vol. 68, pp. 557–70.

Rosenberg, Nathan (1965) 'Adam Smith on the Division of Labour: Two Views or One?', *Economica*, NS, vol. 32, pp. 127–39.

Rosenberg, Nathan (1968) 'Adam Smith, Consumer Tastes, and Economic Growth', *Journal of Political Economy*, vol. 76, pp. 361–74.

Ross, Ian Simpson (1972) *Lord Kames and the Scotland of his Day*. Oxford: Clarendon Press.

Rossner, Philipp Robinson (2008) *Scottish Trade in the Wake of the Union (1700–1760): The Rise of a Warehouse Economy*. Stuttgart: Franz Steiner.

Rothbard, Murray N. (1988) 'The Myth of Free Banking in Scotland', *Review of Austrian Economics*, vol. 2, pp. 229–45.

Rothschild, Emma (1992) 'Adam Smith and Conservative Economics', *Economic History Review*, vol. 45, pp. 74–96.

Rothschild, Emma (1995) 'Social Security and Laissez Faire in Eighteenth-Century Political Economy', *Population and Development Review*, vol. 21, pp. 711–44.

Rothschild, Emma (2002) *Economic Sentiments: Adam Smith, Condorcet and the Enlightenment*. Cambridge, MA, and London, England: Harvard University Press.

Rubini, Dennis (1970) 'Politics and the Battle for the Banks, 1688–1697', *English Historical Review*, vol. 85, pp. 693–714.

Sakamoto, Tatsuya and Tanaka, Hideo (2003) *The Rise of Political Economy in the Scottish Enlightenment*. London and New York: Routledge.

Samuels, Warren J. (1977) 'The Political Economy of Adam Smith', *Ethics*, vol. 87 (3), pp. 189–207.

Samuels, Warren J. and Medema, Steven G. (2005) 'Freeing Smith from the "Free Market": On the Misperception of Adam Smith on the Economic Role of Government', *History of Political Economy*, vol. 37, pp. 219–26.

Samuelson, Paul A. (1977) 'A Modern Theorist's Vindication of Adam Smith', *American Economic Review, Papers and Proceedings*, vol. 67, pp. 42–9.

Samuelson, Paul A. (1980) 'A Corrected Version of Hume's Equilibrating Mechanisms for International Trade', in John S. Chipman and Charles P. Kindleberger (eds), *Flexible Exchange Rates and the Balance of Payments: Essays in Memory of Egan Sohmen*. Amsterdam, New York, and Oxford: North Holland, pp. 141–58.

Samuelson, Paul A. (1992) 'The Overdue Recovery of Adam Smith', in M. Fry (ed.), *Adam Smith: His Place in the Development of Modern Economics*. London and New York: Routledge.

Santayana, G. (1904) 'What is Aesthetics?' *Philosophical Review*, vol. 13, pp. 320–27.

Sargent, T. J. and Wallace, N. (1982) 'The Real-Bills Doctrine versus the Quantity Theory: A Reconsideration', *Journal of Political Economy*, vol. 90, pp. 1212–36.

Schumpeter, Elizabeth Boody (1938) 'English Prices and Public Finance, 1660–1822', *Review of Economics and Statistics*, vol. 20, pp. 21–37.

Schumpeter, Joseph A. (1954) *History of Economic Analysis*. London: George Allen & Unwin.

Sechrest, Larry J. (1991) 'Free Banking in Scotland: A Dissenting View', *Cato Journal*, vol. 10, pp. 799–808.

Seligman, Edwin R. A. (1903a) 'On Some Neglected British Economists, I', *Economic Journal*, vol. 13, pp. 335–63.

Seligman, Edwin R. A. (1903b) 'On Some Neglected British Economists, II', *Economic Journal*, vol. 13, pp. 511–35.

Semmel, Bernard (1965) 'The Hume–Tucker Debate and Pitt's Trade Proposals', *Economic Journal,* vol. 75, pp. 759–70.

Sen, S. R. (1957) *The Economics of Sir James Steuart.* London: London School of Economics and Political Science, University of London.

Siemens, Robert (1997) 'The Problem of Modern Poverty: Significant Congruences between Hegel's and George's Theoretical Conceptions', *American Journal of Economics and Sociology*, vol. 56 (4), special issue: Commemorating the 100th Anniversary of the Death of Henry George, pp. 617–37.

Simmel, Georg (2004) *The Philosophy of Money*, ed. David Frisby. 3rd edn, London and New York: Routledge.

Sinha, Ajit (2010) 'In Defence of Adam Smith's Theory of Value', *European Journal of the History of Economic Thought*, vol. 17, pp. 29–48.

Skinner, Andrew (1995) 'Pufendorf, Hutcheson and Adam Smith: Some Principles of Political Economy', *Scottish Journal of Political Economy*, vol. 42 (2), pp. 165–82.

Skinner, Andrew (1998) 'Adam Smith: The Philosopher (and the Porter)', *Discussion Papers in Economics*, no. 9807. Glasgow: University of Glasgow.

Smith, Craig (2006) 'Adam Ferguson and the Danger of Books', *Journal of Scottish Philosophy*, vol. 4, pp. 93–109.

Smout, T. C. (1963) *Scottish Trade on the Eve of the Union 1660–1707*. Edinburgh and London: Oliver & Boyd.

Smout, T. C. (1964) 'The Anglo-Scottish Union of 1707. I: The Economic Background', *Economic History Review*, NS, vol. 16, pp. 455–67.

Spengler, J. J. (1970) 'Adam Smith on Population', *Population Studies*, vol. 24, pp. 377–88.

Stabile, Donald R. (1997) 'Adam Smith and the Natural Wage: Sympathy, Subsistence and Social Distance', *Review of Social Economy*, vol. 55, pp. 292–311.

Steedman, Ian (2004) 'British Economists and Philosophers on Marx's Value Theory, 1920–25', *Journal of the History of Economic Thought*, vol. 26 (1), pp. 45–68.

Steel, W. A. (1896) 'William Paterson', *English Historical Review*, vol. 11, pp. 260–81.

Stettner, Walter F. (1945) 'Sir James Steuart on the Public Debt', *Quarterly Journal of Economics*, vol. 59, pp. 451–76.

Stimson, Shannon (2004) 'From Invisible Hand to Moral Restraint: The Transformation of the Market Mechanism from Adam Smith to Thomas Robert Malthus', *Journal of Scottish Philosophy*, vol. 2, pp. 22–47.

Swingewood, Alan (1970) 'Origins of Sociology: The Cast of the Scottish Enlightenment', *British Journal of Sociology*, vol. 21, pp. 164–80.

Taylor, W. L. (1955) 'Gershom Carmichael: A Neglected Figure in British Political Economy', *South African Journal of Economics*, vol. 23 (3), pp. 251–5.

Taylor, W. L. (1956) 'Eighteenth Century Scottish Political Economy: The Impact on Adam Smith and his Work, of his Association with Francis Hutcheson and David Hume', *South African Journal of Political Economy*, vol. 24 (4), pp. 261–76.

Teichgraeber III, Richard Fredrick (1978) 'Politics and Morals in the Scottish Enlightenment'. Ph D thesis. Waltham, MA, Brandeis University.

Teichgraeber III, Richard Fredrick (1987) '"Less Abused Than I Had Reason to Expect": The Reception of the Wealth of Nations in Britain, 1776–90', *Historical Journal*, vol. 30, pp. 337–66.

Thomson, Herbert F. (1965) 'Adam Smith's Philosophy of Science', *Quarterly Journal of Economics*, vol. 79 (2), pp. 212–33.

Thomson, Herbert F. (1970) 'Lauderdale's Early Pamphlets on Public Finance (1796–1799)', *History of Political Economy*, vol. 2 (2), pp. 344–80.

Thornton, Henry (1802) *An Inquiry into the Nature and Effects of the Paper Credit of Great Britain*. London: F. and C. Rivington.

Thornton, M. (2007) 'Cantillon, Hume, and the Rise of Anti-Mercantilism', *History of Political Economy*, vol. 39, pp. 453–80.

Thweatt, William O. (1983) 'Origins of the Terminology "Supply and Demand"', *Scottish Journal of Political Economy*, vol. 30, pp. 287–94.

Tortajada, Ramon (ed.) (1999) *The Economics of James Steuart*. London and New York: Routledge.

Townsend, Dabney (2001) *Hume's Aesthetic Theory: Taste and Sentiment*. London and New York: Routledge.

Tribe, Keith (1978) *Land, Labour and Economic Discourse*. London: Routledge and Kegan Paul.

Tribe, Keith (1999) 'Adam Smith: Critical Theorist?' *Journal of Economic Literature*, vol. 37, pp. 609–32.

Vickers, Douglas (1957) 'Method and Analysis in David Hume's Economic Essays', *Economica*, NS, vol. 24, pp. 225–34.

Viner, Jacob (1927) 'Adam Smith and Laissez Faire', *Journal of Political Economy*, vol. 35, pp. 198–232.

Wasserman, Max J. and Beach, Frank H. (1934) 'Some Neglected Monetary Theories of John Law', *American Economic Review*, vol. 24, pp. 646–57.

Waterman, A. M. C. (1991) *Revolution, Economics and Religion: Christian Political Economy, 1798–1833*. Cambridge: Cambridge University Press.

Waterman, A. M. C. (2002) 'Economics as Theology: Adam Smith's Wealth of Nations', *Southern Economic Journal*, vol. 68, pp. 907–21.

Waterman, A. M. C. (2005) 'The Oldest Extant Undergraduate Essay in Economics?' *Journal of the History of Economic Thought*, vol. 27, pp. 359–73.

Watson, Matthew (2005) 'What Makes a Market Economy? Schumpeter, Smith and Walras on the Coordination Problem', *New Political Economy*, vol. 10, pp. 143–61.

Welch, Patrick J. (2006) 'Thomas Carlyle on Utilitarianism', *History of Political Economy*, vol. 38 (2), pp. 377–89.

Wennerlind, Carl (2005) 'David Hume's Monetary Theory Revisited: Was He Really a Quantity Theorist and an Inflationist?' *Journal of Political Economy*, vol. 113, pp. 223–37.

Wennerlind, Carl and Schabas, Margaret (eds) (2008) *David Hume's Political Economy*. London and New York: Routledge.

West, E. G. (1964) 'Adam Smith's Two Views on the Division of Labour', *Economica*, NS, vol. 31, pp. 23–32.

Whatley, Christopher A. (1989) 'Economic Causes and Consequences of the Union of 1707: A Survey', *Scottish Historical Review*, vol. 68, pp. 150–81.

Whatley, Christopher A. (2000) *Scottish Society 1707–1830: Beyond Jacobitism, Towards Industrialisation*. Manchester and New York: Manchester University Press.

Wilson, Edwin B. (1948) 'John Law and John Keynes', *Quarterly Journal of Economics*, vol. 62, pp. 381–95.

Winch, Donald (1978) *Adam Smith's Politics: An Essay in Historiographic Revision*. Cambridge: Cambridge University Press.

Winch, Donald (1985) 'Review: The Burke–Smith Problem and Late Eighteenth-Century Political and Economic Thought', *Historical Journal*, vol. 28, pp. 231–47.

Winch, Donald (1992) 'Adam Smith: Scottish Moral Philosopher as Political Economist', *Historical Journal*, vol. 35, pp. 91–113.

Winch, Donald (1996) *Riches and Poverty: An Intellectual History of Political Economy in Britain, 1750–1834*. Cambridge: Cambridge University Press.

Winch, Donald (1997) 'Adam Smith's Problems and Ours', *Scottish Journal of Political Economy*, vol. 44, pp. 384–402.

Winch, Donald (2009) *Wealth and Life*. Cambridge: Cambridge University Press.

Witztum, Amos (2008) 'Smith's Theory of Actions and the Moral Significance of Unintended Consequences', *European Journal of the History of Economic Thought*, vol. 15, pp. 401–32.

Wolin, Sheldon S. (1954) 'Hume and Conservatism', *American Political Science Review*, vol. 48, pp. 999–1016.

Wood, John Cunningham (1983) *British Economists and the Empire*. London and Canberra: Croom Helm; New York: St Martin's Press.

Wright, Leslie C. (1953) *Scottish Chartism*. Edinburgh: Oliver & Boyd.

Young, James D. (1983) 'Marxism and the Scottish National Question', *Journal of Contemporary History*, vol. 18, pp. 141–63.

Young, Jeffrey T. (1985) 'Natural Price and the Impartial Spectator: A New Perspective on Adam Smith as Social Economist', *International Journal of Social Economics*, vol. 12, pp. 118–21.

Young, Jeffrey T. (1997) *Economics as a Moral Science: The Political Economy of Adam Smith*. Cheltenham: Edward Elgar.

Youngson, A. J. (1961) 'Alexander Webster and his "Account of the Number of People in Scotland in the Year 1755" ', *Population Studies*, vol. 15, pp. 198–200.

Index